1

SHAKESPEARE'S INVENTION OF OTHELLO

CONTEMPORARY INTERPRETATIONS OF SHAKESPEARE

Derek Cohen
SHAKESPEAREAN MOTIVES

Martin Elliott
SHAKESPEARE'S INVENTION OF OTHELLO

Graham Holderness, Nick Potter and John Turner
SHAKESPEARE: THE PLAY OF HISTORY

Murray J. Levith
SHAKESPEARE'S ITALIAN SETTINGS AND PLAYS

Lachlan Mackinnon
SHAKESPEARE THE AESTHETE

Peter Mercer
HAMLET AND THE ACTING OF REVENGE

Further titles in preparation

Series Standing Order

If you would like to receive future titles in this series as they are published, you can make use of our standing order facility. To place a standing order please contact your bookseller or, in case of difficulty, write to us at the address below with your name and address and the name of the series. Please state with which title you wish to begin your standing order. (If you live outside the UK we may not have the rights for your area, in which case we will forward your order to the publisher concerned.)

Standing Order Service, Macmillan Distribution Ltd, Houndmills, Basingstoke, Hampshire, RG21 2XS, England.

Shakespeare's Invention of Othello

A Study in Early Modern English

Martin Elliott

MACMILLAN
PRESS

First published 1988

Published by
THE MACMILLAN PRESS LTD
Houndmills, Basingstoke, Hampshire RG21 2XS
and London
Companies and representatives
throughout the world

Printed in Hong Kong

British Library Cataloguing in Publication Data
Elliott, Martin
Shakespeare's invention of Othello: a
study in early modern English.—
(Contemporary interpretations of
Shakespeare)
1. Shakespeare, William. Othello
I. Title   II. Series
822.3'3 PR2829
ISBN 0–333–44162–1

Contents

Acknowledgements

My gratitude to Warren Chernaik, who helped before the book was finished, and to Barbara Everett and Elizabeth Brennan, who helped thereafter. Any errors, of course, are my own.

M. S. E.

Introduction
Twentieth-Century *Othello*:
A Critical Survey of Some
Critics

The seminal criticisms of *Othello* from the earlier years of this century infrequently engaged with the text in any detail or at any length. And this very lack of engagement resulted, usually, in work that was powerful opinion rather than substantiated argument. This critical feature is evident in, for example, G. Wilson Knight's 'The *Othello* Music' (*The Wheel of Fire*, London, 1930). This superb essay is still, I find, the closest we have to a definitive interpretation of the play; but in his treatment of the characters as 'suggestive symbols rather than human beings' (p.97) Wilson Knight does tend himself to write 'poetically' – and often movingly – rather than with any textual analysis. In considering Othello's language he writes truly of its picturesque exoticism, its solidity, above all its predominant quality of 'separateness' which keeps image from image, the heavens from the human, and Othello from the world of Venice. Moreover, he writes of the dramatic value of this style – which is that its solid but sentimental character is bound to provoke the attack of the *un*solid and cynical Iago: 'a spirit of negation, colourless and undefined' attempts 'to make chaos of a world of stately, architectural, and exquisitely coloured forms' (p. 119). All this is fundamentally true, and does much to illuminate the play's main dramatic movement as well as its symbolism. At the same time, however, Wilson Knight supplies little in the way of a textual demonstration of what he says. And there are occasions, indeed, when he seems to be celebrating Othello's style rather than exploring it. He writes of 'the exquisitely moulded language, the noble cadence and chiselled phrases of Othello's poetry' (p. 106), attempting to define it in terms of other crafts. Or he describes it as having 'an architectural stateliness of quarried speech, a silver rhetoric' (p. 103). On the whole, these accumulated cross-references tell us more about Wilson Knight's 'poetic' response than they do about the literary means by which Othello was invented. Moreover, Wilson Knight's central metaphor of Othello's 'music' remains curiously undeveloped in his essay. 'Music' as the literary expression of the muse is etymologically just; but it also has suggestions of sound rather than literal sense; and it was F. R. Leavis, not Wilson Knight, who (indirectly) developed the metaphor's implications when he defined Othello as an ignoble character disguised in beautiful language. Indeed, Leavis elsewhere, in 'Mr Eliot and Milton', asserted that terms such as 'music' and 'musical' are sometimes not 'respectable instruments of criticism' but 'mere confusing substitutes for the analysis . . . unperformed'.[1]

When, however, one considers Leavis's own essay on *Othello* one finds a similar impressionism. This is surprising, given Leavis's stricture on the 'analysis . . . unperformed'. Leavis, like Wilson Knight, quotes frequently; but *his* quotes, too, are left largely unexamined. It seems that Leavis regards Othello's language not only as anti-Bradleyan but as self-evidently so; to the extent indeed that, at one point, Leavis clearly betrays the weakness of his argument. He writes, 'it does not seem to need arguing. If it has to be argued, the only difficulty is the difficulty, for written criticism, of going in detailed commentary through an extended text. The text is plain enough' (*The Common Pursuit*, p. 144). The topic here is Othello's prompt yielding to Iago's suggestions; but the working-method – assertion rather than demonstration – pertains to the whole of Leavis's essay on *Othello*. For example, Leavis quotes Iago's words to Othello beginning 'I would not have your free and noble nature / Out of self-bounty be abused' (III.iii) and observes, 'There in the first two lines is, explicitly appealed to by Iago, Othello's ideal conception of himself . . . ' (p. 145). There is nothing inaccurate in this; but the lines themselves carry a resonant lexicon – *free, noble, bounty* – that demands exegesis. Such an exegesis, of the kind I attempt in Chapters 1 and 2 below, discloses that Shakespeare's deployment of the ideas intrinsic in 'freedom' is crucial to an understanding of Othello's character and his 'fall'. To take another example: Leavis finds in Othello 'a curious and characteristic effect of self-preoccupation with his emotions rather than with Desdemona in her own right' (p. 150); but instead of examining this highly important preoccupation – of such major importance that it has commandeered the whole of my Chapters 4–6 – Leavis merely quotes the last seven lines of 'It is the cause . . . ' (V.ii) and passes on.

Textual analysis is also largely absent from A. C. Bradley's two printed lectures on *Othello* – they focus instead on the play's characters and construction. Their view that 'the character of Othello is comparatively simple' and 'so noble . . . that he stirs . . . in most readers a passion of mingled love and pity which they feel for no other hero in Shakespeare'[2] – a view less provocative in itself than Leavis's polemical response – has received much debate; but Bradley's general remarks (in an earlier lecture in the same book, 'The Substance of Shakespearean Tragedy') on the nature of Shakespeare's four major tragedies are far less controversial. He grandly defines the drama of these plays: the drama of a single, outstanding protagonist who is brought to sudden calamity and death by a 'total reverse of fortune' (*Shakespearean Tragedy*, p. 4) and by his own 'characteristic deeds' (p. 7), whose internal conflict supplies the main dramatic interest, and whose drama impresses us with a strong sense of waste. This definition supplies a firm basis for *any* consideration of *Othello* – eighty years on, the Bradleyan notion of Shakespeare's sense of a tragic moral order, 'a passion for perfection' (p. 28) offset at times by an evil engendered within that same order, is still remarkably resonant when applied to Othello's idealism, Desdemona's innocent goodness and Iago's cynicism. Where Bradley's treatment of *Othello* itself *is* deficient, I feel, is in its lack of stylistic comment, its ignoring of the words by which the tragedy was, after all, created. Bradley quite often pays a kind of homage to Shakespeare by incorporating the dramatic poet's words – without comment – in his own text. For example: Othello 'has felt as no other man ever felt (for he speaks of it as none other ever did) the poetry of the pride, pomp, and circumstance of glorious war' (p. 153). Or again: 'Anticipating the probability that Iago has spared him the whole truth, he (Othello) feels that in that case his life is over and his "occupation gone" with all its glories' (p. 159). What Bradley says in both instances is true; but the statements would have been considerably more substantial had the words *pride, pomp, circumstance, glorious, occupation* – even *gone* – been studied instead of being merely reset in the critic's prose. (The speech in which they occur suggests, in fact, that Othello has been able to use his military career in some degree as a means of self-extension by sight and sound. I study the speech in Chapter 5 below.)

The works referred to above are not to be attacked for failing to do what they never intended. At the same time, it is hardly surprising that much of the other work on *Othello* has purposed not only to support or attack them but also, more importantly, to substantiate or qualify their opinions by more objective means – by closer looks at the text, for example; or by supplying an Elizabethan/Jacobean cultural context to the discussion; or by considering the play as a piece for performance or in relation to Shakespeare's source-material. The need to remember how Othello would have been admired by a contemporary audience for his heroism and nobility as a great soldier has been emphasised by, for example, Helen Gardner's 'The Noble Moor' (*Proceedings of the British Academy*, 41, 1955), Barbara Everett's 'Reflections on the Sentimentalist's Othello' *(Critical Quarterly*, 3, 1961) and William Empson's 'Honest in *Othello*' (*The Structure of Complex Words*, London, 1951) – which finds Othello dramatically 'credible in his period' (p. 244). Kenneth Muir's *Shakespeare's Tragic Sequence* (London, 1972) discerned Othello's self-dramatisation to be the conventional self-projection of an Elizabethan dramatic character; while the need to treat the play as a theatrical text has been emphasised by, for example, Neville Coghill's *Shakespeare's Professional Skills* (Cambridge, 1964) – which states that T. S. Eliot's finding of 'Bovarysme' in Othello's last speech cannot be expressed on stage (pp. xiv – xv), and by Marvin Rosenberg's *The Masks of Othello* (Berkeley, Calif., 1961) which cites actors as well as critics on the sheer impossibility of playing Othello as anything but initially and finally great of heart. The most extensive theatrical account of the play is, of course, Harley Granville-Barker's *'Othello'* (London, 1930) in the *Prefaces* series; while the infrequent references to *Othello* in John Barton's very recent *Playing Shakespeare* (London, 1984) provide some of the closest textual readings I have come across. Another recent work on *Othello* has been a second essay by Barbara Everett, 'Spanish Othello: The Making of Shakespeare's Moor' (*Shakespeare Survey*, 35, 1982), which considers Othello's sense of honour in the light of his having the traits of a Spanish as well as of an African Moor. And the latest full-length study, Jane Adamson's *'Othello' as Tragedy: Some Problems of Judgement and Feeling* (Cambridge, 1980), returns our attention to the play as a tragedy, speaking out against those reductive theories and productions which fail to match up to their subject's grandeur – interpretations of the play in terms of, for example, Christian allegory or covert homosexuality. As for Shakespeare's source-material in the writing of *Othello*, this is most extensively discussed in Geoffrey Bullough's *Narrative and Dramatic Sources of Shakespeare*, VII (London, 1973), which also has a general account of the play and its criticism.

Not all the works referred to in the above paragraph are directly responding to the controversy incepted by the impressionist critics; but they do represent – along with many other works to be mentioned in succeeding pages – an increasingly informed and scholarly exploration of *Othello*. The old controversy *has*, however, been the direct provocation of many of the criticisms attempting to prove Othello's consistent characterisation by a detailed demonstration from the text. Many of these works are discussed in Adamson's and Muir's books as well as in Helen Gardner's '*Othello*: A Retrospect 1900 – 1967' (*Shakespeare Survey*, 21, 1968) and Robert Hapgood's '*Othello*' in *Shakespeare: Select Bibliographical Guides*, ed. Stanley Wells (London, 1973).[3] Here I would like to consider some of the works I have found most germane to my own close examination of the lexicon and syntax. Interestingly, they form in aggregate a critical reaction less to the Bradley – Leavis issue as such than to the work of another early Shakespearean 'impressionist', E. E. Stoll. His challenging view of Othello – that the character is 'not a psychological entity', that Othello lacks a 'predisposition', that his 'fall' depends on the convention of the 'calumniator believed', and that the play is to be admired not for any accurate psychological depiction but for 'the illusion so convincingly created and sustained'[4] – was published with variations through a quarter of a century from 1915, surviving Leavis's attack (in 'Diabolic Intellect and the Noble Hero . . . ') to be a stimulus still today. Stoll's view, moreover, reflected a larger opinion current at the time that Shakespeare was careless of his overall dramatic structures, often giving up psychological plausibility for the sake of brilliant 'theatre' or of plot-necessity. (L. L. Schücking, indeed, memorably expressed that opinion when he agreed, in *Character Problems in Shakespeare's Plays*, London, 1922, p. 113, to define Shakespeare's plays as largely '*bundles of scenes*'.) And it follows, therefore, that the task of demonstrating Othello's consistent character has the commensurate task of demonstrating also Shakespeare's care*ful*-ness as a psychological dramatist. Both these tasks were well undertaken by Derek Traversi's *An Approach to Shakespeare* (1938; 3rd, rev. edn, 2 vols, London, 1969), one of the sentences of which expresses, in effect, the theme of my own investigations. Shakespeare, Traversi states, is 'careful from the first to suggest the presence of certain weaknesses, potential if not yet actual, beneath the impression of strength and consistency which his hero initially presents to the world' (II, 101). (In passing, I would note the semantic difference between Othello's 'consistency' or firmness in the early part of the play and his 'consistent' or constant characterisation throughout the play.) And Traversi also points to Othello's 'habitual tendency to protest rhetorically against the presence of the very weaknesses that are undoing him' (p. 111), as well as to his 'revealing tendency to self-dramatization' (p. 101) – this definition is akin to my own finding of 'self-publication'. Traversi's refutation of Stoll had a parallel in Leo Kirschbaum's 'The Modern Othello' (*English Literary History*, XI, 1944; rep. in *Character and Characterization in Shakespeare*, Detroit, 1962). This states, first, the important artistic truth that 'in order to create probability the dramatist has to make his characters more consistent than people are in real life' (pp. 151–2) and, secondly, that Shakespeare has created Othello as the very consistent type of a romantic idealist given to extreme reversals of feeling. Like Traversi's concise essay, Kirschbaum's economical – and even shorter – piece is, I think, an accurate interpretation of Shakespeare's Othello. Traversi, in particular, investigated the text far more than other critics did; and even Kirschbaum, in his few pages, touched on the occasional small but significant point of lexicon – for example, the contrast between Othello's greeting of Desdemona as his fair warrior (II.i) and the rather less Platonic, more sexually affectionate way he takes her to bed at the start of II.iii: 'Come, my dear love . . . . ' Even this degree of close reading is, however, capable of much further development. For, on the whole, the method used by Traversi and Kirschbaum effects a *registration* of the text rather than the kind of close analysis I shall be attempting.

   It needs to be said that not all later critics discussing the characterisation of Othello have found in favour of consistency. J. I. M. Stewart's essay on *Othello* in *Character and Motive in Shakespeare* (London, 1949) elevated rather than disproved Stoll's view by asserting that naturalism lifts at certain points in the play, and that the play's protagonist is not merely Othello but a conflation, in fact, of two characters – Othello and Iago – who need to be considered symbolically 'as interlocked forces within a single psyche' (p. 109). And a similar view was later expressed by H. A. Mason's *Shakespeare's Tragedies of Love* (London, 1970), which saw a want of 'necessary substance' (p. 158) in Othello that makes him a speaker of beautiful poetry rather than a character. We are, in effect, returned to Stoll when Mason writes of the 'repellent' and the 'attractive' facets of Othello and charges Shakespeare with 'clumsy craftsmanship' (pp. 120 and 69). A more sympathetic view is presented in A. P. Rossiter's 'Othello: A Moral Essay' (in *Angel with Horns*, London, 1961). This examines some of the ambiguity in the word *jealous* ('sexually jealous' and 'suspicious'), proffering an Othello who is unable to cope with such ambiguity and is prone to self-delusion. In rejecting the Bradleyan view of near-total nobility in Othello, Rossiter's essay sets the play beside *Measure for Measure* as a problem play, asserting in a footnote that 'We *should* see Othello more as we see *Angelo*' (p. 206n) – a note that is conducive to discussion rather than finally sustainable. Rossiter's essay also reminds us (as does Muir's, mentioned earlier) of how extensively Coleridge's listing of jealous symptoms in Leontes – 'dread of vulgar ridicule', 'selfish vindictiveness', 'soliloquy in the mask of dialogue', and so on – is also applicable to Othello despite Coleridge's attempt to prove the contrary.[5]

Much of the more recent writing on *Othello* will be referred to later, mostly in the notes to my chapters. I would especially mention two works, however, not because they parallel my own approach in any way but because, using their own methods, they both emphasise the consistency of Shakespeare's characterisation. T. McAlindon's *Shakespeare and Decorum* (London, 1973) demonstrates how Shakespeare makes Othello as well as Desdemona offend against contemporary ideas of decorum from the start: 'Quietly but clearly Shakespeare shows that the marriage – as a rite, a formalised human relationship, and a microcosm of society – was defective' (p. 97). And Harold Skulsky's two chapters on *Othello* in *Spirits Finely Touched* (Athens, Ga, 1976) examine, amongst other ideas, the Aristotelian and Renaissance idea of 'magnanimity' based upon a conviction of one's own high value. In the old truism, one cannot love another if one does not love oneself; and the play demonstrates that all Othello's apparent early belief in his intrinsic merit is gainsaid by his later actions: 'the flimsiness of Othello's self-esteem strengthens him in his conviction of Desdemona's infidelity' (p. 170). Skulsky's account of Othello's failure to be magnanimous has some affinity with my own exploration of 'freedom' in the play; and his conclusion that Othello's actions 'have grown directly and inescapably out of ingrained traits of personality' (p. 244) is certainly in accordance with my own. Both Skulsky's and McAlindon's discussions of *Othello* in terms of Renaissance morality supplement, in some degree but from other directions, my investigations into Othello's language.

When Hapgood in his survey, mentioned above, said that, 'In their concern for consistency, critics have failed to put the two extreme views of the hero together in one fully worked-out pattern' (p. 163), he might be taken as proposing the want of a full-length work in which Othello's nobility and his ignobility are reconciled and in which this reconciliation is demonstrated throughout the text. These objectives were the concern of Robert Heilman in his book *Magic in the Web* (Lexington, Ky, 1956). Like Skulsky, Heilman discerns in Othello a lack of confidence beneath the apparent firmness. He also writes of

> the qualifications of character that Shakespeare has patiently, and on the whole very unobtrusively, dramatized – the unripeness of his sense of his own past, the flair for the picturesque and the histrionic, the stoicism of the flesh unmatched by an endurance of spirit, the capacity for occasional self-deception, the hypersensitivity to challenge, the inexperience in giving, the inclination to be irritable under responsibility and hasty in the absence of superior authority, the need to rely on position. (pp. 144–5)

And yet this careful summary, in its abstract terminology, serves to suggest the curiously amorphous nature of Heilman's work. His most substantial findings are those based upon a close reading of the brawl-scene (II.iii), where he discerns that Othello reacts not so much to a dereliction of military duty as to a personal affront (pp. 142–4); and in chapter 5 he writes illuminatingly of the 'positional assurance' that Othello constantly seeks. Again, however, Heilman's close reading of the brawl-scene – founded largely upon Othello's use of the pronouns *me/my* – is not characteristic; and his book as a whole leaves much scope for a further, much more detailed exploration of the text. As for another full-length treatment, G. R. Elliott's *Flaming Minister* (Durham, NC, 1953), that leaves even more scope than does Heilman's. It is thorough in that it goes through the play scene by scene; but in doing so it effects little more than a retelling of Othello's drama – the text remains undisturbed.

My concern in this book is to define and examine Shakespeare's inscription of Othello's undoubted nobility by certain traits that help to explain, motivate, prefigure the murder of Desdemona. I shall be attempting to demonstrate what other critics have also been concerned with – the fact that the murderous Othello of Acts III – V *does* develop from the noble Othello of Acts I and II – but I shall be doing so by a means of extensive lexical and syntactical analysis that has not been attempted hitherto. There are, however, certain works on Shakespeare's use of language that have influenced my thinking on this working-method, and I would like here to acknowledge my indebtedness to them. William Empson's work – not only 'Honest in *Othello*' but also 'Honest Man' and other essays in *The Structure of Complex Words* – showed me that the analysis of a past time's lexicon is also a study of the history of ideas, and that this can clarify a literary work not only internally but also in relation to its period. (I would indicate, however, that Othello's leaning upon 'honesty' is part of a larger tendency to lean upon the repetition of single words which Empson has not brought out.) Again, Giorgio Melchiori's 'The Rhetoric of Character Construction' (*Shakespeare Survey*, 34, 1981) encouraged my awareness of the controlled use of language that Shakespeare gives to Othello; while Molly Mahood's *Shakespeare's Wordplay* (London, 1957) did much to turn my attention to the dramatic irony present in many of the key words that Othello utters. She writes, for example (pp. 47–8), that in Othello's 'Put out the *light* and then put out the *light*' the light is, finally, not only the taper and not only Desdemona's life (which *is* briefly relumed as she returns from apparent death) but, above all, the light of Othello's own integrity. For Hilda Hulme's compilation of her scholarship in *Explorations in Shakespeare's Language* (London, 1962) I have a special affection. I have not set out to emulate her searchings in Elizabethan manuscript records; but her way of lexical definition and the rigorous dramatic application of her findings have been a methodological model. Her book shows strongly the critical advantage of concentrating on small, or apparently small, points of lexicon – since, after all, a literary work of any description is an aggregate of such points. I only wish that her references to *Othello* had been more frequent. Apart from Melchiori's essay, the main precedent for my study of Othello's syntax is Madeleine Doran's 'Iago's ''If – '': Conditional and Subjunctive in *Othello*' (*Shakespeare's Dramatic Language*, Madison, Wis., and London, 1976). This demonstrates that Shakespeare has given to Othello an habitual utterance of wild hypotheses, of absurd postulations in the form of *if*-clauses which function, in effect, as extreme statements of the impossible. It is Iago's major

syntactical achievement to suborn Othello with his very own
speech habit: by infecting Othello's consciousness with *if*-clauses –
skilfully introduced and ugly in their hypotheses – of Iago's own.
This syntactical finding opens up the text to a remarkable degree. It
brings one close to the sense of Shakespeare at his desk, so to speak,
and actually engaged in his literary craft.

I am also indebted, of course, to the several editions of the play I
have listed at the beginning of the Bibliography. In the main I have
used them corroboratively; but Alice Walker's notes and glossary in
the New Shakespeare edition that she co-edited with John Dover
Wilson (Cambridge, 1957) have been particularly useful on occasion as a main source. All the listed editions, in fact, have added to
my religious, social and artistic knowledge of Shakespeare's
period. To conclude, I would mention Paul A. Jorgensen's findings
in Elizabethan theatrical culture in *Redeeming Shakespeare's Words*
(Berkeley, Calif., 1962). His lexical inquiries are much less dic-
tionary-based than mine; but his idea of word-redemption certainly helps to define the major activity of the following pages.

A note on the texts used. Throughout this study, F refers to the text
and through line-numbering of *The Tragedie of Othello, the Moore of
Venice* (or, where stated, of other plays) in Charlton Hinman's *The
First Folio of Shakespeare: The Norton Facsimile* (New York, 1968).

Q refers to the First Quarto as in Charlton Hinman's *Othello:
1622*, Shakespeare Quarto Facsimiles no. 16 (Oxford, 1975).

The act, scene, line references relate to Peter Alexander's *The
Collected Works of William Shakespeare* (London, 1951; paperback
reprint 1981).[6]

My main lexical guides have been *The Oxford English Dictionary*,
referred to henceforth as *OED*; and the near-contemporary but
independent compilation, Alexander Schmidt's *Shakespeare-
Lexicon*, referred to as 'Schmidt'.[7] In references to these sources, the
lexical entry and part of speech are omitted except in cases of
ambiguity (e.g. where the lexical entry is not exactly the same as the
form of the word cited in the text, or where a given word can belong
to more than one part of speech). Where there is no ambiguity, the
number/letter of the definition immediately follows mention of the
source. Abbreviations of the parts of speech have been standard-
ised as follows: adj. (adjective), adv. (adverb), interj. (interjection),
prepos. (preposition), sb. (substantive), v. (verb). And note

'comb.' (in combination), 'pl.' (plural) and 'ppl.' (participial). Where there is more than one lexical entry for the same word and part of speech in the *OED*, this is indicated, as in the source, by a superior figure following the entry or abbreviation. Such superior figures are not to be confused with those signalling endnotes.

Except in two respects, I have reproduced the texts of F and Q as originally printed. The exceptions are 'long s' – replaced by 's' – and the italicisation of in-dialogue names: these are not typographically distinguished. The names of speakers are spelt out in full, using F spelling.

To keep the number of endnotes to a minimum, repeated page references to the same source are given parenthetically in the text. Shakespeare editions are designated by the name of the editor only (with 'Walker' standing for the New Shakespeare edition of *Othello*); for references to other sources, a short title is also given. Full details of all the works in question are given in the Bibliography, which lists Shakespeare editions first.

1

'But to be free, and bounteous to her minde'

In this chapter I shall be considering the play in relation to one of Othello's grand announcements. In the following lines he announces a motive and intent of being free and bounteous to Desdemona's mind:

> Let her haue your voice.
> Vouch with me Heauen, I therefore beg it not
> [Q *Your voyces Lords: beseech you let her will*
> *Haue a free way, I therefore beg it not*]
> To please the pallate of my Appetite:
> Nor to comply with heat the yong affects
> In my defunct, and proper satisfaction.[1]
> But to be free, and bounteous to [Q *of*] her minde:
>
> (F610–15; I.iii.260–5)

As far as the immediate context is concerned, of course, Othello *is* practising the stated bounty: he supports his wife's wish that she accompany him, as a kindred spirit, on the Cyprus expedition. But the last of the lines quoted above does, I think, have a resonance that extends beyond the context to signify in the play as a whole. This resonance derives in part from the sounds of *free, and bounteous* and *minde*: slow, easy vowels after the heavy consonance heard in the preceding three lines. The motive and intent is released from context to ascend, at it were, as a momentous standard against which Othello's verbal and physical actions can be judged.

Obviously, as the play moves into Acts III – V all this resonant promise is to be drastically unfulfilled. Less obvious, however, is another fact: that the announced generosity is made to coexist *almost immediately* with its opposite – a *lack* of generosity. It will be seen that Shakespeare has, in fact, inscribed into Othello's utterance a series of lines or passages the gist of which is not to be

1

bounteous to Desdemona's mind. That mind is, rather, to be denied; while Desdemona herself is to be dismissed, on occasion, from Othello's presence. This tendency is to some extent realised even at moments of apparently shared content – that is to say, importantly, before Iago's slanders begin. It is then further developed as a contributing motive in the striking and dismissal of Desdemona in IV.i. And it culminates to participate in the final dismissal by murder.

The phrase *free, and bounteous* is one of several doublets in the speech the opening lines of which are quoted above. In the following the components mean differently from each other: *free, and bounteous*; *defunct, and proper*; *speculatiue, and offic'd* (Q *speculatiue and actiue*). In the following they probably do not: *serious and great*; *corrupt, and taint*; *indigne, and base*. When discussing the doublet-form, Empson declared not only its 'satisfactory form of padding' but also its appeal to 'the dictionary interest in words that was so strong in the Elizabethans';[2] and in *free, and bounteous* particularly, I think, can be heard a strong suggestion of hendiadys – the rhetorical figure in which the simple co-ordination asserted by *and* is worked against by a more-than-simple idea. Shakespeare was using the figure in *Hamlet* and *Othello* much more frequently than in his other plays; and its occasional sounding in Othello's utterance keeps well with the subtly articulate Othello who orates with skill before the Council and in his last long speech – to take but two examples. Here *bounteous*, deriving from Old French *bontif*, denotes the being good to others as well as the being munificent in a material way (see *OED* 1). *Free* seems to mean more. It sounds from a long history of social and moral associations. It concerns the moral qualities that the free man had the time and opportunity to cultivate and which the peasant, or base man, or in earlier centuries the villein tied to an estate, could not. Hence *free* as 'Noble, honourable, generous, magnanimous' (*OED* adj., I.4). This was disappearing in the seventeenth century but seems still to be working here. Othello declares a motive more complex than simple generosity. The whole clause *But to be free, and bounteous to her minde* opposes the idea of self-indulgence expressed by *please* and *comply*. Othello wishes to be good and generous to Desdemona's mind in accordance with the way of a free and ranging spirit. He intends to treat Desdemona with that same 'free, and open Nature' that even Iago acknowledges in him (F745; I.iii.393). Moreover, the existence of this *free/base* axis is supported lexically by Othello's use a few lines later of *indigne, and base aduersities.*[3]

There is, in fact, some remembrance of *The Franklin's Tale* here. Shakespeare may well be presenting in Othello an idealistic aspiration towards that same generosity in marriage that Chaucer showed Arveragus actually achieving. Chaucer, of course, stated the moral and social associations of *free* more explicitly. He opposed the idea of a gentle knight's 'franchise and all gentillesse' to that of 'cherlyssh wrecchednesse', the kind of behaviour to be found among churls or other men of a lower degree.[4]Arveragus, crucially, in his testing-time is able to put his *gentillesse* into practice. His wife, foolishly, has sworn to submit to a would-be lover on the establishment of an apparently impossible condition; and when that condition *is* established Arveragus insists that his wife should keep her assignation rather than be guilty of bad faith. Much distress is caused both husband and wife by this noble marital generosity; but in the event it inspires even people of lesser degree – the amorous squire and his clerk accomplice – to act in a like noble manner; the result being that all churlish and vicious bonds are cancelled. So the Franklin, the freeman, demonstrates the morally beautiful effect that an example of true freedom can produce throughout society in all manner of men: 'Which was the moste fre, as thynketh yow?'[5] With respect to Shakespeare's characterisation of Othello there are two instances in particular that have a strong echo of Chaucer's tale. One of these is the *diminutio* with which Othello prepares to tell the Council of his wooing – 'Rude am I, in my speech' (F420; I.iii.81). This compares with how the Franklin prepares *his* narrative: 'I yow biseche, / Have me excused of my rude speche'.[6] Both characters win sympathy by an admission of little rhetorical skill; both then utter rhetoric of a very high order. Even more suggestive however – and more germane – is the concern for good name that Arveragus and Othello have in common. Arveragus swears to his wife 'to take no maistrie/Agayn hir wyl'; but she in return must respect his 'name of soveraynetee', for 'That wolde he have for shame of his degree'.[7]Accordingly, when Dorigen sets out to keep her assignation she is warned, upon pain of death, to keep it secret. The potential for a parallel with *Othello* is clear. One of the major difficulties that Othello cannot endure is his wife's (apparent) public shamelessness, her flaunting on the sea-bank of her relationship with one of his officers, her flagrant besmirching of his good name. If Dorigen *had* told of her assignation she would, one assumes, have been put to death by her husband despite his love and magnanimity: in some degree, therefore, *Othello* can be seen as a reworking of *The Franklin's Tale* – a reworking in which Desdemona, supposedly, is a Dorigen who does renege against her husband's name for sovereignty; and in which Othello is an Arveragus who, faced by a renegade (as he thinks), can no longer be free and bounteous but must put her to death. (The lexical parallel between Othello and Arveragus is not discussed at all in Ann Thompson, *Shakespeare's Chaucer: A Study in Literary Origins*, Liverpool, 1978.)

Of course, Shakespeare's characterisation of Othello in a psychological drama is infinitely more complex than Chaucer's 'typification' of Arveragus in a moral tale; and this is disclosed in the way that Shakespeare almost instantly qualifies his hero's generosity. In examining the context further, one finds that Othello's assertion of a bounteous motive has been provoked by Desdemona's use of ambiguous *Rites* in the following passage:

> if I be left behind
> A Moth of Peace, and he go to the Warre,
> The Rites, for why [Q *which*] I loue him, are bereft me:
> And I a heauie interim shall support
> By his deere absence. Let me go with him.
>
> (F605–9; I.iii. 255–9)

Now, these words of Desdemona have dismayed some critics: 'Is not this, whether we read "rites" or "rights", rather indelicate coming from the lips of Desdemona? Juliet (*Rom. & Jul.* III.ii.8) might, to herself, speak of the "amorous rites", but for Desdemona to do so before the Senate of Venice! Impossible!'[8] All the same, most critics and editors still understand 'love-rites'; and certainly Desdemona's frankness in so referring to physical conjugality – a felicitous frankness, which describes a husband's absence in the funereal terms of *bereft, heauie* and *absence* – accords both with her downright leaving of her father's house and with her directness, later, in pleading for Cassio. However, to assert 'There is no serious doubt that "rites" . . . is a reference to the consummation of marriage'[9] is to exclude much of Shakespeare's richness. For Desdemona can be interpreted differently. Shakespeare has set up an antithesis between *Peace* and *Warre*; and the *Rites* may well be the rites of war – the common practices or the formal observances (*OED Rite* 2 and 1b) of the soldier's life. They contribute to the fascination of Othello's 'valiant parts' (F603; I.iii.253) – *parts* being Othello's military personal qualities, his military business and function, his military conduct and acts (*OED, Part* sb., II.12, 8, 11). It is to these that Desdemona has consecrated herself in marriage. The rites of war, in Othello's words, made Desdemona wish to be a man herself in order to practise them (in one interpretation of 'she wish'd / That Heauen had made her such a man' at F507 – 8; I.iii.162 – 3). They are the rites in which a moth of peace, merely fluttering around the light of distant military exploits, could never participate. They are the rites that Othello narrated and which Desdemona wept and loved him for. An early Jacobean audience would have been acquainted with atrocity-stories deriving from the Turkish sack of Cyprus, which occurred some three decades before Shakespeare used it as background for *Othello*. Those auditors, one assumes, would have strongly remarked this heroine's intent to risk the frightful dangers of a Turkish siege.[10]

In that intent Othello can discern the valiant parts of the Desdemona he is later to call his 'faire Warriour' (F958; II.i.180) – though that address is made complex by its undertone of *sexual* encounterer. (It is worth noting that Desdemona's use of *parts* is devoid of all the vulgar meaning already available in Shakespeare's time – *OED, Part* sb., I.3.) It is to Desdemona's valour, her adventurous spirit, that Othello refers when he speaks of being generous to her mind. Desdemona's mind is not her wish – though she is firmly 'of a mind' to go with her husband; nor is it her mind in opposition to her body; it is her spiritual being, her feminine equivalent of Othello's military idealism. One might, of course, observe that Othello's generosity could have been put to a more sensible use: he might have refused to second Desdemona's request – and yet have been bounteous in supplying an explanation of that refusal. The expedition, he might justly have said, would be too dangerous; the shipboard presence of a woman might be resented by the sailors as an ill-omen; the presence of the general's wife, and the need to consider her safety, might encumber the general. Nothing of this does Othello proffer. Unlike Cinthio's Moor in the tale on which the play is partially based, Othello is untroubled by the prospect of exposing his wife to the danger of a sea-voyage. As for the *military* danger that she would embrace – which is not applicable in Cinthio – Othello gives it not a thought. Like Tamerlane, whom Knolles reports as taking his wife on the conquest of China, Othello agrees to take *his* wife on a dangerous enterprise.[11]

One might observe also, however, that Desdemona's removal to Cyprus does serve to solve the problem of her lodgement. Othello's deep concern about this would seem to have been clearly marked by Shakespeare:

> Most humbly therefore bending to your State,
> I craue fit disposition for my Wife,
> Due reference of Place, and Exhibition,
> With such Accomodation and besort
> As leuels with her breeding.

(F583–7; I.iii.235–9)

Ridley writes, 'the passage seems overloaded with words expressing "suitability" – *fit, due, besort, levels,* and perhaps *accommodation'*. He suspects that 'there has been some confusion, resulting in redundancy.'[12] The point is, I think, that this overloading is an authorial intent. Othello is made to repeat himself by tautology. *Disposition* means 'Arrangement' (*OED* 1.2). *Reference* means 'Assignment' (*OED* sb.,2). *Exhibition* means 'Maintenance, support' (*OED* 1.1) or 'allowance' (Schmidt) – the sense of 'show' seems not to have developed at this time other than in the verb, and Shakespeare's usage seems always to have kept close to the Latin sense of 'holding out'. *Accommodation* means 'Room and suitable provision' (*OED* 7). *Besort* means 'Suitable company' (*OED* sb.). *Place* seems to be 'high rank . . . dignity' (*OED* sb., III.9). Othello is made to disclose his concern that Desdemona should be treated, in his absence, with the respect due both to her degree and to her new position as the general's wife. Beneath the humility there is a strong assertion of *his* worth. At the same time, all this tautology, together with the insistence of Latinate polysyllables ending in *-ion,* declares some anxiety. These words all fit into the scansion; but the dignity can be marred, the utterance made clumsy, by an emphasis on the morphemic repetition. Additionally, the *semantic* repetition suggests that Othello, in his anxiety, believes such repetition to be an effective means of argument in itself. A more extreme form of this repetition – a single word sounded again and again – will feature largely in Othello's speeches as something of a substitute for inquiring thought. Here, disguised in a lexical variety, it discloses Othello's awareness of an awkward situation. Othello has to *craue* not merely in a formal sense but because Desdemona's fit lodgement has become a matter of urgency (after *OED, Crave* 5). She has become unhoused in a vulnerable way. The Duke, who has implied that Othello is one of the 'broken Weapons' that men use rather than their 'bare hands' (F519–20; I.iii.174–5), is to suggest, with an attempt at a similar compromise, that Desdemona be accommodated at her father's house – to lodge where she formerly resided, and from where this very night she has stolen away! It is a suggestion unacceptable to all parties concerned. Desdemona's expressed wish to accompany Othello does, therefore, overcome a very difficult predicament.[13]

Othello, then, responds to his wife's wish that she share his military life and practices. He does so immediately, gladly and with some relief that Desdemona need not be left behind unhoused and vulnerable. Almost as immediately, however, he then perceives himself to be – or considers himself to be – vulnerable in his own turn to the alternative meaning of *Rites*. It is as if he hears how the syntax of *Rites, for why I loue him* can be disambiguated into 'rites of love' by a reference back of *loue* in the sexual sense alone. These are the rites that Claudio, in *Much Ado* frankly and publicly refers to: 'Time goes on crutches, till Loue haue all his rites' – with knowing associations of crotches and of dispensing with crutches to stand upright (*Much adoe about Nothing*, F752–3; II.i.322–3). Othello realises that his being 'wived' while on a desperate military expedition must expose him to the opinion already voiced for us in Iago's 'blacke Ram' and 'Barbary horse' and in Rodorigo's (F spelling) 'grosse claspes of a Lasciuious Moore' (F96, 124 and 139; I.i.89, 112 and 127). Othello desires not to have his warrior's reputation smirched by the contemporary popular prejudice that moors and blackamoors were possessed of an arrogant libido – a prejudice that Shakespeare exploited in his invention of Aaron in *Titus Andronicus*. So long as Othello followed his career of a military monk, a kind of Knight of St John, he could avoid such smirching – there is no suggestion at all of his ever having been a brothello, even in youth. But now, with his new wife as his fellow-in-arms after a benighted marriage, he is aware of a stereotypical idea that he fears exists in the senate and, so to speak, in the audience. The idea must be dispelled.[14] In this respect, the wording of Othello's phrase *proper satisfaction* is most apt. Schmidt here reads 'own', as in the Duke's earlier use in 'our proper Son' (F406; I.iii.69); but this (Schmidt, *Proper* 2) insufficiently registers Othello's meaning. *Proper* here is more akin to Aemilia's usage in ''Tis proper I obey him; but not now' (F3482; V.ii.199) – i.e. 'fit, suitable' and 'in conformity with

rule' (*OED* adj., III.9 and II.4). Othello emphasises that the gratification of his sexual instinct is and would be legal and, moreover,
intrinsically valid, since sexual gratification is a central property of
marriage. There would be nothing of indecorous behaviour,
Othello says, on this expedition. The companionship of husband
and wife must, by definition, be honourable.

The whole clause, *Nor to comply with heat the yong affects / In my
defunct, and proper satisfaction*, is one of the most discussed – and
emended – passages in *Othello*. Furness has four pages of notes on
the glosses of editors – and that is only to the end of the nineteenth
century. Among the editions I have consulted from the present
century, only those by Hart and Ridley (Ardens old and new)
respect the authority of F and Q. The most common emendations
are of *my* to *me* or of *defunct* to *distinct*. Nuttall, a recent commenter,
observes, 'Quite obviously the sentence is a mess' and proposes
that the mess is deliberate, expressing an Othello who hesitates and
stammers. Most critics agree as far as 'mess', but attribute it to error
in transcription or in the printing-house itself. More challenging
than any emendation, however, are Hilda Hulme's wise words: 'we
should be prepared to postulate, although we know that it cannot
be wholly true, that Shakespeare himself intended what is in the
original text(s)'. And if one strays not at all from F and Q at this
point one finds a meaning that is *almost* adequate and quite in
keeping with the context – one that at least 'airs' the issues. *Defunct*,
probably chosen by Shakespeare in part for its consonance and
assonance with *defend* in 'And Heauen defend your good soules'
two lines later, probably refers not to a general condition of
Othello's sexual life but to a specific dramatic circumstance that
affects his marriage. There is an antithesis between 'making
enough' (Latin *satis*, 'enough', and *facere*, 'make' or 'do') and 'non-
performance' (Latin *fungor*, 'perform', hence *defunct*). That is,
Shakespeare is opposing two words whose components mean
much the same and which have several consonants in common. So
defunct is attracted to qualify *satisfaction*. This linkage is supported
by the meaning. The doing enough, or the making enough, to form
a proper marriage – the consummation – has not been effected.
Defunct as 'dead' and 'No longer in existence' (*OED* adj., A and B)
refers to the interruption of Othello's wedding-night, and to the
subduing of Othello's marital urgency by the military urgency of
the imminent departure for Cyprus. The *satisfaction* has had to be
stinted. (Indeed, since I.ii opens with Othello talking to Iago out-

side the inn of the Sagittary to which he has newly brought his bride, one may assume that the *satisfaction* has probably not even begun.)[15]

I said an *almost* adequate meaning. The difficulty is that it too, like all others, requires an emendation: in this instance 'in my defunct *but* proper satisfaction'; so that Othello can be read first as disclaiming in himself any irresponsible stoking of a youthlike ardour, secondly as recognising that his marriage rites must be interrupted, and thirdly as insisting all the same on the validity of his satisfaction. In this reading *heat* is not an unarticled and abstract noun but part of an adverbial phrase, *with heat*: 'fervently, ardently' (*OED*, *Heat* sb.); and *comply* is not an element of a verb 'comply with' but a verb in itself meaning 'fulfil, accomplish' (*OED* v.¹,1). According to the *OED* this was a new usage *circa* 1600. Othello's meaning – with the emendation of *and* to *but* – is thus, 'Nor fervently to accomplish the interrupted but valid consummation of my legally-effected marriage' – *yong affects* being the 'desire, or appetite' (*OED*, *Affect* sb., lc) that the vigorously mature Othello understandably feels for his young wife. A similar meaning ensues if one acknowledges the comma in Q after *heat* to mark a parenthesis ending on *satisfaction*. If so, then the verbal action is contained in *comply with* and means 'be complaisant (const. *with*)' (*OED*, *Comply* II.1).

In considering the most popular of the traditional emendations – 'Nor to comply with heat – the young affects / In me defunct – and proper satisfaction' (I quote from Alexander) – one discerns a particular virtue: that of echoing two other instances in the text. Since it is the young affects that are here defunct, there is perhaps some prefiguring of Othello's later thoughts on being declined, though not much, into the vale or vault of tears (F1896–7; III.iii.269–70). And, again, there may be a link with Iago's soliloquy on 'her Appetite' as being able to play the God with Othello's 'weake Function' (F1473–4; II.iii.336–7). This last is usually taken as a reference to Othello's mental activities (after Schmidt, *Function* 2). But Iago has a habit of taking up Othello's words and using them to him or of him in a derogatory way – compare Iago's *her Appetite* with Othello's *pallate of my Appetite* in this same speech – and this habit may well be working here. Othello's disclaimer of any youthful, immature ardour – he is certainly not alluding to any deficiency of passion – is sneeringly played on in Iago's talk of how dominated in fact Othello *is* by appetite, by Desdemona's wifely will.[16]

As for Othello's own talk of *the pallate of my Appetite* —

> I therefore beg it not
> To please the pallate of my Appetite:
> Nor to comply . . .

— this pleasing is differentiated by *not* . . . *Nor* from the fulfilling of the young affects. Othello's agreement that his wife should accompany him is not caused by an excessive desire for marital union; nor is it caused by a sexual gourmet's inclination to an inessential sampling. Othello is careful to unfix any figure of a moor given over either to passion *or* to dalliance.

So far, then, Othello's speech is apt and decorous. The emphasis is on Desdemona's valiant mind — and hence on Othello's — with which the *good soules* of the senators, their most important parts, should feel an affinity:

> And Heauen defend your good soules, that you thinke
> I will your serious and great [Q *good*] business scant
> When [Q *for*] she is with me.
>
> (F616–18; I.iii.266–8)

The introduction of *Heauen* is apt: it accords with Othello's earnestness of tone in denying any 'low' motives. There is no disrespectful admonition of the councillors either, since *defend . . . that you thinke* means 'forbid that you should think' rather than any idea that the councillors need to be defended (*OED, Defend* v., I.1–3; cf. Modern French *defenser*, 'forbid'). Importantly, too, the ideal of marriage as a union of true minds is implied in a terminology of respect.

In the second part of his speech, however, Othello becomes immoderate:

> No, when light wing'd [Q *light-wing'd*] Toyes
> Of [Q *and*] feather'd Cupid, seele [Q *foyles*] with wanton,
>   dulnesse
> My speculatiue, and offic'd [Q *actiue*] instrument [Q *instruments*]:
> That my Disports corrupt and taint my businesse:
> Let House-wiues make a Skillet of my Helme,
> And all indigne, and base aduersities,

Make head against my Estimation [Q *reputation*].
(F618–24; I.iii.268–74)

Shakespeare has made Othello pick up Desdemona's phrase *Moth of Peace* and turn it from a gentle disparagement into an extreme attack: from a description of a gentlewoman's futile and peaceful existence to a derogation of the physical character of marriage. A toy was 'A thing of little or no value or importance'; plural *Toyes* amounted to a singular 'act or piece of amorous sport, a light caress' (*OED, Toy* sb., II.5 and I.1). Both these senses maintain the inessential idea declared by *pallate*. Othello emphasises it with *light wing'd*: the toys are either light and winged or light*ly*-winged as in Q. In either version they have a fluttery quality akin to that of the moth. Further, the sexual trivia either belong to, or are linked with, a Cupid whose own wings are rendered as their component feathers – and those feathers supply even more an impression of insufficient gravity. The wings do not make Cupid ubiquitous; they merely make him light. Meanwhile, his irresistible nature, his sheer power, are not entertained. Nor is his accuracy: if the light winged toys are Cupid's arrows as well as his sports, then those arrows are instruments of wantonness, not an undodgeable and heavenly means to holy wedlock.

Those arrows might be more aptly suggested by *seele*. The *OED* defines it as 'prevent from seeing' (*Seel* V.², 2); but the literal sense adds something here. The verb derives from the Old French *cil*, 'eyelash'; and the literal sense is 'To close the eyes of (a hawk or other bird) by stitching up the eyelids'. This allusion – to the royal sport of falconry and to the prince among birds – is appropriate in Othello. The *dulnesse* then becomes a thread, and the arrows become needles. In either instance – whether as thread or as an abstract quality – the dullness is truly *wanton* in being caused by unchastity, or by dalliance, or indeed by effeminacy. All three of these defects are expressed in *OED, Wanton* adj., 2 and 4.

Briefly to consider Q's version: *foyles* assonates with *Toyes* and probably means 'baffles' (*OED, Foil* v.¹, II.4). Additionally, the nominal sense of 'blunt-edged and button-tipped fencing sword' (*OED* sb.,4), which the *OED* first dates at the end of the sixteenth century, may be contributing. Othello may be considering the image of a sword made harmless for use in sports (as Hamlet's is, for example, when he fights the unblunted rapier of Laertes). Othello may have deeply registered the Duke's talk about broken weapons.

He asserts the impossibility of himself, as a great weapon of the State, having the edge taken off his mental and physical faculties. It is worth noting, too, that *foyles* contributes to the recurrent motif of swords with which Othello is associated throughout the play: from his concern for the bright swords' welfare in Act I to his use of swords and his reflections on the 'Sword of Spaine' (F3552; v.ii.256) in the last scene.

Again, briefly to consider the *instrument* or *instruments*: the Q version, *speculatiue and actiue instruments*, seems to refer to Othello's intellectual and physical capacities – particularly, in the latter, to active members such as his arms (*OED, Instrument* sb., 4). F's version, *speculatiue, and offic'd instrument*, seems to refer to the well-housed, well-socketed eye of the great general; or to the mental vision of the great general (*speculatiue:* of 'intellectual or comprehending vision' – *OED, Speculation* i.1). In both senses, the instrument is *offic'd* not only in Othello but by the Venetian State (Schmidt, *Officed*: 'having a place or function').

Although, as is generally recognised, either text makes good sense throughout this sequence, the F version – with *seele, offic'd* and singular *instrument* – is incomparably richer. Ridley, indeed, seems to be on his own amongst modern editors in opting through-out for Q – though several editors choose *instruments* by itself. F's richness consists not only in the details discussed above but also in the development of the image of Cupid: Othello himself is imaged as blindly cupidinous with his eyes seeled. Furthermore, if one considers Othello's instrument to be the aggregate of his virtues as a man, then Othello himself, by extension, can be seen as the instrument. The great general is himself the instrument of Venice and is later to become, as he thinks, the instrument of heaven. Moreover, there are ironical implications. Othello is not just a 'means' by which great purposes are served (*OED, Instrument* sb.,1); he is also shortly to become a person made use of by another (*OED* 1b). Othello will eventually consider himself to have been wrought and perplexed by Iago. (Additionally, *dulnesse* in both F and Q will be instrumental in turning Othello into the 'dull Moore' of Aemilia's description [F3516; v.ii.228]. It will be *wanton* by reason of Othello's 'effeminate' subjection to Iago's slanders.)

This reduction of marriage to a physical and trivial function is continued in *Disports*. This has a physical meaning in 'pastime, game, sport' and a trivial one in 'Diversion from . . . duties' (*OED, Disport* sb., 2 and 1). They are further compounded in *corrupt and taint.* This doublet emphatically declares the impurity of the disports – though *taint* might have the additional sense of 'hit, *esp.* in tilting' (*OED* v.,A II.5). If so, the action would be aimed against Othello's good soldiership (*my businesse*), and would derive from the lists of love. The action of Cupid's arrows may exist here too: the arrows would hit both Othello and his soldiership.

All in all, Othello's anxiety – in Heilman's phrase his need of 'positional assurance'[17] – makes him unfair to Desdemona's mind. He juxtaposes the idea of marriage as sexual indulgence against Desdemona's vision of marriage as a sacred union:

> My heart's subdu'd
> Euen to the very quality [Q *vtmost pleasure*] of my Lord;
> I saw Othello's visage in his mind,
> And to his Honours and his valiant parts,
> Did I my soule and Fortunes consecrate.
>
> (F600–4; I.iii.250–4)

Desdemona talks of Othello's *mind* and demonstrates its influence upon her. But there is no mention in Othello's speech of Desdemona's *heart*, nor of the idealistic (albeit naïve) nature of her love. The elusive 'I saw Othello's visage in his mind' seems to imply an unintended disparagement of Othello's blackness – which Othello probably registers, hence his 'Haply, for I am black' (F1894; III.iii.267); but the intended sentiment is of spiritual love. *Visage* derives from Latin *visus*, which means both 'sight' and 'face': Desdemona declares that her love is not based on sight. She loves him not for his foreign blackness but for the 'white' virtues of his warrior temper. No acknowledgement of that love is in Othello's immoderate speech. Nor is there any mention of *soule* or of consecration. There is no acknowledgement at all that Desdemona's good companionship might actually help Othello in his serious business. Instead, there is an aspersion of marriage in which Othello's own talk of *proper satisfaction* would seem to be revised. It might be a concubine, a mistress, a camp-follower used solely for disport that he is talking about. Desdemona as a wife is not recognised. Her rights, and her idealistic view both of soldierly *Rites* and of conjugal *Rites* (if she means them) are denied.[18] Here, in fact, is a prime example of something to be heard frequently in Othello's utterance: a statement whose implications either contradict or subvert its apparent intent. Those implications the audience or reader comprehends. Othello does not.

This second part of Othello's speech forms one of his frequent *if*-sentences, conditional yet asseverative, as defined by Doran. In these sentences Othello is impelled by a habit of absurd supposition and of formulating conclusions he regards as impossible in practice. Iago is to exploit this habit by introducing into Othello's thoughts *if*-sentences or half-sentences of his own. In this instance the *when* of 'No, when light wing'd Toyes . . . ' is ostensibly a marker of time but in fact equals 'if'. And 'That my Disports corrupt and taint my businesse' acts not only as a clause of result but also as a parenthesis ('if, that is, my disports . . . ').[19] The structure of the *if*-sentence helps to continue the syntactical organisation of the early part of the speech – where all possible fallacy was cleared away by the definition of *not / To . . . Nor to . . . But to*. Here the adverbial clauses are clearly marked by *when* and *That*. Othello's gist may be immoderate, but his delivery is considered. Moreover, the anaphora (repetition of syntactical elements in several clauses) that is written into the main clauses and object clauses of the last three lines –

> Let House-wiues make a Skillet of my Helme,
> And [*let* understood] all indigne, and base aduersities,
> Make head against my Estimation

– confirms this impression of organised power. Indeed, Othello would seem to be so confident in his humorous (and hubristic) hypotheses that he eschews the use of 'should' before *seele* – an eschewal that becomes more marked when it is remembered that *when* here means 'if'. Othello uses no auxiliary, but talks instead virtually in the indicative mood. This is really another way of arriving at Doran's finding of the asseverative conditional, and I would not labour it here – particularly since signals of the subjunctive had vanished from plural verbs by Shakespeare's time and some sense of that mood may be invisibly present. But the use of the indicative where an auxiliary 'should' could and might have been used is to feature notably in Othello's utterance. It is possible that a crucial trait in Othello is being suggested: his inability in emotional matters to distinguish between a reported, or conjectured, or supposed truth and a truth that has been ascertained.[20]

Of course, the long conditional sentence of this speech forms a prime example of dramatic irony. Even to an audience unacquainted with the subsequent course of events, Othello's over-weening announcement would probably signal as inadvertently predictive. Adversities should not be so directly challenged, particularly by a hero in the early part of a drama. For hubris will provoke nemesis. Othello does uncannily foretell his corruption. And he does so not only in accordance with dramatic convention but also in a way that is true to his self-publicising character (the trait of self-publication is essential to an understanding of Othello and is discussed at length in later chapters). Moreover, his prediction is, inadvertently, precise. The toys of Iago's and his own lascivious imaginings *are* to seel or blunt his speculation, whether that speculation be ocular sense or best judgement. He *will* become dull to Desdemona's virtues. And he *will* consider himself to be afflicted by adversities of the most degrading kind. So that one can justly ask whether a dramatic character capable of such anticipation can be intended by his creator to be wholly confident. This is the main theme of Heilman's book on *Othello*. And it is a theme that is to recur frequently in the play, notably in II.i, where Othello's confidence in the present as he lands on Cyprus is qualified by a strange fear about the unknown future. Equally, this long, conditional sentence is interesting for its early sounding both of Othello's concern for his reputation – for how he is esteemed by the world – and of the narrow, masculine, specifically military nature of his sense of honour. The *Helme* is an emblem here of the great general, the man in whom fighting qualities are ideally joined with commanding qualities of mind – the conjunction being officed in the service of Venice and of heaven. In defining the emblematic opposite Othello produces the image of the *Skillet*, or cooking-pot – something structurally similar in being a container made of metal but lacking all the dignity of containing and protecting within a military mould the Othellonian mind. And against the soldier he puts the *House-wiues. OED* defines this in the singular as 'A woman who manages her household with skill and thrift' (*Housewife* 1) – such a woman as the motherless Desdemona was, arguably, in her father's house, where the house-affairs would pull her from Othello's stories (as reported in Othello's address to the council in I.iii). But no recognition of this domestic virtue is present in Othello's speech. Domesticity is for women. It can have nothing of honour, in Othello's conception. For Othello honour is something he has formerly found only in the 'vnhoused free condition' (F230; I.ii.26) of the military bachelor – a man averse not only to the kitchen but to the domestic life in all its respects.[21]

In Othello's immoderation one may the more easily discern Shakespeare's working of the *free/base* conflict. Against the untied man's freedom to be noble is set the bondage of a man bound in by base adversity – that is, by the suspected defamation of Othello's good name by the Council's thoughts. This man reacts, in an unaccustomed circumstance, with some baseness himself. Such a man would be base not only in the sense of 'unworthy' or 'low in the moral scale'; he would be 'Servile as opposed to free' (*OED*, *Base* adj., II.9 and 11). Othello is servile to the dominant demand of his reputation. He is not sufficiently free to think of Desdemona's mind alone. His estimation, in the sense of his judgement, is already affected by the marriage-bond. Already, Shakespeare is touching the note he makes Othello strike in the *base* Judean or Indian image of the last long speech. Like any being low in the scale of morals or creation (*OED*, *Base* adj., II.9 and 8), Othello will be considerably less than bounteous in discarding the pearl that is Desdemona.

Two more of Shakespeare's lexical pointings need to be registered here. First, the rehearsal of *bounteous* for the later 'I greet thy loue, . . . with acceptance bounteous' (F2121–2; III.iii.473–4). Othello will grant to Iago the means of expressing his love by the killing of Cassio: from III.iii Othello is to be far more bounteous in his consideration of Iago's mind than ever he is in consideration of Desdemona's. In this respect, too, Iago's 'I would not haue your free, and Noble Nature, / Out of selfe-Bounty, be abus'd' (F1815–16; III.iii.203–4) has its interest. Iago plays on Othello's earlier announcement of a bounteous motive and intent. He refers to Othello's innate generosity of self; or – this is less likely – he refers to Othello's need to be more generous *to* himself. In either case he works on a conviction in Othello that he *has* been completely and consistently treating Desdemona in accordance with his announcement. The second of Shakespeare's lexical points that need registering is the insistent repetition of *my* in the last few of the lines under discussion: *my . . . instrument*; *my Disports*; *my businesse*; *my Helme*; *my Estimation*. It is generally observed – by, for example, Heilman (*passim*) – that Othello is given to an obtrusive use of the pronouns *me* and *my*. Here the habit is particularly incongruous: all those *my*s work against the announced bounty to Desdemona's mind; they suggest, rather, that Othello is being bounteous to his *own* mind. To conclude the discussion of this passage, it is worth noting that in addressing Desdemona as 'Bounteous Madam'

(F1598; III.iii.7) Cassio confirms a major truth: it is Desdemona, not
Othello, who freely supplies most of the bounteousness in the play.

Shakespeare's point about Othello's lack of such bounty is made
again, briefly, towards the end of this 'trial' scene. Told 'you must
hence to night', Othello and Desdemona differ in their reactions:

> DESDEMONA. To night my Lord? [Not in F.]
> DUKE.. This night. [Not in F.]
> OTHELLO. With all my heart.
>
> (Q628–629; I.iii.278)

For all her warrior mind, Desdemona is distressed at this rough
curtailment of her wedding-night. Q certainly underlines the
alacrity with which, in contrast, Othello dismisses his marital dues
for military duty and the affairs of state. Heilman (*Magic in the Web*,
p. 141), in briefly alluding to this passage, considers Othello's
attitude of 'business first' understandable but expressed with some
'ruthlessness'. This last is probably inaccurate in that it implies a
conscious lack of ruth; but certainly in this little exchange the subduing of Desdemona's *heart* to the very quality of her lord is not
reciprocated. Her lord's phrase *With all my heart* adverbially supports a quick embarkation; it suggests that Othello's heart is subdued to the pleasures of a military expedition rather than to
Desdemona's very quality. Beyond the needs of the military emergency, of reassuring the Senate, and of defending his (unassailed)
reputation, Othello overrides Desdemona's distress.

When Othello lands on Cyprus, there are no senators present
needing assurance; and, anyway, the Turkish invasion fleet has
been dispersed. Othello can loose his emotion at being reunited
with his wife. He can prattle engagingly. He can kiss his wife. He
can refer to his 'content', his 'comfort', his 'too much of ioy'. He can
call his wife 'my Soules Ioy', 'Hony' and 'my Sweet'. Moreover, in
the phrase 'my faire Warriour' (F958; II.i.180) the two senses of *Rites*
are brought together. Othello refers both to his wife's beauty and to
her heroic nature in having endured the storm and in having
arrived earlier than he despite her having started later. (*Before*, in 'It
giues me wonder great, as my content / To see you heere before me'
[F960–1; II.i.182–3], seems to function both as preposition and as
adverb: certainly, both these grammatical functions were available
to Shakespeare.) On the whole, Desdemona must be gratified by a
reception in which both her beauty and her character have been

appreciated and the sacred nature of her marriage implied.

However, throughout this section (F958–95; II.i.180–210) there are small instances of discord in Othello that accumulate into significance. I use the word 'discord' in order to qualify the view of Wilson Knight, for whom this sequence expresses Othello's marriage as one of unqualified harmony.[22] The first of these instances is in the very use of *my fair Warrior*, in which Desdemona's far more direct 'My deere Othello' highlights a comparative distance. True, Othello's greeting may carry something of the courtly convention by which Desdemona becomes a welcomed warrior in *marital* encounter; but still Othello's courtliness has nothing of Desdemona's directness. Othello orates. Desdemona merely greets – and is the more eloquent in her simplicity. True, Othello is to say 'Come my deere Loue' (F1119; II.iii.8); but elsewhere he transfers *deere* to his 'deere heart-strings' (F1892; III.iii.265) and to his arms' 'deerest action, in the Tented Field' (F424; I.iii.85). Not, that is, to a beloved person (*OED, Dear* adj.[1] I.2; Schmidt, *Dear* adj., 4) but first to a vital and inmost part of himself (Schmidt adj., 6) and then to a precious, valuable activity of his military life (Schmidt adj., 3). This contrasting usage is suggestive. The tendons that bind his heart to himself, and his idealistic fighting – these, according to Shakespeare's deployment of *deere*, would seem to mean more to Othello than does his wife. Another instance in which Shakespeare makes Othello use *deere* as 'beloved' is 'Minion, your deere lyes dead' (F3120; V.i.33): the adjective has been turned into a synonym for Cassio; the warmth that Desdemona put into the adjective has been turned to Othello's hate.[23]

Another discord sounds in Othello's

> I feare
> My Soule hath her content so absolute,
> That not another comfort like to this,
> Succeedes in vnknowne Fate.
>
> (F968–71; II.i.188–91)

Once again Shakespeare enriches the drama by presenting in Othello an uncanny ability to foretell the future. Here it is not hubris that is at work – rather its opposite, a humility before whatever might come. Usually the gift of prophecy is given to dying characters – to John of Gaunt, for example, in *The life and death of King Richard the Second*. Here Shakespeare gives something ap-

proximating to it to a hero at his moment of maximum happiness –
his foes defeated by a pro-Venetian Nature, his marriage resumed.
Desdemona certainly hears the incongruity of this extreme joy
conjoined with extreme pessimism; and she is quick with a corrective:

> The Heauens forbid
> But that our Loues
> And Comforts should encrease
> Euen as our dayes do grow.
>
> (F972–5; II.i. 191–3)

In this much healthier prognostication of happiness, Desdemona
would seem to be far more a fair wife than a fair warrior. She looks
ahead to increase and growth, whereas her husband has just envisaged a future of violence and adventurous contrast:

> If after euery Tempest, come such Calmes,
> May the windes blow, till they haue waken'd death:
> And let the labouring Barke climbe hills of Seas
> Olympus high: and duck again as low,
> As hell's from Heauen. If it were now to dye,
> 'Twere now to be most happy.
>
> (F963–8; II.i. 183–8)

It would seem that Othello exemplifies the view that true relaxation
can occur only as a result of great effort and discomfort. For him,
marital calm consists in the cessation of violence – and needs the
contrast of the violence in order to be appreciated. There is, then, a
suggestion of temperamental incompatibility as Othello looks for
emotional extremes in marriage while Desdemona, for all her talk of
risks and travel, looks for steadiness. As for being bounteous to his
wife's mind, Othello seems to perceive only the warrior quality and
nothing of the woman in his apparent readiness to subject himself –
and by implication her – to another such storm as the one they have
just separately survived. There is, in other words, a curious lack of
judgement in his joy. Of course, to Desdemona all this may well be
merely a feature of her husband's unaccustomed and fond garru-
lity:

> Oh my Sweet,

> I prattle out of fashion, and I doate
> In mine owne comforts.
>
>   (F988–90; II.i.203–5)

Doate here means 'act or talk foolishly or stupidly' (*OED, Dote* v.¹,
I.1). Desdemona is not to know what we know in retrospect: that
here is more of the author's dramatic irony; and that Othello *is* to
subject the two of them to a far worse storm of emotion, in which
their marriage will be wrecked.

There are two further indicators of a potential for disharmony.
The first is Othello's talk of *me/my* and *you*, which contrasts to
Desdemona's easy thinking in terms of a couple: *our Loues* and *our
dayes*. The other is Othello's use of the formal *vous* form. Unlike
Desdemona, who always *you*s her lord and husband, Othello has
the choice of either the familiar or the formal form of the second
person singular in addressing his wife.²⁴ His 'see you heere' and
'you shall be well desir'd' (F961 and 987; II.i.182 and 202) support
the idea of distance already suggested by 'O, my faire Warriour'. If
the scene is formal, a public ceremonial, Othello does little to relax it
and make it intimate. True, after Desdemona's wording of her
reproof he uses the plural pronoun of a couple: 'And this, and this
the greatest discords be / That ere our hearts shall make' (F979 – 80;
II.i.196 – 7). But even this, and his kisses, and his endearments, fail
to match Desdemona's quiet instinctiveness.

Not long after this scene, Shakespeare gives Iago an observation
using *deere*: that Othello will 'proue to Desdemona / A most deere
husband' (F1073–4; II.i.284–5). Iago's character means that a sneer is
probably present. Shortly after, Othello is shown dearly taking
Desdemona off-stage or at least behind curtains to bed:

>   Come my deere Loue,
> The purchase made, the fruites are to ensue,
> That profit's [Q *The profits*] yet to come 'tweene [Q *twixt*]
>   me, and you.
> Goodnight.
>
>   (F1119–22; II.iii.8–11)

These lines have been little glossed. Some editors briefly explain
the marital reference; others seem, in their silence, to regard the
lines as uninteresting. By now Othello has ceased his doting endearments and relaxed to join Desdemona in a natural, unforced

kind of marital address. But the lexicon after the first line seems, still, to err from Desdemona's view of marriage as an idealistic and spiritual love. Here, one might have thought, is Shakespeare's opportunity to write for Othello some elevated and romantic sentiments. A word on the calmness of the night perhaps – as in the Belmont scene of *The Merchant of Venice* when Lorenzo instructs Jessica; or a reference to the benign (for once in this play) influence of the moon. Instead, Shakespeare gives Othello a passage of language that belongs, certainly, to the conventional literary lexicon of love – in which terms of sexual love and of finance were often equated, as in the word *spend* for example – but which also has something of a laboured insistence. The general meaning is that husband and wife are now to enjoy the legally acquired, earned pleasure – the proper satisfaction – of the rites of love; but the financial metaphor *is* emphatically inscribed, and one wonders whether Shakespeare might not be making a comment within the convention. *Purchase* is 'Acquisition by payment' (*OED* sb., 6). *Fruits* are 'products, revenue' (*OED* sb., 7a *pl*.). *Profit*, though generally 'advantage or benefit' (*OED* B sb.), is pushed by the metaphor into the meaning of 'That which is derived from or produced by some source of revenue' as in the phrase *profit and loss* (*OED* sb., 4 and 6a). If the third line is a clause of result as opposed to a main clause as in Q, then *profit* might refer to children. The triteness of the extended metaphor is similar to that of Iago's extended comparison, made to Rodorigo, about bodies as gardens and wills as gardeners (F673ff.; I.iii.320ff.).[25] The couplet, too, marking the end of a scene, supplements the reduced sentiment with a facile neatness quite alien to the Othello one has heard hitherto.

Why does Shakespeare make Othello speak of this love-match in terms more appropriate to a marriage by arrangement? Why this incongruity? The reason is, arguably, to suggest that, inside a confident exterior, Othello is feeling some unease. He has nuptial 'nerves'; and instead of acknowledging them he denies them. He attempts to conceal his unease beneath a misplaced jocosity. This cast of thought – the refusal to acknowledge uncertainty – will become crucial in the play's development. It may be, too, that Othello is demonstrating another anxiety in this scene – that same concern for his military reputation that we have heard before. The old conflict between the rites of love and the rites of war re-sounds. Othello cannot delegate authority even to Michael Cassio without reminding him of the 'Honourable stop' to revelry. And when he asks Cassio to speak with him 'Tomorrow with your earliest' (F1118; II.iii.7) he is concerned, probably, first to prove his sense of military duty unseeled and unfoiled and then, secondly, to prevent on Cyprus the thoughts about excessively lusty moors that he suspected in the councillors back in Venice. It is a fine example of Shakespeare's dramatic sense that he makes Iago promptly, on the newlyweds' withdrawal, voice such thoughts: 'Our Generall cast vs thus earely for the loue of his Desdemona: Who, let vs not therefore blame; he hath not yet made wanton the night with her: and she is sport for Ioue' (F1126–9; II.iii.13–17).

Othello is sympathetic as a late recruit into Cupid's ranks, less so for his failure, again, to respond in kind to Desdemona's view of marriage as a consecration of soul to soul. Othello has not even modified his financial metaphor by any reference to Desdemona's being more than the sea's (or seas') worth, as he implied she was at F229–32 (I.ii.25–8). It could well be that in giving Othello such a spiritually poor expression Shakespeare is preparing for the 'brothel' scene – 'there's money for your paines' (F2793; IV.ii.94) – while showing us that Iago is not the only character who indulges, early in the play, in talk of price and trade.[26] interestingly too, in the couplet Shakespeare makes Othello revert from the marital first person plural to *me* and *you* – and, moreover, makes Othello give himself a syntactical priority. A small point, but suggestive.

The word *purchase* has interest from another meaning. It may, in fact, express some authorial comment. *Purchase* could mean 'the catching or seizing of prey; hence pillage, plunder, robbery, capture' (*OED* sb., I.1). This participates in the scheme of hunting-with-hound-or-hawk images distributed through the play.[27] It also reminds us that a plunder *has* been made – by the newlyweds of Brabantio's emotional rights in his daughter, and by Othello of Brabantio's hospitable trust. In this meaning Othello would still be jocular – Desdemona might delight in being her hero's plunder – but in view of Othello's later implication (in his last long speech) of himself as a Turk who has hurt a Venetian, one of the *OED*'s illustrations of *purchase* as 'plunder' becomes remarkably resonant: '1596 Z. J. tr. Lavardin's Scanderberg iii, 91 (The Turks) being scattered and dispersed . . . here and there about purchase and pillage.' It is unlikely that Othello does intend this contemporary meaning; but as an authorial connotation it is suggestive. By the end of the play Othello as a foreigner and barbarian will have robbed and pillaged Venice.[28]

At F1629–93 (III.iii.36–93) Shakespeare enacts another instance of Othello's lack of bounty to Desdemona's mind. Four soundings of *deny* make for a theme of denial. Othello says, 'I will deny thee nothing' and again 'I will deny thee nothing.' Desdemona says, pleading for Cassio, 'I wonder in my Soule / What you would aske me, that I should deny' and then 'Shall I deny you? No: Farewell my Lord.' And in each use *deny* means 'refuse or withold' (*OED* v III.4). Each character asserts his or her intent of being generous to the other's plea or wish. And Othello does in fact grant his wife's wish that Cassio may come; while his wife does in fact accede to his wish to be left to himself for a while. And yet this quibbling on *deny* expresses much tension in the couple. Desdemona, characteristically, is direct in her answers to Othello's peculiar questions. She declares she has been talking with a man that languishes in Othello's displeasure. Obviously Cassio. No other man has displeased. And, though Othello replies obliquely, 'Who is't you mean?', still Desdemona answers straight: 'Why your Lieutenant Cassio . . . . ' To ask for Cassio's reinstatement is certainly premature and forward of Desdemona; but at least she is open about her suit. She prays that Cassio be called back, is answered again in a peculiarly awry manner – 'Went he hence now?' – but again herself answers straight, her oath expressing some impatience: 'I sooth . . . ' – or, in Q, 'Yes faith . . . . ' There now follows a series of plea and evasion that constitutes the couple's first quarrel. Decorous, controlled, even humorous, but still a quarrel. Desdemona's extended questioning, by which she tries to pin Othello to a fixed time for Cassio's interview, is met – or not met – by an equally consistent set of evasions: 'Not now (sweet Desdemona) some other time'; 'The sooner (Sweet) for you'; 'No, not to night'; and finally 'I shall not dine at home: / I meete the Captaines at the Cittadell.' And moreover, when Othello does capitulate to his wife's argument and exclamation, he does so in a way that again evades the issue. He condescends (in the modern sense) to Desdemona. He purports to be amused: 'Prythee no more: Let him come when he will: / I will deny thee nothing.' That is, instead of facing squarely Desdemona's arguments and countering with his own, he retires into vagueness. He attempts to give in on his own terms, as if to say, 'Ah, these women, we must indulge them.' But the admirable – if tactless – Desdemona will not allow him this dishonesty. She exposes it:

> Why, this is not a Boone:
> 'Tis as I should entreate you weare your Gloues,
> Or feede on nourishing dishes, or keepe you warme,
> Or sue to you, to do a peculiar profit
> To your owne person.
>
> (F1676–80; III.iii.77–81)

Admirable Desdemona! What logic! What a Portia this heroine is! And poor Othello! His beautiful soldier has turned on him. She has him in siege. He has surrendered but still she is assailing him with this unwifely weapon of cogent argument. All he can do is re-announce his surrender and beg to be allowed to collect his casualties:

> I will deny thee nothing.
> Whereon, I do beseech thee, grant me this,
> To leaue me but a little to my selfe.
>
> (F1684–6; III.iii.84–6)

That is, to the self that finds it difficult to think in the marital first person plural.

That *Whereon* is cunning. It translates as 'On the basis of which promise of denying you nothing'. It implies that Desdemona must leave Othello not because he has important work to do (no mention of any) but on the grounds of a balance of bounty: he has granted Desdemona's wish; now she must grant his. In other words, Othello ignores or fails to register the substance of Desdemona's argument. As far as he is concerned, he *has* granted a boon.

All this is to say that, overall, Othello *does* deny Desdemona. Perhaps he is not used to argument in a woman; perhaps he is amazed by this precisian Desdemona. Whatever the reason, he has not been free and bounteous to her mind. To her wish, yes, eventually. But not to her argument. Othello does not recognise her presentation of a logic that should be answered in kind. For he makes no attempt to counter Desdemona's pressure with any of the well-founded defences available to him. He might have taken Desdemona's

> In faith hee's penitent:
> And yet his Trespass, in our common reason
> (Saue that they say the warres must make example)

Out of her best, is not almost a fault
T'encurre a priuate checke

(F1662–6; III.iii.64–8)
[Q, more correctly, closes the bracket after *best*].

and destroyed it. He might have said that Cassio's penitence is irrelevant. He might have said that Cassio's neglect of duty when responsible for the town's safety *was* serious enough for a dishonourable discharge. He might have additionally pointed out that Desdemona has no right whatsoever to be interfering in these military matters. She should confine her fair warriorhood to the service of her lord and should not be trying to influence his professional judgement. Had he said any of these he might have made for a more expressive colloquy, a talk of two people in which the opinions and thoughts of each are registered by the other. But Othello does not so answer. Inside the forced jocosity of the dialogue – it cannot be justly called an exchange – there is an irritation that Desdemona healthily allows to emerge but which Othello hides.[29]

What Othello is feeling, in fact, is a temporary draining of his tenderness for Desdemona. Her talk of gloves and dishes, her domestic reference 'is an intrusion comparable to that of the Cassio topic, and it brings Othello's latent irritation to a head.'[30] To revert to a 'draining' figure: Othello is horrified by the resulting emptiness. But, instead of analysing, instead of trying to account for his lesser tenderness, he does nothing but refill that emptiness with a reassertion of love: a reassertion that does not encompass the need of Desdemona's absence that he has just experienced. He does not reflect on that new experience. Instead, he goes in for his usual extremes:

Excellent wretch: Perdition catch my Soule
But I do loue thee: and when I loue thee not,
Chaos is come againe.

(F1691–3; III.iii.91–3)

And in so doing, it seems, he further denies Desdemona's quality of mind. For *wretch*, though a term of endearment, is really a bizarre definition of Desdemona. Othello is still maintaining his indulgent attitude: he still does not recognise her right to be treated as an intelligent being. *Wretch* caused much dissent among early critics,

who thought it unfair but considered the unfairness to be elsewhere than in Othello. Some went against the authority of both F
and Q in emending to 'wench'. Johnson defined the whole phrase
as 'Dear, harmless, helpless excellence'; and Hart (p. 130) has 'An
affectionate term, generally used with pity.'[31] There *may* be a
reference to Desdemona's submissiveness in so promptly obeying
the wish of her husband and leaving him. But this interpretation
ignores Desdemona's zeal in logic. It is this zeal that has provoked
wretch (while it is the prompt obedience, along with some admira-
tion of Desdemona's moral crusade for Cassio, that has provoked
Excellent). By *wretch* Othello means mainly 'little creature (used as a
term of playful depreciation)' (see *OED* 2e, which is illustrated by
this passage). But the depreciation needs to be emphasised.
Remove the playful element and you are left with 'A vile . . . or
despicable person' (*OED* 3) – the kind of person that Desdemona
will shortly have become in Othello's mind. Again, there may well
be some author comment: Shakespeare may be suggesting something of 'One who is sunk in deep distress, sorrow, misfortune
. . . ' (*OED* 2). This also describes, from another point of view,
what Desdemona is shortly to have become. It also suggestingly
Englishes her Italianate name. Othello's denials and dismissals are
increasingly to make that name apt.[32]

The sequence *and when I loue thee not, / Chaos is come againe* is a
variant of the conditional asseverative. *When* seems to denote time
more than it does 'if'; and the sequence combines the present with
the future. Othello is referring to a condition he has just experienced. In his extremist language he is dissimulating his suppressed irritation. The chaos is Othello's way of describing the
emptiness he has felt – *Chaos* being the state of primal emptiness
(after a Greek verb stem meaning 'yawn' or 'gape') rather than mere
confusion. This emptiness, felt momentarily here, is later to
become chronic: 'Me thinkes, it should be . . . that th'affrighted
Globe / Did yawne at Alteration' (F3362–4; v.ii.102–4). Ridley (p.
98n) maintains that 'the verb in both clauses is, in effect, future';
and this future sense certainly sounds yet again Othello's strange
apprehension of unknown fate. Once again he supplies a powerful
dramatic irony to the play with his unknown gift of inadvertent
prophecy. This particular prophecy is realised twofold: first by the
murder of Desdemona in Act V; second, more immediately, by
Iago's first insinuations. It is precisely from this point that they
develop. (Iago's earlier 'Hah? I like not that' (F1628; III.iii.35) is,

strictly, his first insinuation; but the text has no real evidence that it takes effect.) Shakespeare's skilled dramatic juxtaposition here is generally recognised: *Chaos is come again* acts virtually as a cue for the agent of chaos to begin his work. There is, too, a further prophecy and prefiguring in the oath *Perdition catch my Soule*. Its effect is more startling and extreme than conventional. One registers the wording and may justly ask, why does Othello consider that his love entails damnation and loss? Does he have some obscure unease about an unsoldierly weakness in falling in love? The oath rehearses Othello's awareness of deserved damnation after his dreadful folly has been exposed in v.ii. Desdemona's look, he says, will hurl his soul for fiends to catch at. He himself will command his own punishment in hell. Perdition *will* catch his soul. For this chapter the germane point is this: that Othello's unease for his soul and for his love is bound up with his subtle denial of Desdemona's mind – her right to an independence of mind – and with the actual dismissal of Desdemona that concludes this 'denial' scene.[33]

Shakespeare, then, has well established Othello's denial and dismissal of his wife in the early part of the play. From now on they will be working in the context of Othello's doubt and jealousy. They will not demonstrate a new tendency in Othello. They will develop from the earlier instances.

The first development is in the tiny section where Desdemona drops the handkerchief. The main, indeed the only, purpose of this section is to get that handkerchief dropped; but Shakespeare does effect an inscription of character within the stage business. He makes Othello rebuff both his wife's mind and her physical proximity. Othello's faintness of voice has been inquired into by the direct Desdemona; and Othello refers to a headache. He may actually have a headache caused by the stress he is under – a precursor of his fit – or he may be dissembling. In either case he is withholding from Desdemona vital information about his sickness. He makes a covert reference to his (presumed) cuckold's horns – and this naturally must miss Desdemona. In effect Othello is saying, You see, I know all about you. But for Desdemona the headache can be nothing but the result of *watching* (F1919; III.iii.289). Further, when the handkerchief proves too small to bind his head Othello's 'Let it alone' (F1923; III.iii.292) expresses yet again his irritation – even perhaps to the extent of a physical putting-away of Desdemona's hand. In this I am of course interpreting *it* as Othello's head or the binding-activity and not as the handkerchief.[34]

Again Othello distances his wife with *vous* – in 'Your Napkin' and 'Come, Ile go in with you' (F1922 and 1923; III.iii.291 and 292). On landing on Cyprus he held her at arm's length, as it were, to expatiate on his wonder and contentment; here he keeps her there. Come, he says, but he goes only physically with Desdemona to his guests and dinner. He does not go in spirit. Not as one happily in a couple. This *Come* repeats the *Come* of 'Come Desdemona, 'tis the Soldiers life, / To haue their balmy Slumbers wak'd with strife' (after the brawl at F1381–2; II.iii.249–50). Both passages imply a mutuality that on Othello's side does not exist. In both instances Desdemona's inquiry – in the earlier passage 'What is the matter (Deere?) [*sic*]' – is ignored. The earlier, habitual dismissiveness is developed; it becomes purposive.

At F2174ff (III.iv.30ff) Shakespeare truly begins to derive benefit from his careful laying-down of Othello's tendency to deny and dismiss his wife. In this extended passage – concerning a hand, a handkerchief and a tragic hero unique in a head-cold – Desdemona is mystified, provoked and finally walked out on. At the end she has no more information than she had at the start. All she knows is that she stands 'within the blank' of Othello's 'displeasure / For my free speech' (F2284–5; III.iv.129–30). I find that *blank* extraordinarily vivid. Desdemona's reference is to the white spot in the middle of a target (*OED* sb., 2). She reports herself as having been shot at by Othello's anger. There is much pathos in this fair warrior's use of a military image: the military virtue she so much admires is being turned against her. Additionally, *blank* derives from, and is similar to, French *blanc* ('white'); and by association, on the page at least, it is possible to visualise Desdemona's pale face white with shock. At the same time *blank* means 'empty' or 'emptiness': in Othello's displeasure Desdemona finds the coming of chaos, of nothing. As for Desdemona's use of *free* in 'free speech', that is a cunning Shakespearean touch. Her speech has been not only independent but generous on Cassio's behalf. She is freely bounteous to Cassio in the way of a noble – albeit tactless – mind. And, the more free she is, so the less free and bounteous does Othello become. Far, far more than Desdemona's knowledge at the end of this section is her shock. Othello's behaviour was not 'such obseruancie / As fits the Bridall' (F2306–7; III.iv.150–1). Rather, it was suggestive of a putting-away.[35]

The whole business of the hand, in fact, travesties the giving of a hand in marriage:

    OTHELLO.   Oh hardnes [*sic*] to dissemble!
       How do you, Desdemona?
    DESDEMONA. Well, my good Lord.
    OTHELLO. Giue me your Hand.
       This hand is moist, my Lady.
    DESDEMONA. It hath felt no age, nor knowne no sorrow.
    OTHELLO. This argues fruitfulnesse, and liberall heart:
       Hot, hot, and moyst. This hand of yours requires
       A sequester from Liberty: Fasting, and Prayer,
       Much Castigation, Exercise deuout,
       For heere's a yong, and sweating Diuell heere
       That commonly rebels: 'Tis a good hand,
       A franke one.
    DESDEMONA. You may (indeed) say so:
       For 'twas that hand that gaue away my heart.
    OTHELLO. A liberall hand. The hearts of old, gaue hands:
       But our new Heraldry is hands, not hearts.
    DESDEMONA. I cannot speake of this:
       Come, now your promise.
    OTHELLO. What promise, Chucke?

                     (F2175–94; III.iv.31–46)

Desdemona is made to remain in ignorance of the death-sentence passed on her by her husband at the end of III.iii. She is given, in lieu of such plot-collapsing information, a sinister kind of reversed marriage, an un-marriage, a consignment to a strait austerity. This strict life of penitence would be more suited to a religious near-votarist such as Isabella in *Measure for Measure* than to a warm young wife. Desdemona is advised to take it up not because, as in Ophelia's case, all mankind are sinners and she must not breed, but because she herself is sinful, the harbourer of the young and sweating devil in her hand. This earnestly advising Othello, who is also covertly intent on Desdemona's death, prefigures the 'priestish', murderous Othello whose great *Cause* and concern for Desdemona's soul inform the early part of V.ii. At the same time, however, the verb *dissemble* in the first line is an important keyword for the whole of the utterance here. Everything that Othello says, aggressive as it is, is couched in a tone of affectionate banter. Everything he says is highly ambiguous. As a result, much dramatic tension is generated by the fact that we, as audience or reader, receive two sets of meaning from much of the lexicon while Desdemona, not possessed of our knowledge, can receive only one – the 'innocent' one. So, *fruitfulnesse* develops from Othello's talk of the fruits of a wedding – happy married life and children – as he led Desdemona to bed at the start of II..iii. It could mean 'fertility', and had already come to denote a generosity of spirit as well. (This last is Iago's meaning in 'She's fram'd as fruitefull / As the free Elements' – F1467–8; II.iii.330–1.) *Fruitfulnesse* had also, however, come to denote an amorous liberality. Schmidt, and others, draw the attention to 'Nay, if an oyly Palme bee not a fruitfull Prognostication, I cannot scratch mine eare' (*The Tragedie of Anthonie, and Cleopatra*, F129–30; I.ii.49–50). Here, *fruitfull* has reference to sexuality and fertility together – so that even Charmian's remark about scratching her ear takes a heavy sexual innuendo. Thus, right from the start, Othello's talk offers a duality of interpretation, the one 'good', the other 'bad'. And it is indicative of Desdemona's general innocence, as well as of her specifically uninformed condition, that she should offer her lack of age and her lack of sorrow as reasons for the sanguine character of her palm – that she should have registered only the innocuous sense of Othello's talk. Again, *liberall* could mean in a 'good' sense 'munificent, bounteous' (Schmidt, *Liberal* 6); but in a 'bad' sense it could be 'licentious' (*OED, Liberal* A adj., 3). Equally, in a 'bad' sense, it could be used 'of women profuse in their favours' (Schmidt 6 again, citing this passage). The point is that Desdemona, who meant 'licentious' when she called Iago 'a most prophane, and liberall Counsailor' (F938–9; II.i.162–3), does not take that meaning from Othello's speech. Yet again, the same dualism pertains in *Liberty*. It could be merely 'freedom from restraint' (Schmidt 1); or it could be 'licentiousness' (Schmidt 3) or 'licence' (*OED* sb., 5). And *franke*, too, conforms to the pattern. While Desdemona responds to the meaning of 'liberal, bountiful' (Schmidt, *Frank* adj., 3), Othello's real meaning is the masked sarcasm of 'open, using no disguise' (Schmidt 2) – Desdemona's hand, Othello obliquely states, is at least moistly honest in declaring her licentious nature.

All these ambiguous near-synonyms belong to the lexical family of *free, and bounteous*; and in view of her husband's announced intention with regard to her mind Desdemona has no reason to feel alarmed by them or, indeed, to perceive any of her husband's distress. Othello finds it hard to dissemble, but his dissembling is effective. Even his more explicit talk of incarceration may be attributed to reasons other than sexual jealousy. Desdemona's innocent remark about having felt no age – a truth, by the way, that the overwrought Othello could easily misinterpret as referring to a motive in Desdemona's disaffection – might after all have provoked the older Othello to pass amused observations on the hot-bloodedness and new-fangledness of youth. And his prescriptions of fasting and prayer, of correction and religious offices, are much in the character of the pilgrim soldier whose austere valour helped to fascinate Desdemona in the first place.

Interestingly, through all these prescriptions Othello is made to refer back to the listing of

> 'Tis not to make me Iealious,
> To say my wife is fair, feeds well, loues company,
> Is free of Speech, Sings, Playes, and Dances [Q *well*]:
> Where Vertue is, these are more vertuous.
>
>   (F1799–802; III.iii.187–190)

He is made to refer back to the activities in which he detected – perhaps overprotestingly – the proof of his wife's virtue. Now, instead of enjoying *company* she must suffer a seclusion from it – and particularly from that kind of company which is 'Sexual connexion' (*OED* sb., 2 [1386–1616]) and which you might 'cohabit (with)' (*OED* v., 3b [c. 1400–1680]). Instead of feeding well she must fast. Instead of singing she must pray. Instead of demonstrating her accomplishment in the discipline of a musical instrument she must submit to 'corrective punishment or discipline' (*OED*, *Castigation* 1) – and lots of it. Instead of dancing she must put herself to religious exercise, the saying of offices. The parallel between these passages is strong, and supplies a good example of Shakespeare's rich economy in characterisation, his way of developing material already inscribed.

I said Desdemona shows no alarm and perceives nothing of Othello's distress. That is not to say she is not mystified. Othello's final, cryptic words about marriage certainly elude her. In the sense that heraldry is the job of a herald or messenger, Othello says, the hand's message in our new heraldry derives only from the hand and not from the heart. Marriage now is no longer a guarantee of love. In the old days hands were sincerely given in matrimony; now merely from the hand's habit of promiscuous generosity. Whether Desdemona understands all this or not, her response – 'I cannot speake of this' – sounds a certain impatience. She is perhaps a little irritated by the insistent teasing of this husband of hers, particularly since she has the more important matter of Cassio to press. The point is, Desdemona would not have been impatient or irritated at all if Othello for once had behaved freely and bounteously to her mind – if, that is, he had been frank and liberal instead of merely using those two words in an incomprehensible condemnation. But by now Shakespeare has well established that this candour is precisely what Othello does not practise with Desdemona. As ever, Othello denies her right to information. As ever, he circumlocutes. The hand is held, brooded on, condemned and sentenced. But it is never actually reasoned about. There is nothing for Desdemona to catch hold of in turn: no line directly to the effect, This hand you gave me but your heart is false.

Further, this established inability to speak true to Desdemona is again used by Shakespeare when he pulls Othello from hand to handkerchief. The gypsy's reported warnings about the handkerchief do, of course, alarm Desdemona. Or perhaps it is Othello's insistence, his very manner, that she finds the more alarming. The fact that Othello, when he gave the handkerchief to Desdemona, did not warn her of its significance is not developed by Shakespeare. Othello's extreme declaration that to lose or give the handkerchief away must entail 'such perdition, / As nothing else could match' (F2215–16; III.iv.67–8) is met by Desdemona's 'Is't possible?' There is an amount of childlike wonder in this response, perhaps even shock, which yet maintains a gist of disbelief. Not a challenging disbelief, more a wish *not* to believe. Now, *perdition* has featured recently once before in Othello's utterance – *Perdition catch my Soule / But I do loue thee* – and its re-sounding of a specifically Christian allusion here, amongst so much reference to magic and superstition of a largely pagan kind, serves to complicate and enrich our sense of the Moor's spiritual being. He is a sincere Christian, idealistic and austere; and yet his atavistic susceptibility to pagan magical practices supplies an alarming as well as an exotic facet to this commander of Christian, European forces who prides himself on his reason. Desdemona's response is not, however, to this cultural mixing. Rather, it is to the sheer extremism of what she has been told. She would prefer not to believe in the handkerchief's antecedents. She would prefer not to believe that its loss – and it *is* lost – must involve her in such a frightful punishment as perdition: not just loss but a damnation worse than any other. (The *OED* lists 'loss' as a peculiarly Shakespearean meaning of *perdition*. The meanings of 'damnation' or 'destruction' derive from Middle English.) In this talk of the Egyptian or gypsy there is, in fact, something of Othello's traveller's history and courtship as reported in Act I: the same exoticism, the same effect of wonder – 'She swore in faith 'twas strange: 'twas passing strange'; and of fright – 'She wish'd she had not heard it' (F505 and 507; I.iii.160 and 162). The difference is that Desdemona's fright is now directly for herself, neither vicarious nor for Othello; and it does not prevent in Othello a suspicion that this time she disbelieves.

He meets this with no argument. Rather, he attempts to smother all possibility of doubt with layer upon layer of assertion. First he asserts simply that ''Tis true.' Then he asserts that the handkerchief has had magic worked into it. Then he asserts the authority of the sibylline manufacture – by another dealer in magic, who had had two hundred years' experience in the natural ways of the universe ('that had numbred in the world / The Sun to course [Q *make*], two hundred compasses' – F2219–20; III.iv.70–1).[36] Then he adds that the silkworms themselves were blessed in their production of the handkerchief's raw material – thereby mixing another Christian allusion to this detailing of an occult practice. All this he then supplements: the finished handkerchief, or the silk used for the handkerchief, was dipped in a particularly horrid preparation of 'Mummey, which the Skilfull / Conseru'd of Maidens hearts' (F2223–4; III.iv.74–5). This is a notable piece of wife-frightening. Look what happens to naughty maidens and then imagine what might happen to a naughty wife. Of course, the full import of it must widely miss the innocent Desdemona; but its effect is signalled in Desdemona's 'Indeed? Is't true?' Her fright is caused as much by Othello's inexplicably threatening behaviour as by his macabre tale in itself. At the same time, the implication of the tale must alarm: if Desdemona is the maiden, or young wife, then Othello is the mortician who receives her heart in this unromantic way.[37] Othello then places the last of his assertions: the magic of the handkerchief is not just true, it is 'Most veritable'. It is intensely and absolutely true, with all the authority that a long and Latinate word can give it.

That Desdemona has not dropped dead, or has not straight confessed her licence, must amaze Othello. The handkerchief is not lost, she says, but what if it were? Of course, the fact that she lies, out of fright and indignation, supplies the poignant irony that

Desdemona's one single instance of not being direct and honest is to contribute largely to her death – when Othello compares her statement with the ocular proof of the handkerchief's being in Cassio's possession. And the fact that she lies as a reaction to Othello's oblique but powerful threats – to his lack of bounty to her mind – is a notable instance of how Shakespeare so works his drama that a plot-necessity derives naturally from Othello's character, as well as from Desdemona's here. From now on the dialogue of this segment consists in Othello's attempts to command his wife – 'Is't lost? Is't gone? Speak, is't out o'th'way?' (F2230; III.iv.80) – and his wife's scared defiance. This defiance develops into a renewal of Desdemona's pleading for Cassio – and the whole develops into an exchange of volleys, with Othello, eventually, storming off. It is an exchange that is particularly strong when Q's extra lines are interpolated. Othello's four soundings of the word *handkerchief* – without any speculation on the word – are extremely effective. To this has his thinking reduced. It will be seen in later chapters that Othello is given to using the repetition of single words to shape even his most considered and sustained speeches; here his syntactic habit sounds in almost its lowest form – the simple, distressed repetition of a single plereme with attendant article. As such it rehearses the even simpler repetitions of the 'epilepsy' segment in IV.i. The dialogue is as follows:

> DESDEMONA . . .
>> This is a tricke to put me from my suite,
>> Pray you let Cassio be receiu'd againe.
> OTHELLO. Fetch me the [Q *that*] Handkerchiefe,
>> My minde mis-giues.
> DESDEMONA. Come, come: you'l neuer meete a more sufficient
>> man.
> OTHELLO. The Handkerchiefe.
> DESDEMONA. I pray talke me of Cassio. [Q line]
> OTHELLO. The handkercher. [Q line]
> DESDEMONA. A man that all his time
>> Hath founded his good Fortunes on your loue;
>> Shar'd dangers with you.
> OTHELLO. The Handkerchiefe.
> DESDEMONA. Insooth, you are too blame.
> OTHELLO. Zouns [Q's version of F's *Away*.] *Exit Othello*.
>> (F2238–50; III.iv.88–99)

The pressure on Othello will, shortly, dismiss him from his senses for a while; here it dismisses him from Desdemona. As for Desdemona herself, she is left in a state of wonder: 'Sure, there's some wonder in this Handkerchikfe [*sic*]', she says (F2253; III.iv.102). By *some wonder* she means something miraculous, beyond rational explanation, something supernatural (after Schmidt sb., 1: 'a miracle'). She is also left, however, in a state of bewilderment. 'Why do you speake so startingly and rash?' she asked (F2229; III.iv.79). As might now be expected, her question falls on the stage unanswered.

Towards the end of IV.i. Othello's denial and dismissal of his wife consists not only in the physical assault which 'would not be beleeu'd in Venice' (Lodovico at F2636; IV.i.238) but in his verbal behaviour as well. He not only strikes Desdemona but orders her out of his sight. At Lodovico's request he calls her back and insults both her and Lodovico – 'What would you with her, Sir?' – with his pointed ambiguities in *turne* and *obedient*:

> you did wish, that I would make her turne:
> Sir, she can turne, and turne: and yet go on
> And turne again. And she can weepe, Sir, weepe.
> And she's obedient: as you say obedient.
> Very obedient:
>
> (F2650–4; IV.i.249–53)

He changes Lodovico's 'call her backe' into 'make her turne' for the sake of a sexual reference. So far, *turne* has featured in *Othello* as Iago's word. Iago has used it in 'I follow him, to serue my turne vpon him' (F46; I.i.42), where Iago's purpose is to follow his own requirement (*OED, Turn* sb., V.30 and 30b); and in 'will I turne her vertue into pitch' (F1486; II.iii.349). Othello makes the word much stronger. On top of the immediate sense that Desdemona can be made to turn around in her walk he loads several additional meanings. Desdemona can 'revolt' (*OED, Turn* v., V.30c) against her lord and husband. She can become 'sour or tainted (VI.46b). She can 'shift the body (as on an axis) from side to side' and 'twist or writhe about' (III.6a). Above all, she can be shaped or turned (after II.4) as on a lathe, to serve any man's purpose. With some, not necessarily all, of these nuances, Othello virtually declares that Desdemona, at his command, would serve Lodovico sexually, as she would any man. Othello prefigures the 'brothel' scene – but with himself in

Aemilia's role as the bawd. In all this turning, however, he implies, Desdemona is capable of continuing her life of apparently *un*turned virtue. In her deceit Othello discerns her as the type of a Venetian lady in being adept at a trick, a wile, an artifice (*OED, Turn* sb., IV.2). Her wifely obedience is only a cover for her truer obedience to other men. She is the kind of wife who, in Iago's words, will show her pranks to heaven but not to her husband (F1818–9; III.iii.206–7). It is this Desdemona – a delusion – whom Othello then dismisses with nothing of courtesy: 'get you away: / Ile send for you anon' and 'Hence, auaunt' (F2656–8; IV.i.255–7). That the real Desdemona has already been dismissed from, denied in, Othello's mind can be taken as understood.

By this stage the whole male population of Venice has become implicated, in Othello's view, in his wife's treachery. Much discourtesy sounds in Othello's treatment of Lodovico. As far as Othello can tell, Lodovico is probably another Cassio, less extravagantly spoken, but still another representative Italian, a probable chamberer, who hides disports beneath a serious demeanour. Othello's repetition of *Sir* in the last displayed quotation and in the continuation –

> proceed you in your teares.
> Concerning this Sir, (oh well-painted passion)
> I am commanded home: get you away:
> Ile send for you anon. Sir I obey the Mandate,
> And will returne to Venice. Hence, auaunt:
> Cassio shall haue my Place. And Sir, to night
> I do entreat, that we may sup together.
> You are welcome Sir to Cyprus.
> Goats, and Monkeys
>
> (F2654–62; IV.i.253–60)

– distances this man, and insults him. Othello parodies the Venetian courtesy that can disguise discourtesy. One thinks of Iago's lexicon in his denigration of Cassio as one 'apt to play the Sir' in the modish kissing of his own fingers (F948–9; II.i.171–2). Shakespeare makes Othello play the sir in a double sense: Othello savagely mocks the sir that is Lodovico; he also pretends a courtesy. Moreover, one also registers that Shakespeare makes Lodovico enter this scene with Desdemona, probably arm-in-arm or even holding hands in their upper-class easy way; that he makes Iago point this meeting of the two Venetians – ' 'Tis Lodovico, this, comes from the Duke. / See, your wife's with him' (F2602–3; IV.i.210–11); and that he makes Desdemona call Lodovico 'cozen', i.e. kinsman (Schmidt, *Cousin* 2) – or, as Othello must hear it, 'fellow member of the closed Venetian society that excludes my husband'. It must seem to Othello that Lodovico knows all about the infidelity of Desdemona, this female intimate whose tricks he knew back in Venice and who has made this outlandish marriage with the general.[38] Furthermore, the whole of Cyprus must know of Othello's cuckoldry by now. Consider how Desdemona (in fact, Bianca) came bauble-like to Cassio on the Cypriot sea-bank as he was speaking with certain Venetians and fell upon his neck and lolled and wept and shook him and pulled him (in Cassio's misinterpreted account at F2518–25; IV.i.130–9). Could she have been more public? Why, she practically disports on the streets. And consider now, in this scene, how shamelessly it must seem that Desdemona flaunts her feeling for Cassio. She would like to reconcile Othello and Cassio 'for the loue I beare to Cassio' (F2621; IV.i.227). Learning that Othello is to be replaced as governor by Cassio, she is 'glad on't', swearing 'By my troth' (in Q) – which oath may be taken by Othello as an indecent misuse of a marital wording (F2629; IV.i.234). Little wonder, given all this apparent evidence of a barely concealed conspiracy, that the incensed Othello strikes his wife; or that, in his greeting of Lodovico – 'I kisse the Instrument of their pleasures' (F2607; IV.i.213) – he loaded his courtesy with sexual innuendo. The instrument is either Lodovico or, more likely, the mandate he delivers. Othello's greeting, in fact, sounds as a parody of chamberers' language – a parody which is yet informed by his basic simplicity, his native dignity, of speech and action. Othello once saw himself as the military instrument of the State's great business; here he sees Lodovico as instrumental, somehow, in the Duke's and councillors' *pleasures*, those pleasures being not only 'will' (Schmidt, *Pleasure* sb., 2) but also, by implication, amorous gratifications. Wildly Othello implies that Venice is one vast whorehouse and that Lodovico, as any pimp, has brought the directive that Cassio is to *haue my Place*. He cannot reflect that Desdemona, if so enamoured of Cassio, should be *un*happy about a military and political replacement that keeps Cassio in Cyprus while she returns with her husband to Venice. It must seem to Othello as if he is surrounded by people who know all about his horns: by Italian sophisticates who must be barely concealing their laughter behind their handkerchiefs, goats of elaborate etiquette who parade their unholy loves before his very face. Their hypocritical courtesies insult true courtesy just as Desdemona's marrying insults true marriage. Why, even the Duke and the Senate must have been struggling to hide their smiles as he spoke against the love-rites to which Desdemona has proved to be so promiscuously addicted. Othello's parting words, *Goats, and Monkeys*, refer not only to Italian lechery but also to the aping, the monkeying as it were, of an honourable and honest humanity.

On Othello's exit from this scene Shakespeare makes Lodovico ask 'Is it his vse?' (F2676; IV.i.271) – *it* being wife-hitting. Physically, of course, it is not. Such physical violence has never been part of Othello's marriage. (By now the second time-scheme, the 'long' time of Acts III – V, has taken over; so it would be inappropriate to observe that marital violence has hardly had the time to become a use. Indeed, by Lodovico's question Shakespeare contrives to reinforce our sense of 'long' time.) Desdemona has never hitherto been struck or stricken. She is a 'Child to chiding' (F2819; IV.ii.114) – i.e. inexperienced and instantly obedient in being rebuked. But she has been mentally denied before; she has been ordered away before. The action of this sequence – the public humiliation of a wife to match the wife's supposed public humiliation of her husband – is unique in the play. But *some* precedent for its dismissal element has been established by Shakespeare. The real mind of the real Desdemona is, as ever, denied. And it is on the basis of this denial that the actual physical blow is struck.

To advance now to the 'brothel' scene (IV.ii): Desdemona's real self is again denied in Othello's opening description, 'a subtile Whore: / A Closset Locke and Key of Villainous Secrets' (F2710–11; IV.ii.21–2) – though in the syntax it may be Aemilia who is so described. The scene is then dominated by Othello's old trait of quite simply ignoring his wife's questions. The following are the questions put by Desdemona between F2714 and 2766 (IV.ii.24–71):

> My Lord, what is your will?
>
> What is your pleasure?
>
> What horrible Fancie's this?
>
> Vpon my knee, what doth your speech import?
>
> To whom my Lord?
> With whom? How am I false?

Alas the heauy day: why do you weepe?
Am I the motiue of these teares my Lord?

Alas, what ignorant sin haue I committed?

Of these only the second is answered – after a fashion, as Othello
states that his pleasure or will is to look into Desdemona's eyes. The
sequence *To whom my Lord? / With whom? How am I false?* is
particularly critical. If Othello answers these questions, or even
hints at an answer, then Desdemona will deny and attempt to
confute the 'charge' with, arguably, far more success than she
actually does achieve, or fails to achieve, in the final scene. For
Othello is not yet sufficiently worked by a sense of religious sacrifice to bring himself to the murder – which, anyway, like the
marriage must be effected by night. Aemilia would be sent to fetch
Cassio. The handkerchief's theft and leaving in Cassio's lodging
would be discovered. Iago would be sent for. How is Shakespeare
going to avoid this happy ending? How is he to effect Desdemona's
murder – without which the play, featuring as it does potentially
comic conventions such as gulling and mishearing, will lose its
tragic nature? How will he resolve the problem he seems deliberately to have contrived for himself in subjecting Othello to such
specific demands for information? Quite simply, he does so by
exploiting the accumulative effect of all Othello's habitual denials of
his wife and compacting it into one line: 'Ah Desdemon, away,
away, away' (F2735; IV.ii.42). By itself, this single line may sound
unconvincing; but in the context of the Othello utterance as a whole
it has much strength. Shakespeare has earned its use, its economy.
Desdemona's questions and Othello's dismissals of her questions
are the quintessence of the denials that have been going on for
much of the marriage as presented on stage. Away with Desdemona's mind. Away with being bounteous to it.[39]

Of Desdemona's other questions in the scene Othello is not quite
so directly dismissive. Rather, he ignores them. On them he super-
imposes his own voice, his own preoccupations. First, he uses a
ghastly pleasantry: 'Pray you Chucke come hither' (F2715; IV.ii.25)
– when tragic heroes such as Othello, Macbeth and Anthony use
Chucke the endearment signals a denial in some degree.[40] Then he
uses vague denunciation: 'Heauen truly knowes, that thou art false
as hell' (F2732; IV.ii.40). Then he uses the magnificent lament of
'Had it pleas'd Heauen . . . ' (F2742–59; IV.ii.48–65), in which he
declares those afflictions he could tolerate and the one affliction he

cannot tolerate at all. These lines form a major example of Othello's trait of self-publication, a trait that informs the utterance through-out and takes the place, at critical moments, of argument, infor-mation, communication. As an example of this self-publishing the lines are fully discussed below in Chapter 5. Here it is germane to note that they disclose Othello's almost total bounteous concern for his own state of mind and, equally, an almost total neglect of Desdemona's. Directly afterwards Othello turns on the false Des-demona of his delusions:

> Oh thou weed:
> Who art so louely faire, and smell'st so sweete,
> That the Sense akes at thee,
> Would thou had'st neuer bin borne.
>
> (F2762–5; IV.ii.68–70)

Q's version of the first three lines is:

> O thou blacke weede, why art so louely faire?
> Thou smell'st so sweete, that the sence akes at thee,
>   . . . .

In both versions Othello's concern is the difference (as he supposes) between the appearance and the reality of Desdemona. She repre-sents the destruction of the ideal by which a beautiful body must contain and express a beautiful soul. The doublet *louely faire* has an extraordinarily powerful effect in suggesting Desdemona's extra-ordinary beauty. The elision of *and* gives adjectival *louely* an adver-bial nature – hence a tension ensues. (Schmidt does, in fact, define *louely* here as a rare Shakespearean adverbial use.) And this resonance is helped by the fricative in each word. The point is, Othello observes this discrepancy between soul and body, but he does not inquire into it. Rather, Desdemona in the last line is dismissed as her husband stays, so to speak, on her surface. And, again, from Othello's following 'Was this faire Paper? This most goodly Booke / Made to write Whore vpon?' all inquiry is absent. Othello continues to treat externals – *Paper* prefigures Othello's wonder at the smooth, white surface of Desdemona's skin in 'It is the Cause . . . ' in the murder-scene – while the book and volume of Desdemona's mind remain unexamined. In fact poor Desde-mona through much of these speeches is virtually lost sight of. Her

'I hope my Noble Lord esteemes me honest' (F2670; IV.ii.66) is made bathetic, naïve, by the seriousness of the 'charge', on which Othello unfairly fails to brief her. He leaves her in such ignorance that Desdemona has to clutch at any reason she can think of for her husband's tears. She proffers

> If happely you my father do suspect,
> An Instrument of this your calling backe,
> Lay not your blame on me: if you haue lost him,
> I haue lost him too.
>
> (F2738–41; IV.ii.45–8)

The pathos of this is extreme. Othello has never shown the slightest affection for Brabantio. He can feel nothing of Desdemona's sadness in having lost him. Nor has he ever shown any sympathy for Desdemona in *her* loss. The sheer naïveté of Desdemona's attribution shows the desperate mental condition into which Othello's lack of bounty has confined her. She has lost her logic. She has not enough information.

Shakespeare has another means, too, to keep her uninformed. This is Othello's moral indignation:

>   Oh thou publicke Commoner
> I should make very Forges of my cheekes,
> That would to Cynders burne vp Modestie,
> Did I but speake thy deedes. [Q lacks these four lines.]
>   What commited?
> Heauen stoppes the Nose at it, and the Moone winkes:
> The baudy winde that kisses all it meetes
> Is hush'd within the hollow Myne of Earth
> And will not hear't. What commited? [Q – *what committed,*
>   – *impudent strumpet.*]
>
> (F2769–76; IV.ii.74–82)

Othello asserts in himself a modesty akin to that of the chaste stars in 'It is the Cause . . . ' (V.ii). This modesty, he claims, prohibits any definition. At the same time, in *publicke Commoner* he asserts an *im*modesty in Desdemona which goes utterly against the audience's experience of her: we are soon to learn that, to Iago, she cannot even say the word 'whore' –

DESDEMONA. Am I that name, Iago?
IAGO. What name (faire Lady?)
DESDEMONA. Such as she said my Lord did say I was.
AEMILIA. He call'd her whore . . . .

(F2824–7; IV.ii.119–21)

It seems, however, that Othello's inability to speak Desdemona's deeds applies only to when he is being morally indignant and confronting Desdemona. In other contexts his imagination is lewdly indulged at Iago's provocation even to the point of inducing an epileptic fit at one stage. Othello's inability to speak the deeds seems, therefore, to link with the lack of candour with which he has frequently treated Desdemona hitherto. If only, one might wish, Othello could be as imaginatively familiar with Desdemona's actions and mind as he seems to be with the inner thoughts, so to speak, of disgusted heaven and of the moon and wind that refuse to look or hear for the shame of Desdemona's sin. These vivid personifications of the elements – the skies and the earth become virtually populated by three vast, shocked, human presences – provide an example of what Wilson Knight (p. 101) called Othello's 'picturesque' language: language that is essentially pictorial rather than expressive of abstract thought. Shakespeare allows Othello the ability to conjure fantastic presences in his own mind, and to project upon them his own feelings; but he makes him incapable of understanding the ordinary world of human dealings. Another example of this thoughtless, pictorial quality in Othello is in Othello's image of his own glowing, forge-like cheeks that would house the destruction of Modesty. This blushing has some reference back to the turned complexion of Patience in 'Had it pleas'd Heauen . . . '; the forges have some reference forward to the Promethean fire of 'It is the Cause . . . .' Othello elevates himself not only by comparing his own disgust with that of the elements but also by assuming within himself the presence of a quintessential ideal of modesty.

In the rhetoric of the speech, too, there is a characteristic habit of Othello's working to keep Desdemona uninformed. This, again, is the simple repetition of words – here that of *What commited*? In F the lines I have quoted are preceded by an earlier 'What commited? / Committed?'; so there are four occurrences of the question in all. Othello seizes Desdemona's reasonable and most central question – *Alas, what ignorant sin haue I committed?* – and brutalises it. He provides no answer, but interprets Desdemona's inquiry as yet more evidence of her immodesty. He sees Desdemona not at all; he 'sees' only the *impudent strumpet*. *Impudent* meant considerably more in Shakespeare's time than the 'disrespectful' or 'cheeky' of Modern English. It denoted more precisely, too. Othello is asserting that Desdemona is immodest, unblushing, indelicate (*OED, Impudent* adj., 1 [obsolete by 1732]). She is a true strumpet in the way she can flaunt yet deny her sin, in the way she can turn and turn and yet go on. The word was acquiring something of its modern meaning but, conversely, was much closer to its Latin origin of *pudendum*: 'privy parts' – literally, 'that of which one ought to be ashamed' (*OED*). All of Desdemona's modesty is denied in Othello's announcement of shameless sexuality.

To stay for a while longer on Desdemona's want of answers from Othello: it would seem that Shakespeare has deliberately set this off against the veritable bounty of answers given *to* Othello. His rhetorical questions are directly replied to by Desdemona:

> OTHELLO. Why? What art thou?
> DESDEMONA. Your wife my Lord: your true and loyall wife
> (F2725–6; IV.ii.34–5)

and:

> OTHELLO. Are not you a Strumpet?
> DESDEMONA. No, as I am a Christian.
>   If to preserue this vessell for my Lord,
>   From any other [Q *any hated*] foule vnlawfull touch
>   Be not to be a Strumpet, I am none.
> OTHELLO. What, not a Whore?
> DESDEMONA. No, as I shall be sau'd.
> (F2778–84; IV.ii.83–7)

Moreover, Othello's demands for information are fully and immediately met by Aemilia in the prelude to the 'brothel' scene. I say 'demands' – in fact Othello's questions are assertions in effect. They expect and require the answer 'yes'. The heavy dramatic irony is that Aemilia's repeated and emphatic negatives fail to affect Othello's thinkings. All evidence for the defence – indeed, the very possibility of a defence – is dismissed in this Kafkaesque 'trial' and conviction:

OTHELLO. You haue seene nothing then?

AEMILIA. Nor euer heard: nor euer did suspect.

OTHELLO. Yes, [Q *and*] you haue seene Cassio, and she together.

AEMILIA. But then I saw no harme: and then I heard,
    Each syllable that breath made vp betweene them.

OTHELLO. What? Did they never whisper?

AEMILIA. Neuer my Lord.

OTHELLO. Nor send you out o'th'way?

AEMILIA. Neuer.

OTHELLO. To fetch her Fan, her Gloues, her Mask, nor nothing?

AEMILIA. Neuer my Lord.

OTHELLO. That's strange.

(F2688–99; IV.ii.1–11)

The juxtaposition comments strongly in itself. While keeping his wife in ignorance, Othello is copiously informed by both wife and Aemilia yet manages to reject such inconvenient knowledge. With facility, he misinterprets: Aemilia must be lying because Aemilia must be a bawd.

Of course, something of Othello's lack of bounty to Desdemona's mind derives from the fallacy, in *his* mind, that Desdemona already knows. Why brief her when her information is more than his own? By her shameless behaviour in public she has shown herself capable of showing her infidelity to the world. Why go into details then? In this respect, when Othello says that Desdemona is honest 'as Sommer Flyes are in the Shambles, / That quicken euen with blowing' (F2761 –2; IV.ii.67–8), he is referring not only to a lack of chastity but to the flies' and Desdemona's straightforward shamelessness, a kind of honestly unabashed quality. (See *OED, Honest* adj., 3a and b; and Schmidt, *Honest* 4 and 1.)[41] This is akin to the frankness of Desdemona's hand in humidly disclosing her amorous disposition. Flies openly taint the meat as they deposit their eggs, and Desdemona is quite open, it seems, about bestowing her affections: she has practised them on the sea-bank with Cassio and alluded to them before Lodovico and her husband. To Othello she is flylike in the honesty of her dirt. More than other Venetian ladies, it seems, she does show the edge of her pranks to her husband. When Othello again dismisses her – again by walking out on her – he leaves her with a picture in words of herself that, in his opinion, she must be familiar with: a picture of 'that cunning Whore of Venice, / That married with Othello' (F2788–9; IV.ii.90–1) by wooing him with tears, with kisses or sighs, and with seeming worship.

Once Othello has evolved a religious cause to pull him to the point of uxoricide, he can be allowed some bounty to his victim's need of information. Once he can re-enter the bedchamber as a moral vigilante, there is little chance that any truth will penetrate his armour of ideals – particularly when that armour is further proofed with rage. Accordingly, Shakespeare permits Desdemona some answers. 'Who's there? Othello?' she asks – and actually receives a direct reply: 'I Desdemona' (F3263–4; v.ii.23). After two more *un*answered questions she tries again: 'Talke you of killing?' and again is directly answered, 'I, I do' (F3276–7; v.ii.34). From now on Desdemona's enlightenment looms. As Othello shakes and gnaws his nether lip and rolls his eyes – while managing to address her much as a priest might have done – Desdemona asks the same question she asked after the brawl: 'What's the matter?' She was not answered before. But now, when it is too late, Othello does become narrowly bounteous. Not to Desdemona's mind in the sense of her idealism and purity, but to her Christian need of confession before death. In urging her to prepare for death, Othello does at last enunciate what the matter is and has been: 'That Handkerchiefe / Which I so lou'd, and gaue thee, thou gau'st to Cassio.' And again: 'By Heauen I saw my Handkerchiefe in's hand' (F3295–7 and 3314; v.ii.50–2 and 65).

There it is. The simple specific actual fact. The simple specific actual fallacy. But this information is far too lately arrived. Desdemona's denials can be met by Othello's reference to what he thinks was an ocular proof. Desdemona's declarations that this proof is not the proof of a gift, but only of Cassio's having found the handkerchief, can only exacerbate Othello's rage as this seeming strumpet now compounds her guilt by perjury. And the chief witness, Cassio, can no longer be called because of his supposed death. Moreover, Desdemona's shock at this death, and her panic, can be taken as evidence of a strumpet's guilt: 'Alas, he is betrayed, and I vndone' (F3333; v.ii.80).

Associated with the final dismissal – by murder – of Desdemona are three further instances of Othello's lack of bounty. Desdemona's request to say one prayer is refused on the ground that the time for prayer is past. That is to say, the announced bounty of 'I would not kill thy vnprepared Spirit' (F3274; v.ii.32) is not put into practice. Again, Othello's verbal accompaniment to the murder is set in the dismissive lexicon of 'Out Strumpet' and 'Down Strumpet' (F3334

and 3336; v.ii.81 and 83). The two conventional exclamations *Out*
and *Down* suggest, respectively, exclusion and an assignment
down to hell as Desdemona is physically sudbued. Thirdly,
Othello's confession to Aemilia, 'She's like a Liar gone to burning
hell, / 'Twas I that kill'd her' (F3398–9; v.ii.132–3), also fits into the
lack-of-bounty scheme. It denies Desdemona's motive to absolve
Othello from the responsibility for the crime: a motive expressed in
her answer to Aemilia's demand to know who has done the deed –
'No body: I my selfe, farewell: / Commend me to my kinde Lord: oh
farewell' (F3392–3; v.ii.127–8). This strange return from apparent
death – a short recovery commensurate, one is told, with fracture of
the larynx or cardiac arrest – would seem to have been written by
Shakespeare to emphasise the degree to which Othello lacks in
bounty. Desdemona's instinct in death is to love her lord even to
the point of charity. For Othello, however, this charity must be
denied; it must be ungenerously interpreted as yet another example
of Desdemona's mendacity.[42]

Othello's maltreatment of Desdemona – inscribed as it is within
his character – not only assists the movement of the tragedy but also
supplies a major theme: the denial and dismissal of women in
general by their men. Both Aemilia and Bianca are made to suffer,
in this theme, by Iago and Cassio respectively. Just as Othello
humiliates Desdemona in public, so Iago does Aemilia. On Cyprus,
as Othello's landing is awaited, Iago asserts that Aemilia is garru-
lous and that, when not speaking, she is nagging in her thoughts
(F869ff.; II.i.100ff.). Of course, this is far less serious than Othello's
physical attack and vituperation. But Iago's virtual bewhoring of
Aemilia – she is amongst those described as 'Huswiues in your
Beds' who 'go to bed to worke' (F882–3 and 886; II.i.111–12 and 115)
– does set something of a precedent for Othello's actual bewhoring
of Desdemona. Iago's view of women as cold, businesslike prosti-
tutes who make all-but-clients of their husbands differs, of course,
from Othello's obsession – in which an excess of female amorous-
ness predominates. But both male characters, in their respective
ways, demean their wives. Iago's pleasantries, and the jesting
couplets that follow them, express the bluffness that everyone
seems to expect from honest Iago. As a kind of lady's fool or
shipboard jester he has a licence to utter it. But the source of the
humour is not pleasant. It is an extreme and dismissing misogyny.
What Desdemona turns away from with her dissembling laughter
is in effect a dismissal and denial of virtuous women such as she.

Iago's talk is not just a collection of 'old fond Paradoxes' (F913; II.i.138). Fools may laugh at them in the alehouse, but they form an abusive opinion of women that Shakespeare has carefully written into the core of the play. As Desdemona says, Iago should not be learned of; he is a 'most prophane, and liberall Counsailor' (F938–9; II.i.163); and she speaks, unknown to herself, a jesting truth that Othello is to prove incapable of discerning for himself.

Like Othello, too, Iago maltreats his wife in his actual deeds. Aemilia confirms this treatment when she admits her ignorance of why Iago wants the handkerchief: 'I nothing but to please his Fantasie' (F1934; III.iii.303). *Fantasie* here seems to be 'caprice' or 'desire' (*OED, Fantasy* 6 and 7). Like Desdemona, Aemilia – until V.ii – thinks it proper to obey her husband; and she does whatever her husband bids her despite his contemptuous dismissal of her mind. Her obedience is such that her duty to her mistress is overridden for much of the play. She is glad to find the handkerchief and would, indeed, have directly stolen it earlier but that Desdemona reserved it 'evermore about her' (F1930; III..iii.299). Aemilia uses the handkerchief in an attempt to win her husband's favour. Since she is treated like a whore, she will behave like a teasing one. That is to say, she talks in terms of money or of a gift: 'What will you giue me now / For that same Handkerchiefe' (F1942–3; III.iii.309–10 – Q has a question mark). But her teasing is in vain. Iago treats her abruptly. Along with her sudden compunction on behalf of Desdemona she is dismissed. She wants to know what Iago intends with the handkerchief. 'Why, what is that to you?' Iago says. And again, 'Be not acknowne on't: / I haue vse for it. Go, leaue me' (F1955 and 1959–60; III.iii.319 and 323–4). Schmidt reads 'Be not acknowne on't' here as 'do not confess to the knowledge of it' (Schmidt, *Acknown*) – i.e. as advice how to react when Desdemona discovers the handkerchief's disappearance. The *OED* (*Acknow* v., 4d), also citing this passage, is in accord: 'To be *acknown*: To be (self-)recognized or avowed in relation to anything; hence, to avow, confess, acknowledge (*to* a person).' For the theme of this chapter another meaning would have been attractive, that of *acknowne* as 'apprized, informed (*of*)' (*OED* v., 3): did the *OED* not list this as obsolete (last used by Caxton in 1490), it would have reinforced one's sense of Iago barring Aemilia from a knowledge of his purpose, of Iago telling her she is to remain in ignorance. As it is, Aemilia is ordered to lie for her husband, while her interest on behalf of her mistress is rebuffed as irrelevant and intrusive. Once again, a woman's right to know is denied and the woman dismissed.

It is arguable that Iago's maltreatment here is responsible in part for Aemilia's words of marital revolt in the second part of IV.iii. She starts frivolously enough, asserting – in prose – a potential in herself for adultery, not for material gain but certainly for the world. Much more seriously, however, she then utters a long speech of blank verse that acts as a kind of manifesto on behalf of fallen wives in general. This speech, along with the Willow Song and several other lines in the scene, is not in Q:

> But I do thinke it is their Husbands faults
> If Wiues do fall: (Say that they slacke their duties,
> And powre our Treasures into forraigne laps;
> Or else breake out in peeuish Iealousies,
> Throwing restraint vpon vs: Or say they strike vs,
> Or scant our former hauing in despight)
> Why we haue galles: and though we haue some Grace,
> Yet haue we some Reuenge. Let Husbands know,
> Their wiues haue sense like them: They see, and smell,
> And haue their Palats both for sweet, and sowre,
> As Husbands haue. What is it that they do,
> When they change vs for others? Is it Sport?
> I thinke it is? and doth Affection breed it?
> I thinke it doth. Is't Frailty that thus erres?
> It is so too. And haue not we Affections?
> Desires for Sport? And Frailty, as men haue?
> Then let them vse vs well: else let them know,
> The illes we do, their illes instruct vs so.
>
> (F3059–76; IV.iii.84–101)

This speech has much interest in expressing the worldliness in Aemilia's character that is so opposite to the idealism in Desdemona's. Aemilia uses a possibly vulgar lexicon at times – as Hilda Hulme has demonstrated, *lap* could mean the female genitals – of a kind that Desdemona has never used in the play. She also insists on the opinion that any fault in a wife must be derived from a similar fault in the husband, while taking for granted the fact that such fallen wives are numerous – a fact that Desdemona finds it difficult to believe. Much of the speech is concerned with husbands' philanderings and is therefore irrelevant to Desdemona's situation –

perhaps Aemilia is speaking from her own marital experience. Nor, one notes, has Othello scanted Desdemona's former having in despite – perhaps again Aemilia is speaking from experience, perhaps Iago was as avid of her jewels and purse as he has been of Rodorigo's. But there are specific conditions that do relate to Desdemona. These are a husband's breaking-out in peevish jealousy (Aemilia has suffered this too, when Iago suspected her with the Moor); a husband's throwing restraint upon his wife; and, of course, his striking of her. The keywords in the speech as a whole are, I think, *galles*, *Grace* and *Reuenge*. The first of these denotes 'biles' and, by implication, the rancour that was supposed to derive therefrom (Schmidt, *Gall* sb., 1 and 4: both cite Aemilia's usage here). The ecletic word *Grace* here denotes a 'blessed disposition of mind, virtue' (Schmidt sb., 9, again citing Aemilia). It refers to the gentleness of women; and it links with the theme of noble generosity, the free man's or free woman's ability to rise above the baser emotions. *Reuenge* seems to encompass both the desire and the power to retaliate, to redress wrong by wrong. From these central words derives Aemilia's gist: which is that women, like men, are human; they can overcome their gentler dispositions and avenge their marital injuries as their husbands' bad examples instruct them.[43]

Until Aemilia starts this speech the tone of the scene has had a degree of intimacy. Desdemona's hurry not to displease her lord, her apprehensions of death, her start at the wind's knocking, the unease that makes her broach the topic of adultery in the first place – all this cannot quite dispel the quiet atmosphere of feminine companionship. The setting of a quiet, feminine bedtime ritual is, indeed, a welcome change from the masculine 'noise' of the scenes involving Othello and Iago. During the speech, however, a mental and emotional separation of the two women occurs. From its own experience of Desdemona the audience is aware of how little Desdemona can subscribe to Aemilia's opinion. They know she has nothing of gall and revenge; they know she has much of grace – too much, some might say – towards her lord. Her own specifically Christian state of grace Desdemona sounds in her short response to Aemilia's speech:

> Good night, good night:
> Heauen me such vses send,
> Not to pick bad, from bad; but by bad mend.
>
> (F3077–9; IV.iii.102–3)

This directly opposes Aemilia's 'manifesto'. Desdemona declares her own desire is to be instructed towards *goodness* by bad example. There is, in fact, a fascinating contrast between the development of this scene and that of the scenes involving Iago and Othello in Acts III and IV. Of course, there is absolutely nothing similar between Aemilia's motives as she speaks to Desdemona and Iago's as he speaks to Othello. Though we know Aemilia's low opinion of the marriage – 'I, would you had neuer seene him' (F2987; IV.iii.17) – we also know her clear conviction, voiced in IV.ii and V.ii, of her mistress's virtue. But Aemilia's assertion of worldly knowledge *is* similar to Iago's. Just as Iago presented a low opinion of wives in Venice, so too does Aemilia of husbands – and of wives. Just as Iago juxtaposes his cynicism against his master's idealism, so too does Aemilia juxtapose hers against the idealistic girl who is her mistress. In the play's dramatic structure the parallelism between these two exchanges serves to emphasise the wide contrast between their respective effects. Iago's cynicism is adopted; Aemilia's most certainly is not.

The prevalence of Desdemona's fine idealism and love is strongly expressed earlier in the Willow Song scene. There too Shakespeare suggests that this quality in Desdemona is to be associated with a fatal submissiveness?

> my loue doth so approue him,
> That euen his stubbornesse, his checks, his frownes,
> (Prythee vn-pin me) haue grace and fauour [Q *in them*].
> (F2988–90; IV.iii.18–20)

There is some resonance here of Iago's remark to Othello, that 'when she seem'd to shake, and feare your lookes, / She lou'd them most' (F1824–5; III.iii.211–12). Iago was suggesting a pretence in Desdemona; but in reality Desdemona's love for Othello's military aspect – his valiant parts – may well be inextricably linked with a certain capacity in her for fearful excitement. In a telling variant sense of *grace* Shakespeare declares that even Othello's masculine 'roughness, harshness' (his *stubbornesse*) is a quality in him that she finds well-pleasing (Schmidt, *Grace* sb., 2).[44] This is perhaps a more 'psychological' way of expressing the selflessness that Desdemona earlier defined for example in 'his vnkindnesse may defeat my life, / But neuer taynt my Loue' (F2874–5; IV.ii.161–2) – the selflessness that made Desdemona excuse Othello's rage and call herself, instead of Othello, an 'vnhandsome Warriour' (F2308; III.iv.152). Again within the Willow Song scene, Shakespeare effects a contrast between the attitude of Aemilia and that of Desdemona in the very 'Song of Willough' itself. The song concerns a swain who shares in Aemilia's pragmatism: 'If I court mo women, you'le couch with mo men' (F3026; IV.iii.55); and it concerns a woman who, like Desdemona, cannot bear to censure her man: 'Let no body blame him, his scorne I approue' (F3021; IV.iii.51). All in all, Shakespeare uses the scene to emphasise, again and again, the sheer extent of Desdemona's bounty to Othello's mind. It is a bounty that acts as an opposite to Othello's *lack* of bounty and dramatically complies with that lack in assisting the approach to murder. The extraordinarily generous Desdemona of the Willow Song scene also acts as a precedent for the extraordinarily generous Desdemona who, despite her 'guiltlesse condition' and despite her having been 'falsely, falsely murder'd', yet struggles in her death-agony to assume the responsibility for her husband's deed in the final scene. (I refer to her last four lines before she dies at F3393; V.ii.128.)

But the different attitudes of the two women as shown in the Willow Song scene do not preclude their being members, both, of a sisterhood: the sorority of wronged wives. Moreover, Aemilia's revolt against Iago, when it happens, is not the sexually expressed one on her own behalf that she spoke of in her 'manifesto'; it is a revolt of idealism on the behalf of her virtuous mistress – this makes the kinship closer. Aemilia's stand against Iago, maintained despite her (possible) sense of her own impending death – a sense uncannily like Desdemona's – is one of the finest examples in Shakespeare of a secondary character achieving greatness:

> Good Gentlemen, let me haue leaue to speake:
> 'Tis proper to obey him; but not now:
> Perhaps Iago, I will ne're go home.
>
> (F3480–2; V.ii.198–200)

Although too late, Aemilia emerges from her pragmatic moral dubiety to die in a good cause: the exposure of a male conspiracy against the life of a virtuous woman, the rebuttal of the idea that female virtue can be denied and dismissed.[45]

A paragraph now on Bianca. She too exemplifies the theme of a woman denied and dismissed. Even this minor character must enact Shakespeare's principle, particularly strong at this point in his writing-career, that the women characters must be evicted from the love and confidence of flawed males – I am thinking here of Ophelia, Cordelia, the also flawed Lady Macbeth. As far as the plot of *Othello* is concerned, Bianca is necessary for the 'Othello-encaved' scene IV.i. During it Cassio's comments about her can be misheard as being about Desdemona. She can also be seen as having received the handkerchief as a loan from Cassio. She is useful, too, in helping to establish the second time-sequence of the play: 'What? keepe a weeke away? Seuen dayes, and Nights? Eight score eight houres?' (F2332–3; III.iv.174–5). Cassio's emphatically delineated week-long absence contributes, with other means to the same effect, to our sense that a considerably longer period has passed on Cyprus than the thirty-six hours or so of the staged action.[46] But Shakespeare makes a good thematic use of Bianca as well as for his plot. She is fortunate in that Shakespeare does not arrange for her death – he merely makes her suffer Iago's implication of her in her lover's wounding (F3179ff.; V.i.78ff.). But as a result of Cassio's careless way with her she supplements one of the 'truths' of the play: the women have to be distressed by their menfolk and, for much if not all of the time, without knowing why. She guesses that Cassio's seven-day absence has been caused by his having found a newer friend – and this guess is as wrong as was Desdemona's about the cause of Othello's tears ('If happely you my father do suspect' – F2738; IV.ii.45). Bianca, too, is put off: 'Go too, Woman: / Throw your vilde gesses in the Diuels teeth' (F2345–6; III.iv.184–5). She is also dismissed, because Cassio dislikes that the general should see him womaned (or so he proffers), and her repeated request for a rendezvous is refused. As she says, she must be 'circumstanc'd' (F2367; III.iv.202). That is, she must endure her man's maltreatment as best she can and without reason. A little later, she is mocked in her absence as Cassio calls her 'poore Caitiffe' and dismisses all chance of her marrying him (F2491ff.; IV.i.106ff.).

Interestingly, however, Shakespeare then brings her back on stage for the purpose of returning the handkerchief. He makes her refuse to copy the handkerchief's pattern, and he makes her enraged. That is, for the purpose of the plot he makes her assert herself – and in doing so he effects in Bianca much less submissiveness to her 'lord' than either Desdemona or Aemilia (at first) shows to hers. Bianca rails behovingly, in a whorish manner. The point is: the mind of this woman, who *is* a Venetian courtesan, is treated not differently in kind but only differently in degree from that of Desdemona, the chaste Venetian lady of the play.

In this long and ranging chapter I have been concerned to demonstrate two facets of Othello: first, Othello's noble ideal of treating his wife as a free man – an Arveragus – should; secondly, his failure to maintain such generosity in practice. Much of the discussion has been based on the idea of 'freedom' as a noble person's bounteousness of spirit. In the next chapter, a shorter one, I shall be led to consider *free* in another meaning – that of 'unconfined' and 'unhoused'.

2

'But that I loue the gentle Desdemona'

The word *gentle* has a rich ambiguity in Othello's

> But that I loue the gentle Desdemona,
> I would not my vnhoused free condition
> Put into Circumscription, and Confine,
> For the Seas worth.
>
> (F229–32; I.ii.25–8)

In Shakespeare's time, *loue* could have a long vowel as in Modern English 'move'; and this pronunciation was especially common in verse for the purpose of rhyme. If this lengthy vowel is present here, in Othello's unrhymed but high style, then *loue* can be made particularly to dominate the line by marking a definite caesura. With this emphasis on Othello's emotional state – on what Spivack has called love's 'slow arrival, its high and permanent residence' – the word *gentle* tends to take a lesser accent and to denote a conventional idea of the woman Othello has chosen for wife: she is 'soft, tender' (*OED* A adj., 5); and she is 'amiable, lovely, full of endearing qualities' (Schmidt adj., 2).[1]

The context, however, suggests that Othello is intended to mean rather more. The *OED* defines *circumscription* as 'The marking out of limits . . . restriction . . . the having well-defined limits' (*OED* 1); but the verbal form's earliest version was *circumscrive* with a denotement of drawing or scrivening a line around something; and as late as 1676 Elisha Coles was defining *circumscription* as 'a writing around'. It is probable that Shakespeare, with his command of Latin and as one of the 'etymological writers' of the time, was aware of the root meaning in *circumscribere*: 'to write around' and is making Othello refer directly to the condition of being bound in by the written laws of Venice – and even, perhaps, by the etiquette books with their soft and set phrases – that both keep in and protect

54

the citizen.[2] Moreover, *Confine* is probably more than just a doubling-up of *Circumscription* as 'restriction' that makes the phrase 'heightened repetition . . . which yet stops short of bombastic tautology'.[3] Like *free, and bounteous* and *defunct, and proper,* discussed in Chapter 1, *Circumscription, and Confine* would seem to express some lexical differentiation. In one sense *Confine*, albeit in the plural, could mean 'borders' and 'neighbours' (*OED* sb.[2] I.1 and sb.[1]). According to the *OED*, the former was obsolete in the written language after 1670, the latter after 1598; but some residue of these senses might well have lingered as Othello declares a reluctance to have committed himself, in circumstances other than love, to the close neighbourhood of two people that is marriage.

Thus a small lexical scheme ensues – of contraction by laws, and of marriage as a contract – in which *gentle* participates as 'Well born, belonging to a family of position' and as 'noble, generous, courteous, polite' (*OED* A adj., 1 and 3). 'Polite' is probably the aptest meaning here, with its association of Latin *politia* ('citizenship') and *politus* ('polished, refined'). (See *OED, Polite* adj., and *Policy* sb.[1].) This genteel meaning makes *gentle* more prominent. Desdemona lives in a condition of civil, indeed metropolitan, life; and into that condition Othello himself must transfer. It is not only because he loves that he comes inside the laws of civil life; it is also because the woman of his choice happens to reside within those laws as a member of the *polis*. The great change that Othello effects in his condition is not only emotionally but pragmatically induced. He submits gladly to being in love; but his coming within the pale of Venetian life is rather more expedient. He comes inside only because his wife is there. Put it another way: Othello loves Desdemona not only *for* her softness, tenderness and lovable qualities but also *in despite of* her citified, civilised and housed condition.

Of course, Desdemona loves Othello precisely for his free and warrior quality and proves, eventually, eager to join him in his literal and metaphorical tents. But the marriage, for the moment, has brought Othello *into* Venice rather more than it has brought Desdemona without. The verbal meaning of· *house* could be, in Shakespeare's time, 'To drive . . . into a house' (*OED* I.1b); and this further points the sheer extent of Othello's disinclination from the walls and roofs of civilisation. *Vnhoused*, really, means uncircumscribed, unconfined. Othello has a belief in the superior virtues of a life lived, militarily and adventurously, as a pilgrimage on which the self might be tested and proved in an alien or heaven-made circumstance instead of being controlled by man-made laws. A housed condition would be, for Othello, a morally inferior condition.

All this is to say that Othello's happiness in marriage is not totally unconfined and not totally unalloyed. The lines indicate a certain mixture of feelings in Othello on his becoming an in-law of the Venetian State. Ordinarily, he says, he would not have exchanged either the natural beauty of the seas or their shipwrecked treasure for the amenity of the civic laws and the contract of marriage. The reason for this disinclination is that freedom for Othello quite simply does not consist in the city. He values not at all the political freedom for which Venice, as described in, for example, Lewkenor's English account published in 1599, was famous. *Free*, for Othello, does not mean 'Enjoying civil liberty; existing under a government which is not arbitrary or despotic, and does not encroach upon individual rights' (*OED* adj., I.2) – the sort of controlled liberty experienced by the free men and plebeians of Venice and, to some extent, by the peoples of James I's England. Freedom exists for Othello outside the State. Although he serves the State he serves it outside its boundaries. And when he is confined inside the State he calls it the wasting of his arm (F423; I.iii.84). Moreover, since to be free was to be capable of nobility, honour, generosity and magnanimity, it would seem that Othello is setting up a 'wild' or natural nobility to oppose the 'tame' nobility represented by *gentle*. This opposition prefigures the action of the play: the civilisation of Venice is to be damaged by the barbarian autonomy of a man whose dislike of the gentle condition can be worked on for an evil purpose. It is, after all, Iago to whom this dislike is revealed. Moreover, the sentiment is given this additional emphasis: it does not form part of Othello's direct answer to Iago's 'Are you fast married?' (F214; I.ii.11) and Iago's warnings. It is an irrelevant appendix. It does not derive from the stated argument of Othello's marital eligibility. It derives, rather, from some private discussion peculiar to Othello. In this, his first long speech, Othello is already obscuring an issue with his own irrelevant and solipsistic preoccupation.[4]

So, it would seem, there is the beginning of a second conflict here. Just as Othello's bounty becomes qualified by his loss of freedom, so his marriage contains already a potential for the groom's unrest. Furthermore, this develops on several occasions into a certain cavalier attitude with respect to Venice and Venetians. Indeed, a paradox has been written into the play almost at the beginning. The fact of the marriage seems to confirm Othello's recognition of Venetian law; but the manner of the marriage, its furtiveness and its offending of Brabantio, is itself evidence of how much Othello has remained outside, of how much he is ready to ignore Venetian *moeurs*, if not as yet her actual statutes. He has abused Brabantio's hospitality. He denies Brabantio's right to have some say in the disposal of his daughter – and remember that Brabantio has by no means been a tyrannical father: none of the 'wealthy curled Deareling of our Nation' (F286; I.ii.68) has been forced upon Desdemona.

Much of Othello's purblind treatment of Brabantio and Venetian customs is expressed in his use of one particular word: *spight*. Iago has warned that the magnifico is well-loved – presumably by the Duke and councillors – and has as much influence as the Duke. He will effect a divorce, or exert the utmost rigour of the law to restrain Othello (Iago says). To all of which Othello replies,

> Let him do his spight;
> My Seruices, which I haue done the Signorie
> Shall out-tongue his Complaints.
>
> (F221–3; I.ii.17–19)

That is, Othello dismisses or does not even consider the motives of Brabantio's understandable pursuit of his possibly abducted daughter. This pursuit is caused, for Othello, by 'A strong feeling of . . . hatred or ill-will; intense grudge or desire to injure; rancorous or envious malice' (*OED, Spite* sb., 2). Schmidt, too, reads 'malice, ill-will' as Othello's meaning here, not the more neutral 'disposition to thwart and disappoint the wishes of another' (Schmidt, *Spite* sb., 1 and 2). Othello's sense of *spight* would have been a true description of Iago's motives, but it does not truly register Brabantio's. The magnifico is not merely a wronged and innocent old gentleman; but underneath the wild assertions and the outrageous racial insults that Brabantio utters against Othello a genuine grievance does exist. Marriages without parental consent, and secret marriages, were matters of public debate in England *c.* 1604. Indeed, a canon law of that year condemned both practices. Lawrence Stone in *The Family, Sex and Marriage in England 1500–1800* writes,

The canons of 1604 stipulated that a church wedding must take place between the hours of 8 a.m. and noon in the church at the place of residence of one of the pair, after the banns had been read for three weeks running. Marriages performed at night, in secular places like inns or private houses, or in towns or villages remote from the place of residence, would subject the officiating clergyman to serious penalties. The canons also forbade the marriage of persons under twenty one without the consent of parents or guardians.[5]

Of course, the introduction of such canons might imply the ubiquity of irregular marriages in England in the early seventeenth century. Indeed, Stone (pp. 32–4) discusses the ambiguity of a situation where the Church recognised lay marriages made by oral contract (akin to the pre-contract that Shakespeare used in *Measure for Measure* to make respectable the bedding of Angelo and Mariana) but where the civil courts recognised only marriages made in church. The point is this: one cannot be certain that a London audience would have responded with total sympathy to a benighted and unblessed marriage except where the parents were known to have been cruel and unreasonable. And these Brabantio was not. Whether Othello is, in Iago's phrase, 'fast married' in a church with the banns having been properly read (it seems unlikely) or whether he is bound by a lay betrothal, Shakespeare does not clarify. The obscurity is to his dramatic purpose – which is to present the very secrecy of the wedding, Brabantio's shock and Othello's reaction to that shock. It is interesting, too, to observe how much this secrecy is counter to the Venetian emphasis on publicity as disclosed in Lewkenor (*The Commonwealth and Gouernment of Venice*, pp. 194ff.): the couple, ideally, were allowed no mutual sighting until the dower and arrangements had been settled; thereafter the bride by gondola was much shown in public to 'make her marriage apparent and manifest to all men' (p. 195). Again, one cannot know how far, if at all, this Venetian practice was known to Shakespeare or his audience. But its contrast to Desdemona's actual transport 'at this odd Euen and dull watch o'th'night' with 'a Gundelier' (F136 and 138; I.i.124 and 126) is extreme. Another contrast, and one more accessible, is that between the benighted nature of the marriage and Othello's unshadowed confidence in what he seems to consider the propriety of his action. It needs emphasising that Othello is given the use of *spight* some time before he has heard Brabantio's charges and insults. His discernment of *spight* in Brabantio is based on Iago's

> He will diuorce you.
> Or put vpon you, what restraint or greeuance,
> The Law (with all his might, to enforce it on)
> Will giue him Cable.

(F217–20; I.ii.14–17)

The only premise on which this early discernment of malice in Brabantio – as opposed to an understandable resentment – can be justified in Othello is if one takes Brabantio and not Rodorigo to be the pronoun *he* of Iago's 'he prated, / And spoke . . . scuruy, and provoking termes / Against your Honor' (F210–12; I.ii.6–8). This premise seems unlikely.[6]

Brabantio's complaints about the seduction and theft, as he still sees it, of his daughter, have some justification; but his cause is largely lost in his pantaloon behaviour before the Council. From his charges of witchcraft, from his immoderation, one might hear not a councillor of superior judgement but a foolish elderly man driven by, in the Duke's word, 'moderne' ideas – that is, commonplace, vulgar superstitions not appropriate in a person of education. (See *OED, Modern* adj., 4; and Schmidt.)[7] Moreover, as Brabantio says himself, the 'generall care' of the Turkish threat is as nothing to him compared with his own 'perticular griefe' (F386ff; I.iii.52ff). Little here, then, of the sage governor – either of Venice or of himself. All the same, Othello's allusion to Brabantio as *this old man* in his first speech to the Council does disregard the dignity intrinsic in Brabantio's office:

> Most Potent, Graue, and Reuerend Signiors,
> My very Noble, and approu'd good Masters;
> That I haue tane away this old man's Daughter,
> It is most true: true I haue married her;
> The verie head, and front of my offending,
> Hath this extent; no more.

(F415–20; I.iii.76–81)

Othello, of course, is eager to extinguish the charge of witchcraft. Hence his careful definition. But he seems not to allow for the fact that the old man of his allusion is one of those powerful, important signiors who should be reverenced; and that the old man of his allusion has been provenly a good master to Othello in opening up his house to him in a nobly generous way. Brabantio's reaction is extreme and lacking in dignity – but it is no more so than the cunningly effected marriage that has provoked it. And the Duke is quite prepared to listen to the complaints of this 'gentle Signior' of whom he he says, 'We lack't your Counsaile, and your helpe tonight' (F384–5; I.iii.50–1). Already, it seems, Othello's marriage into the gentle condition is exposing him to the threat of Venetian gentles with their circumscription. Not until he learns the identity of the accused and hears Othello's defence does the Duke defect from Brabantio's cause. It is the present use that the Council has of Othello, not his past services, that causes Brabantio's complaint to be out-tongued. In any other circumstance than the military emergency Brabantio's powerful position as an elder statesman might well have had more effect. Despite his comic element – his tendency to fulfil the potential of his name by brabbling, contending noisily – he is not just the *old man* of Othello's description.[8] And, indeed, in Shakespeare's juxtaposition of that short phrase with the extraordinarily long entitling of the councillors there may well be a deal of author's comment. In insulting one of their number Othello insults them all. They are all old men for him. In taking on Brabantio – in the 'cutting-out' expedition of the marriage – he has taken on Venice and the government of Venice. And he is defeating them. The councillors are not so *Most Potent* that they can dispense with Othello's service. They are not so *Graue*, i.e. weighty, important, influential (*OED*, *Grave* adj.[1], A 1) that they can control Othello beyond their military commission. Collectively, they may be held 'in high respect or esteem' or venerated 'as being of an exalted or superior kind' (*OED*, *Reverence* v. 2b): individually, Brabantio has certainly not so been held. As for their nobility, well, it might be said that their republican rank is matched (without their knowing it) by Othello's royal descent. Only *approu'd good* seems to sound with no tonal ambiguity. According to the *OED*, *approu'd* could be adjectival only; but an adverbial 'provenly' may be indicated here. Schmidt in this instance reads 'proved to be so by experiment' (*Approve* 2). So, the *Signiors* have demonstrably been good *Masters* to Othello in the past and he trusts they will continue to be so by acknowledging the propriety of his marriage. If *approu'd* is adjectival, then the signiors have been tried and tested in their service to the state and, on the establishment of their noble quality, have been elected by the republic to the Council. (See *OED, Approved* ppl. adj.) In either case Othello's use of *good* is direct: a man who declares only virtue in himself addresses the virtue of the council.

So, in the heavy premodification of *Signiors* and *Masters* one might hear not only overt respect but also a covert *dis*respect. To the orator's skilled winning of his auditors by a flattering address Othello has added a portion of parody. The flattery is a little *too* flagrant to be sincere only. Shakespeare is arranging for Othello to relate a *précis* of his history: he gives Othello the oratorical equivalent of a written history's dedication, in which the author (or speaker) deplores his poor talent and rudeness of speech and extravagantly lauds the virtues of the dedicatee. Mock-modesty belongs in this convention – and, by extension, a possibility of mock-respect. Othello works upon the Council with a rhetorical skill that suggests a certain relaxation. He knows the Council's need of his military expertise, and he spends some time, very subtly, not in defending himself against the charge but in mentioning – incidentally as it were – the depth of that expertise. He mentions his military experience since the age of seven, his close acquaintance with all things warrior. He knows too that Brabantio's charge can be simply disproved – by the witness of Desdemona. He can relax. Through his solemnity he can allow the smallest amount of amusement to gleam.

Phonetically, few lines in Shakespeare are more 'noble' than those in which Othello entitles the signiors. Shakespeare's intricate working of assonance and consonance – a main means to his poetic resonance – is particularly marked in them. There is [v] in *Graue, Reueren'd, very* and *approu'd*. There is [r] in *Graue, Reueren'd, very, approu'd* and, probably, *Masters* (with short *a* and 'rolled' *r*). There is [p] in *Potent* and *approu'd*. There is [g] in *Graue* and *good*. There are [m], [s] and [t] through *Most* and *Masters*. In *Most, Signiors* and *Masters* there is [s] or [z]; while [n] sounds in *Potent, Reueren'd, Signiors* and *Noble*. These are the principal examples of consonance – a feature more subtle than alliteration. As for assonance, there is [u:] as in Modern English 'move' in *approu'd* and *good*. There is also a sound somewhere between Modern English *law* and French *beau* in *Most, Potent* and *Noble*. There is also syllable-play in the first syllables of *Reueren'd* and *very*. To supplement these 'noble' phonetics, moreover, Shakespeare has put them into a syntax of parison: two phrases of parallel structure with intensifier/adverb (sometimes understood) + premodification + noun. Again, these two

lines include no verbs at all. Thirteen words, and not an action-
word amongst them. The lines practically stand still with Othello's
earnestness.[9]

And yet inside the very extreme of this deviation from the norm
(a norm established by the rest of the speech) exists the potential for
parody. With so much on one side, there is room on the other side
for a hint of the opposite: for the attitude expressed by Othello's
maltreatment of Brabantio in the marriage and by Othello's use of
the phrase *old man*.

In the rest of the speech Othello's phrase *some nine Moones wasted*
has an ambiguous interest:

> Rude am I, in my speech,
> And little bless'd with the soft phrase of Peace;
> For since these Armes of mine, had seuen yeares pith,
> Till now, some nine Moones wasted, they haue vs'd
> Their deerest action, in the Tented Field:
>
> (F420–4; I.iii.81–5)

Othello is referring primarily to the waxing and waning of the
moon. In another conventional denotement of the lunar month he
will use the phrase *changes of the Moone* (F1794; III.iii.182). *Wasted*
has a neutral sense, as in *The Tragedie of Ivlivs Caesar*, 'Sir, March is
wasted fifteene dayes' (F679; II.i.59); and *some nine Moones wasted* is
parenthetical to *now*. Othello says in effect: until now, some nine
months passed (see Schimdt, *Waste* v. 1c, which cites this passage).
However, the phrase *seuen yeares pith* in the previous line is syntactically similar enough to set up an opposition: of *seuen* and *nine*; of
yeares and *Moones*; and, most importantly, of *pith* and *wasted*
despite their disparity of grammatical function. *Pith* is 'strength' –
with perhaps some nuance, lingering from its Old English meaning
of 'pith of a tree or vegetable', of 'central' or 'essential' part (*OED*
sb., 5 and 4). This opposition brings in the stronger senses of *waste*
which, as Schmidt discloses, are common elsewhere in Shakespeare. There is a connotation that the nine months passed at peace
in Venice have been squandered. There is also the connotation – by
which *wasted* removes to qualify *Armes* or their *pith* – in which
Othello's strength has dwindled or decayed through nine months
of inactivity. Conversely, that strength has been weakened *by* the
nine months of peace. (See Schmidt, *Waste* v., 2 and 1b; and *OED*,
Wasted, ppl. adj., 2b and 2.) To use Desdemona's phrase, and to

apply it to her husband, Othello has been a moth of peace in Venice for nine months: he has lived off the memory of wars, his own stories of wars, instead of actually following the wars in the present. The only expedition available to him has been the marital one of the night now passing – a night he certainly has not wasted. (Interestingly, during this same speech Othello may well be defining the marriage in military terms: 'The verie head, and front of my offending' (F419; I.iii.80). The general sense of 'highest extent or pitch' (*OED, Head* sb., IV.41, *Head and front*) may be strengthened, by the military lexicon elsewhere in the speech, into a phrase suggesting 'Advance against opposing force' and 'foremost line or part of an army' (*OED, Head* sb. III.29, and *Front* sb., II.5a).) Indeed, given that the pith of his arm is seen by Othello as an essential virtue, one may entertain a nuance of *wasted* as 'morally marred' (*OED* ppl. adj., 3). With this at least kept in mind, one may better understand the facility with which Othello comes later to condemn Venetian morality. Intrinsic in Othello, it would seem, there is an impatience with the *dolce vita* by which a soldier, like any Anthony, may be unmanned.

Another ambiguous interest belongs to *soft*:

> Rude am I, in my speech,
> And little bless'd with the soft [Q *set*] phrase of Peace;
>
> (F420–1; I.iii.81–2)

Othello might have added, 'Rude, that is, as are the rudely throated cannon I command and which Venice needs so much' (see F1998; III.iii.359). *Soft* could, and can, be 'low, quiet, subdued' and 'melodious, pleasing to the ear, sweet' (*OED* adj., I.3). Othello refers to the modulated tones and customs of aristocratic Venice, the courtly queen of the Adriatic famed for her civil skills. So Othello flatters the signiors with a speech that decidedly is not *rude*, or unrefined (Schmidt, *Rude* 3). However, *soft* might be sounding as 'weak, effeminate, unmanly' and 'involving little or no hardship; easily endured' (*OED* adj., III.14b and I.2). The result is this: that Othello's winning humility can be heard as accompanied by a certain pride, a warrior's sense of superiority, hence a disparagement of things and men civilian. Again, in Q this implication of disparagement sounds more strongly. *Set* here derives from the verbal form meaning 'write', and refers to a form of speech that is prescribed – i.e. 'before-written' – formal and imposed. (See Schmidt v., 14; and

OED, ppl. adj., I.3b, 5d and 2.) Othello is betraying an antipathy towards Venetian *pre*scription that joins his antipathy towards Venetian *circum*scription. The etiquette that might govern society in Venice, or advocacy in Venice, or an address to the Council in Venice – all those social, rhetorical and formal skills of language imposed on a Venetian are foreign to Othello's nature. *Set*, in fact, sounds so strongly as to emerge from ambiguity and to express openly the autonomist Othello's scorn. For this reason it is probably less to be preferred than *soft*.

If retained, however, it certainly acts as a fine description of the Duke's facile couplets to Brabantio later in this scene:

> When remedies are past, the griefes are ended
> By seeing the worst, which late on hopes depended.
> To mourne a Mischeefe that is past and gon,
> Is the next way to draw new mischiefe on.
> What cannot be presern'd [Q *preseru'd*], when Fortune takes:
> Patience, her Iniury a mock'ry makes.
> The rob'd that smiles, steales something from the Thiefe,
> He robs himselfe, that spends a bootelesse griefe.
>
> (F550–7; I.iii.202–9)

These are the Duke's set phrases of speech, the facile sentences by which he imposes peace without satisfactorily settling the issue that caused its disturbance. The Duke still refers by implication to Brabantio's *Iniury*, to Brabantio as *the rob'd*, and to Othello as *the Thiefe*; yet he has decided against Brabantio in the necessary interest of the State. Brabantio's sarcastic reply in kind – i.e. in facile couplets – shows how little he feels his grievance has been redressed. Desdemona stole willingly to her wedding. But this fact has hardly lessened Brabantio's sense of having been beguiled. Contrast the Duke's prescribed language – his clichés expressed in a set rhyming-scheme – to Othello's command of a persuasively pacific language: Othello's scorn of the *set phrase of Peace* would seem to be just. His own eloquence, based on a subtle use of rhetoric, particularly self-depreciation, is far more effective.[10]

Later in this scene Othello continues his implied disparagement of Venetian life:

> The Tirant Custome, most graue Senators,
> Hath made the flinty and Steele Coach [Q *Cooch*]

of Warre
My thrice-driuen bed of Downe. I do agnize
A Naturall and prompt Alacartie [Q *alacrity*],
I finde in hardnesse, and do [Q *would*] vndertake
This present Warres against the Ottamites.

(F577–82; I.iii.229–34)

True, Othello is once again reminding the Council of his military
prowess – but, really, there is no need of such a reminder. True, too,
that *most graue* acknowledges the councillors' state and importance.
But Othello contrasts the compelling custom of warfare – the only
tyrant he would submit to – with the peaceful customs of Venice.
These make you soft or set, not only in your phrasings. And by this
contrast Venice is subtly mocked. Not intentionally: it is as if
Othello's exuberance at the success of his marital expedition, and at
the prospect of war, is allowing his ambiguous attitude to his
employers to slip through. In the next two lines, however, that
attitude becomes less ambiguous. Venice is equated with the
marriage-bed, and both are denigrated in *thrice-driuen bed of
Downe*. Othello is shortly to be insulting conjugal love as *wanton
dulnesse* (as discussed above in Chapter 1); and this phrase
rehearses that insult. It is a remarkably packed description. The
OED reminds us, as do editors of *Othello*, that *driuen* refers to the
separating out of lighter feathers from the less light by means of a
current of air – the lighter ones being accumulated into beds of the
utmost luxury (*OED, Driven* ppl. adj., 2). For this particular bed the
already soft feathers have been sifted thrice; this supplies a further
extreme of softness. These feathers, too, are akin to the *light wing'd
Toyes* and the wings of *feather'd Cupid* (F618–9; I.iii.268–9) with
which Othello is to asperse conjugal love. Both Venice and marriage
become a feather-bed state. They are soft, effete, unmilitary. They
are circumscribed and prescribed by laws and have lost their pith.

Moreover, there is probably a contrast intended between the
couch – given the usual emendation of *Coach* or *Cooch* – and the
bed. A couch was not necessarily a sleeping-fixture: it furnished
sleep without canopy or hangings (*OED, Couch* sb.,[1] 10). The pairing with *bed*, therefore, is not merely an example of Elizabethan/
Jacobean copiousness. Othello is distinguishing between the permanence and formality – the word *set* returns to mind – of the civil
life and the portable, 'camp-bed' life of the military hard man. In
the one life is virtue, occupation; in the other, sybaritic existence –

comfort, luxury, *otium*.

Again, this disparagement of Venice is possibly maintained in Othello's use of *Naturall*. This, of course, is one of the most ambiguous words in the English lexicon. In one sense, Othello's alacrity is 'innate', 'consonant with' his character (*OED, Natural* adj., II.8 and 9). Thus the habit of hardness that Othello has acquired – he refers to it with affectionate amusement as a tyrant – is based upon a native inclination. More comfort for the Council, then. However, Othello's alacrity may also be 'Based upon the innate moral feeling of mankind; instinctively felt to be right and fair' and 'not artificially made', 'free from affectation . . . or constraint' (*OED* I.1, 6 and 7b). This eagerness (the repetition of *prompt*'s sense in *Alacartie* emphasises that eagerness) is not a quality that Othello has felt for his civilian life in Venice. In Venice, he implies, natural vitality is vitiated by peace.[11]

The confine of Venice and of marriage becomes an emotional imprisonment in

> Think'st thou I'ld make a Life of Iealousie;
> To follow still the changes of the Moone
> With fresh suspitions?
>
> (F1793–5; III.iii.181–3)

Othello is not, of course, referring to himself as an astronomer. To observe the skies scientifically might well have delighted the speculative mind; and a close attention to the sun's passing through two hundred solar years certainly brought wisdom to the Sybil, whom Othello is later to describe in III.iv. Here the image supplies two comparisons. The jealous man will espy his wife as obsessively as the astronomer will the moon in its sphere. And a wife will be moonlike, lunar, in being apparently both chaste in temperament *and* fickle in her changings. This was a paradox for which the youthful Donne, intellectually at least, considered a woman to be 'the most delightfull thing in this world'.[12] Not so for Othello, however. Despite the power of the moon-image, a sequence of main stresses can be heard on *Life*, on *still* and on *fresh*. Othello is reacting not to the idea that he might be jealous, but to the idea that he might be jealous, ignominiously, for any length of time. It is Iago's postulation of the man who 'dotes, yet doubts' and who *'euer feares'* (emphasis added) cuckoldry that has provoked him. And Othello echoes Iago's *euer* in his own use of *still* as 'always'. (See Schmidt adv., 1; and compare 'But still the house Affaires would draw her hence [Q *thence*]' – F492; I.iii.147.) In fact, the changing nature of the moon or woman and the *un*changing nature of the husband's observation are most subtly opposed. To be permanently uncertain about his wife's fidelity is a condition Othello would not tolerate. The mere thought of that condition makes him uneasy. Even the moon, Othello's companion in his own movements as a free man, is now seen as describing a circumference to confine him between perplexing opposites. To be always waxing and waning in certainty? To think at times that a wife is constant, at others that she is inconstant – constant only in her inconstancy? This must be unendurable. It is a paradox, this moonlike nature of a woman, that Othello is to express later in his savage 'demonstration' to Lodovico: 'Sir, she can turne, and turne: and yet go on / And turne again' (F2651–2; IV.i.250–1). There is something else too: the possible connotation of moon as month and therefore as the female cycle ('menses' from Latin *menses*, plural of *mensis* 'month'). There is perhaps a sense of a husband suspecting any cyclical cessation in his wife that might arouse the question, 'Am I the father?'

This husband will not merely spend a lifetime in jealousy. He will make of his *Life* a vocation in that emotion. He will be ridiculous, imperfect. He will be an especially degraded kind of sublunary creature. Naturally Othello – who is essentially *super*lunary in his ideals – will not allow himself to be lowered to this moon-calf existence. For him the moon is a co-mate of his tented travels, not an overseer of his confinement in a mundane, constantly renewing (*fresh*) emotion. When, a few lines later, he declaims 'Away at once with Loue, or Iealousie', he is postulating less a dismissal of either of those two emotions than a release of himself from a marital and Venetian/human prison.[13]

Once Othello is actively jealous, much use can be made of the fear of confinement so carefully inscribed. It is from Othello's view of Venice and Venetian marriage as a bed with too much 'give' that the attack on *Chamberers* develops:

> Haply, for I am blacke,
And haue not those soft parts of Conuersation
That Chamberers haue: Or for I am declin'd
Into the vale [Q *valt*] of yeares (yet that's not much)
Shee's gone.
>
> (F1894–8; III.iii.267–71)

The bed of thrice-sifted feathers stops being symbolic and becomes a literal bed in a Venetian bed-chamber. *Chamberers* were gallants who frequented ladies' chambers (*OED, Chamberer* 4) instead of battlefields: boudoir boys, lizards of the lounge. They spend their days on the beds of over-refined softness – and are as much slandered by Othello, with as much unjust generalisation, as are the Venetian ladies by Iago. Their *Conuersation* is not just our modern 'speaking with' but one's 'Manner of conducting oneself in the world or in society' (*OED, Conversation* 6). But in context the further and more specific meaning of 'Sexual . . . intimacy' (*OED* 3) is peripherally present. (Literally, *Conuersation* is a 'turning with', from Latin *convertere*. Compare Desdemona's attributed ability to turn and turn again – F2651–2; IV.i.250–1.) There are references back in *soft* not only to the soft phrase of peace but also to the bed's thrice-driven, volupt's quality. Othello's blackness here seems to be equated with a lack of civilisation – a lack that Desdemona apparently deplores and which Othello, since civilisation equals decadence, must extol. The landscapes' rudeness in Othello's travels is preferable to elaborate manners that mask a predilection to 'chamber' – i.e. 'indulge in lewdness' (*OED, Chamber* v.).

In this same speech Othello declares,

> I had rather be a Toad
> And liue vpon the vapours of a Dungeon,
> Then keepe a corner in the thing I loue
> For others vses.
>
> (F1902–5; III.iii.273–6)

Here the sense of confinement is developed in images of physical housing. The chamber becomes Desdemona herself. She has acquired internal corners. Corners in Shakespeare could be regions and directions, or quarters and parts of the world, or angles of parks and gardens. Above all, however, a corner in Shakespeare is 'The angle as part of the interior of a room' (see Schmidt, *Corner* 4, 5, 2 and 3) and this would seem to be the metaphorical meaning here. (None of the editions I have consulted supplies any comment.) Desdemona's body is spoken of as the chamber in which lewdness occurs, to which chamberers resort, in which Othello is entrapped. He finds intolerable the thought that a corner, a secret place, might be reserved therein for others' sexual uses. Additionally, Desdemona's *corner* is part of a *thing*. According to the *OED* (sb.[1], II.10), *thing* was not necessarily perjorative. It could, in fact, denote commendation. But the reference to 'Privy member, private parts' (II.11: c.1386–1762) needs to be registered. (Compare Iago's comment to his wife, 'It is a common thing' – F1939; III.iii.307.) The *OED*'s last date obviously does not refer to the spoken language: the meaning is common enough today. It may well be that Othello, under stress, is being made to betray a lesser decency than we have been used to – and without Iago's help.[14]

One last point about *corner*. In its links with Latin *cornu* ('horn') it has a further aptness in this tirade against possible cuckoldry. *The Merry Wiues of Windsor*, much concerned in its own way with suspected wives, has a reference to a jealous husband as a *peaking Curnuto* (F1741; III.v.63).

Another kind of chamber is the *Dungeon*. This could mean the tower or donjon of a castle (*OED* sb., 1); but *vapour* and the ground-level *Toad* declares for a 'dark subterranean place of confinement' (*OED* sb., 2). It says much for Othello's sense of extreme imprisonment in Desdemona and marriage that an actual dungeon existence should be preferable. Inside such a dungeon Othello would be breathing in the unhealthy exhalations; he would be infected as by the poisoned vapours of Venetian *moeurs*; as a toad he would himself be poisonous. As a toad, too, he would be low in the order of bestiary, with no self-awareness, let alone a soul. Othello is saying, in effect, toad-ignorance is bliss; and this prefigures his 'I had beene happy . . . So I had nothing knowne' (F1988–90; III.iii. 349–51). The irony is, of course, that he already is living underground, so to speak. He is already enclosed by delusion and living off the vapours of slander and suggestion.[15]

Q's *valt* maintains the confinement-motif more than does F's *vale*. Like *Dungeon*, it has an up and a down meaning. 'Arched roof or ceiling' is inappropriate as something declined into (*OED, Vault* sb.[1], 1). The meaning here is 'lower or underground apartment' with an 'arched roof' or, particularly, 'burial chamber . . . usually altogether or partly underground' (sb.[1], 2 and 3b). A man near this vault of his years – even if not *that* near – might possibly be less ardent than a younger man like Cassio in sexual matters. Othello, whose body is subordinated to the business of his soul, would have an especial horror of any receptacle in which imperfect flesh might further corrupt and threaten his virtue. This vault is not one of the antres or caverns before whose vastness Othello stopped in wonder during his travels. It is another of the chambers in which he feels cornered. The Greek word for vault is the source of 'chamber' via Latin *camera* or *camara* – from this there derive two rooms: the Venetian vaulted room which might be Desdemona herself and which is filled in the imagination by vaulting Venetian gentlemen; and the room in which Othello sits by himself registering the slander-vapours and which takes on the atmosphere of a tomb.

F's *vale* has nothing of this. It may be linked to the watery vales, the troughs, that Othello's bark may descend into at F965–7 (II.i.185–7), having climbed 'hills of Seas'. In both vales danger would threaten: in one, cuckoldry; in the other, drowning. In the *vale of yeares* the sense is not of confinement but rather of emptiness – the valley of death, the bourne of no return, deserts of vast eternity. It belongs, as *valt* does not, to the familiar geological and moral landscape of Othello's pilgrimage. It suggests, if not confinement, at least a want of the free condition.

Shakespeare, then, is now gaining advantage from Othello's carefully inscribed preference for the unhoused, free condition. Othello's dislike for the easy furnishing and customs of a life that is housed and civilised – a life lived in confining rooms – grows to an apprehension about chambers, corners, vaults, dungeons. There is claustrophobia – or at least something claustrophobic – in the way Othello's imagination dwells so frequently in images of physical or spiritual confines.

At F2714ff. (IV.ii.24ff.) – the 'brothel' scene – this housed condition has worsened even more. Othello sees himself as a client of his own wife. The marital bedroom has become a room in a bawdy-house with Aemilia as a bawd. Inside this 'brothel' confinement are further confining images: of steeping, of captivity, of the cistern in

> Had it pleas'd Heauen,
> To try me with Affliction, had they rain'd [Q *he ram'd*]
> All kinds of Sores, and Shames on my bare-head:
> Steep'd me in pouertie to the very lippes,
> Giuen to Captiuitie, me, and my vtmost hopes,
> I should haue found in some place [Q *part*] of my Soule
> A drop of patience
>
> (F2742–8; IV.ii.48–54)

and

> But there where I haue garner'd vp my heart,
> Where either I must liue, or beare no life,

The Fountaine from the which my currant runnes,
Or else dries vp: to be discarded thence,
Or keepe it as a Cestern, for foule Toades
To knot and gender in.

(F2752–7; IV.ii.58–63)

Steep means to 'involve deeply in a state or condition' (*OED* 3c); but *to the very lippes* brings in a literal immersion in the sense of 'soak in water' (*OED* 3c). In this extreme confinement all one could do is breathe and suffer the awareness of one's condition. As for *Captiuitie*, this Othello has already experienced – according to his summary of his warfaring in I.iii. He could probably endure it again with a certain amount of patience. (The phrase *in some place of my Soule* nicely echoes *a corner in the thing I loue*: the use by others of that corner – as Othello imagines it – destroys the place where patience might reside.) What Othello cannot endure is that the symbolic bedroom into which he has put all his stock of idealism should have been profaned. What he cannot endure is that the well or spring of his river of life should have been fouled up. The bond of marriage has become an unwelcome bondage. *Knot* relinquishes all sense of the true-lovers' knot, or remembers it only with savage irony. The meaning points to a merely physical intertwining. *Gender* as 'copulate' (*OED* – obsolete by 1634), or perhaps as 'generate', seems to denote the mindless, merely animal activity by which a species contrives its survival with no recognition of the individual. Desdemona and Othello in the 'brothel' room, Desdemona with Cassio and other Venetian 'toads', have become subhuman. They are reduced to the muddy vesture of their flesh. This cistern, or tank, is the latest development of the dungeon, the vaporous rumours of which have condensed into the despair in which Othello is steeped.

The cistern is the more horrible in its contrast to what it was: a fountainhead of ideal love that newly supplied the single source of Othello's life. This contrast remembers the crucial premise on which Othello entered matrimony: *But that I loue the gentle Desdemona*. That premise is now destroyed. The sheer degree of Shakespeare's concentration on the housed/unhoused theme is disclosed as Othello laments as any immured prisoner might.

Othello's figurative claustrophobia informs how he views others. Desdemona's hand should suffer a *sequester*, a seclusion (*OED* 3) or enclosure (F2183; III.iv.37). When Othello attempts to know what

Iago is thinking he talks of a monster confined:

> Alas, thou eechos't me
> [Q *By heauen he ecchoes me*];
> As if there were some Monster in thy thought
> Too hideous to be shewne
>
> (F1713–15; III.iii.110–12)

and

> didd'st contract, and purse thy brow together,
> As if thou then hadd'st shut vp in thy Braine
> Some horrible Conceite [Q *counsell*]
>
> (F1720–2; iii.iii.117–19)

It may be that Iago contracts intransitively on learning that Cassio was Othello's go-between. Or it may be that *contract* and *purse* both have *brow* as a direct object. In either case Iago has confined a monster just conceived (it would seem) and struggling to be delivered. *Conceite* may be touched in some degree by the notion of conception and birth as Iago apparently labours not to let this monster forth. Conversely, *Conceite* may have the denotement of thought alone, and nothing of physical conception. *Purse* here, as 'contract, to draw together the (lips, brow, etc.) . . . ' was a newish usage, with a metaphoric force that by now has weakened (*OED* v.,4). A purse of soft leather or of cloth would wrinkle as its 'mouth' was drawn tight by the strings. Iago's forehead is wrinkled tight with the effort of shutting the monster up where it belongs. Again, Othello's use of *purse* supplies an interesting example of how two characters can use a word in their respectively differentiated ways. For Othello the purse is essentially a container. For Iago, who harps upon *purse* at F692ff. (I.iii.337ff.), it is a means to money: Rodorigo will increase his credit with Desdemona (supposedly) by putting money in his purse; Iago thence will benefit.

   This passage of the play will not be discussed in any other chapter. I shall digress for a paragraph here to discuss the *Monster*. Though Othello's suspicions are obviously aroused by Iago, it is Othello who realises the actual monster as a physical animal and installs it in Iago's brain; and it is from this creature of Othello's imagination that Iago develops his 'greene-ey'd Monster', the animal embodiment of jealousy (F1781; III.iii.170). Many critics have tried to identify this vivid creature as variously a crocodile or a tiger or even as a mouse.[16] In fact, the image derives much of its strength from its blend of the vividly coloured particular with the vague – though there is definitely something feline about the way this monster plays with its prey ('doth mocke / The meate it feeds on'). Othello's earlier version of the monster has a similar physicality. Schmidt's reading of 'something monstrous', i.e. something shockingly unnatural, unjustly reduces the image to an abstraction (*Monster* sb.). The point is this: that a fine example is supplied of Othello's alacrity in crystallising something particular and definite around Iago's *ifs* and innuendoes. A fine piece of evidence is also supplied for the argument that Othello is the main originator of his own tragedy and that Iago's function is hardly more than to rouse him. Another point about the *Monster* is this: that Othello would probably be thinking in terms of the monsters he has seen on his travels – the cannibals and the men whose heads do grow beneath their shoulders – but that the lexicon of *shewne* and *shut vp* suggests a narrower range of reference than a simply wild and abominable being. This monster is so hideous and un-natural as to defy public spectacle. Also, the specific reference to time in *as if thou then hadd'st shut vp* indicates the actual moment of violent encaging: that is to say, Othello refers not to a state of imprisonment but to the violent action of imprisoning; and this seems to reinforce the hideousness of an animal that must be flung so precipitately from sight. A kinship can be observed, therefore, between this monster of Othello's present imagining and the 'fixed Figure' he is to imagine later (F2749; IV.ii.55). This later monster is principally an example of the species 'cuckold', the 'Horned man' whom Othello himself declares to be a 'Monster, and a Beast' (F2442; IV.i.62). But it is also fixed and pointed at, an object of scorn; and it therefore assumes the semblance of a type of effigy, a vilely painted representation that might for example be viewed by the vulgar at a fair. In other words, when Othello imagines a monster in Iago's brain he is probably thinking already in terms of his reputa-tion, of how he is shown to the world. There is a large irony here, of course. Having caused the figure of the horned general to be no longer *shut vp* in Iago's brain, Othello suffers the more for its release. It fixes in his imagination and provides much of the moti-vation for the monstrous act of uxoricide. Iago in his mean little plot could hardly have foreseen such a shocking outcome – a bonus beyond his dream. To return via the *Monster* to the theme of confinement one can observe as follows: that the monster is essentially a metropolitan monster. As Iago puts it, 'Ther's many a Beast then in a populous Citty, / And many a ciuill Monster' (F2443–4; IV.i.63–4). It needed the circumscription and confine of Venice, the bonds of marriage – and the malignity of a Venetian – for Othello to conceive of this monster. Before such hideousness, such unsightliness, the morally and physically deformed creatures whom Othello met abroad become in retrospect as nothing.

3

'Who can controll his Fate?'

Othello asks 'Who can controll his Fate?' towards the end of the play, when his decisive action of revenge has proved destructive of innocence (F3565; V.ii.268). The question functions, in fact, as an assertion; and it seems to derive from a sudden realisation in Othello about man's inability to shape his destiny. The implication is that until now Othello *has* considered himself to be in control, to some extent, of his own fate.

The implication would seem to be correct. Othello has managed to control the events of his life or, in adverse circumstances such as captivity, to endure them. He has mastered the hazards of war and travel and proved his virtue and efficacy amongst alien peoples. In his own words to Gratiano, 'I haue made my way through more impediments / Then twenty times your stop'; and such military prowess against such odds has been a principal means whereby he has made his own destiny. One might add that in the enterprise of his marriage he showed much autonomy in deciding his fate; and that in his suicide, too, he is to demonstrate once again a characteristic control.

Inside this heroic nature, however, Shakespeare has inscribed for Othello the ability to see himself as 'a heauenly effect in an earthly Actor' – I use Lafew's phrase from *All's Well, that Ends Well* (F915–16; II.ii.23–4). It enables Othello to discern in his actions a divine as well as a Venetian service. It allows him a view of himself as one sublimely controlled *by* Fate.

It is not, this ability, a prime cause of Desdemona's murder. But it certainly does nothing to prevent it. It is linked with Othello's idealism and with his inexperience of human dealings; and it certainly assists the murder in ushering Othello to the recognition of a respectable *Cause*. Moreover, this tendency to remove responsibility in a sublime direction is accompanied by a tendency to move it laterally. That is to say, Othello is able to share out at least some of the responsibility for his actions among other characters in the drama.

75

He first discloses a susceptibility to motives other than his own in the description of his courtship. Initially, Othello says, it was Brabantio who caused him and Desdemona to meet so often:

> Her Father lou'd me, oft inuited me:
> Still question'd me the Storie of my life,
> From yeare to yeare: the Battaile, Sieges, Fortune,
> That I haue past.
> I ran it through, euen from my boyish daies,
> To th' very moment that he bad me tell it.
>
> (F473–8; I.iii.128–33)

The syntax of single subject and three verbs in the first two lines – of one man propelling several activities – suggests something of Brabantio's insistence; and *he bad me tell* reinforces that suggestion. Brabantio, it seems, has a pleading characteristic – which is strongly marked in his daughter, too, when she persistently pleads on Cassio's behalf. Moreover, the pre- and post-modifications supplement Brabantio's insistence – while supplying much of the noble certainty of Othello's rhythm: *oft; Still* (= 'unceasingly'); *From yeare to yeare; through; euen; very*. These do not quite take over the tonics from the verbs and nouns, but they certainly take significant stresses. They help to slow and dignify the lines. The paradox ensues that much of Othello's (slightly amused?) grace under pressure derives from his pointed delegation of responsibility. Othello – or so he claims – did not voluntarily tell his seductive tales; nor did he even voluntarily visit the magnifico's house. He did so only because Brabantio, the old man and citified Venetian, demanded to know every detail of every military operation, to have a full coverage of Othello's life and fortune. All this narrative, Othello says, was nothing of his responsibility. He was fulfilling his host's importunate desire to have him as a guest for vicarious experience. If Desdemona, overhearing, was allured by the tales and wished to hear more, it was her father who had dragged them from Othello in the first place.

According to Othello, then, it is Brabantio's insistence that should be seen as the first cause of the events culminating in the marriage. Othello as a guest could do nothing but submit. Othello says in effect, 'Had I not been in Brabantio's house, I should not have put my tongue to such narrative art.'

Further into this same speech Othello details the circumstances in which he announced his love to Desdemona. His own actions are clearly described. He observed Desdemona's interest in his stories:

> Which I obseruing,
> Tooke once a pliant houre, and found good meanes
> To draw from her a prayer of earnest heart,
> That I would all my Pilgrimage dilate,
> Wherof by parcels she had something heard,
> But not instinctively [Q *intentively*]
>
> (F495–500; I.iii.150–5)

Schmidt reads *pliant* as 'convenient'; but it probably means the time that Othello was able to ply or shape to his own positive purpose. How he used that time is suggested in *found good meanes*: he found his way to an effective method of drawing Desdemona out. Presumably his means was a mingling of that same persuasiveness and amusement that the Council hears during this speech. (Othello does 'woo' the Council with his summary. He does incline them in his favour.)

Again, in his stories to Desdemona he

> often did beguile her of her teares,
> When I did speake of some distressefull stroke
> That my youth suffer'd
>
> (F501–3; I.iii.156–8)

Beguile here is 'take or draw from one in a pleasing manner' (Schmidt). Othello's usage corrects the Duke's earlier sounding of the word:

> Who ere he be, that in this foule proceeding
> Hath thus beguil'd your Daughter of her selfe,
> And you of her . . . .
>
> (F402–4; I.iii.65–7)

The Duke means 'rob . . . of', in a bad way (Schmidt, *Beguile* 1). In this wordplay Othello is encapsulating the whole purpose of his speech. He is to destroy Branantio's charge of witchcraft with a calm account of what he did actually win the lady with.

Othello, then, frankly acknowledges his own responsibility in the courtship. He clearly demonstrates his positive movements.

At the same time, however, Othello also contrives to make it clear that, in Brabantio's words, Desdemona 'was halfe the wooer' (F522; I.iii.176). Brabantio bases this finding solely on Othello's summary; he is, in fact, responding justly to the following sentences in which Desdemona is the activating subject:

> These things to heare
> Would Desdemona seriously incline:
>   . . .
> She'l'd come againe, and with a greedie eare
> Deuoure vp my discourse.
>   . . .
> She gaue me for my paines a world of kisses [Q *sighes*];
> She swore in faith 'twas strange
>   . . .
> She wish'd she had not heard it, yet she wish'd
> That Heauen had made her such a man. She thank'd me,
> And bad me, if I had a Friend that lou'd her,
> I should but teach him how to tell my Story,
> And that would wooe her.
>
>   (between F490 and 511; I.iii.145–66)

One has to be careful here. These extrapolations may, erroneously, give the impression of a forward miss only too eager to compromise herself – the less-than-innocent Desdemona that might be proffered to counter the opposite view of Desdemona as a 'saint'. They may suggest that Brabantio's household was an unusual one or, indeed, that it was a typical Venetian household in which a resting soldier was unsafe from the wiles of a daughter who virtually propositioned her father's guest behind her father's back. Such a view, of course, ignores the dramatic situation. Othello does not have the advantage enjoyed by his actual historical contemporary, Sebastiano Veniero. That great soldier commanded the Venetian forces at the Battle of Lepanto; he married the Venetian princess Cecilia Contarina, and in 1577 was actually elected Duke. Although in Venetian terms he was a foreigner, he did in fact hail from the Italian peninsula: he was, that is, Caucasian. Desdemona's directness in revealing her love to Othello – a directness to be sounded again in her plea to go with Othello to Cyprus and again in her pleading on Cassio's behalf – is in fact evidence of her sensitivity. She is aware that Othello is unlikely to be acceptable to her father or perhaps to the Council in any social capacity other than guest. She is courageous, not bold, in overcoming her modesty – a modesty referred to by Brabantio's 'A Maiden, neuer bold' (F435ff.; I.iii.94ff.) – in the higher interest of a virtuous love that transcends the apparent impediment of racial difference. When Othello says, 'Vpon this hint I spake' (F511; I.iii.166) – *hint* is 'suggestion' or 'occasion' (*OED* sb., 2 and 1) and seems more appropriate than Q's *heate* – he is pointing the decorous nature of the initiatives taken under Brabantio's roof.[1]

This mature, careful – and black – man is hardly at fault, then, in the caution of his courtship in its early stage. As Eldred Jones has summarised, 'Because of his isolation in Venetian society and the prevailing attitudes, Othello puts himself into the hands of Desdemona, the one who really belongs to the society.'[2] As Othello says, he can be found in her report. Let her witness the proper course of his wooing. Additionally, of course, Desdemona is to witness the absence of any witchcraft on Othello's part. As it transpires, she does not have to directly, since the careful delineation of Othello's speech has already had the effect of dispelling Brabantio's charge. But the accusation of witchcraft was no light matter: the procuring of love by blackly magical means was punishable by imprisonment on a first conviction, by death on a second.[3] Othello's careful demonstration of a mutual wooing, a shared initiative, is directly provoked by his urgent need to defend himself. It says much for Othello's rhetorical control of others' responses in this scene that the wild accusations with which Brabantio attacks him are reduced to a precise, indeed mathematical, truth: 'If she confesse that she was halfe the wooer . . . . '

There is therefore nothing to censure Othello for in his apportioning of responsibility. But his ability so to apportion needs recording. His account of his courtship is essentially careful – and one can note that he puts a certain emphasis on 'How I did thriue in this faire Ladies loue' rather than on how 'she (did thrive) in mine' (F470–1; I.iii.125–6). One can note, too, the emphasis on a mutually natural magic in the incantatory repetitions of

> She gaue me for my paines a world of kisses [Q *sighes*]:
> She swore in faith 'twas strange: 'twas passing strange,
> 'Twas pittiful: 'twas wondrous pittifull.
> She wish'd she had not heard it, yet she wish'd
> That Heauen had made her such a man.

They declare not only Othello's entrancing of Desdemona but also Desdemona's entrancing of Othello. Again, one can note that Othello describes Desdemona's ear as *greedie* and that she did *deuoure vp* his discourse. These words combine both a passivity and a violent activity in Desdemona, while presenting in Othello an amused, quasi-paternal wondering at her youthful appetite for his history. All such emphases as these are understandable, for the reasons outlined above. The point is this: that Shakespeare, having inscribed this recognition of Desdemona's intitiative, can use it later in developing Othello's jealousy. A potential for mistrust – a potential more strongly put in Brabantio's 'Looke to her (Moore) if thou hast eies to see: / She ha's deceiu'd her Father, and may thee' (F645–6; I.iii.292–3) – is thus subtly expressed. Othello's jealousy has something to work on in Desdemona's initiative. Othello will be able to distort her courage into the boldness of the strumpet, 'that cunning Whore of Venice, / That married with Othello (F2788–9; IV.ii.90–1). He will be able to review her sighs and wonderings as wiles and beguilement – in the 'bad' sense of that word. He will be able to establish a total responsibility for the marriage on his wife.

In the murder-scene Shakespeare makes great dramatic use both of Desdemona's apparent ability to lie and of Othello's ability to assign responsibility outside himself:

> O periur'd woman, thou do'st stone my heart,
> And makes [Q *makest*] me call, what I intend to do,
> A Murther, which I thought a Sacrifice.
>
> (F3314–8; V.ii.66–8)

The same syntax, with Desdemona as the motivating subject, is present here as in the sentences quoted earlier. It is Desdemona's fault that Othello can no longer offer her up as a sacrifice. The alabaster stone – spoken of in 'It is the Cause . . . ' at the start of V.ii – has left Desdemona's skin for Othello's heart, petrifying all sorrow in him. Or, alternatively, the seat of Othello's emotions has been assailed and he enraged by a stone-hurling adultress who, biblically speaking, needs stoning herself. It seems that Desdemona, who dragged Othello down into mankind by marrying him, has dragged him down even further: she has reawakened in him the sublunary loss of control he so much despises.

Moreover, this tendency to assign responsibility elsewhere also helps to explain Othello's dependence on Iago's honesty. This dependence is as much a plot-necessity as is Desdemona's being kept uninformed; and it likewise derives not from a plot-contrivance – though the honesty itself *is* heavily emphasised – but from Othello's character.[4] A syntax recurs in which a subject other than Othello supplies the premise of Othello's action:

> O, I were damn'd beneath all depth in hell:
> But that I did proceed vpon iust grounds
> To this extremity. Thy Husband knew it all.
> (F3408–10; v.ii.140–2)

> . . . 'twas he that told me on her first.
> An honest man he is, and hates the slime
> That stickes on filthy deeds.
> (F3419–21; v.ii.150–2)

> 'Tis pittiful: but yet Iago knowes
> That she with Cassio, hath the Act of shame
> A thousand times committed.
> (F3499–501; v.ii.213–5)

Othello is made yet again to justify the murder by a reference outside himself for his authority. The same purblindness pertains in

> Will you, I pray, demand that demy-Diuell,
> Why he hath thus ensnar'd my Soule and Body. [Q ?]
> (F3605–6; v.ii.304–5)

Here Iago continues as the activating subject, the entrapper. Othello's question would have been more apt had he asked why the snare was so easily entered and allowed to work so efficiently. As it is, Iago's suggested status as a demi-devil further diminishes Othello's responsibility (in Othello's mind). Even though Iago as a non-commissioned ancient must belong to a lower or 'demi' order of devils, and even though he can be only half a devil in having a human identity, still the snare can be regarded as an instrument of hell before which Othello's *virtù* must be inadequate. The view that ' "Devil" is a cliché in this play, a tired metaphor for "very bad", as "angel" is for "very good" ' and that 'Theological conceptions help us . . . little . . . '[5] omits the landscapes of heaven and hell – and of heaven on earth and of hell on earth – by which Othello's imagination has been dominated with particular vividness through the play. The description of Iago specifically as a demi-devil does in fact disclose a remarkable consistency in Othello's characterisation: just as Othello has been able to see himself as the instrument of a heavenly *Cause*, so he is now able to view Iago as a hell's equivalent.

The theme of Othello's ability to discern authority for the murder elsewhere than in himself is continued by his use of *wrought* and *Perplexed*:

> Of one, not easily Iealious, but being wrought,
> Perplexed in the extreame . . . .
>
> (F3656–7; v.ii.348–9)

Wrought as 'overwrought' probably needs to be retained as a connotation;[6] but it is more germane to read the verbal form 'to be wrought', the passive of 'to work'. The denotement is that Othello's will and mind have been acted upon; that he has been influenced, prevailed upon, induced, persuaded by subtle and insidious means; that he has been brought into a particular mental state by an external agency. Here I am paraphrasing the *OED* article on *Work* (v., B I.14a). Or, Othello has been operated upon and, again, acted upon – here I paraphrase Schmidt's definition (*Work* v., 3b), which cites Othello's usage. Some sense is also present of 'work' as 'agitate, stir, move, excite, incite' (*OED* v., B I.14b). *OED* finds this a new metaphor first written in *Macbeth*: 'My dull Braine was wrought with things forgotten' (F266; I.iii.149–150). Importantly, *but being wrought* opposes *not easily*; and this opposition confirms the idea of hard work and intricate design that I think is expressed in *wrought*. Like Othello, Iago finds an alacrity in hardness; and without the ancient's ability to engineer or work his superiors to his own pattern Othello would not have been brought to jealousy in the first place or kept to it so assiduously. In these lines, therefore, Othello is summarising a truth. Much of his final long speech is a plea for a fair and just report; and it would be perfectly just to report that Othello *has* been extensively and cleverly worked. At the same time, however, Iago's ability is to work his victims along the grain of their own weaknesses; and Othello makes no mention of this in his summary of himself as a worked victim. There is some reference back by Shakespeare (one surmises) to Iago's 'Worke on, / My Medicine workes' (F2421–2; IV.i.44–5) in Othello's literal fall in the trance-scene: the contrast thus effected between Iago's active and Othello's passive use is interesting. Earlier, in speaking to the Council in Act I, Othello countered Brabantio's charge that he 'wrought vp on' (F447; I.iii.106) Desdemona with a dram or mixtures by carefully pointing the degree to which Desdemona helped to work the situation by being, as Brabantio recapitulates, half the wooer. Here, in speaking to Lodovico, the representative of the Council, Othello asserts in *being wrought* not only Iago's cunning but his own helplessness. He halves responsibility. Of course, he has just been apprised of the intricacies of Iago's plot – what happened, why, how and when – and his sense of having been wrought is hardly surprising. But, equally, his quick apportioning of blame is characteristic and remarkable. What one misses in him is the ability not only to answer but even to raise the question that Shakespeare implicitly puts: how is it that Iago found such an extremely malleable quality in material that must have seemed so intractable? The general has been given to hardness, to flinty and steel couches, to a sword of icebrook-tempered steel, to rough quarries, to rocks. In Iago's working he has been Venetian-soft, with only rare and ineffective attempts at resistance.[7]

Perplexed can be more briefly dealt with. In the clausal hierarchy of the sentence it is more 'powerful' than *being wrought*; but it is, I think, semantically weaker. Strictly, it is a participial adjective, but something of the passive mood in *being wrought* prevails: Othello has not merely been in a perplexed state; he has also experienced Iago's perplexing. The word derives from Latin *plectere* ('to plait') and the prefix denotes a quality of thoroughness (from Latin *per* 'through'). The active form, stronger than in Modern English, was 'To fill (a person) with uncertainty . . . to trouble with doubt; to distract confuse, bewilder, puzzle' (*OED, Perplex* v. 1). Once again Othello sees himself as a passive victim. Not only was he actively wrought; he also was distracted and bewildered, filled to the extreme with doubt about Desdemona's honesty, by Iago's plot.

Brabantio's invitations and demands, Desdemona's hints and share in the wooing – these, then, for Othello established the process by which he met, fell in love with and married Desdemona. And it was Iago's honest concern that established the process by which Desdemona, as it were, became killed by Othello. To use Iago's words, Othello considers he was 'tenderly . . . lead' (F747; I.iii.395) throughout: he thought he was being guided by the friendship and the loyalty proffered him. Shakespeare has invested in the early Othello an inclination to share the responsibility for his own actions amongst others; and in making the later Othello so dependent on Iago's honesty Shakespeare is able to capitalise on the careful investment.

Another authority that helps the murder of Desdemona or, at least, does nothing to hinder it, is Othello's Fate. Most of the characters in the play – as indeed in Shakespeare's work as a whole – talk at some time or other about their destinies, their futures. These fictional characters reflect, after all, a culture that gave much credence to the influence on men and women of the stars in their spheres. In *Othello*, however, the references other than Othello's are made on the whole to Fortune – to something less dire, less fell and fatal than Fate itself. So, the Duke gives Brabantio some commonplace advice, when urging him to accept his daughter's marriage: 'What cannot be presern'd [Q *preseru'd*], when Fortune takes: / Patience, her Iniury a mock'ry makes' (F554–5; I.iii.205–6). Here Fortune is a force that might herself be influenced or, at least, offset – as she is also in the Duke's command to Othello a little later in this same scene: 'you must therefore be content to slubber the glosse of your new Fortunes' (F574–5; I.iii.225–6) *Slubber* is to 'soil' or 'sully' (Schmidt 1; and *OED* v.1). Both Brabantio's bad fortune and Othello's good fortune might be modified, then, in the way their results are received. Moreover, *glosse* in both Schmidt and the *OED* (*Gloss* sb.[2], 1) denotes a lustre that is superficial, of the surface; and this suggests the temporary nature of any state of good fortune that one might be enjoying at the moment. If Fate is prescriptive and irreversible by man, the Wheel of Fortune at least supplies some variety and may even position you benignly for a while. Iago, for example, urges Cassio to consult Desdemona – 'And loe the happinesse' (F2261; III.iv.109). The happiness here is not a grand demonstration of Fate. It is (besides an imminent pleasant encounter) the chance happening, the good hap, of conveniently happening across Desdemona just when Cassio needs her. Fate for Iago consists in incidents, often coincidental, that provide a man with opportunities. What he makes of those opportunities is his own choice. Fate for Iago is his own will; while the stars and the fateful properties of the universe are merely 'you euer-burning lights aboue, / You Elements, that clip vs round about' (F2114–15; III.iii.477–8). Here Iago is emulating Othello's vow 'by yond Marble Heauen'; but, though the permanence of the influential stars is suggested in some degree by *euer-burning*, the infinity of the universe is hardly reflected in *clip*. Indeed, *clip* denotes something of the opposite, something finite. It means not only to surround closely, constrain, to grip tightly, but also in a connotative way to curtail (*OED* v.¹, 2 and 3, and v.²). The elements – as much earth and fire, the sea and air as the heavens – are seen as mundane. They possess or express nothing of the virtues that Othello valued in his unhoused, unclipped condition, nor any of the idleness and vastness that Othello registered in the deserts and the antres (F485; I.iii.140). There is nothing here of Othello's idea of a heaven bestowed on earth and distributed through the elements as in a chrysolite. For Iago the elements, along with the stars and with Fate and Fortune themselves, would seem to be restrictive rather than exerting in any way a final authority. Iago's remark to Rodorigo that 'Our Bodies are our Gardens, to the which, our Wills are Gardiners' (F673–4; I.iii.320) is specifically concerned with the influence of reason upon a person's instinctive life; but still the reference implies, too, something of Iago's view of Fortune: as something predetermined by the humorous disposition of a man's body upon which, however, a man such as Iago can set the true virtue, or power, of his own volition.

Desdemona, conversely, is essentially submissive to Fortune, particularly since for her it is represented by her husband. In her first speech she talks carefully of the 'dutie' that her mother owed to her father and that she, now, may profess to the Moor her lord (F533; I.iii.186–9). But *dutie* hardly describes what Desdemona feels for Othello; and soon, less constrainedly, she speaks of 'My downeright violence, and storme of Fortunes' (F599; I.iii.249) that took her to love the Moor and to live with him. In Q's variant, *scorne of Fortunes*, Desdemona seems to be referring either to her scorn for the wealth of Venetian suitors or to her scorn for a prescribed, Venetian future. The latter seems more likely. In F, of course, there is an ambiguity too – but a much richer one, which makes F's version preferable to Q's. On the whole, the usual interpretation of F is to hear the initial *My* as stretching across to define Desdemona as the storming subject. She has acted, uncharacteristically, in attempting to take over her own fortunes; and the reason for this is that the storming has been a joint activity. Desdemona would not have stormed her fortunes without Othello. It was the onset of love, and the difficulties intrinsic to that love, that caused the storming. Othello, it can be said, develops this notion of Desdemona's intitiative – her going out to meet chance – in his image of her as an

untamable bird: she is to be divorced to 'prey at Fortune' – i.e. she is
to survive alone as best she can by taking whatever happens along.
(See F1894; III.iii.267). Meanwhile, it can be said, the initiating
activity of Desdemona, and the identification of her fortunes with
the person of Othello, are confirmed by Desdemona herself in

> to his Honours and his Valiant parts,
> Did I my soule and Fortunes consecrate.
>
> (F603–4; I.iii.253–4)

Explicitly she states – it would seem – that she stormed her fortunes
and took charge of them for the single purpose of making them
sacred by a submission to Othello's idealistic soldiership. She
states, that is, a particularly strong periphrasis of the marriage-
contract. The idea of worship – of an honourable acknowledgement
and respect – through the body becomes a sacring of the soul and
fortunes to the husband; and the periphrasis rings true of Desdemona throughout her utterance. Despite her moments of dissent
and argument – notably when she attempts to help Cassio's fortune
– she is, essentially, obedient to her husband and therefore, by
definition in her case, submissive to her fortunes. Once she has
made them sacred to her husband she can no longer storm them.[8]

This is an extremely attractive reading of *storme of Fortunes*. The
idea of Desdemona assailing her destiny fits with the references to
valour and soldiership in the rest of the speech; and the image is
particularly apt in a young woman who wished, once, that heaven
had made her to be a heroic pilgrim-soldier. There is, however, a
difficulty with the reading which derives from two specific lexical
findings. First, the military metaphor of storming – on which the
reading is crucially based – is dated by *OED* as 1645 for both noun
and verb. By 1645, of course, there must have been many violent
assaults on strongholds during the English Civil War; and, though
OED is not an absolute authority, still its finding is highly plausible. (The relevant definitions are sb., II.5 and v., 6.) Secondly, an
examination of Schmidt discloses that Shakespeare's many uses of
storme were never other than in the literal or figurative senses of
'tempest' or, for example, 'tumult, disturbance'. Of especial interest is *The Tragedie of Troylus and Cressida*, F502–3 (I.iii.46–7):
'valours shew, and valours worth diuide / In stormes of Fortune' –
where the figurative storms clearly belong to Fortune. The *OED*
shows that a verbal sense of *storm* (v., 2) was 'To make stormy', and

illustrates this as follows: '1597 SHAKS. *Lover's Compl.* i "I . . . Ere long espied a fickle maid . . . Storming her world with sorrowes wind and raine" '. But this sense of active grief does not apply to Desdemona's usage. These lexical findings and examples strongly suggest as a whole that Desdemona's *storme of Fortunes* is in fact a figurative version of, for example, a storm of hail; and that this tempestuous fortune is something she has undergone rather than incepted. Moreover, this reading is supported by the submissiveness that Shakespeare elsewhere emphasises in her character. Additionally, of course, the Desdemona who is an object of fortune's storms prefigures the Desdemona who experiences both the actual tempest in her crossing to Cyprus and the emotional storm that leads to her murder. At the same time, this reading allows the possible separation of *My downe-right violence* from *storme of Fortunes*; it does not preclude, therefore, a Desdemona who can embrace with downright, or straightforward, vehemence (Schmidt, *Violence* 1; and *OED, Violence* sb., 5) the tempestuous onset of love.

The *storme of Fortunes* crux supplies a fine example of how a small point of lexicon, when closely examined, can enrich or confirm one's interpretation of a character. For there *is* in Desdemona a strong tendency to respond to Othello as if he were a fortunate or, indeed, heavenly effect. She holds, to an extreme, a belief in the husband as a moral guide; and she deviates from it only in her moral exhortation on Cassio's behalf. (Othello, of course, acts to some extent on this belief in the early part of the murder scene.) This belief illuminates 'Nay, we must thinke men are not Gods' (F2305; III.iv.149), where the fact that *not* negates *Gods* – instead of negating *thinke* – seems to imply that Desdemona *has* been thinking of Othello as virtually divine. Again, here and in later scenes, when Desdemona is struck and bewhored, Desdemona's 'fateful' feeling for her husband survives all the humiliations he inflicts. They are 'my wretched Fortune' (F2835; IV.ii.129), things to be endured. All she *can* do – terribly irony – is supplicate Iago: 'What shall I do to win my Lord againe?' (F2863; IV.ii.150). By the final scene that fortune has turned *fatall*: 'your'e fatall then / When your eyes rowle so' (F3282–3; V.ii.40–1). *Fatall* here not only means 'deadly' but also connotes Desdemona's habitual response to Othello as her Fate.

Cassio's attitude to Fortune is, understandably, less crucial. He talks of 'Fortunes Almes' (F2277; III.iv.123), becoming a beggar who waits on Fortune to bestow something to his advantage. Again,

when he talks of 'high Seas, and howling windes, / The gutter'd-
Rockes, and Congregated Sands' (F830–1; II.i.67–8) – and of their
abeyance of their deadly natures, 'letting go safely by / The Diuine
Desdemona', he is asserting not only the power of the elements but
also another power: that of the goddess–passenger. Desdemona
herself, as a deity, becomes Fate. Over the congregated consonants
of the *gutter'd-Rockes, and Congregated Sands* the goddess passes
wondrously on long vowels. (Arguably, *Desdemona* here is pronounced with the stress on the second syllable.) Cassio's language
is again a conceit; but it seems to express a truth that is felt and not
merely intellectual. Cassio, I think, needs to revere; and his need
leads him to revere both Othello and Desdemona. This need can
coexist with what a critic has recently called 'his libertine foppery',
his chamberer's manners.[9] It is natural that Cassio sees Desdemona
as a divine beauty, by extension a classical goddess of love, Venus
or Aphrodite, enchanting the elements and arriving at her proper
home – the isle of Cyprus described in 1603 by Knolles: 'The people
therein generally liued so at ease and pleasure, that thereof the
island was dedicated to *Venus*, who was there especially wor-
shipped, and thereof called CYPRIA.'[10] It seems natural too that, a
little later in this scene, Cassio looks to Othello to 'Giue renew'd fire
to our extincted Spirits' (Q has also 'And bring all Cypresse comfort'
– F845; II.i.81–2). Besides the sexual pleasantry carried over from the
preceding lines ('blesse this Bay with his tall Ship' and 'Make loues
quicke pants') there is a reinforcement of Cassio's passivity. *Extincted* means 'extinguished' or 'quenched' (*OED, Extinct* v.,1 and
2; and Schmidt, *Extincted*). Speaking on behalf of himself, Montano
and three other gentlemen, Cassio proffers that their valours have
been doused by the contention of the sea and sky. We need, he
claims, Othello's spark to reinvigorate us. This is fine dramatic
language in heralding and enhancing the eventual arrival on the
Cypriot stage of the play's martial hero. But it also places, im-
plausibly, all the fire in Othello and nothing of fire in Montano and
the gentlemen – whom Cassio himself a few lines earlier was greeting as 'the valiant of the warlike Isle' (F801; II.i.43). By itself this
point would probably not signify – particularly since Montano
himself voices hopes for the safe arrival of 'braue Othello' who
'commands / Like a full Soldier' (F790ff.; II.i.34ff.). But in conjunction with the other points made above it does seem to suggest that
Cassio is akin to Desdemona in this: that he too sees his very
fortunes as incorporated in the man to whom he owes love and

service. Both wife and lieutenant, having 'lost' Othello, seek instinctively to find him again – ironically, with the help (as they think) of the very man who has plotted their loss. (Cassio to Iago: 'You aduise me well'; Desdemona to Iago: 'Good Friend, go to him' – F1450 and 2864; II.iii.316 and IV.ii.151.)[11]

Among the major characters of *Othello* who comment on their fortunes, then, Shakespeare has made something of a spectrum. At one end is Iago. He is in *Othello* what Edmund is in *King Lear*. For Edmund, 'Sphericall predominance' is usually in fact the mundane 'surfets of our own behauiour'; there is no such thing as 'heauenly compulsion' or 'an inforc'd obedience of Planatary influence' (*The Tragedie of King Lear*, F447ff.; I.ii.113ff.). Here the influence of the planets is transferred either to overeating (or its equivalent) or to the internal humours: a man 'sicke in fortune' should blame the internal destiny of a humorous predominance. All this has some similarity to Iago's speech beginning 'Vertue? A figge, 'tis in our selues that we are thus, or thus. Our bodies are our Gardens, to the which, our Wills are Gardiners . . . ' (F672ff.; I.iii.319ff.). While Edmund reacts to Gloucester's talk about planetary portents of civil disorders, Iago reacts to Rodorigo's 'I confesse it is my shame to be so fond, but it is not in my vertue to amend it.' (Rodorigo means *vertue* as 'power' or *virtù*. Iago, I think, deliberately misreads 'moral virtue' in order to promulgate his own policy of will and reason.) Both men emphasise self-responsibility. The bastard and the neglected ancient – perhaps they both feel excluded from the natural regulation of the universe and set themselves by reflex against it.

Further along the spectrum, in the middle, are Desdemona and Cassio. They are removed from the 'new men' such as Edmund and Iago whose attitudes are based (those men might proclaim) on science. They might tentatively subscribe to the view of Cassius that 'Men at sometime, are Masters of their Fates' (*The Tragedie of Ivlivs Caesar*, F238; I.ii.139–41), since both have sometime influenced their fortunes to some degree in having Othello enlist them in his service. But only *at sometime*. Excluded from that fortune, they do not turn against it; rather, they wish to be re-enlisted.

At the other end of the spectrum is Othello. If at first he circles on a small Wheel of Fortune turned by Ancient Iago, he very quickly leaves it. He is soon stretched on another wheel, the 'wheele of fire' perceived by Lear (*The Tragedie of King Lear*, F2796; IV.vii.47). Wilson Knight, in his book of that title, saw all of Shakespeare's tragic heroes racked thereon. In the case of Lear, it is a hellish wheel whose constituents are the ingratitude of two daughters and his own maltreatment of a third. In Othello's case it becomes the vast wheeling of the spheres as well as something hellish. For Othello differs from his wife and lieutenant not in the passion of his imagination and activity alone but in the strength and intimacy of his astral awareness. I propose now to examine the authority of the heavenly bodies and Fate in Othello's thinkings.

In his own comments on the tragedy Othello is given the revealing phrase *ill-Starr'd wench*:

> Oh ill-Starr'd wench,
> Pale as thy Smocke: when we shall meete at compt,
> This looke of thine will hurle my Soule from Heauen
> And Fiends will snatch at it.
>
> (F3572–5; V.ii.275–8)

Othello is aware of having committed not merely a crime but a damning offence against heaven. This awareness does not, however, prevent a coexistent belief: that Desdemona is dead as a result of having been born under the influence of an unlucky star. Again, Othello's summary 'vnluckie deeds' (F3651; V.ii.344) may in one sense be true, since the murdering and the maiming have, certainly, been extremely unfortunate. But, *vnluckie* was a much stronger word for Shakespeare than it is for us now. Today a person or thing can be unlucky and not be necessarily in the grip of Fate. One can dismiss bad luck as the merest chance, beyond all 'because'. For Othello here the deeds themselves have been produced by bad fortune: they are themselves *ill-Starr'd*.

This attribution to ill-hap is particularly curious in that it follows so closely on Cassio's talk of the handkerchief: 'he [Iago] dropt it for a speciall purpose, / Which wrought to his desire'. Shakespeare would seem to be deliberately juxtaposing these two attitudes: on the one side, a reminder of Iago's working of the future to his own pattern – specifically of Iago's working his own will even on the magically worked handkerchief; on the other, Othello's insistence on Fate. Indeed, the implication from Othello seems to be that Iago *is* that Fate: Othello catches Cassio's *wrought*, quoted above, and uses it to summarise his own condition of being wrought by Iago and perplexed in the extreme. Iago in his role as a demi-devil or fallen god has been working his special purpose out; and Othello has been snatched up in the workings. In this sense – that is, as a secondary implication – Othello's uncontrollable Fate becomes Iago in *Who can controll his Fate?* – an Iago who survives Othello's sword-thrust and whose reasons are to remain unknown to his victim.

So the general truth of Othello's *ill-Starr'd wench* and *vnluckie deeds* needs to be qualified. Compare these phrases with Lodovico's 'rash, and most vnfortunate man' (F3584; v.ii.286). Lodovico's *rash* (= 'given to act without due consideration or regard for consequences' – after *OED* adj., and adv., 2) asserts Othello's responsibility for the murder of Desdemona inside the framework of a terrible misfortune in a way that Othello's phrases do not. (Shakespeare, I think, uses Lodovico's expression of anger *and* pity in order to modify Aemilia's earlier findings of an ignorant gull and dolt.) Yes, Othello meekly assents to Lodovico's description. And, yes, Desdemona's look will hurl Othello's soul from heaven – this Othello knows. But his own summarising phrases are not inclusive enough. They do not in themselves register the truth that Desdemona has *not* been smothered by an inauspicious star and that one of the dreadful deeds at least, though certainly unlucky, *has* been perpetrated through a responsible Othello's gullibility and rage.[12]

As might be expected, Othello's vision of an authority in Fate has been early inscribed in the utterance. It seems to be expressed in the phrase 'disastrous chances' at F479 (i.iii.134). When Edmund in *King Lear* says, 'We make guilty of our disasters, the Sun, the Moone, and Starres' (*The Tragedie of King Lear*, F449–50 i.ii.113–14), he is using *disasters* in the sense that survives today of 'calamities'. For Othello, however, I suspect that Shakespeare intended another meaning, one associated with *disaster* as 'obnoxious planet' (*OED* sb., 1). The first part of the word declares 'removal, aversion, negation, reversal of action' (*OED*, *Dis-* prefix, 4); the second part derives from Latin *astrum* ('star'). This substantive meaning was not obsolete in the written language, according to the *OED*, until 1635. *Disastrous* therefore could have the precise signification of 'ill-starred, ill-fated; unfortunate, unlucky' (*OED* adj., 1 [–1790]) as well as the more general and neutral meaning. Hence the *chances* become not merely the chances of our modern, slight usage but the prescriptions of Fate. The escapes in the breach, the captivity and the slavery – these were the signs of Fate's working and testing of Othello. Moreover, the 'mouing Accidents' (in the line following

disastrous chances) are not the chance happenings that emerge from
an arbitrary combination of factions; they are disasters, mishaps
(after *OED*, *Accident* 1c). That is, they are again the purposeful
workings of Fate. (Q has *moouing accident* – an abstract noun akin to
Fate or Fortune.)

Compare Brabantio's 'This Accident is not vnlike my dreame'
(F156; I.i.143). For Brabantio his dream does not betray his own
worries about his daughter's future; rather it foretells what Fate has
contrived for him. Dreams were not considered to be expressions of
anxiety or preoccupation as they are today; they were considered to
be portents, omens. In Brabantio's speech, the *Accident* of Desdemona's revolt and departure is not a random occurrence but a
fatal and foretold event.

Given Othello's vision about Fate, his earlier references to Fortune lose the conventionality they might have from sounding thus
early in the play. Three passages can be compared. The first is

> my demerites
> May speake (vnbonnetted) to as proud a Fortune
> As this that I haue reach'd.
>
> (F226–8; I.ii.22–4)

There is ambiguity here. If *reach'd* is 'arrived at' (after *OED* v.[1], 9),
then a pre-existent status is implied upon which Othello, as it were,
happens. However, Othello is denoting a more active participation. He is, after all, speaking in private to his trusted officer and
before Brabantio has brought his charge; he is not yet speaking in
front of the Council and having to refute the charge of seduction by
demonstrating the shared responsibility for the marriage. Rather,
there seems to be something of 'reached for' or 'achieved' present
here. There may indeed be something of another sense, which the
OED states became obsolete in the seventeeth century, of obtaining
by seizure, of laying hold of. (This is noted in *OED* v.[1], 4b and c, but
not in Schmidt.) Again, Othello's pride of Fortune (a fortune that I
take to be the marriage itself and not a matching and fortunate past)
strongly suggests a pride in achievement. One's impression is of an
Othello who, by Marvell's account in 'An Horatian Ode upon
Cromwell's Return from Ireland', might be Cromwellian:

> So restless Cromwell could not cease
> In the inglorious arts of peace,

But through adventurous war
Urged his active star.[13]

In Othello's own words, it is a *Pilgrimage* that he is on: a proving journey in which he has ridden, so to speak, his own destiny.

In the second passage *past* has a similar ambiguity: in 'the Battaile, Sieges, Fortune, / That I haue past' and 'She lou'd me for the dangers I had past' (F475–6 and 512; I.iii.130–1 and 167). It is a transitive verb and refers to the hazards and fortune that Othello has experienced, undergone, endured, put up with, suffered (I paraphrase *OED, Pass* v., B II.32). The implication here is passive. However, the first part of the article in the *OED* reads, 'To go or come through in the way of a course of study or treatment, experience or suffering', and this implies more of activity. The *OED*, in illustrating its article with Othello's first *past*, does not attempt to differentiate these nuances. And both, indeed, richly contribute. If in the end one receives a stronger impression of passivity, it is on the strength of the syntax and lexicon elsewhere in this same speech: Othello speaks of being taken by the insolent foe, of being sold to slavery and of some distressful stroke that his youth suffered. In context, of course, this emphasis is understandable: Othello now *is* defending his marriage to the Council and carefully demonstrating the subjection to Fortune that aroused Desdemona's love.

From these two passages, then, one might deduce that Othello moves between alternative opinions on his Fortune. Always he is strongly aware of it; but sometimes it is something to be endured, at other times something to be influenced. Shakespeare has made his characterisation even more complex than one expected. It would seem – so far – that the alternation depends on the stress – or otherwise – that Othello is under at the time. Relaxed, he has some pride in his own authority. Under attack he can readily indicate external enforcement.

Then, however, one meets the third passage:

I feare,
My Soule hath her content so absolute,
That not another comfort like to this,
Succeedes in vnknowne Fate.

(F968–71; II.i.188–91)

Here is Othello's first sounding of the word *Fate* as opposed to *Fortune(s)*. It implies something more awful and absolute than Mistress Fortune – who is often a strumpet but sometimes may bring good hap and prosperity. It is what the gods have determined for one. It is one's doom. It is odd and perverse that Othello should sound this knell at precisely the moment when he should be most happy – when, in fact, he declares that he *is* most happy. And, of course, Desdemona is aware of this perversity, correcting all this talk of Fate with her own reference to the benign heavens. Why does Shakespeare make Othello, at this juncture, talk like this? Of course, what Othello says expresses a Renaissance commonplace – a fear of the unknown which, in its most common and extreme form, was a fear of death. Montaigne's solution – shared by many, hence the ubiquitous death's-heads – was to reflect continually on one's own inevitable demise.[14] But the context is important. And here Othello seems to shiver in the very warmth of his joy as if with a premonition. As if he discerns in his cup of happiness – not yet Leontes' spider of jealousy, of course – but certainly something alien and fatal stirring somewhere in the depths. As if in all this emphasis on his *Soule* he suddenly sights the skull in which it is seated. This flash of pessimism – at a time when, as Desdemona says, he should be optimistic – declares an awareness of fatal authority which is unusual rather than commonplace. At the same time there is much irony present. Not in Othello, but in Shakespeare's implied comment. Not another comfort like to this reunion on Cyprus *will* succeed: but this discomfortable future will be caused not by unknown Fate but by Othello's own behaviour when he is put into doubt.

This unusual fatal sensitivity recurs in:

> Perdition catch my Soule
> But I do loue thee: and when I loue thee not,
> Chaos is come againe.
>
> (F1691–3; III.iii.91–3)

I have already discussed this with reference to Othello's tendency to deny and dismiss his wife (see above, Chapter 1). Here it is germane to note the extraordinary cosmic scale of Othello's re-action. These lines have a terse but widely-ranging finality that is frequently peculiar in Othello. (Cf. 'Looke heere Iago, / All my fond loue thus do I blow to Heauen. 'Tis gone' – F2094 –5; III.iii.448–50.)

There is a balance between the first sentence (before the colon) and the second; and, again, within the second sentence. And there is, as well, a repetition of the movement discerned in the passage previously discussed: as an extreme content was followed by a premonition of someting fatally less, so now an assertion of love is followed by an ambiguous expression whose syntax negates that love. The whole is made especially memorable and cohesive by assonanace and consonance ([k]) and by the parison of *loue thee*. Othello has experienced for the first time the emptiness caused by a small marital conflict, and he looks ahead to entertain the awful possibility of *not* being in love with his wife. (By analogy with *Succeedes in vnknowne Fate* [= 'will succeed'], *Chaos is come* probably means 'shall have come'. But Othello also has in mind the chaotic state that even this slight conflict induced in him.) There is much ambiguity. It is possible that Othello is being solipsistic, the conventionality of his lover's feeling being redeemed by his passionate extremism and his imaginative preconstruction of the event – *Chaos is come now*. This last is especially characteristic. Or, equally, he may be stating that any cessation of his love for Desdemona will be demonstrating a wider, metaphysical catastrophe, the end of the world – since it is impossible that he, Othello, could ever stop loving his wife of his own volition. In this reading a considerable authority for Othello's loving is attributed to an external natural order of things. In either instance Chaos – with its reference back to *Perdition*, which is not only 'damnation' but also 'loss' and 'destruction' after Latin *perdere* – declares the emptiness that existed (so to speak) before the Creation and out of which creation ensued. The very principle of Love – which is *the* creative principle – would need universally to be destroyed before Othello himself could stop loving. (I take it that this principle is what Wilson Knight denotes when he mentions 'the foundations of human values' in his brief discussion [*The Wheel of Fire*, p. 116] of this passage.)

Against all this, Shakespeare's irony makes us hear – particularly in retrospect – the flat statement produced by Othello's syntax. *When* as a marker of time rather than an *if*-equivalent suggests not only a volatile element in Othello's loving capacity but also what is going actually to happen. When Othello comes to hate Desdemona, then emptiness and disorder do fill him. Destruction does dominate. In the very wording of his grand asseveration he rehearses his tragedy. There is further irony too. It is from this very moment that

Iago begins to work successfully upon the Moor with his effective slanders. It is as if Iago, with his demi-devil's antennae, has registered the negative currents in the Moor's declaration. It is at this moment that Iago begins to suggest that chaos *has* come, a more mundane chaos, involving Michael Cassio and the Moor's wife.

Othello's cosmic sensitivity informs – or misinforms – his early reaction to his supposed cuckoldry:

> Oh Curse of Marriage!
> That we can call these delicate Creatures ours,
> And not their Appetites? [No question mark in Q.]
>
> (F1899–1901; III.iii.272–4)

and

> Yet 'tis the plague to [Q *of*] Great-ones,
> Prerogatiu'd are they lesse then the Base,
> 'Tis destiny vnshunnable, like death:
> Euen then, this forked plague is Fated to vs,
> When we do quicken.
>
> (F1904–8; III.iii.277–81)

These dubious assertions rehearse Othello's later attempts to alchemise his revenge into a divinely inspired execution. He talks not of the curse of his marriage but of marriage in general. He uses the plurals *we, ours, vs, we,* and *these, their, they; Creatures, Appetites, Great-ones;* and the collective plural *the Base.* The reference is to all great men and their wives. Desdemona's infidelity becomes another example of the working of Fate. It is Othello's fate to kill Desdemona 'else shee'l betray more men' (F3245; V.ii.6) – the men probably being the *Great-ones* like Othello. First, marriage is said to be ill-fated by reason of a curse: some malign force has pronounced upon it. The nature of that curse is suggested in the ambiguity of *delicate.* Wives or women in general are 'Endowed with fineness of appreciation'; they are 'Fine: not coarse'; and they are 'Delightful . . . dainty . . . lovely, graceful, elegant'. (See *OED* adj., III, II and I.1d.) They are also, however, 'Given to pleasure or luxury' (I.2b). They have *Appetites* that cannot be satisfied by one man. Othello here is not talking about love. He is talking about the 'determinate desire to satisfy the natural necessities, or fulfil the natural functions, of the body' (*OED, Appetite* sb., 3) and 'inclination' or 'fancy' (sb., 1 and 2). (There may, indeed, be something of a development here from Othello's earlier talk of Desdemona's greedy ear and her devouring up his discourse.) *Creatures* such as Desdemona are not only women as distinct from men but examples of 'an animal; often as distinct from "man" ' (*OED, Creature* 2). That is, they are sexual predators. Thus Othello's phrase *delicate Creatures* – which primarily denotes something akin to Cassio's 'shees a most fresh and delicate creature' (F1132; II.iii.20) – is qualified by a connotation nearer to Iago's 'Ile warrant her, full of Game' (F1131; II.iii.19). And in the sentence as a whole Othello sounds the same paradox that Lear sounds:

> Behold yond simpring Dame, whose face betweene her Forkes presages Snow; that minces Vertue, & do's shake the head to heare of pleasures name. The Fitchew, nor the soyled Horse goes too't with a more riotous appetite: Downe from the waste they are Centaures, though Women all aboue: but to the Girdle do the Gods inherit, beneath is all the Fiends. (*The Tragedie of King Lear*, F2563–9; IV.vi.118–28. Prose in F and the Quarto of *Lear*. For consistency I quote from F. Alexander follows modern practice in setting the passage as verse.)

This degrading of women to a beast-status helps to explain Othello's restriction of cuckoldry-as-plague to great men – which prevails, I think, despite the universality apparently implied in *destiny vnshunnable* and *vs*. When men such as these marry they must, by definition, marry beneath them: not so much in a social sense as in the sense of marrying beneath their species. Their marriages must be of man and female beast. Base men, being less inclined to reason and being therefore more beastly themselves, are less likely to suffer from a moral discrepancy. They are more *Prerogatiu'd* than the great, more 'privileged, exempt from certain evils' (Schmidt, *Prerogatived*), in being less fastidious. Othello's use of *prerogatiu'd* is, of course, savagely ironic.

Moreover, this *forked plague* is fated to the great man at birth. *Quicken* means primarily 'receive life . . . become living' (*OED* II.6). The growth of cuckold's horn is predetermined and inevitable. At the same time *forked* probably has a secondary meaning: it probably refers to the bifurcate anatomy of man, to the fact that horns are a symptom of an illness that starts below the waist. The physical sense of a plague is not the main sense here; but Shakespeare's England had an extreme abhorrence of bubonic plague (endemic in cities such as London), and this helps to strengthen one's awareness of Othello's disgust. In marriage, it would seem, the great man consorts not only with a being inferior to him but also with the certainty of contagion by moral and physical disease. (Given the sexual nature of Othello's topic, there may well be a reference to the plague of the French pox – a subject much alluded to in the near-contemporary *Measure for Measure*.)[15]

Othello's 'vision' of this universal 'truth' is arrived at with astonishing ease. Othello has not had to reach for it. He contrives with alacrity to see himself as involved in a cosmic action: Fate has decreed that he, as a husband, must suffer a universal as much as a personal destiny. He may wish to hide or flee from that Fate, he may try to avoid it as something obnoxious or as he might a blow (*OED, Shun* v., 2, 3 and 2b). His efforts will be in vain. The destiny is *vnshunnable*.

From the swift arrival of this 'vision' derives most of one's sense of Othello's folly – while the tragic resonance in the passage derives from the disparity of the 'vision' from reality as witnessed by the audience. The mistake is a potentially tragic one: despite Othello's restricted thinkings, one can feel pity for a character so emotionally afflicted.

Othello also refers to his Fate in his talk about the handkerchief in III.iv. He uses the clause '(when my Fate would haue me Wiu'd)' (F2211; III.iv.64). He is speaking of what his mother said, but the actual words and syntax of the report would seem to be Othello's in spirit. *Wiu'd* is a participle acting as an adjective to describe *me* more than it is part of an active verb. In either case the syntax supplies a sense of passivity in Othello and omnipotence in Fate. *Would* implies a wish on the part of Othello's Fate (*Would* here being the equivalent of Modern English 'would like to'). On the whole it would seem that Othello was not to have any say in his marriage. To Fate he ascribes the function of a tyrannical father.

In this same speech there is an insistence, too, on another authority: that of the fate wrought into the handkerchief. From this insistence derives the curiously fussed character of Othello's.

> She [the 'Aegyptian'] was a Charmer, and could almost read
> The thoughts of people. She told her, while she kept it,
> 'Twould make her Amiable, and subdue my Father

Intirely to her loue: But if she lost it,
Or made a Guift of it, my Fathers eye
Should hold her loathed [Q *lothely*], and his Spirits should
    hunt
After new Fancies. She dying, gaue it me,
And bid me (when my Fate would haue me Wiu'd)
To giue it her. I did so; and take heede on't,
Make it a Darling, like your precious eye:
To loose't, or giue't away, were such perdition,
As nothing else could match.

                              (F2204–16; III.iv.57–68)

The actions of several people are defined in a flux of short clauses –
some in main clauses, others in subordinates, others in subordinates of subordinates. The effect is one of jostle, of anxiety, as
Othello tries to fetch the fatal pedigree of the handkerchief: *She told
her; while she kept it; if she lost it, / Or, made a Guift of it; dying;
She . . . gaue it me; And bid me; (when my Fate would haue me Wiu'd);
To giue it her; I did so; and take heede on't; To loose't; or giue't away.*

In all this fuss, Shakespeare gives Othello a rare instance of
syntactical imprecision: *her* in *To giue it her* refers to a non-existent
substantive 'wife'. The implication is that the wife exists in the
adjective *Wiu'd*. Additionally, the impression of fuss derives from a
pronominal frequency (approximately 40 per cent). The thirty-
seven uses of *it, she/her, my/me, I, him* and *yours* crowd the utterance. There is much busyness. The pronouns contribute to the high
proportion of syllables having a lesser stress. That is, the passage
lacks the frequent primary accents more commonly heard in
Othello's lines – the primary accents that slow and dignify the
utterance.

There is also a remarkable frequency of verbs here (twenty-one,
including the present participle *dying*). None of the verbs is passive
and few are auxiliaries. Othello uses most of them in proffering
significant action by people in his past. Interestingly, however, this
action is not volitional; with the possible exception of the *Charmer's*
– though even she, like the Sybil, could only foresee the future, not
control it – it is wrought by an external force. And it is the sense of
this force – of Fate – that informs the passage, making it descriptive
of a chain of stern premises and unavoidable conclusions. (The
passage is, in fact, a syllogism: from two premises about the
charmer and Othello's mother a conclusion is arrived at concerning

Desdemona.) The use of a logical structure to express the irresistible power of Fate as decreed in the stitching of the handkerchief – a kind of prescription – makes for a very powerful effect.

What has caused all this pronominal, verbal – and parenthetical – busyness? Mainly, Othello's neurotic need to demonstrate to Desdemona the authority of the handkerchief. The charming Egyptian – the gypsy (*OED, Egyptian* B sb., 2) whom the *OED* would endow with a spell-casting ability (*Charmer* 1) but whom Othello endows the rather with the ability of a seer – impressed that authority on Othello's mother. Othello's mother impressed it on Othello. Now Othello is concerned to impress that authority on Desdemona. It is an authority virtually hallowed by tradition: by sybilline lore, by the testament of a seer, and by the awful potency of a parent's deathbed announcement.

But Othello's insistence is also explained in the content of the handkerchief's authority. Othello's eye – or rather his father's eye extended by analogy to Othello when the handkerchief was handed down – should hold his wife loathed if she loses the handkerchief. The auxiliary *should* was capable of much nuance in Shakespeare's day – perhaps more so than today – and here there is a rich ambiguity. Othello seems to mean that his father's eye *would* hold his mother loathed; but one senses that an even stronger compulsion is being declared. Othello could equally have used 'must' in order to emphasise the inevitability of his mother's perdition.[16] Here is another external agency with which Othello's responsibility might be shared. If he falls to hating Desdemona it is on the basis of her having lost or given away the handkerchief. He himself is held by the power potential in it. He himself is bound to loathe Desdemona, to consign her to *such perdition* as nothing else could match – the kind he earlier postulated for himself in his speech on Chaos. And his *Spirits* too, like his father's, are bound to *hunt / After new Fancies*. These spirits are the actual substances, the natural, animal and vital fluids formerly supposed to permeate the blood and chief organs of the body (*OED, Spirit* sb., IV.16). The elements in Othello must obey the natural magic in the talismanic handkerchief. And, ironically, he does pursue new fancies: the unprecedented ideas and fantasies suggested in him by Iago. (The *new Fancies* that Othello senior would have been forced to hunt would have been amorous inclinations – *OED, Fancy* sb., 8b [– 1712].)

In pressing upon Desdemona the handkerchief's importance, therefore, Othello is not just trying to frighten her and overcome her doubt. He is also asserting the authority that makes his own thinking that much easier, his own doubt less. That the handkerchief had a sibylline manufacture, that even the silkworms were consecrated to the breeding of a special silk, that the dye used was a magically associated mummy – all these confirm the fateful influence of the handkerchief by which, Othello insists, Desdemona and his own love for her are bound.[17]

The pre-murder references to Fate are beautifully concluded as Othello voices his thoughts in 'It is the Cause . . . . ' The sweet subject of 'So sweet, was ne're so fatall' (F3260; V.ii.20) might be Othello's kiss, or the taste of Desdemona's lips, or Desdemona's breath, or Desdemona herself; but, whichever it is, its fatality consists not only in its being destructive or deadly in our modern meaning of *fatall*; it also consists in being 'Allotted or decreed by fate', in being 'inevitable, necessary', and in being 'ominous'. (According to the *OED* the first and third of these older meanings are now obsolete – see *Fatal* adj., 1, 3 and 4.) What Othello means is that there never was a kiss, or a taste, or breath, or a woman in which such sweetness was conjoined with such a terrible ordained doom as adultery and its punishment by execution. In this sense *fatall* is being deployed closely to its Latin association *fatum* – literally 'that which has been spoken' – and to the primary sense in Latin of 'sentence of the gods'. By this association Othello is again possessed of an external authority. He is again defining himself as an instrument authorised and compelled – in this instance by the retributive gods. Desdemona becomes *their* victim, not Othello's alone.

A little earlier, with less subtlety, the same idea is expressed in Othello's 'your vnblest Fate highes' (F3121; V.i.34). Here the Fate is an 'unhappy, cursed, wretched' one (Schmidt, *Unblessed* or *Unblest*). It is also unblessed in being damned: Othello shows nothing of the concern for Desdemona's soul he is to show, at first, in her presence. The concern now is for dispatch. *Highes* seems to be a spelling-variant of Q's *hies*, meaning 'hastens' or 'hastens on' (after *OED, Hie* v., 2 and 2b); while Q's 'your fate hies apace' omits the damnation but adds to the urgency with an adverb denoting speed. In both versions the action of Fate and of Othello are to be the same. Desdemona's deadly and unavoidable doom – her consignment to hell – approaches in the person of the authorised Othello: 'Strumpet I come'.

Othello's view of Fate is summed up in his own words, 'Who can control his Fate?' (F3565; v.ii.268). In context Othello's rhetorical question is a reaction against his resolve, barely formed and quickly eschewed, to escape with the sword of Spain past his guard, Gratiano. His purpose, one conjectures, is flight, or the pursuit of Iago, or a suicide unconfined and unhoused – or indeed a confused amalgam of all three. In the play as a whole, however, the question does not react against a previously held view. Rather, it expresses what Othello's view has been all along. Who can control a Fate that consists in an external, impersonal and uncontrollable force?

And who can control a Fate that is so often and so strongly exerted by the moon? There is no evidence of Othello's being a votarist of astrology; but to assert as Wilson Knight does that in Othello's 'picturesque' language the stars and planets are 'sublimely decorative' – despite the fact that they 'elevate the theme' and 'raise issues infinite and unknowable' – seems to understate Othello's peculiar relationship with, in particular, the moon.[18] The moon in Shakespeare's time was the nearest reminder of the quintessential, of the heavens that thrived in an ideal state above the lunar sphere. Everything beneath that sphere was mutable, earthbound, mundane, imperfect, blemished – sublunary – unless affected by a supernal grace. By virtue of his idealism, the spiritual home of Othello is somewhere in the heavens above the moon where perfection is possible. It follows that the moon has a special place in Othello's imagination – as the closest neighbour in the skies and as the light and taper of his pilgrimage. It follows too, given Othello's stance on external authorities, that he should be imaginatively sensitive to the pull of lunar influence; and that, the murder committed, he should think upon this powerful co-mate of his:

> My wife, my wife: what wife? I haue no wife.
> Oh insupportable! Oh heavy houre!
> Me thinkes, it should be now a huge Eclipse
> Of Sunne, and Moone; and that th'affrighted Globe
> Did [Q *Should*] yawne at Alteration.
>
> (F3360–4; v.ii.100–4)

Here Othello confronts the appalling fact that Desdemona is dead. It is a fact he finds 'intolerable, insufferable' (Schmidt, *Insupportable*, which cites this meaning in two further uses of the word by Shakespeare). But a near-literal meaning may be present here:

Othello cannot support the heavy burden of his wife's death and of his own distress. This near-literal meaning is continued into *Oh heavy houre* – where, however, there is an additional association with Christ's crucifixion, when darkness covered the earth and earthquakes rent it.[19] The hour of Desdemona's death has a universal heaviness that cannot be supported. There is a development of Othello's words 'Chaos is come again' (F1693; III.iii.93) as he states that the planets themselves should lose the support of the power that retains them in their courses. They should become extravagant, in the original sense of wandering from their allotted place in the great scheme of Nature: the result being that the hitherto impossible event of a double eclipse, of both sun *and* moon, should monstrously happen. After such an act as Desdemona's death, the sun and the moon should be darkened – a development of 'Put out the Light' (F3246; V.ii.7). Chaos should be come again; and the earth should gape, open widely (*OED, Yawn* v., 3c) in a vast, concomitant earthquake. *Alteration* thus becomes not *the* alteration of Desdemona's physical death alone but, in Muir's words, 'the change brought about by Desdemona's death' – a cosmic matter.[20] The lack of an article suggests a change into otherness of the whole body of the world: Doomsday.

However, another reading of the passage is possible – a reading in which the sympathetic action belongs not in the eclipse and quake but in the murder. The coming of Chaos may be the cause as well as the result of the appalling event just past. It may be that Othello looks out from the death-chamber and is dismally astonished to find that the authority of external chaos is not apparent. *Me thinkes* (i.e. it seems to me) that a double eclipse ought to be happening – so why is it not happening? why is my Fate not speaking? The murder then becomes as much a response to an unnatural chaos as would be the earthquake.

This reading is secondary; but it needs to be registered in view of what Othello is shortly to say:

> It is the very error of the Moone,
> She comes more neerer Earth then she was wont,
> And makes men mad.
>
> (F3375–7; V.ii.112–15)

This is Othello's response to the news, as he thinks, of Cassio's murder by Iago. Here the sense of eclipse and of heavenly sympathy is gone. Othello declares the direct, causative influence of the moon. I use the word 'influence' in its original and specific meaning of 'power which flows from the stars and affects the fate of man'.[21] The moon has wandered, has made a fatal deviation from its course (*Error: OED* 1; Schmidt 2), has turned men lunatic. To lunar predominance Othello attributes the murderous propensity of men at the moment. It is in the moon's error, and not in any independent aberration of his own, that Othello discerns Desdemona's fate and the supposed fate of Cassio. That Desdemona's light should have been put out is a natural response to the double extinction of both the sun's light and the moon's.

There is much certainty in Othello's statement of the moon's error. In the dramatic context this statement is not merely an evasive reply to Aemilia: it is also Othello's confirmation to himself of an old belief. *Very* may be functioning in either of two ways. It may be adverbial: it is 'solely' an error of the moon that makes men mad – something explicable in man's science. Or it may be intensive: it is 'indeed' the error of the men. (I read 'solely' after one of Schmidt's definitions of *Very* as 'only'. 'Indeed' is after *OED* I.3 and II.8.) *Very* derives from Latin *verus* ('true') and supplies here a hint of amazing paradox. This is a truthful error: it naturally arranges for the appalling death of an adulteress.

Othello's certainty is also expressed in the terse vowel sounds in *very error*; in the effect of [r] and [m], which helps to bind three lines already assured in their rhythm; and in the unequivocal syntax – three main clauses whose single subordinate, 'then she was wont', supports rather than suborns the certainty.

Moreover, I would suggest, a certain intimacy is implied: between hitherto nomadic Othello and the erstwhile and female companion of his nights. Othello knows the ways of this companion more than he does the ways of his wife. He is more at ease with them. The heavenly body is more familiar to him than that of his wife – which has been, in his fantasy, familiar elsewhere. In this implication even *She*, a conventional reference to the moon as female, is reclaimed from poetic convention and made fresh. This intimacy was suggested too in the 'brothel' scene when Othello asserted that 'the Moone winks' (F2773; IV.ii.78). He asserted, that is, that the moon closes its eyes at Desdemona's strumpetry (*OED*, *Wink* v., 4). This movement of disgust is included with heaven's holding of its nose and with the wind's hiding in shame. Though clouds may have obscured the moon as Othello looks out from the 'brothel', he is suggesting not merely the state of the night but also an emotional condition that he himself has imagined upon the natural and supernatural elements. So, the very calmness of the night is suffused with a sense of shame. The point is, these elements are intensely perceived. They are given human features. They are reacting as scandalised friends and neighbours. If Othello likes an unhoused condition, it is partly because he has such allies in the natural and supernatural village just above the earth. In the moon's instance, the closing of its eyes would seem to be an idea from which develops its share in the looked-for double eclipse in the final scene.

A final point on these moon passages. In the first passage quoted the syntax is precise. Othello indulges his emotions in some degree, but he retains the clausal discipline of his sentence:

> Me thinkes, it should be now a huge Eclipse
> Of Sunne, and Moone; and that th'affrighted Globe
> Did [Q *Should*] yawne at Alteration.

It has the simple strength of a main clause followed by two *that*-clauses: these act as complement to the 'It seems to me' sense of the main clause. This precision highlights the oddity of F's *Did*. The modern editions I have consulted eschew this for Q's *Should*; and, since the page in F (vv4^V; or p.336 of the tragedies) was set by the revisionary 'Compositor B', it is probable that *Did* is not authorial but an example of creative printing. If, however, it *is* Shakespeare's recension, then it is probably signalling in its small way something important to Shakespeare's invention of his hero. The normative or putative sense of *Me thinkes* and *should* is left behind. Othello advances into the indicative – an indicative made strong by the intensive *Did*.[22] This would not be the only place in the text where, by a small matter of verbal mood and auxiliaries, Shakespeare demonstrates in Othello an ability to transform something that is optative or supposed into an established fact. Indeed, such a process constitutes much of Othello's tragic error. Certainly, the use of *Did* conveys an attractive syntactical oddness, a semantic *Alteration* from the expected.

The whole of this 'moon' scheme, and much of Othello's relationship with Fate and the stars, is summarised in the assertion, 'Nature would not inuest her selfe in such shadowing passion, without some Instruction. It is not words that shakes me thus

. . . . ' (F2416–18; IV.i.39–40). The context of this is Othello's fit, but the opinion expressed derives generally from his fatalism. I use 'fatalism' with care, referring not to any immobile submissiveness but to Othello's ability in perceiving as he thinks the workings of Fate; to his active participation in its design; to his ability in perceiving it as an authority for action. In the passage *inuest* means 'besiege' (*OED, Invest* v., 7) – more violent than Schmidt's reading of 'array' or 'dress'; while *Instruction* is authoritative direction as to action (after the sense described in verbal *Instruct* – *OED* I.3). Othello sees *Nature* as working through him – *Nature* being the great creative regulator of all things. He declares that such an eclipsing of his senses and reason does not result from Iago's words alone but has an external authority – which is truth. He declares that his own disorder expresses an actual moral disorder that must be existent without. (This vividly-put conventional idea is a 'pathetic fallacy' in reverse.) The self that is being besieged and instructed is not Othello as such but Nature *her selfe* as represented in Othello. He is being wrought by Nature. He is at the same time the theatre in which nature works.

Finally, another small point of syntax leads one to this chapter's conclusion. F's advance of *Should* into *Did* – discussed above – has some rehearsal in this passage, where *would not* leads to *is not*. The surmise of the first sentence does not impede Othello from making an apparently logical advance to a statement of fact in the second. The passage appears only in F and, again, may be Shakespeare's recension. If so, it supplies in microcosm another example of Othello's broader thinkings: thinkings that compel him with alacrity from supposition to an established fatal authority for murder.

4

'I must be found' (i)

A recent paper has demonstrated that Othello's final extended speech repeats the rhetorical structure of his two speeches to the Council in Act I. All these speeches share rhetorical features such as captatio, excusatio, anaphoric elements, ornatus, peroration and action-pointers (words indicating specific movements on stage). So 'Othello's last speech is no histrionic exhibition: it is the recovery of his real self through the return to the rhetoric that he has made his own.' And between these early and late speeches the rhetoric is much reduced as Othello loses himself. In the epilepsy-scene, indeed, Othello's language disintegrates into exclamations and oaths; while the rhetoric of 'It is the Cause . . . ' is merely 'a sequence of short sentences held together by disjunctives . . . and punctuated by action pointers'.[1]

It needs to be emphasised, however, that in several important instances Othello's rhetoric does not reduce. To some extent the full, proud nature of the speeches to the Council and of the final speech derives from their function in a public occasion. Othello is orating, acting as his own advocate in unofficial courts of law. He uses, therefore, a fuller rhetorical range than in the main body of the play – where, for example, he can eschew captatio and excusatio in the absence of any need to capture attention or win sympathy and a good hearing. What is truly remarkable throughout the play is not so much the reduction of the rhetoric as its proportionate maintenance. Even in a domestic setting it is nearly always present. And nearly always it is more than adequate in expressing Othello's thinkings. He demonstrates, in fact, a superb command of language – an extraordinary syntactical assurance – almost continuously throughout the play.

This syntactical assurance is, of course, astonishing in a character who for much of the play is ostensibly in a state of excruciating doubt. How to explain this discrepancy? The answer, I think, exists in the fact that much of the syntactical assurance is linked with the major characteristic of Othello's utterance: his habit of self-publication.

Some such quality has been discerned by other critics in Othello; but usually they discern it in his final speech and isolate that for their discussion. Inside the 'conventional *genre*' and 'common convention' that Holloway and Bradbrook define in a hero's final report upon himself there is, in Othello's 'Soft you; a word or two . . . ', something more than a final advocacy. The speech is so *full* of Othello, so concerned with the publication of himself for Venice and posterity, that it exceeds the dramatic function of a hero's just putting of his case. The final speech needs to be considered – and has often been considered – otherwise than in terms of *genre*. And equally it needs to be considered not as an isolated instance of self-justification or self-dramatisation but as the final repetition in a pattern of self-publication that Shakespeare has carefully inscribed into the utterance almost from the first line.[2]

Holloway and Bradbrook were reacting to some extent against Eliot's account of Othello as a self-dramatiser in his final speech. In fact, Eliot too was stressing a convention: 'the attitude of self-dramatization assumed by some of Shakespeare's heroes at moments of tragic intensity', which is 'not peculiar to Shakespeare' but conspicuous in, for example, Chapman and Marston as well. Eliot's main point is that Shakespeare makes it 'more integral with the human nature of his characters'. Eliot's next point, of '*bovarysme*', of Othello's 'will to see things as they are not', is less apt: Madame Bovary is a fantasist who tries to turn her banal self and life into the simulacrum of a romantic novel; while Othello's self and life have *been* those of a romance. But in his point about integrity Eliot seems to be hinting at the consistency in Shakespeare's invention of Othello that I shall be examining in this chapter. Specifically I shall be examining whether Othello's consistent self-publication contributes in any way to the murder of Desdemona.[3]

My term 'self-publication' differs from 'self-dramatisation' and from 'histrionics' – another popular description of Othello's speech[4] – in eschewing any idea of insincerity, of falsity; and also in emphasising Othello's extraordinary need to impress himself upon his listener whether in a public or in a private dramatic situation. If Othello does dramatise himself, it is largely inside the plot set for him by Fate, the moon, Iago, Brabantio and Desdemona – as discussed in Chapter 3 – and in his references to himself in the third person towards the end of the play. As one who publishes himself –

I use the word 'publish' in the sense of making generally, sometimes formally, known, as in Dekker's advice to his gull to publish
his suit of clothes in St Paul's aisle as he might a suit in law[5] –
Othello is a singular example among the host of Shakespeare's
characters in the sheer degree of his publishing-activity. Most of
the heroes and heroines make themselves known to us: it is part of
their dramatic task to do so. But none more than Othello imposes
upon his or her fellow *dramatis personae*.

In I.ii, for example, Shakespeare gives Othello a number of words
which singly would be insignificant but together amount to a
veritable lexicon of self-publication:

> My Seruices, which I haue done the Signorie
> Shall out-tongue his Complaints. 'Tis yet to know,
> Which when I know, that boasting is an Honour,
> I shall promulgate [Q *provulgate*]. I fetch my life and being,
> From Men of Royall Seige [Q *height*]. And my demerites
> May speake (vnbonnetted) to as proud a Fortune
> As this that I haue reach'd. For know Iago,
> But that I loue the gentle Desdemona,
> I would not my vnhoused free condition
> Put into Circumscription, and Confine,
> For the Seas worth.
>
> (F222–32; I.ii.18–28)

Out-tongue is a variation on the idea of the 'voice potentiall / As
double as the Dukes' that Iago has attributed a few lines earlier to
Brabantio. The Duke has in reserve at Council meetings the power
of a double or casting vote; Brabantio has a similar latent power,
possibly because of being 'much belou'd'; he can therefore, it
seems, be virtually as powerful as the Duke when he so elects.
(Most editors read *potentiall* as 'powerful' in accordance with *OED*,
Potential A adj., 1, and Schimdt. But the idea of 'latent' was already
available from Middle English [*OED* adj., 2] and enriches the meaning here.) Othello's variation is stronger in that the meaning is
packed inside a verb – a syntax of action – and because the image of
a tongue is thus reclaimed from standard synecdoche. It becomes
the more vivid. The verb too is stronger than, for example, the verb
in 'What this Gentleman will out-talke vs all' (*The Taming of the
Shrew*, F820; I.ii.244). The abstract *Seruices* shall be all but tangible
in speaking for themselves.

Out-tongue (defined in *OED* as 'exceed in power of tongue') seems not to be what Brook says it could be, an example of 'verbs resulting from the functional conversion of nouns,' such conversion being 'often found only in the compound, not in the simple word', since *tongue* was available to Shakespeare as 'utter . . . say' (*OED* v., 3). But it certainly exemplifies Shakespeare's frequent invention of new verbs by prefixing *out-* to old ones. The verb has the additional strength of novelty. In its auxiliary it also has the strength of Othello's certainty: *shall* here indicates not only futurity but more assurance than, say, 'will' or 'might'. The speaking-power of Othello's public service will defeat Brabantio's complaints by publishing Othello's worth.[6]

A little further into the passage, the verbs in *'Tis yet to know* and *For know Iago* denote more than a passive reception of information. The first, meaning 'to be known', denotes the divulging of Othello's royal ancestry, a fact that might have been of crucial importance in its effect on Othello's judges. The second use, either in the imperative mood or in the sense of 'you must or need to know', sounds in the main clause on which there depend the important subordinates concerning *Circumscription, and Confine* discussed in Chapter 2. Othello publishes, or betrays, to Iago and to us his disinclination to be bound by Venetian laws and customs. Iago, of course, responds by 'knowing' and by putting his knowledge to use. It is a knowledge that he summarises to Rodorigo in his phrase *erring Barbarian* (F707; I.ii.354). A man whose life has been voluntarily outside the pale – and who for Brabantio as a son-in-law is quite beyond the pale – of civilised society, has strayed (*OED, Err* v., 1) into a moral and emotional territory new to him. Iago's knowledge will assist him in putting his *wits* (derived from Old English *witan* 'to know') to work upon the bias of this outsider.

Honigmann has written that Othello's talk of his royal derivation and of his deserving Desdemona is 'something very like boasting, thinly disguised as a modest man's unwillingness to boast'.[7] Conversely, one should note that Othello has *not* previously disclosed his royal ancestry; and that now he does mention it he mentions it but briefly and is justified by the dramatic context. He is not boasting: he is preparing his defence against Brabantio's imminent attack on his marriage. We should be impressed by a royal reticence, not a lack of it: by a past and present reliance on the true nobility of personal acheivement rather than on the advantage of birth.

(Interestingly, *boast* until about the mid-1700s could mean 'threaten' [*OED* v., 1]. This is not, of course, the meaning here. But in Shakespeare's soldiery a boasting that includes both vaunts and threats is particularly common; and if a comparison is made with, for example the vaunts and threats of both Henry (in Act I) and of the French lords (III.vii) in *Henry V*, then Othello comes across as a most atypical soldier – though, of course, the dramatic situations *are* rather different. Again, in the primary sense of 'boast', one does not agree with Iago's interpretation of the speech to the Council that Othello was 'bragging, and telling her fantastical lies' and 'prating' when he told his history to Desdemona. [Presumably, Rodorigo has reported 'Her Father lou'd me . . . ' to Iago. Iago's opinion is expressed to Rodorigo at F1006–7; II.i.219–20.] Rather, Othello was retailing marvellous truths. Iago's terms are in themselves slanders, and tell us more about Iago's cynicism and envy than about Othello.)

But to refute the critical charge of 'boasting' is not to disclaim in Othello the ability to promulgate. *Boasting* and 'promulgation' are different from each other. As Othello implies, *boasting* is dishonourable promulgation: something indecorous. In this sense Othello means that he will *not* 'make known by public declaration' (*OED, Promulgate*) his royal ancestry. But he does privately – the qualification is important – confide it to Iago. And the word *promulgate*, a strong example of the self-publishing lexicon, does much to demonstrate the intimating nature of this speech. It denotes a formality and ceremony of announcement; and formality and ceremony are marked even in this private intimation. These qualities, I think, are more important in the word than its property of public declaration; and Othello *is* capable of making even the most informal of occasions ceremonious. Ross considers that *promulgate* has 'inappropriate connotations of publication by authority';[8] but, then, in many of his announcements Othello *is* moved – as he thinks – by the authority of Fate (see above, Chapter 3). In Q's *provulgate*, alternatively, there is a suggestion of the vulgar ear, the ear of the populace, which Othello – one surmises – would be akin to Coriolanus in disliking. In Q, however, there is a fine dramatic irony: Othello does reveal himself to the vulgar Iago.

A short final point about *promulgate* as a verb of self-publication derives from the meaning of its Latin root: 'to expose to public view' (*OED*). It may be that Shakespeare is already rehearsing one of Othello's major preoccupations – a concern for the true fixing of his figure in the world – as Othello quietly promulgates his virtue to Iago and to us.

From the stately, Latinate quality of *promulgate* or *provulgate* Shakespeare passes us to the terseness of the 'native' *fetch* and *speake* (both derived from Old English). Neither of these verbs takes a tonic, but both contribute to the sounding strength of their sentences. *Fetch* is primarily 'derive' (*OED* v., I.6) with some connotation of a source 'more or less remote' and the deriving of a pedigree (I.6c). I also read, however, a more physical sub-meaning: that of 'go and bring' or 'call for', as defined in other contexts by Schmidt. Othello as it were would summon his ancestry to attest or publish his worth.

Speake . . . to is more ambiguous. In the sense of 'talk to' (*OED*, *Speak* B II.13a) Othello is claiming that his *demerites* may converse with the good fortune of his marriage – that is, he deserves the marriage. This seems to be the main meaning. In the sense of 'attest, bear testimony to' (B II.13f) Othello is claiming that already, in his ancestry and royal rank, he has received a fortune as proud as that of his marriage. In the first reading *demerites* means 'deserts' of a laudable kind, 'merits' (*OED*, *Demerit* sb., 1, obsolete in the written language, according to the *OED*, by 1731. The sense of 'ill-deserts' [sb., 2] does not seem to apply here). In the second it is returned more closely to the Latin or Greek origins of *merit* meaning 'share, part': Othello has already shared in a fortune commensurate with marriage to a magnifico's daughter. In the first reading the worth of Othello – and of Desdemona – is emphasised. In the second Venice is disparaged. In both a feature characteristic of Othello is expressed.

The demerits-speech repeats the out-tonguing ability of the services: evident virtues will witness for Othello and show him forth. The adjective (*vnbonnetted*) functions strongly in this showing-forth. (I say 'adjective': it has adverbial connotations too.) It has been much glossed. Does the verb *to bonnet* mean to don one's bonnet? or does it mean to doff it? Both *OED* and Schmidt define a Shakespearean, intransitive sense that equates with 'off-cap'. Most editors follow this, and take *vnbonnetted* therefore as ' "*without taking the bonnet off*", i.e. "on equal terms" '(Ridley, p. 16n). Hart's note (p. 21) reads, 'the word may well mean what it should mean (i.e. with hat on), and therefore, I take it, it *must* mean that'. Hart also cites Cotgrave's definition in 1611 of French *bonneter* as 'put off his cap unto'. Walker (p. 147n) says, 'the sense required is plainly "as an equal" '; and she cites the following passage from *The Tragedy of Coriolanus*, where, she says, *Bonnetted* is 'took their caps off': 'those, who hauing been supple and courteous to the People, Bonnetted, without any further deed, to haue them at all into their estimation, and report' (F1228–31; II.ii.24–6). But, as Ridley observes, *Bonnetted* here could equally mean 'put their caps back on'. Indeed, I think it *does* mean that: the people have been flattered, there is no further need of courtesy, the caps can be put back on.

The traditional view of *vnbonnetted* is probably correct, however. Othello claims for his merits the right to remain covered before the Duke and Council. He is referring to a carefully defined and – one imagines – a jealously guarded prerogative that allowed, for example, the Duke of Alva in the mid-sixteenth century to remain covered in the presence of the Spanish monarch.[9] At the same time it is possible to read – particularly in F's bracket – a certain humour and a hint of courteous modesty. The demerits will insistently publish Othello's worth – but they will do so decorously, their bonnet off. Such a relaxed self-assertion keeps with the respectful yet at times subtly scornful Othello – the complex Othello – of Act I. It is nicely rendered by Kenneth Muir in the Penguin note as 'without my hat on, with all due modesty',[10] Additionally, of course, the theme of Othello's self-publication is strongly expressed in this reading: Othello's demerits do not need any covering or concealment; they can be published forth, bareheaded, for the better viewing of their self-evident value.

I come now to the sentence used for this chapter's heading. It sounds in

Not I: I must be found.
My Parts, my Title, and my perfect Soule
Shall manifest me rightly.

(F236–8; I.ii.30–2)

A few lines after Othello's *demerites* speech the dramatic situation has changed. Lights announce the threat of what seems to be Brabantio's search-party. The auxiliary in *may speake* – which denoted a future ability at need and, possibly, when permitted –

changes to an auxiliary that denotes assurance about the immediate future in *Shall manifest*; while *must be found* confirms the arrived necessity of Othello's self-publication. Othello's own search for certainty will cause him to encave himself in order to spy on and overhear Cassio in IV.i; here, however, Iago's advice of 'You were best go in' is dismissed with full confidence. Othello will not retire into a housed condition either in a literal or in a figurative sense: he will not go indoors, and he will not hide his virtue within the Venetian walls of the Sagittary. He must be found not only in the sense of being discovered by the search-party but also in the sense of having his right and deserving revealed and established – and not just to Brabantio. In a general way Othello seems to be using *find* in the meanings of 'To . . . come to a knowledge of . . . by experience or trial'; '*Law*. To determine, and declare (an issue) to be so and so'; and 'deliver, "bring in" (a verdict)'. These three definitions are in *OED* v.¹, I.6, II.17. and 17d. The roots and the meanings of the verbs *to find* and *to found* are different (the verbs derive respectively from Old English and from French and Latin); but Othello's sense is well on the way to expressing a need that he himself should be seen to be well-founded and his actions valid. Despite the passive mood, *must be found* does in fact denote a positive act. The passive marked by *he* is less than the active assertion of *must* (which here denotes both necessity *and* intent). In staying upon the street Othello becomes as actively engaged in the discovery of Othello as is Brabantio. Additionally, the phrase *perfect Soule* lifts Othello's case from a merely pragmatic to an absolute justification. *Soule* here is more than Walker's 'clear conscience' and more even than Ross's 'absolutely unblemished conscience'.[11] Othello is not merely conscious of having done no wrong: he is conscious of having done right. By a marriage based on an ideal love Othello's soul has been throughly fulfilled, completed. This meaning derives from the Latin *perficere* ('to accomplish, complete thoroughly'). In becoming thus fulfilled Othello's soul is in a 'state of complete excellence . . . faultless' and of 'supreme moral excellence . . . immaculate' (*OED*, *Perfect* adj., B 4 and 4b). There is an absolute quality here which fails to be registered in the critical view that Othello's confidence subsists in his being 'fully prepared' (Ridley, p. 17n). Rather, the confidence is metaphysical. Othello fetches the immaculacy of his case from a quintessential virtue. The fact that *Soule* has an adjective helps to distinguish it stylistically from the unmodified *Parts* and *Title* and so helps to emphasise its metaphysical declaration. *Parts* referring back to *demerites*, are Othello's 'Abilities, capacities, talents' (*OED* sb., II.12) that make up his deserving quality – in rather more worldly terms. *Title* could be the nomenclature of Othello's royal rank but, in view of his lesser insistence on his ancestry, is more probably 'ground of right' and 'Legal right to the possession of property' (*OED* sb., 6 and 7): Othello is asserting the proper nature and legality of his marriage – just as, later, he is to assert the proper nature and legality of his *satisfaction* (F614; I.iii.264).

All these are to combine in manifesting Othello *rightly*: not only 'correctly . . . not erroneously' (Schmidt 2) but also in his legal and proper right – and, moreover, in his being in the right from a universal and ideal point of view. *Manifest*, another verb of publication, means 'make evident to the eye or understanding' (*OED* v., 1). The *OED* suggests that the adjective 'manifest' derives from Latin *manus* ('hand') and *festus* ('struck'), the primary sense being 'palpable'; and this etymology attractively underlines Othello's sense of the almost tangible obviousness of his 'case': the combination of parts, title and soul is to publish him in great strength. Not until the mid-seventeenth century (according to the *OED*) was the noun 'manifesto' used in writing in the sense of the publicising of past actions and of actions to come; but Othello *is* virtually effecting such an announcement. With one curious and significant difference, however. Othello is not announcing his actions and qualities; it is they that are to announce him. Not only is the manifesting to be extraordinarily strong; it is also to have an extraordinary reversal by which Othello becomes the object of the verb. Once again Othello's self-publication is insisted on. He will not be arguing a case, or even asserting his rights and qualities, so much as asserting the sublime self that is the conjunction of those rights and qualities with his soul.

The dramatic function of this self-publication is less to inform Iago – though Iago does make use of Othello's unease about circumscription and confine – than to inform the audience of Othello's character and background as Othello sees them. This information is conveyed in a scene where the image of the thick-lipped lecher full of verbal fustian projected by Iago and Rodorigo in the first scene is dramatically displaced by the real Othello – the Othello whose simple 'declarative sentences' and 'conditional sentences in asseverative form' impress upon us his dignity and assurance.[12]

Something of this assurance is effected by Shakespeare's inscription of the repeated *know*: *'Tis yet to know; which when I know; For know Iago;* and, later in the scene, 'Were it my Cue to fight, I should haue knowne it / Without a Prompter' (F302–3; I.ii.83–4). Not all of these are synonyms or near-synonyms for 'publish'. They do not all participate in publishing Othello. But overall they do participate in the 'know/think' scheme that Jorgensen has demonstrated and which culminates early in the 'temptation' scene.[13] Here I wish to stress the fact that this simple repetition helps to suggest the organisation of Othello's thought. In a very subtle way Othello is playing upon a single word; that he can do so – with such skill that the play is hardly discernible – suggests a certain relaxation in him. Within the increasing emergency of the scene Othello yet has time to deploy a rhetoric made all the more effective by its being virtually subliminal.

A similar syntactical organisation gives a similar impression of assurance in Othello's speeches to the Council in Act I (F415ff.; I.iii.76ff.). Othello details the extent of his *offending* in order to refute the charge of witchcraft; but the expansiveness of his definition seems easily to fulfil his self-publishing bent as well. Easily because of the easy use of *true*:

> That I haue tane away this old man's Daughter,
> It is most true: true I haue married her;
> The verie head, and front of my offending,
> Hath this extent; no more.
>
> (F417–20; I.iii.78–81)

From its final position in the first sentence, *true* transfers to an initial position in the second. This large syntactical reversal is deftly done, and contributes to the rhythmic dignity: a wide and stately caesura has been created within the repetition *true: true*. (Some deft elision too [of a second *it is most*] would seem to have occurred.)

The repetitions of two other words help to structure Othello's utterance later in this same speech. The first word is *little*:

> Rude am I, in my speech,
> And little bles'd with the soft phrase of Peace;
>
> . . .
>
> And little of this great world can I speake,
> More than pertains to Feats of Broiles, and Battaile,
> And therefore little shall I grace my cause,

In speaking for my selfe.

(F420ff.; I.iii.78ff.)

In a strict grammar the first *little* belongs in the complement phrase 'Rude in my speech and little blessed'. But the second line becomes virtually a sentence in itself: 'And little bles'd (am I) with the soft phrase of Peace'. Thus all three examples of *little* sound early in their sentences and all take tonics. All, too, are put into their early position by a syntactical reversal – of, respectively, '(I am) little bles'd'; 'I can speake little of'; and 'I shall little grace'. Furthermore, each *little* is introduced by *and*. Again, the sounds made by *l* in *little* are repeated in each context: in respectively, *bles'd, world . . . Broiles . . . Battaile* and *shall . . . selfe*. So the syntactical repetition is extended and then heightened by consonance. Meanwhile, subtlety is supplied in the varying function of *little*: it is first a minimiser qualifying *bles'd*, then adverbial in qualifying *speake* and *grace*.

All this is hardly contributing to a rudeness of speech. Like the prologue of Chaucer's Franklin (who apologised for his 'rude speche', lack of 'rethoryk', and 'bare and pleyn' style), Othello's 'prologue' prepares us for a skilled narration.[14] The speech is of an utmost refinement and cultivation. Othello's self-depreciation – his be*littling* of himself – is self-publication in disguise. In rhetorical terms, it exemplifies Othello's use of a skilful modesty to produce pathos, a favourable reaction by the audience to the orator's words. At the same time, in referring as it were indirectly to his military prowess Othello is publishing his ethos, the virtue in him that Venice so urgently needs.

There is also, I think, some opposition between the mock-belittlement of *little* and the frequency of intensifying words in the speech as a whole. These words are *most* and *very* in 'Most Potent, Graue, and Reuerend Signiors, / My very Noble, and approu'd good Masters'; *most* again in 'It is most true'; *verie* again in 'verie head, and front'; *deerest* in 'deerest action'; *great* in 'this great world'. I have already, in Chapter 2, suggested a certain elusive humour in Othello's appellation of the senators: to some extent this humour is also present in Othello's alternations between overstatement and understatement. The point is, it is all skilfully done. It greatly suggests Othello's certainty in his self-publication and in his cause.

The other repeated word in this speech is *what*:

> Yet, (by your gratious patience)
> I will a round vn-varnish'd Tale deliuer,
> Of my whole course of Loue.
> What Drugges, what Charmes,
> What Coniuration, and what mighty Magicke,
> (For such proceeding I am charg'd withall)
> I won his Daughter.
>
> (F428–34; I.iii.89–94)

The anaphora packed inside the fourth and fifth lines creates an effect as of incantation. Othello mocks the absurdity of Brabantio's charge by casting on the Council and on us the 'spell' of his own skilled use of language. His magic was not black; it consisted in the way he told his history. Moreover, the four nouns defined by *what* are not all synonymous. *Drugges* seem to imply potions administered for the purpose of 'stupefying or poisoning' (as in *OED, Drug* v² 2). *Charmes* seem to imply magical 'chanting or recitation' (*OED, Charm* sb.¹ 1). *Coniuration* is 'The effecting something supernatural by the invocation of a sacred name or by the use of some spell' (*OED, Conjuration* II.3). Though all these are defined and summarised by *Magicke* as 'Sorcery, witchcraft' (*OED, Magic* sb., 1), they all have meanings in context specifically their own. Just as Othello defined the extent of his offence-by-marriage, so now he lists the available forms of magic he has *not* used. In so doing he informs his utterance with the very rhythm of incantation that Brabantio – presumably – believes he must have sounded in the concoction of his spells. This rhythm is, of course, among Othello's natural gifts as a narrator. And this combination – of intellectual classification with a stylistic informing – discloses the extraordinary confidence with which Othello here presents himself.[15]

These lines also have another of Othello's publishing-verbs – *deliuer*. It means 'give forth in words' and 'make known' (*OED, Deliver* v., IV.10 and 11). The tale to be delivered (Othello claims) will be 'straightforward' (*OED, Round* adj., III.12). and it will be 'Not embellished or rendered specious; plain, direct' (*OED, Unvarnished* ppl. adj., 1). He is correct. There will be no digression in the tale, only simplicity and concision. At the same time, some sense of the tale's sublime nature is anticipated in the phrase *whole course of Loue. Course* seems to be 'manner' or 'way' (after Schmidt sb., 3; and *OED* sb., 14 [1583–]) as much as 'progress' or 'proceeding'. One thinks of the infinitive action of the sun *to course*, as witnessed by the Sybil in Othello's words at F2219–20 (III.iv.70–1). Othello describes his wooing, his ideal love, as belonging in the region of the spheres. Or at least he seems to imply this. *Whole* seems not only to refer to everyting said and done; it has an absolute quality. The wholeness of Othello's love has assisted the perfecting of his soul.

Before considering the tale itself, one needs to note that Shakespeare maintains the lexicon of publication in the rest of the 'prologue'. The relevant words are *speake of, finde, confesse, present* and *report* in

> I do beseech you,
> Send for the Lady to the Sagitary,
> And let her speake of me before her Father;
> If you do finde me foule, in her report,
> The Trust, the Office, I do hold of you,
> Not onely take away, but let your Sentence
> Euen fall vpon my life
>
> (F457–63; I.iii.114–20)

and

> And tell [Q *till*] she come, as truely as to heauen,
> I do confesse the vices of my blood,
> So iustly to your Graue eares, Ile present
> How I did thriue in this faire Ladies loue,
> And she in mine.
>
> (F467–71; I.iii.122–6)

Interestingly, Othello does not say 'speake *for* me', in the sense of 'make . . . a plea . . . on behalf of' (*OED, Speak* B 10a). *Speake of* is 'discourse upon' (B 11a) in a more general way. In speaking of Othello – Othello implies – Desdemona will merely have to tell the truth about him for his virtue to be evident. The expression rehearses Othello's 'Speake of me, as I am' in his final extensive speech (F3652; v.ii.345), where he asks that Lodovico should report him justly – with no extenuating defence and no prosecuting malice.

In *finde* the legal sense of bringing in a verdict is present; and a particular legal sense of *foule* is probably denoted – that of 'Guilty of a charge or accusation; criminally implicated' (*OED, Foul* adj.,

II.7b). But Brabantio's 'Oh thou foule Theefe' and the Duke's'this foule proceeding' (F279 and 402; I.ii.62 and I.iii.65) bring Othello's *foule* also into a scheme in which the word means 'Morally or spiritually polluted' (*OED* adj., II.7). *Finde* reminds one of Othello's resolve and need that he *must be found*, that he must be established and defined as unblemished, morally right in his actions and in himself.

The other three words are near-synonyms of, for example, *manifest* and *speake of* in the lexicon of self-publication. But *confesse* has its denotement of a religious earnestness and truth. Amongst its origins are Latin *con*-(intensive) and *fatērī, fass* 'utter' or 'manifest' (*OED*). (But the earnestness is mixed, I think, with the humour of Othello. He implies, If I *had* any vices of the blood . . . . His amusement is also present perhaps in the otherwise standard synecdoche of *Graue ears*: to him the councillors must seem translated by their serious attention – 'all ears'.) Again, *present* denotes a formal stating or delivery (*OED* v., I.8a and II.11); while the noun *report* is '*Law. A formal account of a case' and 'an account, more or less informal, of* some person' (*OED* sb., 3c and 3). These religious and legal nuances enrich the general publishing-nature of these words. The ceremonious dignity of the publishing-lexicon – strongest in such words as *promulgate* – is here maintained.

Now to consider Othello's tale itself. Whether Shakespeare conceived it as a 'cover' for Desdemona's off-stage journey from the Sagittary, or whether the dramatic hiatus was specifically designed to allow the story, one cannot tell; but in either case dramatic necessity and the necessity of character-invention are marvellously combined. Othello is given a chance to assert his cause in an extensive piece of oratory. Reactions to it are probably more mixed than is generally allowed: the Duke's 'I thinke this tale would win my Daughter too' (F517; I.iii.171) may be read and played with a realist's briskness as well as with wonder; and Iago dismisses it, as reported to him by Rodorigo, as 'fantasticall lies' (F1006–7; II.i.219–20) – typical travellers' tales, based on fantasy more than on experience. Our own reaction, too, needs to include a sense of Othello's transfer to Brabantio and Desdemona of some responsibility for the wooing – a transfer discussed above in Chapter 3. Above all, though, we need to be impressed – impressed, that is, not as by a traveller's tale proceeding from the teller's fantasy of himself but by Othello's own romantic wonder at what has happened to him. Also, I think, by the sheer assurance and organisation of his telling. Given its wonder, it is remarkable how short Othello's actual *précis* of his life-before-Desdemona is in the larger account of his courtship: twelve lines suffice for the 'Storie of my life':

> Wherein I spoke of most disastrous chances:
> Of mouing Accidents by [Q *accident of*] Flood and Field,
> Of haire-breadth scapes i'th'imminent deadly breach;
> Of being taken by the Insolent Foe;
> And sold to slauery. Of my redemption thence,
> And portance in my Trauellours historie.
> [Q *And sold to slauery, and my redemption thence,*
> *And with it all my travells Historie;*]
> Wherein of Antars vast, and Desarts idle,
> Rough Quarries, Rocks, Hills, whose head [Q *heads*] touch heauen,
> It was my hint [Q *hent*] to speake. Such was my Processe,
> And of the Canibals that each others [Q *other*] eate,
> The Antropophague [Q   *Anthropophagie*], and men whose heads
> Grew [Q *Doe grow*] beneath their shoulders.
>
> (F479–90; I.iii.134–45)

The wonder consists not in the facts – there are no facts as such – nor in the extensiveness of Othello's travels – the foe's insolence suggests the malignant Turk of Othello's last speech, hence the East or Asia; the cannibals suggest the Caribbean New World – but in the actual telling. Violence and travel are raised into a quintessence of romantic and spiritual adventure. The *Accidents*, or events of Fate, moved Desdemona in the telling as well as moving Othello's life. These events on the sea, on rivers or in inundations (*OED, Flood* sb., 1, 3 and 4) and on dry land or on battlefields (*OED, Field* sb., I.1 and I.6) are expressed in the all-encompassing phrase *Flood and Field* – whose consonance and whose long vowels (*Flood* as in Modern English 'food') help to detain us at this abstract rendering of the elements water and earth. In Q these elements actually cause the events. In F they may do so but primarily supply a natural theatre of action. The *haire-breadth scapes* have their urgency impressed upon us by the novelty of *haire-breadth* (according to the *OED* a Shakespearean new metaphor) and by the elision of *i'th'imminent*; but they do nothing to specify whether the *breach* is a gap in fortifications (the usual gloss) or the equally likely 'breaking of waves on a coast or over a vessel' (*OED* sb., I.2 – apparently another neologism: cf. 'you tooke me from the breach of the sea' in *Twelfe Night, Or what you will*, F630–1; II.i.19). The resonant ambiguity of earth and water, of land-imagery and water-imagery, prevails.

Even the *Insolent Foe* is less an actual soldier or soldiers than a collective noun suggesting a quintessence of enmity: one of the 'indigne, and base aduersities' (F623; I.iii.273), perhaps, that Othello is soon to postulate. *Slauery* resounds too. As servitude it is the opposite of Othello's *'free condition'* (F230; I.ii.26) and has ironical connotations. From the generosity that the free man can cultivate Othello is soon to descend to that kind of slavery that is emotional – 'Conduct befitting a slave; ignoble, base . . . behaviour' (*OED, Slavery* 2). Also, he is soon to be 'entirely subject to . . . some power or influence, (*OED* 3b), that of Iago. (Cf. Lodovico's 'cursed Slaue' and, indeed, Othello's 'O cursed, cursed Slaue!' [F3595 and 3576; V.ii.295 and 279]. Both of these may be referring to Othello's subjection.) Again, *redemption* conveys nothing of the details of Othello's ransom (*OED* has *Redemption* 2: 'The action of freeing a prisoner . . . or slave by payment; ransom'); and it is possible that Shakespeare chose the word not only for its complexity of sound – an actor might linger the more on a word ending on a possibly disyllabic *-ion* and so express more a sense of wonder – but for its complexity of meaning too. Nuances of 'Deliverance from sin and its consequences by the atonement of Jesus Christ' (*OED* 1) were available to Shakespeare. In the context, of course, it is impossible to read this meaning into Othello's words: he is *not* viewing himself as a Christ-figure imprisoned by the Romans and redeeming the world by his sufferings. But the pairing of *redemption* with *Pilgrimage* (fifteen lines on in this speech) lifts both words into a spiritual lexicon. *Pilgrimage* is redeemed from being a commonplace term for a soul's progress through the world; and in *redemption* can be read something of Othello's awareness (or delusion) of a Fate moving his life, of his being purchased back in a grand design.

So far Othello's tale has been, on the whole, a military abstract. The eloquence has derived not from argument as such but from a lyrical evocation of dangers – lyrical in that Othello as it were hymns his epic of soldiery. His exploits in themselves – in Othello's mouth – are speaking of him.

This same epic lyricism endows the *Trauellours* or *Trauells* history. Both words were closer in Shakespeare's day to 'travail' or 'labour'; and there is probably some connotation of Othello's travels as sought-for hardships in which Othello's pilgrim soul might be proved. Hence *portance* (F), far from being 'seriously out of character' since Othello is 'the last man to expatiate on his own creditable behaviour under stress; (Ridley, p. 29n), demonstrates Othello's pride in his having spiritually come through. *Portance* is not so much Othello's 'bearing' or 'behaviour' (*OED*) in a civilised world as the tested hardness of a monkish explorer discovering himself in the wild.

This spiritual resonance is maintained into the phrase *Antars vast, and Desarts idle*. F's *Antars*, probably a misspelling, has the phonetic interest of its second short *a* and its rolled *r* – these supply assonance and consonance with *Desarts*. More germane to my theme, however, is the fact of the post-modification. Both *vast* and *idle* are placed to take the tonics: they mean more than do the geographical features they describe. *Vast* might well signify not only immensity but also emptiness – a 'void'. This 'void' derives from the meaning of Latin *vastus* and links with the emptiness that Othello fears in 'Chaos' (F1693; III.iii.93) – which derives in turn from the Greek meaning 'gape'. As for *idle*, the denotements seem to include not only 'worthless' and 'useless' but also the modern meaning, available to Shakespeare, of 'Not engaged in work, doing nothing' (*OED* adj., 2, 3 and 4). The *Desarts*, which are wildernesses of any kind, not merely wastes of sand (*OED* sb.²), are empty not only of people but of cultivation: they are not being put to use. (Interestingly, the Middle English meaning of *idle* was 'void' – *OED* adj., 1.) The antres and the wild places, therefore, indicate a landscape devoid of moral value in itself. It is the opposite of the useful and occupied Othello. It has value only in that it supplied a testing-ground for Othello's strength.[16]

In the next line, *Rough Quarries, Rocks, Hills, whose head* [Q heads] *touch heauen*, the adjective takes no tonic but has the force of being an only adjective: it extends the idea of landscape as a testing-ground. It also extends the idea of 'idleness', since *rough* could mean, of ground, not only 'Difficult to traverse' but also 'uncultivated' (*OED* adj., I.3). Again, the *Quarries* are not man-made excavations denoting industry and use; they are the plural of a 'large mass of stone or rock in its natural state, capable of being quarried' (*OED* sb.², 2) but not necessarily having been so. So, the idleness

and uselessness persist. The *Hills*, however, do function as something more than a test of religious character: since their heads touch
heaven (unlike those of people whose heads grow beneath their
shoulders), it is possible that Othello achieved some elevation by
their means and came to a closer knowledge of heaven in windy
high places. Certainly, in this line and its predecessor the biblical
resonances and the implication of Othello's religious view of himself are strong. Ross cites the strangers and pilgrims on the earth
who 'wandered in wildernesses and mountains, and dens, and
caves of the earth' (*Hebrews* 11:13, 38–9). One might also think of
Jesus Christ himself, who suffered in a wilderness and on a moun-
tain in Matthew 4.[17]

Othello's next subject, the monsters he has met, also resonates
with his sense of wonder. He is not just trying to impress his
audience; he is also expressing his own response to marvels. He is
still alive to the memory of them. From publications such as *Geor-
graphia universalis*, which contains a charming drawing of men
with heads in their torsoes – one sitting at ease, the other lifting an
arm in greeting – and Raleigh's account of discovering Guiana, in
which he wrote of, 'a nation of people whose heads appear not
above their shoulders', people in late-Renaissance London might
well have been aware of such monsters. Othello yet has the stature
and mystery of a man who has actually encountered them. The
same impression is made by Othello's talk of the man-eaters. Both
the words *Canibals* (from the Spanish) and *Antropophague* (from
Greek through Latin) entered the English language midway
through the sixteenth century; and contemporary publications suggest a knowledge in Shakespeare's London of the barbarous practice they signify. Hart cites not only the translation of Pliny's
Natural Historie by Holland (probably Shakespeare's major inspira-
tion in the writing of Othello's *précis*) but also books by Greene and
Dekker among others which mention anthropophagi by name.
Geographia universalis also contains a drawing of them – two very
ordinary-looking men are busy chopping up a third. Again, similar
drawings in England probably gave Londoners a visual depiction
of what the word *Antropophague* – literally 'man-eaters' – described.
When, therefore, Shakespeare gives Othello his threefold definition – *Canibals, that each others eate, Antropophague* – he is probably
concerned less with explanation than with emphasising Othello's
own reminiscent marvelling. *Antropophague* in particular is a
lingering word that can be used virtually to bring the utterance to a

wondering halt. As Wilson Knight (*The Wheel of Fire*, p. 100) has written, it is one of the 'rich, often expressly consonantal, outstanding words' that help to characterise the '*Othello* music'.[18]

The strength of the morality that guided Othello in his wars and travels has its counterpart here in a strength of syntax. The earlier structuring repetition – of *true, little* and *what* – is maintained in the repetition of *Wherein* + 'speak' + frequent *of: Wherein I spoke of . . . of . . . of . . . of . . . of* and *Wherein of . . . It was my hint to speake . . . and of.*

The first *Wherein* relates to *Storie* (or *it*, either word occurring in the lines preceding the *précis*); the second relates to *Historie*. This structure supplements the certitude with which Othello effects a reasoned classification of his adventures into two separate but similar groups: his talk of war, his talk of travel. He is given an ability to organise his material – a rhetorical ability.

Later in this same speech Othello's wonder sounds afresh. He speaks of the last journey he has made: his discovery of the new world of female emotion, of a young woman not only beautiful but spiritually responsive to his own vision of himself:

> My Storie being done,
> She gaue me for my paines a world of kisses [Q *sighes*]:
> She swore in faith 'twas strange: 'twas passing strange,
> 'Twas pittifull: 'twas wondrous pittifull.
> She wish'd she had not heard it, yet she wish'd
> That Heauen had made her such a man.
>
> (F503–8; I.iii.158–63)

Just as Othello's earlier journeys had been in a moral landscape, so now this new world of kisses or of sighs engages him in a spiritual, not a (merely) sensual, adventure. This is the engagement that Leavis seems to miss. In this world Desdemona sees Othello's visage in his mind; and Othello intends to be bounteous to *her* mind – the mind that in Bradley's phrase is 'ardent with the courage and idealism of a saint' (though 'of a young girl' might be more apt).[19] These kisses or sighs have a prelapsarian freshness; for Othello they are the first ever to have happened on the earth (as well as being, possibly, the first he has literally experienced). True, Othello is transferring some initiative for the courtship onto Desdemona; true, arguably, that his devotion is less than his flattered acceptance of devotion (as Heilman, *Magic in the Web*, p. 171, suggests) and that this account of Desdemona's response contributes to Othello's 'impressive manifestation of a noble egotism' (Leavis, *The Common Pursuit*, p. 142). All this does not detract from Othello's sublime vision of a newly found land. The phrase *for my paines* has nothing of the sarcasm expressed in Modern English usage. Here it denotes an instance of the hardness, the taking-trouble (*OED, Pain* sb., 5 [1528]) that appeals to Othello and which he refers to here with some humour. His narration to this beautiful young woman was really no trouble at all. And his reward has been an experience unparalleled. Shakespeare's use of *a world* is highly apposite: it looks back to the moral and geographical mapping that formed Othello's old life; it also expresses the value Othello places on his wife and on love. The wife is more perfect (in Shakespeare the absolute can have degrees) than 'one entyre and perfect Chrysolite' (F3416; v.ii.148); while the world of love is worth more than all the shipwrecked treasure of the sea *and* the sea's own permanent and intrinsic *virtù* ('Seas worth' – F232; i.ii.28).

Othello's rhetoric, therefore, not only manipulates the Council's response but is also informed by Othello's emotion. The girl who was increasingly stricken by the strangeness of the story – its exotic otherness – and who felt more and more a retrospective concern for the narrator in his hardships; the girl who, moreover, was divided between her terror and her urge to heroic emulation – such a girl must have appealed not only by her spirit but by her touching vulnerability. The repetition and the varying intensifiers in the passage last quoted help to express Othello's wonder at Desdemona's wonder. The language rings with the prospect of Othello and Desdemona as a couple travelling together and enriching wild things and wilderness with their love. Othello encapsulates the reciprocity:

> She lou'd me for the dangers I had past,
> And I lou'd her, that she did pitty them.
>
> (F512–13; i.iii.167–8)

The reversal of subject and object and the use of the simple co-ordinate *And* expresses what for Othello was a very simple process. Something of Heilman's 'flattered acceptance' may be present – but then Othello would hardly be attracted by a girl who *diminished* his sense of himself.[20]

Othello's final lengthy speeches in this act, 'The Tirant Custom

. . . ' and 'Let her haue your voice . . . ', have already been discussed above in Chapters 2 and 1 respectively. The one advertises Othello's liking for hardness, the other his high seriousness; and both are based on a precision of syntax. Both maintain Othello's theme of self-publication in their gist and logic. This logic, to speak now of Othello's utterance throughout Act I, is a supreme organising-principle. The rhetoric is inside as a skeleton, not outside as a scaffold for the clambering of figures. And even when the adjectives and nouns proliferate, as they do in Othello's disparagement of love in favour of military duty, still important lexical differences are made, still the exactness of the argument prevails. The syntax – the arrangement of the words with one another and, particularly, the connection of the clauses – expresses the certainty of Othello's thought.

Shakespeare, then, has developed *I must be found* as a compelling need in Othello to find himself, as it were, to others. Shakespeare can use that need at several crucial moments as Othello flees from doubt during and after the 'temptation' scene. Frequently Othello publishes himself to Iago or to Desdemona when he might have inquired on his own behalf into Iago's reports or informed Desdemona of the specific details of the 'charge'. These frequent relapses – into a dramatically very useful habit which furthers the plausibility of *Othello* by helping its plot to derive from character – are expressed in a series of 'manifesto' speeches from III.iii to the first part of the murder-scene.

The first of these speeches is:

> Why? why is this?
> Think'st thou, I'ld make a Life of Iealousie;
> To follow still the changes of the Moone
> With fresh suspitions? No: to be once in doubt,
> Is [Q *once*] to be resolu'd: Exchange me for a Goat,
> When I shall turne the businesse of my Soule
> To such exufflicate, and blow'd [Q *blowne*] Surmises,
> Matching thy inference. 'Tis not to make me Iealious,
> To say my wife is faire, feeds well, loues company,
> Is free of Speech, Sings, Playes, and Dances [Q *well*]:
> Where Vertue is, these are more vertuous.
> Nor from mine owne weake merites, will I draw
> The smallest feare, or doubt of her reuolt,
> For she had eyes, and chose me. No Iago,

Ile see before I doubt; when I doubt, proue;
And on the proofe, there is no more but this,
Away at once with Loue, or Iealousie.

                    (F1792–808; III.iii.180–96)

There is a dramatic irony here from two sources. First, the speech succeeds a lengthy passage of inquiry in which Othello presses for information about the contents of Iago's mind. A near-constant harping on *know* and *thinke* culminates in the intense precision of:

I prythee speake to me, as to thy thinkings,
As thou dost ruminate, and giue thy worst of thoughts
   [Q *the worst of thought*]
The worst of words [Q *word*].

                    (F1741–3; III.iii.135–7)

Here the verbal and nominal variety in the form of *thinke* reflects the precision with which Iago should answer. *Ruminate* as 'muse, meditate, ponder' (*OED* v., 4) seems to denote a deeper and more sustained mental activity than *thinke*. *As thou dost ruminate* can mean not only 'as soon as you have your thinkings' but also 'that is, as to your most secret thoughts'. Additionally, Iago must not attempt to mince his matter – as the gulled Othello thought he did after the brawl – but must rather utter his thoughts directly, no matter how bad they may be. Othello is pressing the theme most notably expressed a few lines earlier in his description of Iago's frightening 'stops', or hesitations, as 'close dilations'. *Close* as 'exact' was not available until the later seventeenth century: the meaning here is 'secret' (as in *OED* adj., 1.4). The *dilations* are 'dilatations', defined in *OED* 3 (in the singular) as 'amplification, enlargement'. Walker (p. 181n) mentions that they were 'physiologically used for expansion of the arteries (believed to be air-ducts and including the windpipe)' and that a movement from the heart is indicated. Iago's hesitations may try to retain what the just man would prefer to keep small and close: in effect they enlarge and betray it. (In Q the 'denotements' or indications have a lesser richness.) Othello now wishes that these stops should be eschewed. He wants an exact and instant disclosure, continuing to press with 'What dost thou meane?' (Q has merely 'Zouns', a mark of early exasperation) and '[Q *By heauen*] Ile know thy Thoughts'. The irony is this: that Othello, having learned something of Iago's insinuations, does not insist that Iago either explain or substantiate them. And the irony is seconded by the fact that *Why? why is this?* is hardly functioning as an interrogative at all. On hearing it, an audience might well anticipate a close interrogation of Iago as to his meaning, his sources of information and how he came by that information. Instead it hears a long speech in which Othello reacts not to the suggestion of Desdemona's infidelity but to the suggestion that he, the quick and decisive warrior, would long continue in a state of uncertainty about that suspected infidelity. In other words, the audience hears Othello react against Iago's hint of an Othello who might *euer* suspect –

> Riches fineless, is as poore as Winter,
> To him that euer feares he shall be poore.

This reaction is pointed by Othello's answering use of *still* (*OED* adv., 3: 'always'), of *fresh* and of *Life* as both a lifetime and a vocation. It is further pointed by the usage – twice – of *once*: he announces he would 'immediately' act 'as soon as' made suspicious. Furthermore, this publication of himself as the man of action is replicated in the last four lines of the speech. After an emphatic *No*, the main movement is insistently marked for time: *before, when, on the proofe*. This, together with the lexical limitation and repetition reflects Othello's view that to test a wife's fidelity is a merely temporal matter. Othello smothers the ambiguity intrinsic in *doubt* and *proue*. *Proue* as 'try, test' (*OED, Prove* v., B I.1) progresses easily in Othello's facile thinking into *proofe* as 'issue, result' (*OED, Proof* sb., B II.7) untainted by any residue of *doubt*. This speedy disappearance of *doubt*'s premise repeats its earlier disappearance from 'to be once in doubt, / Is [Q *once*] to be resolu'd', where *resolu'd* is the past participle of *resolve* as 'To free (one) from doubt or perplexity . . . (common in 17th. c.)' as in *OED* v., III.15. (Further connotations of *resolve* as 'separate . . . into . . . component parts'; as 'untie, loosen' [1558–1609]; as 'melt, dissolve'; and as 'undergo dissolution' [*OED* v., II.6, III.10, IV.21 and 22] supply superb ironies. Othello will not separate out Iago's pieces of evidence for a just examination. He will himself become separated out, untied, dissolved. Once in doubt he suffers a vast dissolution.)

Ostensibly and in its implication, then, the passage expresses two divergent meanings. Othello uses the word *doubt* four times in the speech overall. Ostensibly he denies the existence of doubt in himself and asserts how he would deal with it. But the very frequency of the word suggests that doubt is already troubling him. If one understands *jealous* as the *OED*'s 'distrustful of the faithfulness of wife . . . or lover' (adj., 4), then one can say that Othello in being doubtful is already jealous in a general way and that this will qualify the truth of Othello's 'not easily Iealious' in his final speech (F3656; V.ii.348). The point is, I think, that Iago dares to speak plain – 'Looke to your wife' – only when Othello *has* betrayed this doubt. Iago declares that Desdemona is a typically Venetian woman in being unfaithful and prankish; that her easy deception of her father is being matched by an easy deception of her husband; and that in marrying a man not of her own race, temperament and rank ('Clime, Complexion, and Degree' – F1858; III.iii.234) she has acted against nature and must now revert. All this comes *after* Othello's long speech. And it does, in fact, develop from it – from the doubt aroused by Iago and nourished by the uncertainties about Venetian life that Othello has disclosed in Act I. This last is important. Consider Othello's declaration

> 'Tis not to make me Iealious,
> To say my wife is faire, feeds well, loues company,
> Is free of Speech, Sings, Playes, and Dances [Q *well*]:

This implies that Iago has said something concerning Desdemona's beauty and her social life. He has not. Othello delineates a social life as a proving-ground of virtue in his wife (a kind of housed equivalent of the moral landscape in which he himself was proved – a 'roomscape' which, however, on Othello's terms must be inferior); but in his very delineation he protests too much. Impelled by doubt, he parades before himself the kind of *dolce vita* in which a wife might the more easily be covertly unchaste. The love of good food, of company, and of good talk, the enjoyment of singing, of making music and of dancing, these are the features of Venetian life that Othello has already disparaged as effete and luxurious – the features of a civilisation he has implied to be an oversoft bed of down, a featherbed state (F577ff.; I.iii.229ff.). Later he is to castigate them as the soft parts of social intercourse (F1895; III.iii.268). He himself is not adept at them. They are the accomplishments of the chamberers he so much despises. As Walker has written,

This enumeration of Desdemona's attractions gains in signifi-

cance when it is related to the context where Shakespeare met it –
a passage in Cinthio's Introduction where the company is
warned against the snares of beautiful courtezans whose plausible accomplishment (*sembianze di virtù*) conceal evil minds:
singing, playing, dancing well (*leggiadramente*), pleasing talk
(*dolcemente favellare*) and composing amrous trifles are mentioned as the acquired graces which deceive simple men.[21]

Under Othello's talk of his wife's social life are two propositions:
Desdemona may share all the social graces of the immoral woman
but is not thereby defined as immoral; indeed, her social graces
only make her the more chaste. The first of these propositions is
sound; the second is dubious. Importantly, Othello has supplied a
theme for Iago to work on in this overstatement. The matter is no
longer that of Desdemona's possible leaning towards Cassio; it is of
Desdemona as a general immoralist. The anxiety that Othello does
not acknowledge in himself is betrayed to Iago. Iago, in the rest of
this scene, is to work virtually from a sense of *company* as 'Sexual
connexion' (*OED* sb., 2 [1386–1616]) and as, verbally, 'To cohabit
(with)' (*OED* v., 3b [c. 1400-1680]).

Othello betrays something else too: a curiously 'low' – and un-
provoked – chain of thought in *Goat*. From the writing of Clemen
and Morozov we are aware of how Iago's use of bestial imagery in
the early part of the play becomes Othello's usage in the middle
part.[22] The assumption in general is that this image-transfer expresses the infection by Iago of Othello's mind. It needs emphasising, however, that, though Iago freely utters his beast-images to
Rodorigo and Brabantio, he begins to utter them to Othello only
when Othello has himself initiated such an image.

To digress for a paragraph on *Goat*: arguably, Shakespeare gives
Othello the word not just for its association with lechery and
horned cuckoldry but also because a goat (Latin genus *capra*) was
considered to be capricious, whimsical: to entertain Iago's in-
ferences must be (Othello claims) to behave in a capricious way.
Additionally, goats being symbolic of wickedness at the Day of
Judgement (Matthew 25: 32, 33), would presumably be wicked
enough to entertain the *exufflicate . . . Surmises*. The adjective, as
was noted by early critics, could well derive from 'exsufflation',
defined in *OED* 2 as '*Eccl.* The action of blowing, performed by a
priest . . . at baptism, by way of exorcising the devil, or by the
person baptized in token of renouncing the devil' (1502–1858).

Othello could well be defining Iago's surmises not only as 'fly-blown', 'tainted' or 'inflated' but also as having been blown free into the air by an act of exorcism: that is, they are devilish, renounced by one person somewhere and now roaming for a new habitation. Othello postulates a goat not only on the grounds that lechery in another person is the more suspected by someone given to lechery himself but also on the grounds that jealousy on insubstantial evidence must result from a goatish lack of judgement that tempts the Devil. Iago, however, when he turns Othello's word back upon Othello, strips it of all denotements save that of lechery: 'Were they as prime as Goates' (F2051; III.iii.407). The important point – returning to my theme – is this: having omitted to dismiss or inquire into Iago's insinuations, Othello discloses in his defensive self-publications not only a general doubt about his wife's social behaviour but also the hint of a certain potential for degradation from his (impossibly) idealistic standards in his own thinkings. These publications betray a way ahead for the opportunistic Iago. He sees how Othello may be worked.

Iago also works on the implications of Othello's *her reuolt*. The nominal form of 'To draw back from a course of action . . . to return to one's allegiance' (*OED* v., 2b) seems more apt in context than the *OED*'s substantive 'movement of strong protest against, or refusal to submit to . . . ' (sb.[1], 1b). Othello postulates the idea of Desdemona's return to the kind of 'wealthy curled Deareling of our Nation' (Brabantio at F286; I.ii.68) her father had wanted her to marry. Iago echoingly observes, 'Her will, recoyling to her better iudgement, / May fal [Q *fall*] to match you with her Country formes' (F1864–5; III.iii.240–1). (One may also note here Iago's cunning deployment of *her better iudgment*, which plays on Othello's concern for his own *best iudgement* heard by Iago in the brawl-scene – F1326; II.iii.198.)

Consider, too, how Othello's 'For she had eyes, and chose me' is answered by Iago's remark that when Desdemona 'seem'd to shake, and feare your lookes, / She lou'd them most' (F1824–5; III.iii.211–12). Iago suggests that Desdemona's response to Othello's appearance, or his glances or gazes (*OED* sb., 1 and 2) was less simple than Othello supposes. Consider, again, how Othello's later line 'And yet how Nature erring from itselfe' (F1854; III.iii.231) is manipulated in Iago's talk about 'Foule disproportions' (F1861; III.iii.237) in Desdemona that have offended against decorum and congruity. Perhaps Iago here is reinterpreting *reuolt* in the Shakespearean sense of 'Revulsion of appetite' (*OED* sb., 2c). Of much interest is the fact that Shakespeare makes Othello's *Nature* and *erring* echo Brabantio's lexicon: 'She is abus'd . . . corrupted . . . For Nature, so prepostrously to erre' (F397–9; I.iii.60–2); 'She, in spighte of Nature' (F437; I.iii.96); and

> It is a iudgement main'd [Q *maimd*], and most imperfect.
> That will confesse Perfection so could erre
> Against all rules of Nature
>
> (F440–2; I.iii. 99–101)

This echo across such a distance of time and from Venice to Cyprus strongly reverberates. It would seem that Othello was much more affected by Brabantio's allegations of unnatural practice than his calm and dignity at the time suggested. In brooding upon those allegations Othello is not so much self-publishing as thinking aloud; and, when Iago supplements *Foule disproportions* with 'Thoughts vnnaturall', it is little wonder that Othello, shocked by this over-explication, gives Iago one of his frightening *lookes* (thus eliciting Iago's 'But (pardon me) . . . '). It would seem that Shakespeare has contrived a deliberate scheme of 'errant nature': a doubt concerning his racial disparity from Desdemona is installed in Othello's mind, is dredged up by Othello and is then held out by Iago, adventuring prematurely, as a reasonable argument for revolt. This scheme is paralleled by another scheme, of *Monster* as 'Something extraordinary or unnatural' (*OED* A sb.,1). Iago's vivid monster in

> Oh, beware my Lord, of iealousie,
> It is the greene-ey'd Monster, which doth mocke
> The meate it feeds on
>
> (F1780–2; III.ii.169–71)

suggests that jealousy is an emotion that errs against Nature. Iago conjures up in the imagination a beast different from its fellows in ridiculing its prey – beasts ordinarily devoid of emotions and soul would not so behave. Or, conversely, Iago's monster may belong to the centaur species, its cruelty being supplied by its human upper half (*OED Monster* A sb. 3). In either instance something more than the savagery conventionally perceived in wild animals is being denoted. And, once again, Iago is extending an idea first voiced by

Othello – in this case in Othello's postulation

> As if there were some Monster in thy thought
> Too hideous to be shewne
>
> (F1714–15; III.iii.111–12)

Othello has seen the unnatural anthropophagi, the cannibals, the man-eaters. He has spoken of them openly. The fact that he can imagine behind the bars of Iago's furrowed brow a monster worse than they, one too abominable for display, does more than exemplify Othello's characteristic extremism of thought: it also betrays the force of his anxiety.[23]

Shakespeare maintains Othello's self-publication in the soliloquy that concludes this first exchange of the 'corruption' scene:

> Why did I marry?
> This honest Creature (doubtlesse)
> Sees, and knowes more, much more then he vnfolds.
>   . . .
> This Fellow's of exceeding honesty,
> And knowes all Quantities [Q *qualities*] with a learn'd Spirit
> Of humane dealings. If I do proue her Haggard,
> Though that her Iesses were my deere heart-strings,
> I'ld whistle her off, and let her downe the winde
> To prey at Fortune. Haply, for I am blacke,
> And haue not those soft parts of Conuersation
> That Chamberers haue: Or for I am declin'd
> Into the vale [Q *valt*] of yeares (yet that's not much)
> She's gone, I am abus'd, and my releefe
> Must be to loath her. Oh Curse of Marriage!
> That we can call these delicate Creatures ours,
> And not their Appetites? [Q has colon] I had rather be a Toad,
> And liue vpon the vapour of a Dungeon,
> Then keepe a corner in the [Q *a*] thing I loue
> For others vses. Yet 'tis the plague to [Q *of*] Great-ones,
> Prerogatiu'd are they lesse then the Base,
> 'Tis destiny vnshunnable, like death:
> Euen then, this forked plague is Fated to vs,
> When we do quicken. Looke where she comes:
> If she be false, Heauen mock'd it selfe:
> Ile not beleeue't.
>
> (F1872–4 and 1889–911; III.iii.246–7 and 262–83)

Othello is given only two soliloquies of any length (the other is 'It is the Cause . . . '). This one demonstrates why. The comparative simplicity of Othello's mind is as well expressed in private or public dialogue as in solitary communications to us, the audience. Indeed, several of Othello's great speeches that occur ostensibly in a context of colloquy with Iago, Desdemona or Aemilia are in effect monologues. As shown in Chapter 1 above, Othello seldom talks *to* Desdemona even when he is apparently conversing *with* her: he tends, rather, to talk *about* her – about, that is, the monstrous strumpet Desdemona of his convinced imaginings and not the real Desdemona known to us. Othello's free and open nature – the noble naïveté that thinks all men honest unless they be Turks – leads to an uninhibited utterance: so that Othello's most intimate confidings differ very little, if at all, from his public promulgations. The self-analyses of Hamlet and the self-registrations of Macbeth – their introspections – are much less evident in the manifesting Othello. Hence 'manifesto', rather than soliloquy, becomes Othello's norm.[24] In this first of Othello's soliloquies the interrogative form of the opening *Why did I marry?* contains an exclamation – a specific version of the earlier 'O miserie' (F1786; III.iii.175) – rather than a self-questioning. And when Othello does speculate, in the six lines beginning *Haply, for I am blacke,* he speculates on the possible reasons for Desdemona's disaffection and not on whether she *has* disaffected in fact. That is, *Haply* ('perhaps') seems to refer to Othello's blackness, to his lack of chambering-skills, and to his seniority in years, rather than to the assertive *She's gone, I am abus'd, and my releefe / Must be to loath her.* Or, conversely, the sentence can be read as starting on a 'perhaps' but moving as it goes into a series of declarations. Certainly, it is difficult to hear Othello as saying 'Perhaps my relief must be to loathe her' or 'Perhaps I am abused' in the syntax of this sentence.

This movement – call it an easy forgetting of the postulative for the assertive – one feels to be characteristically Othello's. There were hints of it already in the 'Why? why is this? . . . ' speech discussed earlier in this chapter. In that speech the conditional sense caused by auxiliary *would* in *Think'st thou, I'ld make . . . ?* soon vanished. Thus: '*Tis not to make me Iealious* instead of "Twould not be to make . . . '. Thus: *Nor from mine owne weake merites, will I draw / The smallest fear* instead of ' . . . would I draw . . . ' And in the soliloquy, similarly, the conditional sense of

If I do proue her Haggard,

> Though that her Iesses were my deere heart-strings,
> I'ld whistle her off

vanishes too. True, on Desdemona's reappearance Othello's sense of 'if' and of the subjunctive returns:

> Looke where she comes:
> If she be false, Heauen mock'd it selfe:
> Ile not beleeue't.

But the strength of this asseverative conditional (in which *Heauen* either mocks its own self or itself mocks – like Iago's green-eyed monster – at Othello and at the whole neo-Platonic concept whereby Desdemona's beautiful body must express a beautiful mind) might have sounded more plausibly had it not been qualified by Othello's several earlier statements in the soliloquy. The emphasis on Iago's honesty and insight, the generalisations about the *Curse of marriage* and the *plague to Great-ones*, the raising of the *I had rather be a Toad* preference – these lessen one's confidence that Othello will *not beleeu't*. It is germane to note that in publishing Othello's fears and hypothese to us they supply little of the inquiry we might have expected.

Much of Othello's energy in this speech belongs in fact to the hawking-image – to the punishment he would inflict on his wife. This image needs examining. The *OED* has *Haggard* as 'wild, un-tamed' (adj., 1) and preambles according to Cotgrave's definition of French *hagard*: 'orig. said of a "falcon that preyed for her selfe long before she was taken" '. This implies that Desdemona, in Othello's mind, was immorally inclined before her marriage and has brought the immorality with her into the marriage. At this stage Othello's revenge (he claims) would consist in divorce and disgrace – no more. Hart (pp. 144–5n) says, 'Against the wind . . . was the proper flight for a hawk. Down the wind had a proverbial signifi-cation, equivalent to deliberate, reckless fortune.' There would be no sustenance or harbour provided by Othello. There would be, in Desdemona's own words, 'beggerly diuorcement' (F2872; IV.ii.159). But specifically the metaphor declares Desdemona as a hawk beating her wings at the mews wall and wanting to come back in after one of her stoops on Cassio. The hawk-image suits Othello's utterance, of course, since hawks were 'noble' birds and hawking was an activity of aristocrats and royalty; but, in the sense that a hawk was essentially a warrior used in the serious and great business of making war on other birds, the image of Desdemona as such underlines the attitude of Othello to his wife that was succintly sounded in 'O, my faire Warriour' (F958; II.i.180). Othello discloses in this metaphor the trait that is fundamental in him and to the action of the drama. He allows little breath to the Desdemona who is wife and woman. When he is not seeing Desdemona as a representative corrupt Venetian beauty he sees her as a being trained, unsuccessfully, in his service.

The divorce would, in fact, have some similarity to the cashiering of the actual warrior Cassio. The blamable brawler 'shall loose me', says Othello at F1333 (II.iii.205) – loose being 'lose' rather than 'unleash'. Similarly, Desdemona will lose Othello's keeping if proven haggard. Again, if Cassio cannot be received back into Othello's love and service, Cassio shall 'shut my selfe vp in some other course / To Fortunes Almes' (F2276–7; III.iv.122–3) – while Desdemona would be 'set free' (OED, Let v.¹, 8) to suffer a like dependence on Fortune's whims away from Othello's love. Shakespeare, it seems, is pointing the similarity of these two 'cashierings', the one effected, the other threatened. Not only a military peremptoriness but also a subjugation of love to something apparently higher is common to both. The earlier 'Cassio, I loue thee, / But neuer more be Officer of mine' (F1370–1; II.iii.240–1) – properly decisive, given Cassio's instigation of the brawl as revealed by honest Iago – is echoed in *Though that her Iesses were my deere heart-strings, / I'ld whistle her off,* – where an abrupt dismissal despite all love is seen as a future possibility. In the first statement the higher thing is military necessity, since Cassio has fallen from ideal soldiership; in the second it would be a necessary divorce, since Desdemona would have slipped from her status as an ideal wife.

The comparison of *Iesses* with *deere heart-strings* suggests in Othello both an awareness of the emotional tearing that might be expected and, at the same time, an incomprehension of that tearing's effect. Jesses are straps fastened around a hawk's legs for the attachment of the leash. *Heart-strings* were the tendons or nerves that in old notions of anatomy were supposed to brace and sustain the heart (OED sb. pl., 1). They were indeed *deere*, most intimate and precious. The image becomes extraordinarily cruel when one considers that Desdemona's enforced flight would tear out or damage Othello's heart – which is to say, his emotional capacity.

The uncompromising sentiment is akin to that expressed in the ambiguous 'I do not thinke but Desdemona's honest' (F1851; III.iii.229) – in which the meaning might well be 'My whole mental faculty is based on Desdemona's virtue' – and to several other assertions of whole-hearted love (the adjective is freshened by its context). In the terms of the metaphor Othello acknowleges the terrible maiming or indeed emotional death he would be bringing upon himself; and yet, still, he is prepared *to* bring them on – as if he thinks the essential Othello would survive. He still maintains the simplistic thinking of *Away at once with Loue, or Iealousie.* He still, moreover, keeps at the front of his mind what he would drastically and decisively do in the eventuality of Desdemona's guilt. He spares little energy to consider – in the dozen last words of the speech – the eventuality of her innocence.

5
'I must be found' (ii)

The fact is that Othello entertains the idea of Desdemona's guilt far more than he does that of her innocence. This is confirmed by his next great speech of publication – the 'Occupation' speech. The apparent discussion implied by the balance of

> I thinke my Wife be honest, and thinke she is not:
> I thinke that thou art iust, and thinke thou art not
>
> (F2030–1; III.iii.388–9)

does not sound in Othello's voiced thinkings to Iago. Othello's sufferings derive from his insufficient knowledge of the *extent* of Desdemona's abuse and not from any uncertainty whether she *has* abused him:

> Thou hast set me on the Racke:
> I sweare 'tis better to be much abus'd,
> Then but to know't a little
>
> (F1977–9; III.iii.339–41)

Furthermore, the various demands for proof – bringing from Iago the reports of Cassio's talking in his sleep and of Cassio's possession of the handkerchief – are demands for a proof of guilt: they are not demands for a proving, or testing, of Iago's case. In the dramatic context, it seems, Othello suspects and almost certainly manhandles Iago; but, even allowing for the violence of Othello's threats, one is faced by the fact that all idea of Desdemona's innocence is absent from

> Villaine, be sure thou proue my loue a Whore
> Be sure of it: Giue me the Occular proofe
> . . . .
> Make me to see't: or (at the least) so proue it,

That the probation beare no Hindge, nor Loope,
To hang a doubt on

. . . .

Ile haue some proofe.

. . .

Giue me a liuing reason she's disloyall.

> (F2002–3, 2008–10, 2032 and 2057;
> III.iii.363–4, 368–370, 390 and 413)

Othello consistently uses *proue* as 'To establish . . . as true' (*OED Prove* v., II.5) and not as 'To make trial of, put to the test' (I.1); and *proofe* as 'That which makes good . . . a statement' (*Proof* sb., b II.1) and not as 'test, trial' (II.4). He betrays, in fact, an illogic of argument – much as he did in his use of *proue* and *proofe* in 'Why? why is this? . . . ' at F1806–7 (III.iii.194-5). Again, *probation* means 'proving, or showing to be true' (*OED* sb., II.4) as opposed to 'testing or putting to the proof' (I.1). This proving must be immaculate. It must have no obtruding 'prop' (*OED, Hinge* sb., 4) and no 'hole, opening' (Schmidt, *Loop*) or 'opening on the parapet' (*OED, Loop* sb.[2], 2[c.1477–1686]) onto which any rope or grappling-iron may be affixed. This siege-imagery is, of course, appropriate in Othello. In another sense of *Loope*, the garment of proof must have no excrescence by which doubt might pull the whole garment off. Othello means to have a proof so evident, an evidence so strong, that no one would even think of questioning it. As for *liuing reason*, that too expresses Othello's need of something incontrovertible. Most editors gloss *liuing* (as 'sound') but let *reason* go. *Reason* here is 'A statement of some fact . . . to . . . prove or disprove some assertion' (*OED* sb.[1], I.1 – ['in common use down to *c*.1600']). It is not a 'reason why'. Othello's brief thoughts about Desdemona's motives have not prevailed. (And since those thoughts – on his blackness, age and lack of soft skills – defined rather than inquired into Desdemona's motives, they would not have supplied any questionings anyway.)

The 'Occupation' speech, then, derives not from doubt as uncertainty or disbelief (after Schmidt, *Doubt* sb., 1 and 2); rather it derives from doubt as a strong suspicion (after Schmidt 3) amounting to a virtual certainty which, however, cannot be demonstrated as palpably true:

OTHELLO. What sense had I, in her stolne houres of Lust?

I saw't not, thought it not: it harm'd not me:
I slept the next night well, fed well, was free, and merrie.
I found not Cassio's kisses on her Lippes:
He that is robb'd, not wanting what is stolne,
Let him not know't, and he's not robb'd at all.
IAGO. I am sorry to heare this? [Q omits question mark.]
OTHELLO. I had beene happy, if the generall Campe,
Pyoners and all, had tasted her sweet Body,
So I had nothing knowne. Oh now for euer
Farewell the Tranquill minde; farewell Content;
Farewell the plumed Troopes, and the bigge Warres,
That makes Ambition, Vertue! Oh farewell;
Farewell the neighing Steed, and the Shrill Trumpe,
The Spirit-stirring Drum, th'Eare-piercing Fife,
The Royall Banner, and all Qualitie,
Pride, Pompe, and Circumstance §f rlorious Warre:
And O you mortall Engines, whose rude [Q *wide*] throates
Th'immortall Ioues dread [Q *great*] Clamours, counterfet,
Farewell: Othello's Occupation's gone.

>   (F1975–2000; III.iii.337–61)

To take the first section first: perhaps one may discern some significance in the frequency of undefined *it* – three examples in the
second line, a fourth example in the sixth. These are not an impersonal usage. The first three examples refer to an unstated 'adultery',
the fourth reference is to an unstated 'that he is robbed'. A similarly
loose pronoun will sound in

>   She dying, gaue it me,
>   And bid me (when my Fate would haue me Wiu'd)
>   To giue it her
>
>   (F2211–13; III.iv.63–5)

where *her* refers back to a non-existent noun 'wife'. Since such
syntactical 'looseness' has been absent from Othello's utterance
hitherto, it may be that Shakespeare is signalling by *her* and *it* a
certain disconnectedness in Othello's thought under stress. (If so,
Shakespeare may well be rehearsing the 'epilepsy' scene – in which
Othello's syntax is certainly less cohesive than elsewhere in the
play.)[1]
    In this first section, too, Shakespeare makes Othello repeat lexical

items of his earlier review of Desdemona's social life. Othello observes that he fed well – by implication, even as Desdemona was feeding well in her adultery; and that he was free and merry – by implication, even as Desdemona was speaking freely with whom she chose and loving company. The review continues, but with a new subject: that of Othello's own state of mind. Once again the inquiry suggested by an initial interrogative – in this instance, 'What sense had I, in her stolne houres of Lust?' – does not occur. We hear instead variations on the theme that to be ignorant is to be happy – a theme that in the two lines starting *He that is robb'd* descends to an Iagoist triteness.

(To digress for a paragraph: this uncharacteristic triteness of expression, clumsily playing on intransitive *robb'd* and transitive *stolne* balances the uncharacteristic sublimity a few lines earlier of Iago's

> Looke where he comes: Not Poppy, nor Mandragora,
> Nor all the drowsie Syrrups of the world
> Shall euer medicine thee to that sweete sleepe
> Which thou owd'st yesterday.
>
> [F1971–4; III.iii.334–7]

Here, several characteristics, while not exclusively Othello's, accumulate into an 'Othello style'. One of these is the elongation and verbless nature of the main clause's subject. Another is the assured structure of the subject – the repetition of *Not . . . nor . . . nor*. Another is the rhythmic contrasts effected by the juxtaposition of poly- with monosyllables. There are also consonance, particularly of [m] and [p], sibilance, of [s] and [z] and general assonance – these on the whole sound more intensely than elsewhere in Iago's speeches. Additionally, Iago *thou*s Othello – speaking ostensibly to him but in an aside – expressing not only the familiar contempt he elsewhere disguises inside polite *you* but also the rhythmically detaining sounds in fricative *th* and in the consonantal cluster of the inflection *-st*. Also, extreme *Nor all* and *Shall euer* would more naturally be Othello's than Iago's, as would also the evocative ambiguity of *drowsie Syrrups*, by which the liquids 'medicated, or used as a vehicle for medicines, [*OED, Syrup* 1a, citing this passage] not only induce drowsiness but are themselves, decorously, made drowsy. The fact that the primary origin of *syrup* in Arabic was not necessarily known to Shakespeare does not stop one from remarking how much less apt in Iago's utterance *Syrrups* is than it would have been in Othello's – cf. the 'Medicinable gumme' of the 'Arabian Trees' in the last long speech. I digress to make these points because, while editors generally have observed Iago's uncharacteristic sublimity, none to my knowledge has defined in what it consists.)

Shakespeare makes Othello's self-publication betray yet another way in which Othello can be worked on: in the reference to physical sexual detail in *Cassio's kisses on her Lippes*. Iago, of course, is to play on Othello's preoccupation with the physical in his account of Cassio's dream:

> And then (Sir) would he gripe, and wring my hand:
> Cry, oh sweet Creature: then kisse me hard,
> As if he pluckt vp kisses by the rootes,
> That grew vpon my lippes, laid his Leg ore my Thigh,
> And sigh, and kisse . . . .
>
> (F2068–72; III.iii.425–9)

Iago's image of kisses is quite extraordinary. More commonly kisses are planted on lips, not plucked up. Iago takes the convention of lips-as-roses and varies it with a vivid violence. He declares Cassio's rapacity: Cassio would want to uproot, by implication, Desdemona from her marriage. In Iago's rationale, Cassio as a gardening *will* has effected an illegal permission of Desdemona's *garden* body (see p.85). Othello's 'O monstrous! monstrous!' – 'Deviating from the natural order; unnatural' (*OED* adj., 1) and 'outrageously wrong' or 'atrocroas' (5 and 6) – exclaims against Cassio's supposed words to a succubine Desdemona, 'cursed Fate, / That gaue thee to the Moore'. But Iago's explicit development of Othello's *kisses* reference – an explicit form which also, obliquely but strongly, hints at Iago's possible feeling for the young and handsome Cassio – obviously does much to exacerbate Othello's imaginings. Iago also utilises Othello's *kisses* in his explicit 'lip a wanton in a secure Cowch' (F2452; IV.i.71;. This was probably the first verbal use of *lip* (*OED* v.[1], 1b) in writing: here it powerfully conveys the canker-in-the-rose nature of a false wife's kisses.

Now to consider Othello's self-publication in the 'Occupation' lines themselves. After the three lines about the *Pyoners*, Othello maintains the simple repetition of single words that makes his speech so apparently sure. The seven uses of *not* in the first section helped to shape and stiffen the main clause sequence – even helped the *robb'd* lines with the dignity of a surreptitious repetition. Now, the repetition becomes most obviously that of *Farewell* with or without *the*. There are six soundings, single or double, in initial or final positions, with single or plural substantives. This repetition is strong enough to bind and to move ten and a half lines in which occur, astonishingly, only three verbs (*makes, counterfet* and *is* or *has gone*). In fact, *Farewell*, though technically an interjection, has itself something of a verbal activity, returning to its components as imperative 'Fare you well' or subjunctive 'May you fare well' (*OED, Fare* v.[1], 8 – which, however, acknowledges only the imperative; and *Farewell* interj. – which also includes a sense of 'no more of'). As something of a surrogate verb *Farewell* functions zeugmatically in two of its soundings, yoking *Troopes* with *Warres* and *Steed* with *Trumpe, Drum, Fife, Banner, Qualitie, Pride, Pompe* and *Circumstance*. Overall, the variety in syntactical placing and in context that Shakespeare has given to the six 'Farewells' makes for much subtlety in their simple repetition. The structure is not a simplistic one. Nor, in effect, is another structuring by repetition, that of single pre-modifier + noun, which almost constantly recurs: *generall Campe; sweet Body; Tranquill minde; plumed Troopes; bigge Warres; neighing Steed; shrill Trumpe; Spirit-stirring Drum; Eare-piercing Fife* (these last two, with their participal adjectives, supply a further repetitive pattern); *Royall Banner; all Qualitie; glorious Warre; mortall Engines; rude throates; immortall Ioues; dread Clamours.*

A high frequency of primary accents is effected by these sixteen examples of adjective + noun sounding in the space of only a dozen lines. Hence a strong rhythm. The culmination of the speech is extremely packed too: the duplication of *'s* in *Othello's Occupation's gone* creates an impression of crammed intensity even though the first *'s* is possessive not elisional; while the play on the sounds of *o* help to organise this declaration's force. Elsewhere assonance/consonance is less emphatic: [u:] in *plumed Troopes*; [u] (as in Modern English 'put') or possibly [u:] again in *Trumpe* and *Drum*; [p] in *Trumpe, Spirit, piercing, Pride, Pompe, Occupations*; [k] in *Clamours, counterfet, Occupation's*; [r], of course, riffs through the last seven lines. Even [l] in *Farewell* is made to work unobtrusively, linking with *Tranquill, plumed, shrill, Royall, Qualitie, glorious, mortall, immortall, Clamours, Othello's*. What Othello speaks, in effect, is a symphony of sense with sound – something that Wilson Knight (*The Wheel of Fire*, p. 107), citing it as an example of the

Othello music, called a 'noble apostrophe' and 'this noble eulogy of war'.

The speech has, however, much more of interest. Of especial interest is its position: it immediately succeeds a lament about the distress of imperfect knowledge, yet itself seems based upon a knowledge complete. Again nothing of *Ile not beleeue't* seems to be retained in Othello's mind. Those farewells have much vigour! They also attest something of Othello's tendency to luxuriate in the publishings of his emotion. Shakespeare has created a great irony in thus juxtaposing Othello's strong but wrong assumptions against the truth that the play so far has clearly demonstrated to us. The farewells indicate a willed, indeed wilful, leave taking – as if the military things apostrophised are not faring from their general of their own volition and cannot really see the grounds for his self-cashiering. Othello contrives to celebrate not only the occupation but also his departure from it: since he can no longer luxuriate on the flinty and steel couch of war, he will luxuriate in an emotional distress. All this has taken the place of genuine speculation with alarming facility. Kirschbaum's 'there is something in Othello's character which leads him to believe Iago's calumny'[2] is hardly strong enough in indicating the current that compels Othello into belief. The very fact that Shakespeare makes Othello postulate the sexual knowing of Desdemona by the whole army's rank-and-file (*generall Campe*) suggests that we should be hearing Othello as already imaginatively convinced of his wife's promiscuity. Here is one of Doran's asseverative conditionals in which the conditional has become a postulate.[3] The *Pyoners*, being as auxiliaries the lowest rank of soldiery, are enlisted to show Othello's extremism; being trench-diggers and clearers of ways (*OED, Pioneer* sb., 1), they also parade a sexual connotation. It is *almost* on the premise that he has been taken by the insolent foe again – this time by his own troops, who have tricked him with his own wife – that Othello speaks. Certainly, public knowledge by the army of his cuckoldry – if known to the general – must compromise a general's power to command (I should have thought), while also cancelling his vocation, his desire to follow his 'calling' (*OED, Occupation* 4b). Moreover, the sexual connotations about the pioneers are reinforced by *Occupation* as linked to verbal *occupy*: 'To deal with or have to do with sexually' (*OED* v., 8). As the *OED* and Onions note, the verb was leaving the language and was little used in the literature of the seventeenth and eighteenth centures because of this vulgar employment. (*OED*, adding 'apparently', is less certain than Onions about the reason.) Hilda Hulme comments

> It is noteworthy that the verb *occupy*, 'to cohabit with' was, in Shakespeare's day, in process of being dropped from decent usage, so that the meaning of 'Occupation' which Othello himself ignores would be the more vividly present to the Shakespearean audience. Doll Tearsheet, for instance, cries out that Pistol's claim to being a captain will bring all captains into disrepute; the word 'captain' will become 'as odious as the word occupy, which was an excellent good worde before it was il sorted' (*2 Henry IV*, II.iv.161, Quarto 1600). I do not want to make too much of this tiny point, but it seems to me that there is here another indication of the dangers in Othello's position: he stands at a certain distance from the world of common men; only rarely does Shakespeare allow the audience to identify itself with him; at this point of the play we are listening to his words with ears more sensitive, less noble, than his own.[4]

Possibly. Hulme's comment is highly pertinent. But, though Othello *is* spiritually distanced from common men, one wonders how far Shakespeare means him to be unaware of the common concerns. He is aware of the common *Pyoners*, their rank ways. If Desdemona has been used by them, then assuredly Othello's occupation of her has gone. Of course, Othello does not actually state any belief that his wife has been generally known by the army; but his mind is certainly working in that wild direction; and the possibility remains that Shakespeare, in the topical ambiguity of *Occupation*, purposed to affect his contemporary audience with a sense not of Othello's innocent nobility but, rather, of the sexual anxiety in Othello that Iago has developed.

A further point about Othello's *Occupation* – in its primary denotement. It has not been merely a mundane job. It has expressed and required the virtue of manly qualities and natural efficacy (*OED*, *Virtuous* adj., I.1 and II). It has enabled Othello to fulfil his idealistic concept of what a man should be. (Latin *vir* = 'man', hence Latin *virtus* = 'manliness, valour'.) Now, Othello's idea of his own virtue has been confirmed by Desdemona's perception and worship of it. In marrying him, Desdemona joined herself to Othello as a martial pilgrim. (The fact that Shakespeare gives her a 'purse / Full of Cruzadoes' – Portuguese coins stamped with a cross

[*OED, Crusado*[1]] – perhaps associates Desdemona with another kind of 'crusado': the 'crusader' of *OED*'s *Crusado*[2] [1575 –1625] – F2163–4; III.iv.22–3.) Since, therefore, Othello's virtue has become bound up with Desdemona's, one might have expected that Desdemona's revolt might have affected Othello's own view of his career. He might have come to consider it worthless by reason of its having been corrupted from within. He might have commented on the vanity of soldiership – the meaningless nature of war unless made pure by 'soul'. Not so. Nothing of such an encompassing disillusion is expressed in Othello's farewell to his career. It *is* a eulogy, as Wilson Knight says; but, interestingly, Othello refers to the morality and virtue of soldiership hardly at all. And where he does – in *the bigge Warres, / That makes [sic] Ambition Vertue!* – his reference is pragmatic rather than idealistic. *Ambition,* the soldier's virtue, is 'The ardent (*in early usage* inordinate) desire to . . . attain . . . distinction' (*OED* sb., 1). The soldier's desire to fight for glory, dangerous in civil life and in peace, is made good in war. Moreover, it seems highly probable that Shakespeare used *Ambition* for its connotation of another idea altogether – that of 'Ostentation, display of the outward tokens of position, as riches, dress; vain-glory, pomp' (*OED* sb., 2 [1382 – *ante* 1631]. In this sense it becomes synonymous with (i) *Pride*: 'Magnificence, splendour; pomp, ostentation, display' – *OED* sb.[1]. II.6; (ii) *Pompe*: 'Splendid display . . . magnificent show' and 'ostentatious display; parade, specious or boastful show; vain glory; esp. in phr. *pomp and pride'* – *OED, Pomp* sb., 1 and 3 *c.* 1325–1772; and (iii) Circumstance: 'The "ado" made about anything; formality, ceremony . . . ' – *OED* sb., II.7. These characteristics are preceded by *all Qualitie* and succeeded by *of glorious Warre. Qualitie* seems to be a classifier meaning something like 'properties' (after *OED* sb., II.9a). *Pride, Pompe, and Circumstance,* then, becomes a parenthesis: it defines what essentially the glories of *glorious Warre* have been for Othello.

This is all most odd. We hear a eulogy of war that includes nothing of the exploits summarised in Othello's abstract to the Council. It becomes even odder when one considers the extent to which this already strong marking for ceremony and display is further strengthened. Like *Ambition, glorious* has a connotation that may help our understanding of Othello. The primary meaning – Othello's meaning – is 'entitling to brilliant and lofty renown; conspicuously honourable' (*OED* adj., 3b); but a secondary meaning, 'ostentatious, fond of splendour; proud, haughty; vainglorious' (adj., 1 [1382 – *ante* 1734]), might also have been present in a contemporary audience's minds as Shakespeare, probably, comments on his hero's propensity for parade.

Consider, further, Othello's soldiers. The most important thing about the *Troopes* is, apparently, their being *plumed* – that is, their wearing birds' feathers on their helmets. Of course, just as the *Royall Banner* would be used as a mustering- or rallying-point, so the plumes would be signals of identity. But in neither *plumed* nor *Banner* is this tactical function described. The fact that the plumes are syntactically fixed to the soldiers and only by implication to their helmets suggests the overall splendour of the troops, who, together with the banner – presumably carried by Iago's predecessor as ensign – are seen by Othello as emblems of himself. The psychology of military dress suggests something of the *OED*'s 'in pretentious display' (*Plume* sb., 1b); and the troops, their heights increased by their plumes, in turn augment their general. They increase visually his command and his importance. Heilman's 'a theatrical war, an affair of parade and pageant', is not necessarily exact: Othello's imagination may well be seeing his troops advancing into battle before their plumes have been cut and smirched. But certainly much of Othello's military pride – within this speech at least – seems to have been associated with the publishings of military display.[5]

When, that is, it has not been associated with the noise that the *bigge* wars make. This noise most definitely is not of a mere parade. The steed, presumably, neighs from fear and pain. The trumpet shrills as a signal of military manoeuvre: Charge, Regroup. Its unpleasantly high pitch Othello no doubt has preferred to the effeminate, base chamberer's music of the lute and viol – as he has also, no doubt, the similarly sharp, almost wounding, sound of the *Eare-piercing Fife*. All these noises are the aural equivalent of the 'flinty and Steele Coach of Warre' (F578; I.iii.230): they indicate difficulty, danger, physical discomfort. Only the *Spirit-stirring Drum*, an instrument whose rhythmic music could be used to steady advancing troops, has a sound pleasant as well as military. As for the *mortall Engines* (doubly mortal in being both 'deadly' and themselves subject to the imperfection of earthly existence in contrast to the immortal and rustless Jove – *OED, Mortal* adj., 2 and 1), they are heard for the dreadfulness (in F) or the greatness (in Q) of their sound and not at all for the effect their shot might have on the enemy. They are made stylistically 'noisier', too, by being apostrophised: the only objects of farewell to be preceded by *you* instead of *the*. This directness of address might suggest a special affinity felt by Othello with the cannon. The uncouth coughing in their *rude throates* is not to be equated with Othello's humorously and inaccurately claimed rudeness of speech – which is rude only in being more vigorous and original than courtly and conventional utterance – but they might be dear to Othello in their attempting to realise on earth a godlike sound. *Counterfet* here means 'simulate, resemble . . . (Without implying deceit)' (*OED, Counterfeit* v., 7). The cannon are, as it were, idealistic cannon. The ingenuity of these engines consists in their expressing the most godlike military noise of all. Othello directly addresses what is most symbolic of himself.

According to this speech, then, wars have provided for Othello's visual and aural extension of himself – for self-publication. It is as if, in *Henry V*, the military life was all about the Dauphin's noble palfrey and the Constable's armour (*The Life of Henry the Fift*, F1626ff.; III.vii.1ff.) and included nothing of the facts of battle exemplified in Williams' talk of 'all those Legges, and Armes, and Heads, chopt off in a Battaile' (F1983–4; IV.i.134–5). It is as if soldiers such as Falstaff and Pistol had never campaigned ignobly on the London stage. Even Sidney, the epitome of the honourable Renaissance soldier, detailed the actual horrors of war when he wrote *Arcadia*. Amphialus, having received 'upon the belly so horrible a wound that his guts came out withal . . . pulled up his [enemy's] vizor, meaning with his dagger to give him death'. But such realities do not feature in Othello's vision of his military past. Nor does any sense of tactical reality, of soldiers actually doing their job, following their occupation. The troops, for example, are not seen in conjunction with the neighing steeds as cavalry (*OED, Troop* sb., 3: 'a subdivision of a cavalry regiment commanded by a captain, corresponding to a company of foot and a battery of artillery') possessing the great tactical advantage, in Sidney's words in *The Defence of Poesie*, of being 'speedie goers, and strong abiders'. They are merely deployed as part of an inventoried military accoutrement by which Othello has been noised and seen abroad.[6]

By means of which, also, Othello found *the Tranquill minde* and *Content*. *Tranquill* (the *OED* claims this as the adjective's first appearance) denotes not a circumstance but a deep centre of stillness in Othello's soul as the world turns about him. In the midst of all the noise and spectacle – by implication – Othello's tranquillity used to deepen. It may, indeed, have been created by it. This paradox – of peace discovered in war's commotion – links with Othello's alacrity in hardness, his liking for the flinty and steel premise of the military life. And this, in combination, strongly suggests the conflict, or at least the unease, that Othello has experienced in times of peace. If men can make war, climb indifferent mountains, traverse impersonal deserts, rather than suffer the difficulties of the interpersonal life with women, then Othello's vocation may be a fearful as well as an honourable one. If an absolute idealism is a refuge from the sometimes messy business of human dealing, then it may be that Othello's idealistic career has been a campaign less to fulfil than to avoid himself. The emphasis in this speech on the externals of an army – its spectacle and noise – suggests perhaps the comfort that a deeply uncertain Othello has required and which, away from war, he has lacked. One remembers at this point that Othello, at a moment of utmost peace in the play – the Turks dispersed, his wife in his arms – yet voiced apprehensions about unknown Fate, about a future lack of absolute content (II.i). Perhaps those apprehensions – incomprehensible to everyone – can be explained as Othello's fears, always experienced but never confronted, about his own capacities in a human relationship not ruled by military necessities.

Iago's question 'is't possible my Lord?' can therefore be answered. Yes, it is indeed possible for a soldier's occupation to go when the promiscuity of his wife is commonly known and the soldier's own happy state of *nothing knowne* is ended; when that occupation has done so much to seat the soldier's otherwise insecure self – a self now drastically *un*seated; and when that occupation has expressed so much of a compensating and idealising *pre*-occupation with what Herman Melville, writing about Nelson, termed the 'ornate publication of his person in battle'.[7] Othello's ideal figure of himself *and* his public figure – both these have been damaged (as he thinks):

> My name that was as fresh
> As Dians Visage, is now begrim'd and blacke
> As mine owne face.
>
> (F2032–4; III.iii.390–2)

Those editors who emend *My name* to 'Her name' on the strength of *Dians Visage* but not on F's authority (the sentence does not exist in Q) present an acceptable reading but, I think, do not emphasise enough the sentiment brought forward from the 'Occupation' speech. Othello is concerned more for his own name than for Desdemona's.[8] Furthermore, if one hears rather more of an exclamation in Iago's *Is't possible my Lord?* then one can register why. For Othello's speech has great force. This quality derives from the liguistic decorum – the informing of manner by matter – that Shakespeare has preserved. Othello takes leave of the military means to self-publication in a passage that is itself a lengthy and assured piece of self-publication. We have, in fact, a kind of decorous bombast, in which the extension of Othello by the sights and sounds of army life is reflected by the 'pompus' tautology and by the commanding repetition of *Farewell*. I am not suggesting that the speech overall is bombastic – it is far removed from that. But bombast *is* language padded out, as clothes are with cottonwool, to increase its 'size'; and Iago's report of Othello's style on another occasion as 'a bumbast Circumstance, / Horribly stufft with Epithites of warre' (F17–18; I.i.13–14) *is* lexically germane in regard to the 'stuffing' effect of *Ambition, Pride, Pompe, Circumstance*.

The next piece of self-publishing by Othello is in the 'Ponticke Sea' extended simile. This too is based on a certainty of Desdemona's guilt. It would appear that the conditional of 'If thou dost slander her, and torture me' (F2012; III.iii.372) and the uncertainty of 'I thinke my Wife be honest, and thinke she is not' (F2030; III.iii.388) have been cancelled in Othello's need of conviction. He is prepared to accept Iago's

> If imputation, and strong circumstances,
> Which lead directly to the doore of Truth,
> Will giue you satisfaction, you might haue't.
>
> (F2054–6; III.iii.410–12)

Now, *imputation* here is 'opinion founded on strong circumstantial evidence' (Schmidt 1); but the *liuing reason* or vital proof demanded and obtained – the reports of Cassio's dream and his having the handkerchief – is not received by Othello as evidence merely circumstantial. His demand for ocular proof, his command 'Make me to see't' (F2008; III.iii.3689) or at least provide an equivalent proof, were stated in terms of the sensible and true avouch of Othello's own eyes. But when Othello then responds to hearsay and reported circumstantial evidence with 'Now do I see 'tis true' (F2094; III.iii.448) one has to surmise a special kind of sight in Othello.

Othello has *not* seen it is true. The external authority he needs so much and which he discerns in Iago's honesty – among other things – has made Iago's eyes and vision into his own. His compulsive drive from *Would* to *will* and his entertainment of Iago's *may* in

> OTHELLO.   Would I were satisfied.
> IAGO.   . . .
>   You would be satisfied?
> OTHELLO.   Would? Nay, and I will.
> IAGO. And may
>
> (F2036–41; III.iii.394–8)

have led him into fallacy. Imputation in itself *has* become proof. Indictment, or charging, has become conviction. The process is similar to that of the brawl-scene, in which Cassio was cashiered as a result of Iago's eyes acting as a deputy for Othello's. There is this important difference, however: Othello did actually see some of the brawl but has seen nothing of Desdemona's revolt.

The 'Ponticke Sea' simile, based then on a conviction of Desdemona's guilt, extends Othello's earlier disclaimer of indecisiveness – *Why? why is this?/Think'st thou, I'ld make a Life of Iealousie . . . ?'* – discussed above (pp. 127ff.). The provocation then was in the *euer* of Iago's insinuation of Othello as 'him that euer feares he shall be poore'. Here it is in Iago's 'Patience I say: your mind may change.' Intolerant of any suggestion that he might be less than an instant avenger, Othello protests his decisiveness with, characteristically, an utterance structured to some degree on the forceful repetition of a single word. In this instance, *neuer:*

> Neuer Iago. Like to the Ponticke Sea,
> Whose Icie Current, and Compulsiue course,
> Neu'r keepes retyring ebbe, but keepes due on
> To the Proponticke, and the Hellespont:
> Euen so my bloody thoughts, with violent pace
> Shall neu'r looke backe, neu'r ebbe to humble Loue,
> Till that a capeable, and wide Reuenge,
> Swallow them vp. Now by yond Marble Heauen,
> In the due reuerence of a Sacred vow,
> I heere engage my words.
>
> (F2103–12; III.iii.457–66)

The simile itself, from *Like to* to *them vp*, together with the phrase *Now by yond Marble Heauen*, is not in Q. This may be an omission for 'practical rather than artistic considerations' (Walker, p. 123); or, alternatively, the F text may represent 'the prodigal afterthought of a great poet', as Swinburne thought.[9] Certainly, Q has a considerably lesser interest. Without the references to water and to heaven Othello's oath becomes as bathetic as Iago's succeeding

> Witnesse you euer-burning Lights aboue,
> You Elements, that clip vs round about

– whereas, one feels a contrast was intended. The simile, far from being in Pope's words 'an unnatural excursion in this place', or exemplifying, as Steevens thought, Shakespeare's liking to 'display his knowledge of Holland's *Pliny*',[10] is essentially a signal by Shakespeare of how his hero's mind is working. Othello is not strolling in a Pope-ish – or Iagoist – garden along paths of reason; he is ranging in a wilderness made rank and gross by monsters. And Shakespeare, rather than publishing himself, is as unobtrusive in *Othello* as he usually is. The simile is characteristically Othello's at this juncture of the play in that, as in the 'Occupation' speech, its syntax suggests much mental organisation when one might have expected some disordering caused by doubt. The three soundings of *neuer* in the simile, and the single sounding that precedes it, contribute to this organisation. So too does the thoroughly well-ordered fit of the clauses.

Main clause 1: 'Like to the Ponticke Sea, . . . Euen so my bloody thoughts, with violent pace / Shall neu'r looke backe'.
Main clause 2: '[They shall] neu'r ebbe to humble Loue'.
Adjectival Clause 1: 'Whose Icie Current, and Compulsiue Course, / Neu'r keepes retyring ebbe'.
Adjectival clause 2: 'but keepes due on / To the Proponticke, and the Hellespont'.
Adverbial time clause: 'Till that a capeable, and wide Reuenge,/ Swallow them vp'.

(I define main clause 2 on the basis that *humble* is an adjective not a verb.) Bradley mentioned that the image of the tideless and rushing sea belonged with Othello's talk of the Arabian trees and the pearl in his final speech: in fact, it belongs rather with the empty antres and the idle deserts of Othello's speech to the Council. It belongs in the moral landscape of Othello's travels. Shaw missed the point when he famously observed, 'if Othello cannot turn his voice into a thunder and surge of passage, he will achieve nothing but a ludicrously misplaced bit of geography'.[11] It is the virtuous compulsion of the sea that Othello admires. He regards this as a moral force and is glad to liken it to his own temperament. In so doing, of course, he betrays the primitive nature of his intellect. He thinks – one surmises – that in comparing himself with a natural force he is making himself sublime. In fact, he expresses his degradation. All this mental organisation – all those *neuer*s and that syntactical precision – includes no use of the safer guides, the best judgment. Othello is to become far more *Like to*, far more *Euen so* as, a mass of unfeeling element than he realises in his comparison. He is very soon to act as a passive, compelled, unreasoning force, descended in the hierarchy of Nature to an elemental insensitivity.

This is not to say, however, that Shakespeare is presenting, in Leavis's phrases, 'The disguise of an obtuse and brutal egotism' or 'stupidity, ferocious stupidity'. Shakespeare is presenting much more, and far more subtly, than Leavis's extreme language declares. One critic who discerns this subtlety is Melchiori, whose definitions of the simile as 'a single formal figure of comparison' and as 'a last attempt at disguising an alien passion in a classical pattern' are far more apt. Of particular interest, I think, are the words *single formal* and *attempt*;[12] and I wish now to consider Othello's speech as an example of a trope popular amongst Jacobean and early-Caroline poets in its potential for wit and illumination.

Those poets were capable, when they wished, of maintaining a strict exactitude throughout their extended comparisons. George Herbert, for example:

> But to all,
> Who thinke me eager, hot, and undertaking,
> But in my prosecutions slack and small;
> As a young exhalation, newly waking,
> Scorns his first bed of dirt, and means the sky;
> But cooling by the way, grows pursie and slow,
> And setling to a cloud, doth live and die
> In that dark state of tears: to all, that so
> Show me, and set me, I have one reply,
> Which they that know the rest, know more then I.
>
> ('The Answer', 5–14)[13]

Here the aspiration and the falling-short of a poet or religious acolyte are worked within the accurately observed natural process of vaporisation and condensation – the result being that the *dark state* expresses, with the utmost ease, both the black continent of rainclouds and the author's tears. Not only Herbert's artistry but also his 'scientific' seeing (the two are probably related) lifts the poem far above the conventionality of a rain – tears equation.

Or, for example, John Donne:

> If they be two, they are two so
> As stiff twin compasses are two,
> The soul the fixed foot, makes no show
> To move, but doth, if th'other do.
>
> And though it in the centre sit,
> Yet when the other far doth roam,
> It leans, and hearkens after it,
> And grows erect, as that comes home.
>
> Such wilt thou be to me, who must
> Like th'other foot, obliquely run;
> Thy firmness makes my circle just,
> And makes me end, where I begun.
>
> ('A Valediction forbidding Mourning')[14]

I choose these familiar lines (the last three stanzas of the poem) for their extreme precision. The pair of compasses parallels the couple formed by the pair of souls; and the movement of *th'other* – an oblique running – describes not only a soul-mate's return along the shortest distance of a radius but also a cycle, that of birth and death as raised in the first stanza's 'As virtuous men pass mildly away'. There is too an intellectual play upon the opposition between the immaterial souls' refinement and the material mathematical instrument – which opposition is then resolved in the abstract purpose of the *circle just* for which the instrument is designed. Another fine play is on adverbial *home*, first as a domestic 'to its home' and secondly as 'accurately' or 'closely' in a mathematically measuring kind of way. The point (I do not intend the pun) is this: that Donne, having exactly observed the two movements that the free foot of the compasses can make, uses them to make exact comparisons throughout his conceit.

Or, for a last example, take Shakespeare himself:

HAMLET. Why looke you now, how vnworthy a thing you make
of me: you would play vpon mee; you would seeme to know
my stops: you would pluck out the heart of my Mysterie;
you would sound mee from my lowest Note, to the top of
my Compasse: and there is much Musicke, excellent Voice,
in this little Orgone, yet cannot you make it [Second
Quarto *speak*). Why do you thinke, that I am easier to bee
plaid on, then a Pipe? Call me what Instrument you
will, though you can fret me, you cannot play vpon me.
(*The Tragedie of Hamlet, Prince of Denmarke,*
F2234–42; III.ii.354–63)

In this there is a complex relation of Hamlet to the recorder, of the
recorder's being played to the attempts by Rosencrantz and Guildenstern to sound the Prince. There are further dramatic con-
gruities. Musical instruments, *Hoboyes*, introduced the play-
within-a-play recently curtailed; and the *Pipe* that Hamlet refers to
itself subscribes to a scheme of imagery begun by Hamlet's observation on Horatio:

> And blest are those,
> Whose Blood and Iudgement are so well co-mingled,
> That they are not a Pipe for Fortunes finger,
> To sound what stop she please.
> (F1919–22; III.ii.66–9)

Shakespeare's control of the comparison with which Hamlet
censures Guildernstern is particularly demonstrated in this: that
when he wishes to exploit the pun in *fret* he allows for this change
from a wind- to a stringed-instrument by giving Hamlet the pre-
paratory *Call me what Instrument you will*. The extended tropical
justness is thus maintained – and, of course, expresses the intellectual sensitivity that Shakespeare has written into many of
Hamlet's lines.

Given that such writing was possible, and usual, one can discern
the more clearly certain instances in Othello's simile where a
tropical justness is not sustained.[15] When Othello describes his
thoughts as *bloody* he means not only the murderous intent but also
the provocation by blood as 'passion' (*OED, Blood* sb., II) – as in 'My
blood begins my safer Guides to rule' (F1325; II.iii.197). That is, the
bloody thoughts continue not only Othello's immediately preceding

'Oh blood, blood, blood' but also his preoccupation with the base instinctive part of himself suppressed or avoided in his wars and travels. From these two meanings a double warmth ensues. The thoughts are violently or hotly moving. They are also hot-blooded. And in their heat the equating of the thoughts with the Pontic Sea, whose current is 'extremely cold' or 'Abounding in, or characterized by the presence of, ice' (*OED, Icy* adj., 3 and 1), becomes odd. There is distemperature. Not until the murder-scene itself, in his vague defining of an intellectually justifiable cause, does Othello think in *sang froid* – and then only for a short while. Here too, of course, as in 'It is the Cause . . . ', he is trying to sanction his revenge, by equating it in this instance with the cold, natural and unstoppable virtue of Pontus. But in this equation – or attempt at equation – he either overlooks or ignores an essential dissimilarity between the current of the sea and the current of his thoughts. In the attempt to achieve an extension of his simile – in the attempt extensively to publish himself as a man of cold reason – he compromises intentionally or not with truth. His simile is formally and strongly announced: *Like to . . . Euen so.* Any counter-currents of meaning will be swept away or turned back by the compulsiveness that supplies the simile's main – indeed the only – point of parity. The simile thus forms a linguistic simulacrum of Othello's mental process: a process in which even the possibility of doubt will be overriden by the need of certainty and action. Just as the Sea's current is both active and passive, both compelling and compulsive (*OED, Compulsive* adj., 2 and 1), so too is the *violent pace* of the thoughts – *violent* expressing not only 'great physical force' and 'some degree of rapidity' but also the being 'Due or subject to constraint or force; not free or voluntary; forced' (*OED* adj., A I.4b and 5b [the latter dated 1560–1667]). Othello again contrives that his drive to a bloody revenge shall partake of the same virtue as drives Pontus.

I would not stress so much the disparity between *Icie* and *bloody* were its suggestion of wrong thinking not supported elsewhere in the simile. There are further instances at which the two sides of the figure do not close with the precision emphatically demanded by *Like to . . . Euen so.* Consider, for example, the implied synonymity of the thoughts' returning in *ebbe* with the action declared in *retyring ebbe* (the sea). In ebbing the sea would retire backwards. It would recede. In closely considering how or why the thoughts might do so – instead of pacing back in a more usual way to humble love – one might consider that the precision so formally announced in *Like to* . . . *Euen so* is less evident than in Donne's compass comparison, or in Herbert's parallel with precipitation, or in Shakespeare's trope on the pipe – all of which are effected with much less of ceremonious fuss.

Again, dissimilitude exists in the fact that the Pontic Sea, though tributary to the Propontic and the Hellespont, yet keeps it own identity as a geographical tract of water; while the bloody thoughts are to lose their existence on being swallowed up by the capable and wide revenge. There is much emphasis on this disappearance. *Capeable* is 'Able to take in, receive' (*OED, Capable* adj., 1). *Swallow* . . . *vp* is 'engulf utterly' (*OED, Swallow* v., 10). *Capeable, and wide* (in which *wide* means 'capacious' and 'inclusive' as well as 'extensive' – *OED* adj., 1) doubles up on the sheer capacity of Othello's revenge. From this disappearance too there derives a contradiction: the thoughts, having so throughly been swallowed would not be able to ebb anyway. One assumes that Othello here is using his customary mode of absurd asseveration to exert a savage irony. The thoughts will never return; under a virtuous compulsion they will rush to their predestined conclusion and so die.

It is also possible to wonder why Shakespeare chose *pace* to equate with the Sea's *Current* and *course*. The word was, of course, closer to its Latin origin in Shakespeare's time than it is today; and *Passus* is literally a 'stretch of the legs' (see *OED, Pace* sb.). With the exceptions of 'speed, velocity' and 'movement, motion' (sb.[1], III. 7b and II.4c [the latter dated *c*.1386–*c*.1611]) the various meanings available to Shakespeare seem to derive from the primary meaning of 'A single separate movement made by the leg in walking, running, or dancing; a step' (I.1). A clear demonstration of the animal movement expressed in the word is in Rosalind's 'Time trauels in diuers paces, with diuers persons: Ile tel you who Time ambles withall, who Time trots withall, who Time gallops withall, and who he stands stil withall' (*As you Like it*, F1498–501; III.ii.291–3), where the various paces are 'The action, or (usually) manner, of stepping' and the 'Rate of stepping' (II.4 and 7). Again, Macbeth's 'Creepes in this petty pace' (*The Tragedie of Macbeth*, F2341; V.v.20) denotes yet another way in which time, or a sequence of tomorrows, might transport itself as if on legs. Given all this, it is possible that Shakespeare chose *pace* specifically for its association with legs and feet – an association that Schmidt discerns in all but one of Shakespeare's uses – and for its resultant incongruity with the *current* and *course* of Pontus. That is to say, the thoughts of Othello become so many legged monsters, never looking back but striding as it were along the shores of the Pontic Sea towards a vast cave called Revenge into which, abruptly, they will vanish, legs and all. As such earth-treading creatures they would be *un*like to the Pontic Sea.

None of these dissimilarities would be significant on its own. Their accumulation, however, seems to declare a conscious omission in Shakespeare to make true the agreement of Othello's simile. The kinship of *Compulsiue* with *violent* does not extend into the other parallels. The whole extended simile, in fact, seems to have been written by Shakespeare as an example of Othello's failure to exercise his best judgement. And, when one considers the characteristic commanding organisation that Othello maintains, one begins to consider the figure as a model for his mentality overall. In trying to convince Iago that his mind will never change, Othello publishes himself, with formal strength, in such a way that no awareness of dissimilarity is allowed to qualify the identification of himself with a sublime or natural force or cause. This pattern of thought inside the simile reflects the larger pattern outside: no doubt or inquiry is to be allowed a chance of diminishing Othello's conviction of Desdemona's guilt, his neurotic need of immediate activity. Moreover, a certain bombast, already heard in a part of the 'Occupation' speech, is present here. In *Icie Current, and Compulsiue course* the nouns are semantically though not metrically interchangeable: they both denote movement in a particular direction (see *OED, Current* sb., 1 and *Course* sb., 2). *Course* is used quite often by Othello: the sun that courses its compasses (at F2220; III.iv.71) has a sublime compulsion akin to that of Pontus; while in the 'brothel' scene the reduction of a *course* to brothel-business is effected by Othello with a savage sarcasm. Here, however, emphasis rather than differentiation is served by the doublet – as it is also in the already discussed *capeable, and wide*. Not only does this padded language augment Othello's linguistic 'size'; it also takes up room that might have been occupied by a more 'thoughtful' lexicon and syntax. By tautology, by over-protestation, Othello keeps doubt out.[16]

A Pontus-like movement continues in:

> Now by yond Marble Heauen,
> In the due reuerence of a Sacred vow,

    I heere engage my words.

Schmidt, emending both F and Q to 'word', reads *engage* as
'pledge'. But Othello is not merely pledging his word *to* anything or
anyone – not even to Iago. Rather, he is engaging his words *in* the
vow's reverence, in the sense of enlisting or binding his simile in
the moral obligation of a sacred vow (Schmidt 3 and 2; *OED* v., 4).
As the thoughts are to enter revenge and to be utterly spent therein,
and as the Pontic Sea flooded into a more capacious sea (though,
one needs to add, retaining its own identity), so the mundane
words of the simile arise and enter a high oath by which they are
consecrated. In the actual oath Othello calls heaven *Marble* because,
like his own mind, it will not change. (Schmidt has of *Marble* 'Used
of the heavens (on account of their eternity)'. Walker, p. 234, has
'inexorable'.) By association Othello's mind becomes sublimely
immutable. The oath is an engine by means of which Othello's
revenge is tossed upwards to the cradle of a respectable cause. It
becomes important, therefore, in rehearsing the mental process by
which Othello achieves the deceptive assertion of 'It is the
Cause . . . ' in the final act. It becomes even more important when
one remembers how selective were the thinkings by which Othello
contrived to develop those *words* into the simile.

    Othello's next lengthy piece of self-publication is 'Had it pleas'd
Heauen, / To try me with Affliction . . . '. First, however, I wish to
examine two earlier passages – the 'epilepsy' speech, and Othello's
comments when encaved. These are not promulgatory; they are
famous, indeed, for not being characteristic of the Othello heard so
far; but they contain much of interest.

    The early part of the 'epilepsy' speech appears in both F and Q:

> Lye with her? lye on her? We say lye on her, when they
> be-lye-her. Lye with her: that's fullsome [Q *lye with her,*
> *Zouns, that's fulsome*]: Handkerchiefe: Confessions: Handker-
> chiefe [Q *handkerchers, Confession, hankerchers (sic)*].
>
> (F2412–14; IV.i.35–7)

Othello's harping on *lye* is a quick response to Iago's proffering –
deliberately vague but terse – of *Lye* as the verb used by Cassio in
defining what he did with Desdemona. Compare this response
with earlier quick takings by Othello of Iago's lexical bait: I have in
mind 'think', 'thoughts' and 'know' (F1700ff.; III.iii.98ff.), to which

may be added Iago's speaking hesitations, so speedily seized on by Othello. What Iago does is utter a word laden with apparent significance; Othello immediately lays siege to it, attempting a direct explication of that significance. Othello's response to *Lye* is not therefore, an isolate; it is the strongest instance so far of several such instances – as such it helps to reveal the consistency of Shakespeare's characterisation. Again, it also contributes to the scheme of honesty and lying, truth and slander, that informs so much of the play (and to which even the Clown has contributed with 'for me to say a Souldier lyes, 'tis stabbing' – F2142; III.iv.4.

Most important in the lines, however, is the way that Shakespeare has 'structured' Othello's incoherence by retaining in it one of Othello's major speech characteristics. This particular characteristic is the use of frequent single-word repetitions – I have had occasion several times to note it as a major structuring-device in Othello's utterance. Shakespeare's mad language usually has sense, though not rational argument; and here the incoherence is cohered, as it were, by the simple repetition not only of *lye* but of *Handkerchiefe* and *Confessions* as well. Othello's meaning, in his obsession with *lye*, ranges between that of untruth and that of a sexual knowing; while *be-lye* seems to mean 'calumniate' (*OED*, *Belie* v.², 2); or 'give the lie to, call false, contradict as a lie or a liar; to reject as false, deny the truth of (v.², 5 [1577–1649]); or possibly 'lie around, encompass' (v.¹, 1 [obsolete in *OED*'s record by 1627]). The verb *Lye with* has here, of course, the meaning of 'have sexual intercourse with' (*OED*, *Lie* v.¹, B 1f); for Othello, therefore, the idea of Cassio's lying with Desdemona must be *fullsome*, i.e. morally foul and obscene (*OED*, *Fulsome* adj., 6).[17]

The view summarised by Hart (p. 181n) – 'the Lines here are . . . the disjointed ravings of one on the confines of insanity' – needs, then, some qualification. Disjointed, yes, in the lack of an articulated, jointed syntax. But, just as the utterance is simplified, so that a characteristic lexical repetition comes virtually to *be* the utterance, so Othello's imagination is rendered down, concentrated, so that its basic obsessiveness becomes powerfully clear.

The second part of the 'epilepsy' speech is in F alone:

> To confesse, and be hang'd for his labour. First, to be hang'd, and then to confesse: I tremble at it. Nature would not inuest her selfe in such shadowing passion, without some Iustruction [*sic*]. It is not words that shakes me thus, (pish) Noses,

Eares, and Lippes: is't possible. Confesse? Handkerchiefe? O
diuell.   *Falls in a Traunce.*   (F2414–20; IV.i.37–43)

Of *confesse, and be hang'd for his labour* Walker (p. 195n) writes, 'A
proverbial phrase of obscure origin (*OED confess* 10) = to tell a gross
lie (connected therefore with the quibble on 'lie on' and 'belie'
. . .). Othello is also thinking of Cassio's confession of guilt and the
penalty to be paid.' Some disjointing of sense occurs in Othello's
talk of a judicial punishment when already the private murder of
Cassio has been proposed: 'Within these three days let me heare
thee say, / That Cassio's not aliue' (F2124–5; III.iii.476–7) – but
perhaps Othello is thinking of himself, here as later, as a judge
dispensing punishment. On the whole it is savagery as much as
confusion that is expressed. The phrase *for his labour* is particularly
strong, with a gloating kind of wit. *Labour* is toil, especially when
painful or compulsory (*OED* sb., 1) – so Othello is probably en-
visaging the judicial torturing of Cassio. When Othello published
his stories to Desdemona he was given kisses or sighs 'for my
paines'; when Cassio will have enforcedly published his crime he
will, as a reward for *his* pains, be executed. Again, savagery rather
than confusion alone prompts the reversal of 'First, to be hang'd,
and then to confesse'. Cassio is to have no shriving-time – like
Rosencrantz and Guildenstern he must die unconfessed and
damned since, obviously, he cannot confess after death. The
reversal also prefigures Othello's travesty of justice, a process by
which the accused are sentenced and punished in Othello's closed
'court' without being given a chance to defend.

All this savage emotion makes Othello shake before he falls. But
no matter how vehemently an actor may speak the *Nature would
not* . . . sentence there is no way he can justly disjoint the meaning. This could well be the sententia of a grave signior deliberating
in council, and not the prelude to a fit. I discussed the sentence in
Chapter 3 with reference to Othello's need of an external authority;
here one notes that almost to the very moment of Othello's physical
collapse his publication and coherence are maintained. True, the
tonic segments are longer on the whole, so that the sentence is rapid
and lacks the power to detain us as Othello's blank verse does; but
still the references belong in various themes of the play. *Inuest* as
'besiege' or, indeed, 'attack' (*OED, Invest* v., I.7 [first recorded use
1600]) is more strongly appropriate than the more usually understood 'dress' in view of Othello's occupation hitherto and his pre-

sent bloody thoughts; while *shadowing passion* not only denotes Othello's mental eclipse by blood and passion but also links with the double eclipse and natural disorder mooted immediately after Desdemona'd death. Additionally, in the extension of *It is not words that shakes me thus* Othello is made to sound one of the central themes of the play – that words *are* more than words alone and can pierce a bruised heart with signified reality. In one sense it is Iago's reports and interpretations, Iago's wordplay and lexical nudges, that have increasingly moved Othello; in another the moving agent is not the words but Othello's predisposition to listen to and act on them. So, as far as (*pish*), Othello is made to speak within sense. He can be understood. He makes sense. Indeed, even after (*pish*) Shakespeare makes his utterance relative to other things in the play. For example *is't possible* echoes Iago's reaction to the 'Occupa-tion' speech, 'Is't possible my Lord?' F has no question mark after Othello's clause; but with or without one Othello is heard as still speaking and shaking under Iago's influence. He comments, in effect, on Iago's remembered question, 'Yes, such monstrous things *are* possible.' Meanwhile, in the syntactical reduction of *Noses, Eares, and Lippes* one can hear not only Othello's desire to slice off the named organs but also a larger scheme whereby throughout the play the body is described with synecdoche in terms of a particular part.[18] What Shakespeare has written for Othello, in fact, is not so much disjointed ravings as an obsession that reduces Othello's vision and is reflected in the reductions of syntax and lexicon. Othello is still essentially himself, but com-pressed, diminished finally into the 'Lethargie' that in Iago's words must have its 'quyet course'. This lethargy is the welcoming river of Lethe, in whose oblivion Othello's overtaxed mind can find escape for a while. Thus he is saved by a natural intervention. In his *Traunce* he crosses (*trans*) to another state. Of course, the stage direction does not necessarily have authorial authority – according to Schmidt, 'trance' is a rare word in Shakespeare – but *Traunce* as 'ecstasy' (*OED, Trance* sb., 3b) is highly suggestive. For 'ecstasy' itself, derived from Greek meaning 'displacement' and late Greek meaning 'trance', signifies a 'morbid state characterized by uncon-sciousness' such as 'catalepsy' (*OED, Ecstasy* 2 [obsolete 1647]). The stage direction therefore includes not only a sense of Othello's ecstasy or exit from himself but also a part of Iago's diagnosis, 'My Lord in falne into an Epilepsie / This is his second Fit: he had one yesterday' (F2429–30; IV.i.50–1).

Given Iago's character, it is understandable that some people have disbelieved this diagnosis. It is certainly more to Iago's purpose to announce epilepsy than to state the truth to Cassio – that he, Iago, has been slandering Cassio and Desdemona and that Othello's fit has been caused specifically by shock and emotional distress. And in 1860 a writer on Shakespeare's medical knowledge declared the diagnosis to be 'mere falsehood'. Shakespeare makes Iago describe the 'maniacal excitement which so often follows the fit' caused by the falling-sickness, but, 'When Cassio has been persuaded to withdraw, Iago applies to the patient himself the truthful and correct designation of his morbid state.'[19] Again, though it is possible that Othello inclines to choke with emotion – as on landing on Cyprus and reuniting with Desdemona ('I cannot speake enough of this content, / It stoppes me heere: it is too much of ioy' – (F977–8; II.i.194–5) – there is no evidence in the play that anything in Othello's psyche can be directly attributed to a pathological cause or to any epileptically associated demonaic possession. He is quick to adopt the ruse of a 'paine vpon my Forehead' and of a 'salt and sorry Rhewme' (F1918 and 2196; III.iii.288 and IV.i.48), but this derives from a sense of cuckoldry and of abused love-tokens more than from a (probably suggested) predisposition to headaches. Othello cannot be identified with any generalised malaise, let alone one particular sickness – the plague of great ones is of course imagined and metaphorical: cuckoldry. In this he is unlike Iago, whose choice of imagery might signify an actual ulcerous condition. Iago speaks of a thought that 'Doth (like a poysonous Minerall) gnaw my Inwardes' and of dangerous conceits that 'Burne like the Mines of Sulphure' (F1079–80 and 1966ff.; II.i.290–1 and III.iii.330ff.).[20]

Despite all this, however, I do believe Iago; and the grounds of my belief are supplied in a short paper, 'Othello's Epilepsy', by John P. Emery. This demonstrates that Othello does suffer several specifically epileptic symptoms. Iago asks if Othello has not hurt his head – which suggests the suddenness of Othello's fall and the likelihood of injury. Also, Othello seems to be unaware of his fall – he suspects a mocking reference to cuckoldry's horns in Iago's question: 'Dost thou mocke me?' he asks (F2439; IV.i.60). Again, the epileptic personality tends to be suspicious even without good cause. All these symptoms – suddenness of seizure, total amnesia afterwards, a general suspiciousness – are manifested by Othello, not merely described and attributed by Iago; and they therefore support with actual proof Iago's assertion of the other epileptic symptoms – a foaming at the mouth and a savage madness – that Othello is likely to suffer if the lethargy is not allowed its natural course. It seems, then, that Shakespeare is writing from acute observation and that epilepsy, the falling-sickness at least lexically appropriate in a fallen hero, is explicitly intended. Furthermore, Emery reads Othello's epileptic attack as itself an analogue of the sexual activity by which Othello is distressed; and he declares that the 'medical basis' for this is 'sound'. Modern medical science apparently finds that the tension and the spasms in epilepsy have a close parallel to the movements in and of the body that precede and derive from orgasm. The intuition of science, proved by modern equipment, and the intuition of Shakespeare expressed artistically, would seem to agree.

This argument becomes even more persuasive when one learns that an association of epilepsy with sex was current in Shakespeare's time. James VI of Scotland (later James I of England) owned, in 1580, a work that called sexual intercourse 'a minor epilepsy'; and Shakespeare may have seen a copy of this, or perhaps of another work that Emery cites as current at the time. Certainly the idea, if not the books themselves, had availability. And it seems very persuasive indeed that Shakespeare, who was capable of deploying a characteristic syntax to show his hero's sexual obsession, should also have consciously dramatised in Othello the most appropriate of disorders.[21]

One can register Othello's distress, then, not only as physiological and emotional but also as symbolic. Othello suffers from a falling-sickness of the spirit, from a subjection of his best judgement to blood and passion. Epilepsy is often caused by a toxic effect within the nervous system, and Othello's fall can be seen as a kind of spiritual epilepsy, a poisoning by the vapours of Iago's slanders. These are the narcotics or medicine by which Iago works insensibility in Othello's discrimination and then in Othello himself. For Ross (p. 161n) Othello's fall 'evokes "The Image of Prostration" conventional in the underlying morality play to demonstrate the fall of the once-virtuous beneath the foot of the devil or vice'. To this powerful emblematic image of actual bedevilment – in which Iago may actually place his foot on Othello prostrate – can be added the associations that an audience may have made in addition to the sexual ones. The physiological causes of epilepsy were not known in Shakespeare's day; and the sense of otherness, of the incomprehensible, of the compulsive (if not the convulsive), of something unnatural or even supernatural – this sense could well attach these characteristics to Othello's behaviour. Thus, Shakespeare is probably supplementing his audience's awareness of Othello as foreign to their understanding, an outlander, inside the actual and symbolic investment of his dark skin. Inside this exotic if austere warrior and traveller in far-off lands may be discerned a susceptibility to a frightening and foreign force.[22]

Shortly after Othello's fit comes the 'espial' scene. Just before this Shakespeare writes a little piece of manifesto to Iago:

> Do'st thou heare, Iago,
> I will be found most cunning in my Patience:
> But (do'st thou heare) most bloody.
>
> (F2472–4; IV.i.89–91)

It continues the self-publication of Othello, even to the degree of featuring a variant of *I must be found*. Othello does not merely announce he will be patient in his bloody revenge – thus denying Iago's charge of unmanly haste; he announces that other people, perhaps posterity, will find him to have been so. Once again his need to promulgate himself insistently to Iago is maintained, along with his acute awareness of the figure he makes, his good name. In the 'espial' scene itself, just as Othello is quick to find himself to Iago, so he is quick to supply the misinterpretations that Iago requires. At first, encaved as he is on the stage balcony or perhaps behind curtains, he is a visual witness only. He marks, in Iago's words, the fleers, gibes and notable scorns that dwell in every region of Cassio's face – it is as if poor Cassio's face has become a moving landscape of depravity. Othello interprets Cassio's smiles, gestures and light behaviour 'Quite in the wrong' (Iago: F2488; IV.i.103) by supplying only one meaning: that which strengthens his conviction and continues to exclude all doubt. When Cassio says of Bianca, 'Alas poore Rogue, I thinke indeed she loues me,' Othello's commentary – 'Now he denies it faintly: and laughs it out' (F2498; IV.i.112) – not only is inaccurate but omits to confess Othello's own inability to hear. Othello is stating once again in effect, 'Now do I see 'tis true', when in fact all he sees is the product of his own imagination working on Iago's words. The strength of his need to believe in those words leads him to discern an ocular proof where there is none and to support it with aural assumptions stated as facts.

At the sentence 'Iago beckons me' (Q2517; IV.i.129) it is possible that Othello's sense of hearing comes to supplement his sight. (*Beckons* is Q. F's *becomes* is usually read as corrupt, though it could mean, attractively, that Iago's actions are becoming to Othello's purpose.) According to Ridley (p. 143n) and Schmidt, when Iago beckons he is merely signalling that Othello should closely attend; but the text supports the aptness of *beckon* as 'summon' (*OED* v., 2), since Othello now comes so close he can over*hear* Cassio as well as overlook his gestures. The result is that Othello can complete one of Cassio's sentences (as he thinks):

> CASSIO . . . . I was the other day talking on the Sea-banke with certaine Venetians, and thither comes the Bauble, and falls me thus about my neck.
> OTHELLO. Crying oh deere Cassio, as it were: his iesture imports it.   (F2518–23; IV.i.131–5)

The ocular 'proof' of the gesture suggests Desdemona's words; but if, as seems probable, Othello does overhear the talk of Cassio's seabank encounter, then he has a further cause to feel the public smirching of his name. It is an expert piece of management by Shakespeare and by Iago. From now on Iago's plot depends on Cassio's use of *she* and *her*, instead of a betraying name, until Bianca's arrival. Then Cassio's "'Tis such another Fitchew' (F2532; IV.i.144) confirms Othello's belief that the first fitchew has been Desdemona. A fitchew was not only a 'wanton woman' (Schmidt) but also a polecat – the original meaning – one kind of which is the ferret used to hunt rats and drive out rabbits. A literal coney-catcher. For Othello, then, the word would most aptly describe a wife who hunts and tries to drive out her lover from a crowd of Venetians – particularly on the seashore which, according to Ross (p. 169n), 'As some in the original audience would have known . . . [was] where Cyprian girls were reputed to earn their dowries by prostitution.' (See *OED*, *Fitchew* 1; *Ferret* sb.[1].)

Given Othello's inclination to see what Iago wants him to, Othello's ready acceptance of the handkerchief as evidence is hardly suprising. True, the responses of 'By Heauen, that should be my Handkerchiefe' and 'Was that mine?' (F2544 and 2559; IV.i.155

and 170) seem to supply an implied supposition and an interrogative. The fact is, however, that Othello does not act upon them.
Also, of course, the question is put to Iago – another instance of
Othello's fatal reliance on his ancient's authority. Again, the ready
acceptance of the handkerchief as evidence is hardly surprising,
since the scene managed by Iago – with some help from fortune –
does dramatically realise before Othello the implications of an
earlier exchange:

> IAGO. Her honor is an Essence that's not seene,
>   They haue it very oft, that haue it not.
>   But for the Handkerchiefe.
>
> OTHELLO. By heauen, I would most gladly haue forgot it:
>   Thou saidst (oh, it comes ore my memorie,
>   As doth the Rauen o're the infectious house:
>   Boading to all) he had my Handkerchiefe.
>
> (F2388–94; IV.i.16–22)

Unlike *honor* in women, the handkerchief *can* be seen. Othello
obviously cannot forget it; and it returns to his mind, beating
through his preoccupation with unauthorised kisses and Desdemona naked with her friend abed. Like the raven it is a highly
visible bringer of ill news as it promulgates to all that the plague of
great ones has come to Othello in his housed condition, and that a
fatal event must shortly follow. (*Infectious* here means 'infected' –
OED adj., 3 [–1727].) In its fortuitious return by Bianca to Cassio
before Othello's very eyes, it seems to confirm everything that Iago
has said. Interestingly, Othello's apparent if temporary forgetting
of it, together with his use of *should* and of *Was that mine?*, might
well be intended by Shakespeare to remind us of the sheer flimsiness of the handkerchief's evidence. The possession of the handkerchief by Cassio does *not* have the oracular nature attributed to
the presence of a raven above a house. The tangible, droppable,
losable handkerchief is the only visual and actual piece of evidence
in Iago's case; but it rests upon a column of vapours without which
it would insignificantly fall. Even Othello, fleetingly, has a doubt
and needs to have the evidence confirmed by Iago. But then, again,
perhaps even Iago does not fully realise quite how much the ocular
proof of the handkerchief is supported by another proof: that which
Othello makes by an imaginative response to Iago's words.

Or perhaps by now Iago *does* realise it. With respect to Othello's imaginative response the following lines by Iago are very suggestive:

> his vnbookish Ielousie must conserue [Q *conster*]
> Poore Cassio's smiles, gestures, and light behauiours
> Quite in the wrong.
>
> (F2486–8; IV.i.101–39)

F's *conserue* may express something of the assiduity with which Othello seeks and hoards his proof. He will store and preserve Cassio's behaviour inside his certainty of Desdemona's guilt (*OED, Conserve* v., 1 and 2). But in Iago's sentence Q's *conster* or 'construe' seems to be the only sensible choice – particularly since the relevant page of F (quire vv 1) – was set by the miscorrecting Compositor B.[23] Iago says that Othello *must* misconstrue – this *must* derives not only from Iago's pride in his own plot but also from his knowledge of how Othello in his jealousy responds. (*Vnbookish* refers to Othello's lack of a learned spirit in human dealings, a lack of the wisdom that might be learned from published authorities or from the 'book' of life.) This certainty is such that nothing Othello might say in Desdemona's favour – about her sweetness that might command tasks of an emperor, about her needlecraft and musicianship and her gentleness – can prevent a misconstruction. There is an important point to be made about the manifesto that Othello makes in his response to the 'espial' scene: 'I will chop her into Messes' (F2586; IV.i.196) – i.e. into portions, or gobbets, as for a meal (*OED, Mess* sb., 1; Schmidt 2). From the brawl-scene one learned that men should not carve for their own rage; from the investigation into the brawl one learned that men should not mince matters into more digestible versions; Othello, however, is so far gone in blood and passion that he will permit himself to chop. The important point is this: that Othello's words are markedly similar to his earlier violent manifesto of 'Ile teare her all to peeces' (F2080; III.iii.435); and this earlier, equally violent intent was voiced before the handkerchief was even mentioned by Iago, let alone presented in Cassio's hand. It formed, in fact, a response to Iago's report of Cassio's dream. There is small difference, it seems, in Othello's violent resolve either before or after the ocular proof.

This 'espial' scene presents with particular starkness the great, central dramatic irony of the play – which consists in the increasing divergence of Othello's findings from how he is found by us the audience. In Act I Othello's finding of himself to the Council, to Iago and to us, is attuned to reality. He is manifested rightly. But from the brawl-scene until Aemilia's revelations in Act V almost everything he finds is a delusion. We in the audience discover early on an Othello that Othello himself does not discover until well into Act V; and it is from this central tragic irony that our sympathy derives – a sympathy that extends even when Shakespeare presents Othello at his worst. Othello would not be spying, or striking Desdemona, or murdering her, if his knowledge matched ours; and a sense of impending tragedy develops from the fact that Othello seems to be barred from sharing in our omniscience. The great impediment in the marriage of Desdemona's true mind to Othello's increasingly *un*true mind is this: that the free and open nature that Iago described in Othello continues to find honesty in the seemer Iago while closing, and remaining closed, to the honesty we all know survives in Desdemona. Again and again when inquiry should occur we hear Othello fleeing from doubt instead of examining it; Shakespeare makes him again and again resort to the self-publications and attitudinisings by which we in the audience, with our superior knowledge, must be dismayed.

The self-publishing of Othello in 'Had it pleas'd Heauen . . . ' is ostensibly addressed to Desdemona; but it departs from dialogue to become, in effect, monologue or soliloquy. It needs addressing more to the theatre's heavens than to Desdemona. Thus it serves a major need of the dramatist's plot – that Desdemona should be kept uninformed of the specific 'charge' against her. It occurs in a context of Desdemona's questionings and of Othello's failure to supply any answers, as a result of which Desdemona understands a fury in Othello's words but not the words themselves. The unexplained physical attack of the previous scene is here being matched by an inexplicable verbal violence. Othello assaults Desdemona with his distress. At one point Desdemona, in her frantic search for information, supposes that distress to be caused by Othello's recall to Venice at the possible instigation of Brabantio. This absurd supposition is given much pathos by its sheer distance from the truth, by Desdemona's inability to share in our superior knowledge, by the working of the central dramatic irony in which the unimparting Othello unknowingly rebuffs his own salvation as it stands before him.

In a dramatic situation defined by the absence of any truth the first sentence of Othello's promulgation has, ironically, much of a characteristic syntactical organisation – as if Othello has found a refuge:

> Had it pleas'd Heauen,
> To try me with Affliction, had they rain'd [Q *he ram'd*]
> All kind of Sores, and Shames on my bare-head:
> Steep'd me in pouertie to the very lippes,
> Giuen to Captiuitie, me, and my vtmost hopes,
> I should haue found in some place of my Soule
> A drop of patience.
>
> (F2742–8; IV.ii.48–54)

The repetition in *Had . . . pleas'd* and *had . . . rain'd*, the easy relating of *Steep'd* and *Giuen* back to the second *had*, the easy postponement of the main clause to the final two lines – these suggest an apparent assurance in Othello. They certainly reflect the boldness with which he matches himself implicitly against Job. This allusion is generally recognised – as Ross (p. 183n) says, Job was 'for the Elizabethans a type of patience, suffering God's trials of affliction and hardship'. Othello utters a kind of abstract of Job's afflictions (rather as he uttered in Act I an abstract of his wars and travels). Job's loss of several thousand head of camels, sheep, oxen and she-asses is summarised in *pouertie*; *Shames* could encompass Job's being shunned by his own household; while the *Sores* that rain on Othello's head are reminiscent of the boils that covered Job from crown of the head to sole of the foot. *Captiuitie* in a literal sense was not amongst Job's afflictions, but he certainly shaved his head in his anguish – hence Othello's *bare-head* is probably shorn as well as being bereft of its bonnet. But – and this is interesting – the patience of Job in fact belongs more to legend than to biblical authority. Most of the book of Job describes Job's attempts to justify himself as an upright and righteous man to his would-be comforters (there is, ironically, a deal of Othello in this actual biblical figure). He does not accept his afflictions and attempt to justify God for having visited them upon him. He wishes, indeed, that his life might have a present end. Not until the end of his book does Job repent and learn his fabled patience. To a contemporary audience enforced to church attendance by Statute law, the afflictions of Job were probably as real as his hard-won eventual patience; and Othello's assertions would probably have sounded less extremely than to a modern audience. Job *lacked* patience for much of the time; Othello, somewhere in the essential, Godlike part of him, would have found a drop sufficient to sustain him. Job wishes he had never been born; Othello does not so blaspheme against God's will – rather he makes Desdemona the object of such a wish a few lines after this speech: 'Would thou had'st neuer bin borne'. Whereas Job bitterly complained, Othello would have managed (he claims) to have endured the tribulations sent by God without questioning God's motives.

By this implicit comparison with Job, Shakespeare puts one in mind of Othellos's achievements in the proving-landscape of his travels, in the testing-grounds of war. Here is Othello's alacrity in hardness, with the chances and the accidents now exerted not by fatal stars but by heaven itself. Given Othello's eagerness to prove his *virtù*, his claim to match Job becomes credible. This is the same soldier who, in Iago's earlier account, endured without anger the destruction of his ranks and of his own brother by enemy cannon (F2291–6; III.iv.135–40). Othello's patience in those earlier circumstances would have been particularly admirable: infantry and cavalry would be vulnerable to and perhaps powerless against bombardment by far-off artillery; while the fate of Othello's brother is made the more distressing by his having been blown 'from his very Arme' – i.e. while serving at Othello's side or while being fraternally nursed. One has no cause to question Iago's eye-witness account of Othello's soldierly qualities – its suggestion of military duty taking precedence over emotion has the ring of truth. And, similarly, one can accept Othello's present postulation of a *drop* of patience – *drop* being the smallest appreciable quantity (*OED* sb., 5). The claim may be extreme, but it is not wild.

In the extremism of the sentence as a whole, however, can be read (I think) signs of strain; and these counter the syntactical suggestions of an apparent assurance. The intensive lexicon of *All kind, to the very, vtmost, drop* – even of *rain'd* and *Steep'd* – is characteristic but here seems to have an especial point. Othello has escaped for a sentence into the suppositional world, where absolutes and certainty can exist – the world of Doran's 'asseverative conditional'[24] – instead of confronting the particularly terrible actual and now.

It is tempting to read Othello's change in number from singular *Heauen* to plural *they rain'd* as a possible signal, too, of extremism and strain. This change is of course not present in Q; the force of the implied God in *he ram'd* becomes aptly violent; but the reading is generally eschewed by modern editors (though Ridley opts for *he*). Walker (p. 203) indicates two *Heauen* passages elsewhere that suggest the change in number to be a conventional usage:

> Put we our quarrell to the will of heauen,
> Who when they see the houres ripe on earth,
> Will raigne hot vengeance on offenders heads
>
> (*The life and death of King Richard the Second*, F223–5; I.iii.6–8)

and

> Heauen hath pleas'd it so,
> To punish me with this, and this with me,
> That I must be their Scourge and Minister.
>
> (*The Tragedie of Hamlet, Prince of Denmark*, F2549–51; III.iv.173–5)

Schmidt, however, also shows a few instances of agreed singularity (under *Heaven* 4). So that, although, as Jenkins says, 'the use of *heauen* in plural sense is common'.[25] it may not be always indiscriminatory. It is as if the presence of a plural object in an adjacent clause will retrospectively make *heauen* plural in those cases where a pronominal back-reference occurs. Or, again, it may be that *they* refers politely rather than plurally, that we are hearing an equivalent to *thou* which, usually implying equality or intimacy or even contempt, denotes a ceremonious reverence when used of the Divinity. Certainly, the change in number has an attractive dissonance. *Heauen* becomes not only the home of God but a place inhabited by all the members of the heavenly host. In Othello's lines the reference is particularly sublime, particularly Othellonian. Even if by a paradigmatic or stylistic convention, Othello contrives to cram singular *Heauen* with a plural glory in the interest of his extreme argument. (Cf. 'I haue done the State some seruice, and they know't' – F3649; v.ii.342.)

In Othello's next lines the subject of *to make* is possibly *Heauen* or *they*; more probably, however, it is Desdemona:

> But alas, to make me
> The [Q *A*] fixed Figure for the time of Scorne,

To point his slow, and mouing finger at.
[Q *To point his slow vnmouing fingers at – oh, oh,*]
Yet could I beare that too, well, very well:

(F2748–51; IV.ii.54–7)

The heroic fact of a trial by heaven (by God and his subordinates) is superseded by an affliction more mundane, a shame that is man-made – or woman-made. Not that heaven can be completely excluded from this social shame, since an essential part of Othello's *Cause* in Act V is to be his confrontation with infidelity as yet another divinely sent affliction. Indeed, Othello's failure to define his subject here may, perhaps, suggest something of the ease with which he is to discern that ill-defined *Cause*. Certainly, however, the particular shame in these lines is expressed as mundane, social, public. And especially is it felt to be something degradingly permanent. The earlier, Job-like shames might have been endured in the hope of a triumphant and heroic victory in God's name. But to be made *The fixed Figure* of the cuckold is a hopeless condition not to be endured – except in Othello's second thoughts. The time that scorns is time future as well as time present. The finger is slow because time itself will seem slow to the aware cuckold who must face, as he goes about his daily business, a constant risk of public humiliation. According to Schmidt, *fixed* here is a form of *fix* as 'to set, to place in general' (*Fix* 3); but this neglects to register Othello's central preoccupation. The denotement is of fixity, of being secured against displacement (*OED* v., I.1). The figure will be placed definitely and permanently (II.1). It will be the definitive Othello. The eyes of the present and of posterity will be fixed *on* it steadily and unwaveringly (I.3). The *fixed Figure* therefore has some reference back to Iago's talk of the husband who *euer* fears cuckoldry and to Iago's suggestion that Othello's mind may change from revenge – which provoked Othello's repeated *Neuer*'s in the Pontic Sea speech. The picture of an Othello long in doubt, the picture of an Othello shamed but unavenging, these are succeeded by a third picture not so easily dismissed. F has '*The* fixed Figure' (emphasis added), which declares specifically in what Othello's horror consists. He sees himself not merely as *an* emblem of cuckoldry but as *the* emblem. And not necessarily of cuckoldry alone but of all contemptible qualities – the emblematic composite. The Othello who was married with 'that cunning Whore of Venice' (F2788; IV.ii.90) will become a stock figure synonymous in the public imagination with cuckoldry and gullibility as Job is with patience or affliction. As such he may even feature in the emblem books themselves, *Figure* being 'emblem, type' (*OED* sb., II.2), or in exemplary writings where the *Figure* would be a rhetorical figure (v.21) – this last is less likely. Othello foresees himself as a household name – Othello the Gull – in much the same way as Troilus and Cressida foresee a future in which 'As true as Troylus' and 'As false as Cressid' may be commonplace tags (*The Tragedie of Troylus and Cressida*, F1815 and 1830; III.ii.178 and 192). Additionally, this *Figure* would seem to have developed from the monster that Othello sensed Iago kept within his brain as too hideous to be shown: the monster that was a horned, cuckolded Othello. There is some connotation, therefore, of Othello as a kind of popular attraction, fixed securely as a bear might be, and displayed to the vulgar for a fee. One remembers that the Latin root of *promulgate* is 'expose to public view'. This figure is a promulgation that Othello must detest.

These interpretations of *Figure* are encompassed by the sense of 'image, likeness, or representation' and of 'Represented character' (*OED* sb., II.9 and 11). They are more evocative than the clock-interpretation first voiced in the late 1700s and most recently voiced (in 1984) by the latest editor of *Othello*:

> Othello sees himself as an eternal object of derision, pointed at forever – like the numbers on a clock-face, pointed at by the hour-hand which, though moving, appears to the human eye to be standing still. Compare *Sonnets* 104.9 – 10: 'yet doth beauty, like a dial-hand, / Steal from his figure, and no pace perceiv'd'.

True, something of the clock-idea informs the image. But the exclusive picture of Othello as a clock digit is narrow. Moreover, to insist on it as modern editors do is to be counter-productive: the dial-hand does eventually steal from the figure despite the fact that it moves but slowly or apparently does not move at all; while to see Othello as plural 'numbers', as in the quote above, seems rather to disperse him than to express his being the focus of attention. All in all, the clock-interpretation fails sufficiently to register the publication of Othello (the 'bad publicity') that is intrinsic in *the fixed Figure*.[26]

Furthermore, since this scorned emblem is so contrary to the figure of himself that Othello has published hitherto, one can justly

question the assertion of *Yet could I beare that too, well, very well.*
There would be nothing heroic in such a bearing. There is nothing
heroic in being a figure of scorn. Nor is there a chance of eventual
grandeur in this affliction as there was in the afflictions of the first
part of the speech. The disjunctive *Yet* seems to dismiss the idea
that this particular shame cannot be endured; but Q's – *oh, oh* and
the repetition of *well, very well* suggest respectively a degree of
distress and of possible over-protestation by which the assertion
might be qualified. The syntactical break suggests that Othello is
interrupted by intuition, a second thought; but his finding is debatable rather than true.

The theme of the figure that one makes in the world is, of course,
treated at length in the play; and at this point I wish to digress for a
while to examine it. One side of it, the 'new man's' view, is expressed by Iago: 'Reputation is an idle, and most false imposition;
oft got without merit, and lost without deseruing' (F1392–4;
II.iii.260–1): *idle* because worthless, useless (like the deserts idle
that Othello travelled in): an *imposition* in being bestowed from
without rather than created from within (*OED* 2 has 'attribution';
Onions suggests a germ of 'imposture', after *OED* 6 [1632 –]). Iago
of course, trimming his opinions to suit his plot, *seems* to be engaged in an attempt to reduce Cassio's distress but, in fact,
manages to exacerbate it. The point is, though, that *this* opinion
does seem to signify beyond the dramatic situation; it does seem to
express what Iago truly thinks. As Doran says, 'One has the feeling
that he does despise the reputation on which men like Cassio and
Othello set so much value and which he, in his superior cleverness,
can so easily ruin.'[27] In *Othello*, in fact, the idea of reputation as
something false and imposed is true only of Iago's honesty.
Cassio's military reputation is made suspect, and Othello's name
for command and judgement is astonishingly destroyed. But
honest Iago is alone in being dishonest, the opposite in reality to
the figure that the world has of him. (Even this last reputation,
though, becomes deserved when Iago is defined as being always
honest and true to himself in a cynical and ironic use of *honest*.)[28]

Iago's next lines, 'You haue lost no Reputation at all, vnlesse you
repute your selfe such a looser', express a trite observation that Iago
probably utters for the sake of the relished pun. He does however
convey some suggestion that self-respect and a good opinion of
oneself are important – that indeed they are more important than
the opinion of others. And this definition too must be inadequate

for soldiers such as Cassio and Othello. For them, their honours and their professional reputations must be blazoned forth as heralds of themselves; and the world must share their good opinion.

Cassio defines his lost reputation as 'the immortall part of myselfe' and claims that 'what remains is bestiall' (F1386–8; II.iii.255–6). His reputation is his soul, his divine part, the thing that separates him from the animals and makes him a man, the abstract that, he had hoped, would survive his physical death. This is, of course, a highly elevated view; and it is lowered by what happens next in the drama. Having freely lamented, Cassio is soon reeled in to Iago's control. His sense of a lost reputation is reduced to the sense of a lost position, a position that might be retrieved by the worldly measure of petitioning Desdemona. There is something facile in Cassio's sublimity. With some ease he can descend, or be brought down, to a pragmatic view.

Not so Othello. *His* sense of reputation is more fundamental. His references have nothing of Cassio's near-glibness. They are often implicit, having the strength of suggestion. A notable instance is in Othello's address immediately after the brawl:

> Worthy Montano, you were wont to be civill:
> The grauitie, and stillnesse of your youth
> The world hath noted. And your name is great
> In mouthes (Q *men*) of wisest Censure. What's the matter
> That you vnlace your reputation thus,
> And spend your rich opinion, for the name
> Of a night-brawler?
>
> (F1309–15; II.iii.182–8)

Montano in the Duke's words is 'a Substitute of most allowed sufficiencie' (F571–2; I.iii.224) than whom only Othello is more sufficient (though possibly the mysterious Marcus Luccicos, who is sent for post-haste at F375ff. [I.iii.44ff.] might have been preferred as well). *Sufficiencie* is 'ability' or 'competence' (*OED* 4); and *allowed* is the now obsolete 'Praised, accepted as satisfactory' (*OED* ppl. adj., 1 [– 1728]). Othello has discerned in Montano's reputation the figure of his own younger self, a man whose ability fully to occupy his position is recognised and praised by all. Moreover, the pith of Montano's reputation is a virtue even more specifically to Othello's liking: a virtue that Othello insists on in his use of the near-synonyms *civill*, *grauitie* and *stillnesse*. The *OED* defines *civill* as 'well-ordered, orderly' (adj., 7); *grauitie* as 'serious character' and in later use 'seriousness or sobriety' (*Gravity* I.2 and 3); and *stillnesse* as 'Quietness of temper or behaviour; freedom from turbulence or self-assertion' (*Stillness* 4 [–1745]). In Montano it would seem that the humours have been famously well mixed. He is someone who might have said with as much apparent justification as Othello 'Feare not my gouernment' (Othello to Iago: F1887; III.iii.260); someone who would subscribe to Othello's 'Let's teach our selues that Honourable stop, / Not to out-sport discretion' (F1112–13; II.iii.2–3), which expresses not only the military principle of watch-keeping but also Othello's personal code of behaviour, a general principle rather than a disguised self-praise.

In fact, *your name is great . . .* functions not only to censure Montano but also as a gloss on the word *reputation*. Shakespeare has not made Othello say to the simple effect of 'Worthy Montano, you were wont to be civil; why have you become a night-brawler?' Instead he has written in much lexical marking of Othello's concern with good name. The clause *The world hath noted* indicates that Montano is widely reputed for the mature quality that belies his youth; while the greatness of his *name* refers less to his appellation than to the fame or good repute involved in it (*OED, Name* sb., II.6 and 8). The value of such fame is stressed in its being voiced or known by mouths or men of the most discerning and knowledge-able *Censure* or 'judgement' (*OED* sb., 3); while the *reputation* that is unlaced and the *opinion* that is spent support each other with synonymity. (*Reputation* is 'The . . . being highly regarded or esteemed . . . good report' [*OED* 3] and *opinion* is 'What is thought of one by others . . . reputation' [*OED* sb., 6].) *Rich* declares that the opinion is of great value. Again, *name / Of a night-brawler* denotes reputation, this time in a derogatory sense.

Othello's contempt for Montano's apparent neglect of his reputa-tion sounds in *vnlace* and *spend*. The first of these might mean 'cut up or carve' (*OED, Unlace* v., 3) – in which case it links with 'carue for his owne rage' in Othello's first brawl-scene speech: he who does serve his own anger does risk his reputation. More probably, however, it is a use of the familiar contemporary idea of a personal quality as a garment. Montano is censured for casually – as it seems – treating his hard-won reputation as something to be doffed and donned at will like a suit of armour. *Vnlace* in this meaning is 'undo the . . . laces of (a piece of armour, clothing, etc.)' (OED, Unlace v., 1). Othello is also condemning – though he does not know it –

something that is akin to Iago's view of reputation as an *imposition*. The second verb, *spend*, is also a common contemporary usage and means 'waste' (Schmidt 4). The frequent sexual sense is not present here; but certainly there is a denotement of Montano's having expended something precious and vital to his manhood.[29]

Othello's regard for reputation is implied, then; and this in turn suggests the regard is deep seated. Othello is not overtly 'touchy' about his own reputation: he is not provoked by the scurvy and provoking terms that, in Iago's report, Rodorigo or possibly Brabantio aimed at his honour – ''Tis better as it is' (F209; I.ii.6);[30] nor does he immediately react to Iago's talk of the good name that in men and women is the 'immediate Iewell of their Soules' (F1768–75; III.iii.159–65). The effect is slower, more insidious, emerging much later in 'My name that was as fresh / As Dian's Visage, is now begrim'd and blacke / As mine owne face' (F2032–4; III.iii.390–2). Because Othello's sense of his reputation *is* so integrated with his soul, it is not so much affected by Iago's fluent commonplaces as it might have been.

And, equally, its own effect on Othello is fundamental and powerful. It causes not only the address to Montano but also Othello's disclaimer, before the Council, of any sexual motive in agreeing to Desdemona's company on Cyprus (he fears the imposition of a name for Moorish lechery). It also causes the repeated publications of himself to Iago as a man of decision and action. And it also turned the 'Occupation' speech into a virtual celebration of the noise and spectacle by which the name of Othello was increased in the world's attention. When the Duke defines *opinion* as 'a more soueraigne Mistris of Effects' that 'throwes a more safer voice' on Othello than on Montano (F572–4; I.iii.224–5), it may well be that he is speaking in a double sense: not only about the councillors' opinion of Othello, but also, chorically, about public character and reputation. Othello's concern for these does rule him with supremacy, with something of the power of monarchy, a singular and royal rule (*OED, Sovereign* B adj., 1 and 4).[31]

To return from this digression to the *fixed Figure*: the interrogation of *Yet could I beare that too, well, very well* would appear, all in all, to be justified. The syntactical division – an expostulation is completed by an assertion contrary to what one expects – makes an antithesis that is not resolved. The unfixing of Othello's good name, and the fixing in its place of a name for gullibility and cuckoldry – Othello (arguably) could not bear this 'very well'. True, the theme of a man's good name is to cease in his utterance for a while – until, specifically, his speech to Gratiano in the last scene and his suicide speech; but this silence is caused not by a cessation of concern but by its 'elevation' and generalisation. Until after the murder, Othello's theme will become the good name and well-being of men in general and of a universal chastity. This will be summarised in 'It is the Cause, it is the Cause . . . It is the Cause' (F3240 and 3242; v.ii.1 and 3) – in the threefold sounding of this ill-defined sublimity Shakespeare may well be intending us to hear a parallel with Cassio's threefold (and facile) 'Reputation, Reputation, Reputation' (F1386; II.iii.255). This diffuse elevating of Othello's concern for his good name (something associated with male, heroic militarism) to a higher, even divine, cause whose champion Othello can sorrowfully but heroically become – all this indicates both the consistency and the self-delusion that Shakespeare has written into his characterisation.

The interruption in syntax – and in Othello's thinking – becomes more marked as Othello moves on from the *fixed Figure*:

> But there where I haue garnerd vp my heart,
> Where either I must liue, or beare no life,
> The Fountaine from the which my currant runnes,
> Or else dries vp: to be discarded thence,
> Or keepe it as a Cesterne, for foule Toades
> To knot and gender in. Turne thy complexion there:
> Patience, thou [Q *thy*] young and Rose-lip'd Cherubin,
> I heere looke grim as hell.
>
>   (F2752–9; IV.ii.58–65)

Shakespeare has supplied Othello's usual parison in a sequence of *there . . . thence . . . there . . . heere* and, again, of *where . . . Where . . . from the which*. This helps the passage to cohere. So too does the antithetical sequence of *liue, or beare, runnes, / Or else dries vp* and *to be discarded . . . Or keepe*. But there is a fundamental dislocation inside this coherence. The two main clauses in the first sentence – *to be discarded thence* and *Or keepe it as a Cestern* – are moved to a final position. And this has two effects. First, without *But* – which properly belongs to them – these two main clauses lose their syntactic linkage with what has gone before. They do not achieve the climax that the movement of the subordinates has led us to expect. They seem to have something of the abrupt transition of

Yet could I beare that too . . . And they express similarly something of Othello's emotional confusion. To paraphrase some of his earlier words (II.i): it stops me here, it is too much of distress.

The other effect is that the first *there* the indirect object of 'discarded (from)', is emphasised. The result is a transfer of attention from the fixed figure of Othello to the person or condition in which Othello has fixed his heart. This investment accords with the neo-Platonic idea of the lover dwelling entirely within the cabinet of the beloved's body.[32] The fact that Othello does not actually name Desdemona's body but refers to it vaguely – while perhaps indicating it with an all-encompassing or accusatory gesture – increases the potential of the reference. Shakespeare is able to bring definition into the vagueness with images of a charged and sacred sexuality.

In this respect the scriptural allusiveness is largely created by *Fountaine* and *Cesterne*. Richmond Noble demonstrates that these appear in the Geneva Bible (a copy of which Shakespeare most probably owned) but not in the Bishops' Bible:

> Drinke the water of thy cisterne, and of the rivers out of the middes of thine owne well. Let thy fountaines flowe foorth, and the rivers of waters in the streets. But let them bee thine, euen thine only, and not the strangers with thee. Let thy fountaine bee blessed, and reioyce with the wife of thy youth.
>
> (Proverbs 5: 15–18)[33]

Noble also prints the Geneva note: 'Thy children which shall come of thee in great abundance, shewing that God blesseth marriage and curseth whoredom.' Whether or not Shakespeare consciously used this biblical resonance, he certainly made some modifications. The cistern-as-wife becomes cistern-as-whore. The fountain becomes the source not of the children – which should be Othello's and not the stranger Cassio's – but rather of Othello's vital flow. *Beare no life* denotes the non-endurance of life, as in *Yet could I beare that too*, rather than non-propagation. This resonance is highly effective, of course, in suggesting the spiritual nature of Othello's love. It *is* his whole being that Othello has invested in Desdemona.

Garnerd vp as 'stored' or 'laid up' contributes its effect too. Its total declaration echoes that of the bloody thoughts being propelled until revenge may 'Swallow them vp' – the reversal is characteristically extreme. The *OED* records this usage (*Garner* v., 2 fig.) as the first ever in the written language and does not record a recurrence until the mid-nineteenth century. *Garner* itself, as 'store (corn or other products of the earth)' (v., 1) is not recorded at all as occurring 1474–1837. The extreme and successful novelty of this verbal use (an example of Shakespeare's frequent way of enlivening a noun) would have reinforced the impression of Othello's wholehearted commitment. There may well be a further meaning at work here also: Hulme demonstrates that a garner in Midland dialect is a 'bin in a mill or granary', in which sense Othello's garnering up would become even more intense – he has placed his soul at the very centre of the ideal being that is Desdemona. Moreover, further nuances of 'garner' supplied by Hulme from Stratford records – ' "ii payles ii garners one utyng fate" (this last a vat for steeping grain in the process of brewing) 1593' and ' "a gardner for malt" 1631' – express, as Hulme observes, a linkage of grain and water as symbols of life. They thus dismiss Johnson's pronouncement that 'The "garner" and the "fountain" are improperly conjoined.' Alternatively, if these nuances are eschewed, then *garnerd vp* may be interpreted – given Shakespeare's precision – as a deliberate incongruity. Its 'dryness' in a passage suffused with the idea of wetness (*rain'd, Steep'd, drop, Fountaine, currant runnes, Cesterne*) combines with *dries vp* to suggest Othello's perplexity.[34]

All this publication of distress reveals that Othello's whole life and motivation have come to consist in his unshared occupation of Desdemona as a 'source' (*OED, Fountain* 1). If they consisted in any other source they would cease, the current would no longer run. It is a matter of life or death. Remove the spirituality of that source and the quickening fountain becomes a still 'pond'. This sense of a cistern as a pond is first cited by *OED* (3) as occurring in 1606, in *The Tragedie of Anthonie, and Cleopatra*: 'A Cesterne for scal'd Snakes' (F1147; II.v.95); but it is very appropriate here. (Interestingly, *OED, Cistern* 6 [1702–] is defined, 'the water tank in which grain is soaked'.)[35] As for sexuality, it loses its sacred quality and becomes merely animal. *Knot* as 'unite or gather together (in a knot)' (*OED* v., 4b) excludes spiritual union; while the intransitive *gender* means merely 'copulate' rather than 'beget' in a transitive sense (see *OED* v., 2 and 1). In these two verbs the marital function is displaced by a base promiscuity.[36]

To be *discarded* from the clear fountain of his ideal marriage – this Othello's patience could not survive. (The *OED* states that the primary meaning of *Discard*, a late sixteenth-century word, had its origin in cardplay. It would seem very quickly to have acquired the general figurative meaning [here ppl. adj., 2: 'Cast off, rejected'].) Even less could it survive the maintenance of a mere form of marriage to a whore who must be shared with the chamberers of the cistern. In this very 'brothel' scene Othello is demonstrating such a marriage in the savage pretence of being his own wife's client. Interestingly, this last condition (to keep it as a cistern) joins the earlier two subjectless conditions that Othello expostulated against (to make me a fixed figure and to be discarded) in subjecting Othello to a passivity not in his nature. He is republishing, in fact, the self of his central theme. He earlier denied he would make a life of jealousy, constantly fearing revolt but not acting on it. He denied his mind would ever change to complaisance. Now he declares his intolerance of keeping his marriage as a cistern.

The last lines of this speech form a well-known crux:

> Turne thy complexion there:
> Patience, thou [Q *thy*] young and Rose-lip'd Cherubin,
> I heere looke grim as hell.

The interpretation in which *Patience* (a noun rather than an imperative) turns its face to look *there*, at the world of the cistern, is attractive and valid. Alternatively, however, *Complexion* might mean other than 'Countenance, face' – which in *OED* I.4c is recorded as rare and cited only in this passage. It might mean in fact 'the combination of the four "humours" or the "temperament"' and 'The natural colour, texture, and appearance of the skin . . . of the face; orig. as showing the "temperament"' (*OED* I.1 and 4). Not only blushing but a fundamental shock to the essential being of the rosy-lipped Patience is implied. Such an implication is strengthened by the extreme associations in *Othello* of *Turne*. Othello used this verb to denote the violence and accommodations of Desdemona's strumpetry, the facility with which she can affect (as he thinks) radical changes in her disposition:

> I, you did wish, that I would make her turne:
> Sir, she can turne, and turne: and yet go on
> And turne againe.
>
> (F2650–2; IV.i.249–51)

It is probable that such a recent denotement of violence – the violation of ideals – attaches still to the present usage. Patience, a virtue worthy of a strong man and pilgrim, is essentially of heaven. Now, however, finding that the heaven is a cistern, it must change fundamentally itself. It must radically depart from its own essential property. It must look grim in heaven (*there*) as Othello looks grim on earth (*heere*) – both places being in fact grim *as hell*. Moreover (I think) this reading has the support of the later text. Only a few lines later Othello is to expound several reactions of shame at Desdemona's infidelity, amongst them heaven's stopping of its nose and, a little lower than heaven, the moon's shutting of its eyes. Of this celestial disgust the abstract virtue Patience is to partake as well.[37]

However one reads these lines (and one view, for example, reads in them a direct address of Desdemona), they finally dismiss the patience that Othello claims he would have owned in other afflictions. In the speech as a whole patience and impatience are reviewed in relation to Job-like, religious testings, then to adverse publicity, and then to the smirching of ideals and the banishment from a heaven-on-earth. And the review is peculiarly direct. Two earlier speeches with a similar gist – 'Why? why is this? . . . ' and 'Neuer Iago. Like to the Ponticke Sea . . . ' (F1792ff. and 2103 ff.; III.iii.180ff. and 457 ff.) – were provoked by something specific that Iago said. They were reactions against Iago's insinuations of Othello as a submissive cuckold. *This* speech, however, is not at all a response to Desdemona's immediately preceding lines – a pathetic lament on her and Othello's having lost Brabantio. It seems that those earlier insinuations have so affected Othello that little now quickens him but the need for action and for the frequent publicity of the virtues of *im*patience. And the urgency of that need informs his syntax. To return for a moment to the turning of *thy complexion*: Walker (p. 203), who sees Patience as a cherubic and horrified onlooker, an eye of heaven, suggests some textual corruption 'as the transition is so abrupt'. Alternatively, it may be said, the transition fits well into the pattern of syntactical dislocation that Shakespeare has written into this speech. From the organisation of the long first sentence, Shakespeare moves us to the incompletion of the *fixed Figure* sentence and the interjection of *Yet could I beare that too . . .* ; and then to the assured intricacy of *But there where I haue garnerd vp . . . .* This, in turn, is rendered incomplete and expostulatory by *Turne thy complexion there . . . .* It seems that once again Shakespeare has informed Othello's syntax with Othello's emotion as the characteristic organised nature of the self-publication beings to stop under stress.

By the end of this speech Desdemona is almost as uninformed as ever. She has learned much about Othello's distress and views about patience but nothing of a detailed indictment; and all she will have learned by the end of the scene is that Othello figures her as a 'Whore' and 'Strumpet' and himself as excessively afflicted and scorned. This, however, is the last occasion on which the secondary dramatic function of Othello's self-publishings will consist in the withholding of information from Desdemona and the neglect of independent inquiry. From now on Othello's self-publishings will be concerned with the establishment of a 'respectable' justification for murder to parallel the established virtue of impatience ('It is the Cause . . . '), with a farewell to the Othello that was ('Behold, I haue a weapon . . . '), and with the attempt to refix his figure ('Soft you; a word or two . . . '). These last great speeches will be discussed in Chapter 6.

6

'I must be found' (iii)

At first it may seem that 'It is the Cause . . . ' is not self-publication. It may seem that Othello is thinking aloud rather than particularly addressing his speech – so that the audience overhears (so to speak) his soliloquy. Not so. The speech has five addressees: '(my Soule)', 'you chaste Starres', 'thou flaming Minister', 'Thou cunning'st Patterne of excelling Nature' and 'Balmy breath'. And the audience can listen as before, as if Othello were engaged in one of his earlier monologues to Iago or Desdemona. The *Balmy breath* reference may be exclamatory – in Q's 'A balmy breath' it is merely an observation – but on the whole F supplies Othello with five listeners. Not the kind that audit and respond, but rather the kind that Othello likes, little more than something to set off and frame his monologue – and frequently superhuman, abstract. The principal theme of the self-publication here is that Othello has ascended from looking grim as hell: he now looks and intends to act as sublimely grim as heaven. In addressing his soul Othello is satisfying not the seat of his emotions (*OED, Soul* I.3a) and not just his 'rational principle' (I.5) but, essentially, 'The spiritual part' of himself 'considered in its moral aspect or in relation to God and his precepts' (II.8) – he is satisfying it with the statement of a realised religious cause. And in claiming that 'This sorrows heauenly, / It strikes, where it doth loue', he is maintaining this new figure of himself as a patient but dutifully avenging angel. I say 'new' because this figure supersedes the scorned one that Othello imagined but recently. In fact, this figure of an angelic Othello is not unfamiliar. It resembles the Othello of the deserts and antres, the Othello who made a pilgrimage in a moral wilderness and proved his virtue, the Othello who is alacritous in hardness and quick in the cause of duty. He has served the state of Venice in the performing of difficult tasks; his 'crusader' temperament now leads him to serve – as he thinks – his heavenly part if not the state of heaven itself. (In respect of Othello's 'crusading', he even at one point describes Desdemona's beauty in terms of her ability to impose proving labours of love: 'She might

186

lye by an Emperours side, and command him Taskes' – F2569–70;
IV.i.181.) Thus the whole speech begins and ends on a reference by
which is published Othello's justified self. (F3240–62; V.ii.1–23.)

Attempts to define the pronoun rather than the noun in the first
three lines tend to dull the resonance of *Cause*:

> It is the Cause, it is the Cause (my Soule)
> Let me not name it to you, you chaste Starres,
> It is the Cause.

If *It* denotes Othello's dark countenance glimpsed in a mirror, as in
Fechter's *Acting Edition* of 1861, then the characterisation is made
superficial. Again, if *it* denotes 'blood' in the late-Elizabethan sense
of the source of 'animal or sensual appetite' (*OED*, *Blood* sb., II.6) –
on the basis of a possible back-reference in the immediately succeeding 'Yet Ile not shed her blood' – then *Cause* becomes merely
'that which produces an effect, or is the motive of an action'
(Schmidt sb., 1). One has, I think, to consign *It* to the non-accented
status of an impersonal pronoun, and to concentrate on defining
Cause. For *Cause* has much richness. It is not merely 'ground of
action' (*OED* sb., I.3) but, more strongly, something 'espoused,
advocated, and upheld by a person or party' (II;.11 [1581–]). And
because it is *the* cause Othello's partisanship becomes not just
personal but that of heaven – a fit matter of address to *My Soule*. So,
reason why is functioning much less than reason for. One can
develop *OED*'s 'espoused': Othello is now more married (as he
thinks) to a universal principle than to his wife; and the stars can
remain uninformed – like, ironically, that other chaste star Desdemona – not only because their modesty must be protected but
also because their agent, Othello, is acting on their behalf down
here on earth.[1]

Moreover, this dramatic entrance of Othello as a kind of avenging
angel strongly aware of its identity and function is further suggested in two other ways. The first of these is Q's stage direction
that Othello enters *'with a light'*. As a light-bearer Othello can be
observed as virtually a biblical figure. The second is the scriptural
resonance that *Cause* brings with it – particularly that of Job (again),
who wished to order his cause before God and fill his mouth with
arguments, who had sought out causes and who had not despised
the causes of his servants (Job 23:4; 29:16; 31:13). Further biblical or
scriptural resonances, from Psalm 35:1, 7, 19, 23 in the Book of

Common Prayer and from Psalm 35:7 in the Bishops' Bible, are suggested by Stauffer (*Shakespeare's Derived Imagery*, p. 49). He quotes, 'For without a cause they have privily laid for me a pit full of their nets: without a cause they have made a digging unto my soul.' He compares 'they' with Iago, the unexplained, causeless ensnarer of Othello's soul and body.

The main point about *the Cause* therefore, is its religious sublimity – and, linked to this, its vagueness. When Walker (p. 211n) defines *Cause* as 'offence' and when Muir (p. 214n) reads 'adultery', they are going against Othello's very *lack* of definition. The asserting verb and the definite article of *It is the Cause* do nothing to ascertain what Othello means; while the explanatory 'she must dye, else shee'l betray more men' has a neatness of 'nobility' about it that makes one question not only its premise but also its genuineness as a cause in Othello. The figure of Othello acting on behalf of a heavenly principle (or even pragmatically, out of fellowship) to save either men in general or others of the great ones whose inevitable fate it is to be wedded to inferior womankind – this figure seems too completely realised, too easily and quickly limned, to be a true one. And in the event, of course, it is disproved, since Desdemona is killed out of rage and not for a principle. In fact, this explicitly asserted cause – sounding more as a reason why – is unconvincing as some of Iago's asserted causes are unconvincing. Iago soliloquises of Othello that 'it is thought abroad, that 'twixt my sheets / Ha's [Q; F has *She ha's*] done my Office' (F733–4; I.iii.381–2). This increases to

> Now I do loue her too,
> Not out of absolute Lust, (though peraduenture
> I stand accomptant for as great a sin)
> But partely led to dyet my Reuenge,
> For that I do suspect the lustie [Q *lustfull*] Moore
> Hath leap'd into my Seate . . .
>
> (F1074–9; II.i.285–90)

And eventually Cassio is included: 'I feare Cassio with my Night-Cape [Q *nightcap*] too' (F1090; II.i.301) – this after Cassio's bold courtesy to Aemilia on his landing on Cyprus. None of these claims is plausible; Iago's explanations sound as symptoms rather than reasons, symptoms of Iago's great Cause – which is to pull down, as he can, those superior beings whose very existences threaten his vanity. Both Iago (in *his* self-publication to Rodorigo) and Othello (to Iago, Desdemona, Gratiano and the Senate) express their respective great Causes more fully and accurately in colloquy than in soliloquy. And, just as Iago's asserted reasons are symptoms, so too, in this soliloquy, is Othello's concern for *more men* a symptom: of his need for a cause that his best judgement can approve and champion.[2]

But this vagueness qualifies not at all the certainty of Othello's syntax. Rather, it assists it. The certainty depends, in part, on the non-modification of *Cause*. Not on the incompletion of the sentence (which, completed, would read something like 'It is the cause, not my personal feeling, that compels me to sacrifice my wife'), but on the cause itself remaining unnamed and unexamined. Here in fact is one of the main features of Othello's utterance sounding at a critical time. Here sounds another of those single words that is not defined but instead, by a slow impulsion, informs the speech with (apparent) assurance. It concurrently makes one wonder (in this instance) why it is that Othello needs to sound the word thrice – a word that for him seems to need, in turn, a constant lodgement in an authoritative and simple main clause. At this moment the text-less, unbriefed audiences of 1604 would have been in suspense: the Moor has struck his wife; will he now kill her as planned? All they heard at this crucial entrance was a verbal banner – a slogan – which included nothing of the rage and will to kill they had been witness-ing in Othello hitherto. This slogan must have discouraged their hopes for Desdemona. If Desdemona were to be saved (against the suggestion of the play's billing as a tragedy), the salvation must derive elsewhere than from any illumination or hesitation in her husband. For in Othello there has now recurred a characteristic mental phenomenon. The facility he has earlier demonstrated – in proving what he has not proved, in seeing what he has not seen – is again at work. This time it is not only a need of action that is being served but Othello's spiritual need that his cause be proved and found. Also being served, of course, is his self-figuring. For the figure of Othello the Cuckold has dimmed. It exists in the text of the speech not at all. As with the cause, it is not named – no such mundanity. Similarly, a wife is not a wife, a whore not a whore; instead she is skin and blood, prototype and rose (or a tree). And on the husband the horns have been transmuted into another symbol, a sword of justice.

Furthering all this elevation are the lines that follow:

> Yet Ile not shed her blood,
> Nor scarre that whiter skin of hers, then Snowe,
> And smooth as Monumentall Alablaster . . . .

It is debatable whether *Nor* supplies a real alternative – shedding or scarring. It could be acting as an equivalent for *and*. Or *Nor scarre* might be acting as a participle-substitute 'scarring'. In any case the point is that Othello will not shed Desdemona's blood (the newly euphemistic way of chopping to messes and tearing all to pieces) and he will not disfigure Desdemona's body (*OED, Scar* v., 1) – either by stabbing or by any other means. (This is one of the instances where Shakespeare departs radically from Cinthio. In Cinthio 'Disdemona' is clubbed to death – by the ensign in the Moor's presence – with a stocking filled with sand, and her skull is broken. See Bullough, pp. 250–1.) The cause of this reluctance to scar her – expressed in a far more complex language than is the simple reluctance to shed her blood – is linked not at all to Othello's resolve, earlier, that Desdemona should be strangled. It is, instead, an aversion from spoiling, blemishing a body which, it might have been thought, expresses a concomitant purity of spirit in the accustomed neo-Platonic manner. Othello's 'Be thus when thou art dead, and I will kill thee, / And loue thee after' refers to the exorcism he will have achieved in the execution of his wife. He will have despatched the devil from her along with her soul; so that the purity of her body, *post mortem*, will truly reflect the (new) purity of her soul in heaven. The body will be the earthly representative of a heavenly inhabitant – which is a status roughly equivalent to Othello's. The pure whiteness of the skin, therefore, must not be discoloured.

The *spiritual* affinity that Othello feels with Desdemona asleep here needs to be stressed. Here is *not* 'that characteristic voluptuousness of Othello's' (Leavis, *The Common Pursuit*, p. 149). The registered smoothness is not merely of alabaster, a common contemporary reference, but of *Monumentall* alabaster. *OED* says of *Monumental*, 'In early use . . . pertaining to the tomb, sepulchral'; and this sense is linked to the noun-form, which meant 'sepulchre' until the mid-seventeenth century (*OED* sb., 1). If Othello is not actually comparing Desdemona's skin with the material of a sepulchre – her body entombing her soul – then he is certainly seeing it as the surfaces of a tomb effigy. That is to say, as having a cold and unearthly sheen rather than the milky complexion of the

beautiful late-Renaissance woman. I say 'sheen' advisedly because
alabaster belongs to a species of lime carbonate or sulphate noted
for its 'fine, translucent' quality (*OED, Alabaster* 1); and because
this quality – a shining across, an ability to carry light – would seem
to be important in context. When Othello uses *Light* – in 'and then
put out the Light' (F3246; v.ii.7) and in

> Once put out thy Light
> . . .
> I know not where is that Promethean heate
> That can thy Light re-lume [Q *returne*]
> (F3249–52; v.ii.10–13)

he means life itself, the vital principle, the gift of God – which no
one but God can give or restore – and he means essentially a flame:
life as a brief candle or, in this instance, as a torch not to be relit.
This is an image of fire as well as of light. But in Desdemona's oaths,
'by this light of Heauen' (to Iago: F2864; iv.ii.151) and 'by this
Heauenly light' (to Aemilia: F3037; iv.iii.63), the idea of translucency is supported. While Othello's comparable oath, 'by yond
Marble Heauen' (F2110; iii.iii.464), ignores and as it were puts out
the heavenly light to which even Iago swears four lines later – 'you
euer-burning lights' – Desdemona's innocent utterance is lit by a
radiance as of heaven that is carried across, too, on her body. Her
body is like alabaster because, in its translucency, it expresses the
same chastity and grace as the stars. Or supposedly it does. In the
contrast that Othello thinks he discerns between his wife's illumi-
nated skin and her darkened soul is the essential component of the
Cause. A truly alabaster-like Desdemona will be a Desdemona in
whom the smoothness and translucency of the skin will be matched
by a perfected and lightened soul. That is, this Desdemona will be a
dead but good one. The fixed figure she will make will be accurately
representative. She will be honestly translucent.

Nor is the *whiteness* of Desdemona's skin registered volup-
tuously. Othello's vision is partly that of a man of Moorish pigmen-
tation – a fascination with contrast; even more is it a Platonic vision.
There is, I think, a deliberate otherworldliness effected by the
syntax of *Nor scarre that whiter skin of hers, then Snowe* – i.e. by the
simple dislocation of *whiter* from before *then Snowe*. According to
Abbott, this exemplifies a common Elizabethan usage by which an
adjective is separated from an adverbial phrase by the noun they

are describing:

> it was felt that to place the adjective after the noun might some-
> times destroy the connection between the noun and the adjec-
> tive, since the adjective was, as it were, drawn forward to the
> modifying adverb. Hence the Elizabethans sometimes preferred
> to place the adjectival part of the adjective before, and the adver-
> bial part after, the noun. The noun generally being unemphatic
> caused but slight separation between the two parts of the adjec-
> tival phrase.[3]

It might be considered, that is, that in the 'normalised' syntax of
skin of hers whiter than snow the last three words might seem not to
belong to *skin*. If so, then the correcting syntax errs in turn; for the
separation is effected not by a noun but by a longer noun phrase,
skin of hers, and becomes rather more than Abbott's 'slight'. In fact,
it threatens disconnection. The point is, I think, that a grammatical
explanation of this syntax is inadequate. The fact that Shakespeare
is using an available syntactical alternative does not mean he is
using it arbitrarily, or merely for a better scansion. Rather, the
separation has a stylistic effect. The Platonic form of whiteness, an
ideal that makes even snow's whiteness imperfect by comparison,
envelops and as it were suffocates the breathing skin. From *skin*
Othello abstracts a single characteristic and elevates it. It is a skin
apotheosised, supernal, envisioned already as expressing the
chastity of the heaven to which Desdemona's soul is shortly to
ascend. By the simple device of interrupting his audience's experience of *whiter . . . then Snowe* (a deviation from the norm of
regular declaration established in the speech so far), Shakespeare
induces an unease, a sense of syntagmatic disturbance, a sense that
something is happening that is not in the usual order of thing; and
this reflects Othello's meaning, in which a specialised kind of
whiteness is referred to which is itself outside Nature.[4] How far
Othello is from voluptuousness might be heard, too, in the scriptural allusions of the lexicon here. The commonplace image of
impossibly white skin is made rare, as is the image of alabastrine
smoothness, by Shakespeare's literary skill. Made to hear it afresh,
Shakespeare's audiences might have caught the resonance of Psalm
51:7 – 'I shall be whiter than snow' after being washed by God; and,
indeed, of 2 Kings 5:27, where a leper is 'white as snow' – this may
have sounded an ironical undertone in Shakespeare and possibly

Othello concerning the supposed impurity of Desdemona.[5]
True, Othello bends for a while to the world of the five senses in:

> When I haue pluck'd thy [Q *the*] Rose,
> I cannot giue it vitall growth againe,
> It needs must [Q *must needs*] wither. Ile smell thee [Q *it*]
>   on the Tree.
> Oh [Q *A*] Balmy breath, that dost almost perswade
> Iustice to breake her Sword. One more, one more:
> [Q *Iustice her selfe to breake her sword once more,*]
> Be thus when thou art dead, and I will kill thee,
> And loue thee after. One more, and that's the last,
> [Q *once more, and this the last,   He kisses her*]
> So sweete, was ne're so fatall.
>
>   (F3253–60; V.ii.13–20)

But even the extra kisses of F do little to suggest the addiction to, or luxuriance in, physical gratification that 'voluptuousness' defines. Above all else, these are kisses of farewell.[6] Shakespeare continues to use items from a conventional iconography of physical beauty – as disparaged in Sonnet 130:

> If snow be white, why then her brests are dun
>   . . .
> I haue seene Roses damaskt, red and white,
> But no such Roses see I in her cheekes,
> And in some perfumes is there more delight,
> Then in the breath that from my Mistres reekes.[7]

But, as ever in this speech, their physical properties are more than shared with a spiritual significance not present in the sonnet (the purpose of which is, after all, to praise the mistress for being of the earth). The physically received fragrance of Desdemona's breath is certainly in Othello's mind – *Balmy* being 'Delicately and deliciously fragrant' (*OED* adj., 3) rather than 'Deliciously soft and soothing' (adj. 4, figurative) – and repeats the evocation of Desdemona's physical presence as expressed in

>   Oh thou weed:
> Who art so louely faire, and smell'st so sweete,
> That the Sense akes at thee . . . .
>
>   (F2762–4; IV.ii.67/8–69)

or in Q,

> O thou blacke weede, why art so louely faire?
> Thou smell'st so sweete, that the sence akes at thee . . . .

But just as one is wary of restricting *the Sense* to the sense of smell alone (*OED* sb., I.1) so one may respond to *breath* as something more than literal air expelled from the lungs (*OED* 3). The word *sense* has an unusual variety of meanings in *Othello*, several of them said by the *OED* to be original. Here it seems to be working with some suggestion that *the Sense* represents Othello as a whole in that he himself, rather than his olfactory function, suffers from the degree of sweetness. It is Othello as a whole who aches at *thee* – at Desdemona as a whole expressed through her fragrance. In F, of course, it is a composite of smell and sight that represents Othello. Similarly breath, in the context of apotheosised *skin* and symbolic *Light*, becomes itself other than real. It becomes the spirit of life (*OED* 5; Schmidt 5) that Othello is shortly to stop; while the balminess, in this world of apparent perfection, would seem to have in it at least something of a heavenly redolence – an ideal fragrance.[8]

The balmy breath is further idealised, of course, by its development as an image from the symbolic *Rose*. Desdemona's fragrance is no longer that of a dissembling weed but one of something more complex. Q, in stating that Desdemona is herself a blossom on the Tree of Life, is more consistent than F, where *thy Rose* turns into *thee on the Tree*. This rose is only distantly related to the flowers the poet of Sonnet 130 has seen in gardens but not in his mistress's cheeks. It is a metaphor for a woman of great beauty, excellence or virtue (*OED* sb., II.59); it is an emblem of chastity (the rose-window in churches and cathedrals is a blazon of the Virgin Mary); and it is an emblem of mortality – the 'loathsome canker . . . in sweetest bud' and the fact that 'Roses have thornes' (as in Sonnet 35) and can hurt. As Othello smells it on the tree (its fragrance being its soul, so to speak), so it represents in itself Desdemona, in whom soul is expressed by both balminess and breath. An abstract *Justice*, personified, is made almost to forgo her function by a breath that is soulful as well as physical.[9]

Desdemona as an (apparently) ideal form realised on earth – this is the theme of all these picturings. They are summarised in the Platonic compliment 'Thou cunning'st [Q *cunning*] Patterne of excelling Nature' (F3250; v.ii.11). This is comparable with the earlier 'being like one of Heauen, the divells themselues / Should feare to ceaze thee' (F2728–9 in Q's verse form; iv.ii.36–7). *Patterne* was available to Shakespeare as 'copy; a likeness, similitude' (*OED* sb., 4 [1557–1714]); but much more germane here is 'example or model deserving imitation . . . [or] of a particular excellence' (sb., 1 [late Middle English and surviving today]). Since *cunning* is 'skilfully contrived' (*OED* adj., 2b), the description of Desdemona as a most cunning model in Nature, if not *the* most cunning model that Nature has ever produced, is indeed a compliment. And the compliment is raised, as it were, by *excelling* with its Latin prefix *ex* ('out of'). Nature is 'superior, surpassing' (*OED, Excelling* ppl. adj.). In making Desdemona, she went above herself and made not an earthbound example or copy but an example as of heaven. The verbal element in the gerund, too, makes Nature more active than she might have been in the near-synonymous and available 'excellent': as if Nature were consciously and particularly engaged in the ideal of Desdemona's genesis.[10]

The intensity of Othello's involvement with the Platonic world is emphasised by a comparison of *Thou cunning'st Patterne of excelling Nature* with Cassio's 'hymn':

> he hath archieu'd [Q *atchieu'd*] a Maid
> That paragons description, and wilde Fame:
> One that excels the quirkes of Blazoning pens,
> And in th'essentiall Vesture of Creation,
> Do's tyre the Ingeniuer [Q *Does beare all excellency*]
>
> (F821–5; ii.i.61–5)

Othello needs six words, Cassio needs more than four lines. Othello conceives an absolute ideal, Cassio for the most part keeps Desdemona to a standard of comparison. True, she had to be attained with some effort (*OED, Achieve* v., ii.5b [1393–1618]), but still she was a young unmarried woman of the earth. Also, what she matches or surpasses (*OED, Paragon* v., 2 or 3) is verbal or pictorial portraiture (*OED, Description* 2a or 4) and extravagant rumours or reputation (*OED, Fame* sb., 1 or 2) – more mundane references. Again, what she excels is the flourishes or conceits (*OED, Quirk* 6 or 2) in which she has been pictured. These are the concern of heraldry, or of setting forth honourably in words and proclaiming, or of vaunting publicity – all these associations in *OED, Blazon* v., i.1–3 and ii.4–6, are apt in the military Cassio's mouth. The quirks are above all, however, the productions of versifiers who, presumably like Cassio, attempt to catch a likeness of their lady by a literary means. Not until the last two lines does Cassio use less worldly references – though even then the metaphor is a standard one of artistic style as dress. *Vesture* is both 'clothing' (*OED* I.1c) and 'Metaphorically, the human body as that in which the soul is dressed' (Schmidt). This meaning suggests that *tyre* is 'attire' rather than 'exhaust' (*OED* v.³, and v¹, II). *Ingeniuer* (an idiosyncratic spelling of *ingener*: 'contriver, inventor' – see Schmidt, *Engineer*) is usually read as the artist or blazoner or, indeed, as the imagination. So, like the dyer's hand in Sonnet 111, the *Ingeniuer* is subdued to what he or it works in when attempting to treat Desdemona. Again, since the *Vesture of Creation* is the body's dressing-out of spirit, it is possible to read the *Ingeniuer* as Cassio's way of referring to God or Nature – the Great Artificer. Yet again, Muir persuasively suggests that *tyre* is both 'attire' and 'weary' and that it was suggested by an 'unconscious quibble' on *Vesture*. In this case, the 'immortal' Desdemona outwears or survives, as well as surpassing, the merely mortal artist and his efforts.[11]

In all these readings Desdemona figures as a celestial idea made flesh in an earthly raiment. But even in this Platonic vision there is a subtle difference between Cassio's account and Othello's address. Cassio invests Desdemona with an earthly essence. His imminent further description of the *Diuine Desdemona* by whose beauty the elements are calmed is essentially that of a beautiful woman who, though goddess-like, yet sails on the sea and comes ashore as a virtual Venus only. He is consciously hyperbolic, courtly, extravagant. In reality, as he knows, his goddess 'when she walkes treads on the ground', exactly like the mistress of Sonnet 130. From Othello's address, however, all these worldly standards of excellence and this emphasis on the physical – indeed, pagan – aspect of deity are absent. There is nothing courtly in it. Nor does Othello state directly that Desdemona is divine: his vision of her divinity has been too intrinsic in him for such a simplistic and facile definition.

To summarise the manifesto of 'It is the Cause . . . ': Othello as it were assures the sleeping Desdemona that she will be dying in a good cause. But a definition of that cause consists not in the following direct statements: *else shee'l betray more men*; or *Be thus when thou art dead, and I will kill thee, / And loue thee after*; or *It strikes, where it doth loue*. The straightforward syntax of these sentences derives from a brutal 'reasonableness' and a poverty of descriptive resonance which in turn suggest the poverty of Othello's argument. These statements dispossess the speech of the overall 'ravishingly beautiful' quality that McAlindon hears in it.[12] The beauty is heard – I think – specifically in the repetition of *It is the Cause* and in those lines where Desdemona is described in terms of neo-Platonic idealism. And it is in those lines that a suggestion of the Cause consists. Othello must now continue his pilgrimage not in the landscape of war and travel but in the body of his marriage. Money's assertion that there is a sense in which Othello's 'soul *is* the "cause"'[13] can be modified: Othello's soul has *always* been his cause. Emotions have proved far too untidy to be dismissed at will – as Othello declared they could be in 'Away at once with Loue, or Iealousie' (F1808; III.iii.196); but they *can* be organised and incorporated into Othello's constant concern with the business of his soul. Or so Othello thinks. His new crusade is the purification of his wife's tainted body by the driving-out, in a state of grace, of her tainting but shriven soul. The chastity that is suggested by his wife's physical beauty will then be truly realised. The dramatic function of this speech is precisely to inform us of this spiritual 'advance' in Othello's thinking. Without it, Othello's entrance in itself would have aroused suspense enough to carry the early part of the scene: Shakespeare gives us the speech in order to characterise still further his hero – both his sense of ideal beauty and his capacity for self-deception. Importantly, Othello's long-established practice of self-publication in a crisis makes it entirely plausible in dramatic terms. It would seem that the murder of Desdemona has been brought into Othello's moral scheme. It will be morally beautiful. It will involve much alacrity in hardness. It will be a difficult duty well done.

Shortly after the murder of Desdemona, Othello's elevated figure is determinedly unfixed in a distinctly lowering lexicon by Aemilia. In Aemilia's '(I care not for thy Sword) Ile make thee known' (F3442; V.ii.168) there would seem to be some misunderstanding about Othello's threat with his sword. Othello's 'Peace, you were best' is not a command against disclosure as such – Othello has, after all, disclosed himself as a murderer to Aemilia against the evidence of the momentarily revived Desdemona. It is, rather, a protest against Aemilia's interpretation of events and of Othello's character. Othello is to be found in a lowering way that must both offend his good name and trouble his 'caused' certainty. He is aroused from his stricken condition by the double threat of an alternative range of possibilities and of a degrading terminology. He hears the voice of public opinion and of posterity sounding already another version of events in this furious gentlewoman. Here is the scornful time he feared. If Aemilia intensifies with a pointing finger her descriptions of Othello as a gull and a dolt, then the effect will be of an image – the fixed figure and the slow or unmoving finger of Time – realised and enacted. Before the arrival of other characters on stage (F3444; V.ii.170) Othello hears that he is 'the blackest Diuell', 'a diuell' and 'rash as fire'. Further, Desdemona's marriage is described as 'her most filthy Bargaine' (*Bargaine* being 'compact' – *OED, Bargain* sb., 2). In this Aemilia directly counters Othello's definition of the supposed adulteries – 'filthy deeds', twelve lines earlier in F – by transferring the filth to the marriage itself; while at the same time she repeats the repugnance that Othello heard from Brabantio in Act I and which Iago talked of in 'Foule disproportions' (F1861; III.iii.237). Aemilia, then, negates Othello's great Cause. The murder is no more worthy of heaven, she says, than Othello was worthy of Desdemona; while all notion of honour, spiritual sanction, even of justified revenge, is notably absent from Aemilia's promulgation that 'The Moore hath killed my Mistris. Murther, murther.' Furthermore, Aemilia's address of Othello as 'Oh Gull, oh dolt, / As ignorant as durt' is particularly telling. It has a certain remembrance of Sir Toby's discard of Sir Andrew as 'an Asse-head, and a coxcombe, & a knaue: a thin fac'd knaue, a gull?' (*Twelfe Night, or what you will*, F2369–70; V.i.198–9) – though I am not, of course, suggesting any similarity between the characters of Sir Andrew and Othello. In the comedy *coxcombe* is severally used and played upon as 'head' and as 'simpleton' (*OED, Coxcomb* 2 and 3) for the purpose of verbal wit; in the tragedy the same word is made serious, sombre – 'murd'rous Coxcombe' (F3527; V.ii.237). But, just as the portion of pathos in Sir Andrew is not expressed in Sir Toby's summary, so Othello's large capacity for distress and his (misused) idealism are not expressed in Aemilia's. (I note, by the way, that Empson suggests *Coxcombe* and *Foole* here may refer to Iago – *The Structure of Complex Words*, p. 227.)

His idealism would in fact be exposed by Aemilia – arguably, were she aware of it – as a risky and insufficient quality in the business of living. For a notable consistency can be heard in Shakespeare's characterisation of her. On two occasions she functions as the spokeswoman for that part of our response which is exaspera-

tion, even anger, at the way idealism is inseparable from naïveté in
the persons of Othello and Desdemona. In the *Willow Song* scene
(IV.iii) Shakespeare presented her as an eloquent counterweight to
Desdemona. On the one side Desdemona could not believe that
such wives exist who abuse their husbands. On the other side
Aemilia declared that such wives do exist, and that she herself
would be of their number were the whole world to be gained
thereby – because 'the wrong' of adultery is 'but a wrong i'th'world'
(F3053; IV.iii.77) and not a sin against an impossible ideal of
heaven. Again, on the one side Desdemona prayed,

> Heauen [Q *God*] me such vses [Q *vsage*] send,
> Not to picke bad from bad, but by bad mend.
> (F3078–9; IV.iii.102–3)

One may perhaps read that Desdemona is praying for good usage
from Othello. But the reading would be invalid. Since Othello does
abuse her, Desdemona is praying that God may send her the means
to benefit spiritually by the maltreatment: to improve herself, and
not to respond in kind. This is a conventional Christian morality;
but the fact that Desdemona acts upon it declares the strength of her
idealism, her essential virtue. Her naïveté here consists in believ-
ing that a Christian patience in affliction could ever suffice against
Othello's uncontrollable rage – that same rage that has already
caused him to attack her physically before the representative of the
Venetian government. Against this, on the other side, Aemilia
declared that if wives do ill it is on account of their husbands' ill
example, since wives have sensual feelings and frailties to match
their men's. One may not agree with this extreme view – it is
actually an excuse for adultery, not a reason – but it does plead
implicitly for a pragmatic fairness in marriage; and this the
audience (one presumes) would find more acceptable than over-
acquiescence. (On the Willow Song scene see above, pp. 48ff.)
Similarly, after the murder, Aemilia's indignant realism makes her
outstandingly sympathetic in our ears as she speaks out and supplies the counterweight to Othello's unseeing idealism. The extraordinary social indecorum of her language – not just the diction of
abusive names but also the fact that she *thous* Othello, the man she
has hitherto called *My Lord* and *you* – declares the extraordinary
incongruity of the situation as a whole. For Aemilia, the Moor has
killed her mistress – that is the sum of it. And all respect for rank, for

the natural order of a social hierarchy, is made invalid by that initial monstrous disordering. In her indignation Aemilia is our spokes-woman – Shakespeare's dramatic device against apoplexy – but she also speaks for us in her emphatic demonstration of the truth that Othello should have brought himself to a knowledge of. When the handkerchief is referred to as evidence she immediately asserts what we have always known – the handkerchief's theft – and what Othello has never for an instance entertained: he could conceive of loss, of giving away, but never of criminal activity by a third party. Again, in her immediate assertion of 'Oh she was heauenly true' (F3406; V.ii.138) Aemilia demonstrates a clear-sighted awareness of an ideal where it truly exists. She speaks not merely from a waiting gentlewoman's intimate knowledge of how her mistress has been spending her time but from an intuitive knowledge of Des-demona's essential virtue. Moreover, in actively defending Des-demona's good name, Aemilia herself becomes idealistic. She acts indeed against injustice, against the evil in Iago, for the good that was in Desdemona – and at personal risk. And she dies coming to bliss, as she says, 'So speaking as I thinke' (F3550; V.ii.254). In the compulsiveness of her reaction she is akin to Othello. In her intui-tive faith in Desdemona's virtue, however, she demonstrates some-thing that Othello, for all his idealistic nature, has lamentably lacked.

Of course, the tragedy of the play consists not only in Des-demona's essential purity and Iago's essential nastiness but also in the carefully established essential virtue of the Othello that was once so good – and who, importantly, continues so despite his perpetration of a revolting crime. The fact that Othello can be *justly* addressed as he is by Aemilia supplements our sense of how abysmal has been his fall.

Othello does try to out-tongue Aemilia's portrayal of him. But his assertion

> O, I were damn'd beneath all depth in hell:
> But that I did proceed vpon just grounds
> To this extremity

> (F3408–10; V.ii.140–2)

must alienate an audience – either contemporary or modern – in its uncritical acceptance of death as an unfaithful wife's just punish-ment. Such an acceptance was doubly foreign: not only to the

Jacobean penal code but also in the sense of belonging across the
Channel in an alien code of honour.[14] His claim four lines later,
however –

> had she bin true,
> If Heauen would make me such another world,
> Of one entyre and perfect Chrysolite,
> I'd not haue sold her for it

– has much effect. Not only in Shakespeare's irony – which supports Aemilia's *Gull* and *dolt* – but also in Othello's reversion to the
idealistic language of 'It is the Cause . . . ' – which acts against
Aemilia's 'low' terms. The supposed nature of Desdemona, 'false as
water' (F3404; V.ii.137) – i.e. seemingly transparent but lacking in
structure, promiscuously obedient to whatever might turn her – is
contrasted to Othello's earlier vision. Lexically, there is some
reference back to the world of sighs (Q) or kisses (F) at F504
(I.iii.159) – a place and a moment filled exclusively by Desdemona's
response and by Othello's own vision of love. More immediately,
such another world refers to the world's globe: even if this globe
were formed wholly from one hard crystal, and not partly of false
water, its worth would not have matched the value of Desdemona
in Othello's vision. The sound of *Chrysolite* is so similar to a combination of 'crystal' and 'light' that Othello's earlier talk of Desdemona's alabastrine, white translucency comes to mind. A recent
and admirable essay by Lynda E. Boose on *Chrysolite* comments,

> Shakespeare most probably had never seen a chrysolite but
> fastened on the word for this passage because he was attracted to
> its sound. But he could quite easily have presumed from that
> sound that the word in fact indicated some version of 'crystal', a
> confusion which could logically have arisen from sixteenth-
> century spelling conflations.[15]

Boose suggests that Shakespeares' *Chrysolite* is not 'Pliny's green
gem' of small value but that it derives from the Song of Solomon in
the Geneva Bible and possibly from the chrysolite that formed the
seventh foundation of the New Jerusalem in Revelation 21. It is 'a
translucent white . . . [gem] which would carry with it the abstract
ideas of Desdemona's purity, moral clearness, and chaste fidelity';
and its use contributes to the 'white-translucent-shining-pure-

cold-virginal image cluster' of Act v. It would seem then that, for one last moment, Othello revives the ideal vision of his wife. Just as her skin was symbolically whiter than any whiteness to be seen on earth, so her perfection is more complete even than the perfectest earth – or would have been *had she bin true*. I say 'for one last moment': very soon Othello will have emerged from this world in which idealism mixes with sef-delusion; his vision of Desdemona will have become displaced by a clearer sight of her not as a shining virtue or notable strumpet but as a dead girl 'Pale as thy Smocke' (F3573; V.ii.276).

Of course, *Chrysolite* resonates elsewhere in the text as well. The hardness of stone forms the metaphor in 'thou do'st stone my heart' (F3315; V.ii.66) – whether *stone* be 'harden' or 'kill with stones' (Schmidt v.2 and 1). This hardness is a lesser quality than the chrysolite's however: it belongs (in Othello's specialised scale of emotions) to a revenging murderer and not to the soft-hearted sacrificer whose plan was to kill kindly and with heavenly tears. Again, in Othello's

> Are there no stones in Heauen,
> But what serues for the Thunder?
> Precious Villaine

> (F3529–31; V.ii.238)

the reference is once more to a superior kind of stone. These are the rocks that cause the giant gratings of thunder and which, in Othello's thinking, should be functioning as the thunderbolts sent to strike down Iago. Heaven should not be rude only in her speech; like Othello, her erstwhile champion, she should be decisive and act. Since these heavenly stones will not so function, they lose something of their high value – which is inverted and given to Iago. Iago is a *Precious Villaine* not just in the sense of 'arrant' (*OED*, *Precious* adj., 4) but also, in a connotative sense, because he is highly valued in the world of Satan – where, indeed, he is a 'demy-Diuell' (F3605; V.ii.304). Most resonant of all is the thrown-away 'Pearle' of Othello's last extended speech: another gem of white-ness, value and consistency. The difference, apart from a vast discrepancy in size, is that the pearl is ignorantly thrown away, while the chrysolite is talked of knowingly in terms of sale. The *OED* discloses no contemporary meaning of *sell* that excludes the central concepts of trade or betrayal (the original meaning of 'give' did not survive Middle English). Consider Othello's 'purchase made' and 'profit's yet to come' as he leads Desdemona to the marriage bed for the first time (F1120–1; II.iii.9–10): one wonders whether Shakespeare intends some alloying of Othello's sublimity with this financial vocabulary – especially when the *Seas worth* is considered too:

> But that I loue the gentle Desdemona,
> I would not my vnhoused free condition
> Put into Circumscription, and Confine,
> For the Seas worth.
>
> (F229–32; I.ii.25–8)

The *worth* here is not just the sea's intrinsic virtue (developing into the compulsive merit of Pontus); it is also the sum of its ship-wrecked treasure. It is of course possible that a general of Venice – one of the world's trading and financial centres – might innocently express himself in trading-terms and not be thought akin to the usurious Shylock himself. But a stronger defence of Othello is to hand. The chrysolite and the pearl are mentioned not in terms of the financial price that Venice or the Old World has put upon them but as something perfect and as something not base but (in one reading) worth more than a whole people. Even the treasure is washed, made 'mystical' by its immersion. For Othello, precious stones are a natural wealth informed by spiritual properties; they are not merely the lowest elements in the Great Chain of Being – as Q's Indian might be said to consider them. Brabantio's address of his daughter as 'Iewell' (F543; I.iii.195) signifies the emotional value she had for him before she deceived him in the matter of her marriage; it does not mean that he regarded her as a commodity. Similarly, Othello's *I'ld not haue sold her* denotes that a virtuous Desdemona would have been not only beyond price but beyond all valuation; it does not mean that Othello has the mind of a merchant. Shakespeare does, however, exert the following irony: that a character less idealistic, more susceptible to worldly values, might have proved less suscep-tible to Iago's suggestions – might have been less prone unknow-ingly to 'betray' (*OED*, *Sell* v., 2) his wife and marriage.[16]

Othello's attempt to out-tongue Aemilia has an additional interest: his self-publication is accompanied by the retreat into solipsism, the refusal to confront doubt, that are now established in him. Doubt here sounds in Aemilia's frequent and anguished repe-

tition of 'My Husband?'; and Othello either ignores it or cannot
register it. His reaction is first to assert one of the bases of his deed –
Iago's honesty – and then to utter 'What needs this itterance,
Woman?' (F3423; v.ii.153): i.e. what needs this repetition? (*OED*,
Iterance, and *Iteration* [as in Q] 2). This is as little an interrogative as
was Othello's 'Why? why is this?' to Iago (F1792; III.iii.180). He does
not ask what the repetition means; rather, he asserts it is unnecessary. He is baffled but does not inquire. There is a telling contrast
between his refusal or omission here and his earlier determination
to 'see' Iago's thoughts:

> OTHELLO. . . .
>   Is he not honest?
> IAGO. Honest, my Lord?
> OTHELLO. Honest? I, Honest.
> IAGO. My Lord, for ought [*sic*] I know.
> OTHELLO. What do'st thou thinke?
> IAGO. Thinke, my Lord?
> OTHELLO. Thinke, my Lord? Alas, thou eechos't [*sic*] me
>   [Q *By heauen he ecchoes me*] . . .
>
>   (F1707–13; III.iii.104–10)

The colloquy of which this forms a part is discussed above in
Chapter 4. I quote only the most germane section – in which *eechos't*
supplies a parallel with *itterance*, a comparable lexicon that points
the difference in Othello's reactions. In the one he turns away from
any implication of Iago's dishonesty. In the other he was eager,
already, to meet the proposal of Desdemona's guilt. It is ironic,
moreover, that Aemilia – who repeats herself to demand knowledge
– should be censured by Othello, in whom repetition has usually
worked towards the hindering of a true knowledge. Nothing of
Othello's iteration has expressed, as does Aemilia's, incredulity.
'Desdemona? Desdemona? Desdemona dishonest?' – some such
exclamation has never sounded in Othello.

    Aemilia's fixing of Othello's figure continues in what she says to
Iago: 'Disproue this Villaine, if thou bee'st a man' (F3450; v.ii.175).
A few lines later she is to make frequent accusations of villainy that
include Iago as well as Othello; but her first use must have a
particular shock on Montano and Gratiano, who lack the audience's
knowledge of the play and who make their entrance to hear the
general referred to so indecorously. The shock must be a verbal

equivalent of that effected on Lodovico by the striking of Desdemona in IV.i.

What Othello's reaction might be one does not know: it is not in the text. But his words to Gratiano and Montano disclose his continued attempt to justify the murder. Aemilia's witness that 'My Mistris heere lyes murthered in her bed' and that Iago's 'reports haue set the Murder on' (F3468 and 3470; V.ii.188 and 190) he points and confirms:

> OTHELLO. Nay stare not Masters
>   It is true indeede.
> GRATIANO. 'Tis a strange Truth.
> MONTANO. O monstrous Acte.

He wishes to be found as the murderer who acted on honest grounds – as ever there is no shrinking of his figure. But his confidence *is* extraordinary. It is comparable with that of 'Keepe vp your bright Swords, for the dew will rust them' – no wasted words. His *true indeede* includes nothing of Gratiano's *strange* or of Montano's *monstrous*. And his *Nay stare not Masters* is a more polite version of *What needs this itterance, Woman?* Othello seems confident that Venice will judge the murder as he does. His justness seems to him self-evident. His 'Oh, oh, oh' (F3484; V.ii.201) – what Aemilia calls his roaring – along with Q's stage direction 'Oth. *fals on the bed*', announces the degree of his distress; but, equally, his report to Gratiano emphasises his confident expectation of being well found:

> I scarse did know you Vnkle, there lies your Neece,
> Whose breath (indeed) these hands haue newly stopp'd:
> I know this acte shewes horrible and grim.
>   (F3489–91; V.ii.204–6)

This has an unintentional grotesqueness: unintentional, that is, in Othello. Having despoiled the family of Brabantio by the secret marriage, and having further despoiled it by the murder, Othello inadvertently insults that family by naming the relationship he has enforced on Gratiano. He uncles this senior member of the family; and his first use of that address – to announce his murder of the niece – is hardly in an ordinary family circumstance. There is a conflict – not sensed, I think, by Othello – between Othello's attempt to bring the murder within the Venetian pale of reasonable behaviour and the actual horror of the crime – an actual horror which for Othello *shewes* more than it is. Even if Desdemona *had* been unfaithful, her murder would hardly make Gratiano incline towards this nephew-by-marriage whose very marriage has caused the death of his grieving brother and who now seems bent on the destruction of the family as a whole. Othello's *I scarse did know you* therefore has undertones not intended by the speaker. Othello has but scarcely known any of his new relatives. He has ever but slenderly known his wife. And in general he has scarcely known anything about human dealing.

This condition of scarce knowing it is that supplies the fantasy of Othello's explanation to Gratiano:

> 'Tis pittifull: but yet Iago knowes
> That she with Cassio, hath the Act of shame,
> A thousand times committed. Cassio confest it,
> And she did gratifie his amorous workes
> With that Recognizance and pledge of Loue
> Which I first gaue her: I saw it in his hand:
> It was a Handkerchiefe, an Antique Token
> My Father gaue my Mother.
>
> (F3499–506; V.ii.213–20)

How simple – in more ways than one – is this explanation. It repeats the 'truth' that Othello explained to Desdemona earlier in V.ii. Here in all its distortion is Othello's publication not of himself but of 'objective' facts. The exaggeration of *A thousand times* does more than suggest 'long time' in the play's scheme of 'double time'. It indicates not only Othello's frequent extremism of language but also his *need* to believe. Again, *I saw it* in no way represents the wilfulness of Othello's seeing, his readiness to misinterpret what he saw. Yet again, the inconsistency of *My Father gaue my Mother* with 'Did an Aegyptian to my Mother giue' (F2204; III.iv.56) might be Shakespeare's – but, equally, might be Othello's. As Steevens suggested, the early version might have been a fabrication to frighten Desdemona with magic.[17] Alternatively, in the late version Othello might be neglecting the handkerchief's magic property in order to emphasise its emotional value – the modern term 'sentimental value' is not strong enough. Such a value might more impress Gratiano, in whom talk of magic might have provoked

Brabantio-like accusations of devilry. Indeed, this point can be pressed more specifically. The theme of Gratiano's preceding speech was 'Poor Desdemon: / I am glad thy Father's dead' (F3492–3; v.ii.207), because the murder of his daughter would have made Brabantio commit suicide and so suffer rejection by God – 'fall to Reprobance [Q *reprobation*]' as a result of doing 'a desperate turne'. (See *OED, Reprobation* 3.) Against the sentiment of Gratiano's '*thy* Father' Othello sets the sentiment associated with '*My* Father' (emphasis added). Yes, 'tis pitiful, but the outrage to Desdemona's family cannot be justly compared (Othello implies) with the outrage done to Othello's tender feelings.

Within a few lines of this 'reasonable' explanation the truth is imposed on Othello. Aemilia's account of *her* gift of the handkerchief – to Iago as a kind of love token – demonstrates a new version of events. And Iago's reactions – 'Villanous Whore' and 'Filth, thou lyest' (F3522 and 3525; v.ii.232 and 234) together with his threatening of his wife with his sword – demonstrates a 'new' Iago who makes the new version utterly convincing. Even more quickly than he came to believe in Desdemona's guilt does Othello now come to believe in Iago's. Even more instantly does he attempt revenge. It is as if the energetic exclusion of doubt throughout almost three acts has accumulated an immense and opposite pressure; so that when Iago's reports are disproved – not only by Aemilia's statements but by the ocular proof of the 'new' Iago – Othello is swept from one certainty to another within a very short while indeed.

Othello is hardly of a mind, therefore, to contest Aemilia's further fixings of him: 'thou dull Moore', 'murd'rous Coxcombe' and 'Foole'. *Dull* is particularly resonant. It denotes a slowness of intelligence, foolishness and want of sensibility (*OED* adj., 1 and 2); it also connotes a lack of light and clarity that contrasts to Desdemona's translucency. As for Aemilia's final fixing of Othello as *cruell* – 'Moor, she was chaste: She lou'd thee, cruell Moore' (F3548; v.ii.252) – this must increase Othello's distress in reminding him of his self-deceiving talk about 'cruell Teares' and heavenly sorrow that 'strikes, where it doth loue' (at the end of 'It is the Cause . . . '). There is nothing in Aemilia's line that Othello could justly contest – unless he take offence at Aemilia's further soundings of *Moore*. In this part of the play, from the calling of Montano, Gratiano and Iago to the death of Aemilia, there are five such soundings, four by Aemilia, one by Montano ('take you this weapon / Which I haue recouer'd from the Moore' – F3536–7; v.ii.242–3). These revive the appellation with which Brabantio in Act I and Iago throughout the play have denigrated Othello. It is a reduction of Othello to a race and a sterotype – a fixing of him very low – against which, however, he does not protest until in his suicide speech he protests his Venetian quality and his individualism.

This is not to say that his self-publication ceases until then. On the contrary. The escape of Iago serves the dramatic function of drawing everyone off-stage except Aemilia and Othello. And, while the former loses her life, the latter announces his distress at the loss of his sword and the loss of his honour – they would seem to be one and the same. There is no direction in the text as to how the actor playing Othello should react to Aemilia's eloquent and tuneful death; and that very absence may in itself indicate Othello's self-absorption. In a way he contributed obliquely to Aemilia's death – had his sword found Iago then Iago could not have stabbed her – and the callousness with which Aemilia is ignored may supplement our sense of a *cruell Moore*. Be that as it may, Shakespeare certainly makes Othello speak as a distressed military man rather than as a husband who has just murdered his own wife and is sharing the stage with the last moment of another:

> I am not valiant neither:
> But euery Punie whipster gets my Sword.
> But why should Honor out-liue Honesty?
> Let it go all.

(F3541–4; v.ii.245/6–8)

That *neither* is interesting. It could be a double negative used for emphasis: Most certainly I am not valiant. More probably it refers to the disproving of another quality that Othello thought he had. This quality is likely to be best judgement, or discretion, or reason. And Othello now disclaims it not only in himself but by implication as a general lack in the world at large. Specifically he denies it in Montano, the Governor he formerly admired for the gravity and stillness of his youth. *Punie* means 'weakly' as well as inexperienced and inferior in importance (*OED* adj., A 3b, 2 and 3); while *whipster* denotes Montano as a slight and insignificant person (*OED* 1c). Since Montano has just taken Othello's sword and gone manfully after Iago, and since, also, he was formerly called a substitute of most allowed sufficiency, this description obviously tells us less about Montano than about Othello's state of mind. Othello was given to vociferous abuse of Cassio when he thought Cassio had stolen his manhood in stealing a part of his wife's favour. Now he abuses the man who, he feels, has made a similar theft of his manhood in taking his sword. It would seem that in this one point at least Othello's judgement is still at fault. He was right to disclaim it.

Being disarmed by Montano must, of course, be yet another of the several disorientating experiences that Othello suffers in this scene; and this additional confusion probably contributes to the obscurity of *But why should Honor out-liue Honesty?* The most likely reading, I think, depends on the loss of military honour entailed in the loss of a soldier's weapon, the symbol and tool of his occupation, even while attempting the task of killing an arch-enemy. In this reading *Honesty* is tied by former usage to Iago, to Iago's supposed soldierly inability to lie, his warrant officer's version of virtue — a kind of non-commissioned *Honor* therefore. It may also spread out, though, into a more general meaning: the principle of honesty which is now exposed to have been dead, to have been dishonest, all along. By such an exposure even the worthy Montano has become a whipster.

Another possible reading is of *Honesty* as female chastity (*OED* I.3 [–1634]). In this sense it has already once been used by Othello: 'I do not thinke but Desdemona's honest' (F1851; III.iii.229). Here the reference would be to Chastity as Desdemona, who is dead. The trouble with this reading is that the ideal of chastity, as opposed to its earthly exemplar, is still alive and therefore cannot be outlived. Indeed, there is a critical view that discerns in Othello in this scene some joy that the ideal beloved of his earlier emotion *has* survived in his mind and memory! On the whole I find this reading unpersuasive.

Less so is another reading supported by several editors (for example, Walker, p. 217; Ridley, p. 190n; Ross, p. 238n), in which honour and honesty are the exterior and interior of a quality applied by Othello to himself alone. Sanders (p. 181) translates: why should 'the reputation for honour outlast the possession of honour itself'? This reading suffers doubly, however: first from the fact that the yeoman term *honest / honesty* is never used elsewhere of Othello — by Othello or by anyone else; and secondly from the fact that the premise, which is a clear distinction by Othello between reputation and self-respect, has not sounded hitherto and is not to sound, either, in his imminent talk of having been an (ill-defined) honourable murderer who acted all in honour (again ill-defined). A character who could make such a distinction would have distinguished in earlier acts between fact and fiction, between ocular proof and imaginative interpretation.

When, therefore, Othello says, *Let it go all* – with a heavy stress on *all* – he seems to be dismissing a specifically military honour which can join unimpeded the other illusions of his own good judgement and of Iago's good faith. The parallel with 'Othello's Occupation's gone' (F2000; III.iii.361) in the terse, absolute quality and in the verb supports this military sounding. And the question now arises, as a result, of how far or how little Othello has advanced in his unillusioning. Does his new knowledge include a larger self-knowledge? Or is it rather a mere information, drastically distressing, about the murder of an innocent on mistaken grounds? Does Othello advance into a full awareness of his responsibility for the crime beyond his responsibility for the actual smothering? Or does he remain in his old ways, stressing the basis of Iago's *dis*honesty much as he stressed the basis of Iago's honesty until now? If one compares Othello's rhetorical question and grand dismissal of a vague *all* with Iago's recent words, one has to conclude that Othello's awareness *does* remain limited. Iago said,

> I told him what I thought,
> And told no more
> Then what he founde himselfe was apte, and true.
>
> (F3454–6; V.ii.179–80)

And, since Iago is not to be so forthcoming again, this can be taken as his summary, *his* version of events. Q seems to express the formality of the occasion by scanning these lines, amidst all the commotion of the sequence as a whole, as two regular pentameters. *Founde* declares the finding or verdict that Othello himself arrived at; *apte* means 'appropriate' or 'apposite' (*OED, Apt* adj., 3) with, perhaps, a strong ironical undertone of the verbal meaning 'adapt' (*OED, Apt* v., 1 [current 1540–1672]). Iago stresses the hypothetical nature of his evidence which adapting Othello found to be true. Iago thus declares a case in which the responsibility for Desdemona's murder must be found not in the evidence supplied but in the interpretation. Iago's slow, considered monosyllables present a case that is shrewd and cogent – and one which Othello, with his talk of being ensnared by a devil and of being wrought beyond reason, will fall far short of formulating.[18]

Othello's self-publishing, then, betrays yet again a response not proper to the dramatic situation. Over the double domestic tragedy of two wives slain he utters the obsequies of a lost ideal soldiership. And he continues them, furthermore, to a great extent in the following sequence:

> OTHELLO. I haue another weapon in this Chamber,
> It was [Q *is*] a Sword of Spaine, the Ice brookes temper:
> Oh heere, it is: Vnkle I must come forth.
> GRATIANO. If thou attempt it, it will cost thee deere;
> Thou hast no weapon, and must perforce suffer.
> OTHELLO. Looke in vpon me then, and speake with me,
> Or naked as I am I will assault thee.
> GRATIANO. What is the matter?
> OTHELLO. Behold, I haue a weapon:
> A better neuer did it selfe sustaine
> Vpon a Soldiers Thigh. I haue seen the day,
> That with this little Arme, and this good Sword,
> I haue made my way through more impediments
> Then twenty times your stop. But (oh vaine boast)
> Who can control his Fate? 'Tis not so now.
>
> (F3551–65; v.ii.255–68)

On the death of Aemilia by Iago's dishonest weapon, Othello takes out with no sense of irony – the irony is all in Shakespeare – a sword remarkable for its high Spanish honour, one informed by the ice-cold virtue of waters akin to the coldly reasoned current of the Pontic Sea. Like the word 'complexion', *temper* ranges along both physical and psychological properties. A temper might be the right mixture of essential elements in an object (*OED* sb., I.1, refers to this); or it might be the commingling of emotions and reason in a man's mind (sb., I.3). Since the temper of a man was considered to derive from the mix of his humours, of course, it was still physically based: a man was the sum of how the elements, with a modicum of etherial spirit, were arranged in him. Here, the *temper* of the sword denotes the quality of its steel from one of the Sheffields of the Renaissance;[19] but it strongly *con*notes a temperament, one in which the humours are well mingled to produce discretion, gravity, stillness, judgement – the mark of the ideal warrior. Othello himself has enjoyed a reputation for an icebrook temper. And the sword is not merely a weapon but a symbol, an intrinsic adjunct, of the valiant Othello of hitherto. Its strange ability to sustain itself contributes to its virtually living quality. The Latin components of *sustaine* – *sub* and *tenere* ('hold') – imply a holding-up from beneath, a self-support. The sword lives not on the thigh alone but on its own virtue; and in doing so it sustains, in turn, the opinion that Othello viewed the loss of his first sword as an unmanning measure, that with the sword of Spain he retrieves for a short while his sexual being. Disarmed by Montano, Othello acts by instinct to rearm as soon as possible – with, as it were, his best steel. He hunts after the man once known by the name of Othello. And his *Oh heere it is* sounds not incidentally but as an emotional 'find'. Here is, it seems, the valiant general of old.

According to Granville-Barker it is possible to play Othello as a grimly comic practical joker in the colloquy with Gratiano.[20] If so, the grimness needs emphasis. Othello is speaking out of an old fighting-instinct. Renewed, as he thinks, by the sword in his hand, he deludes himself for a short while into the ability to command any situation that might be resolved by soldiership. He deludes himself into thoughts of escape. Almost at once, however, his intention is dissolved by his sense of psychological confinement. F's 'It *was* a Sword of Spaine' (emphasis added) for Q's *is* suggests Othello's sense of a past lost, his knowledge that no virtue now can flow back from the sword into himself. What use battlefield valour here? Will violence on a third member of Brabantio's family offset his loss of military honour, let alone his uxoricide?

So, the reaction against letting everything go is momentary only. The intention of *I must come forth* gives way to the old craving of 'I must be found'. *Looke in vpon me* and *Behold*, Othello says, using a lexicon of publication. It is, I think, probable that Othello intends this speech to be his suicide speech; and that in his pretence to Gratiano he is summoning a representative of Venice to audit and report his end. But he discovers he is not quite ready. He cannot settle into the rhythm and assurance that he does achieve in the suicide speech itself. He cannot yet manoeuvre himself into the final attempt to fix his figure and atone. He has not the time before commotion re-enters in the persons of Montano with his captive Iago and, in addition, Lodovico and officers. All he can do at the moment is, once again, regret the dear dead days of his military glory, the days when a single arm and the Spanish sword – almost, one feels, a magic sword – contrived for Othello near-superhuman feats of broil and battle.

The regret in these last few lines of the quoted passage is height-ened by this: the sounding of several words that Othello formerly used when occupied still by honour and by innocent love. For example *Arme* might remind one of the time when Othello was newly married and newly reassigned to military expedition (the 'deerest action' of 'these Armes of mine' – F422–4; I.iii.83–5); while *Stop* earlier sounded as 'Honourable stop' (F1111; II.iii.2), i.e. as discretion in a dutiful soldier, before it began to be alloyed in Iago's apparently honest hesitations ('these stops of thine' – F1728; III.iii.124). Again, *Boast* has echoes of 'when I know, that boasting is an Honour', uttered in the full pride of Act I. (F224; I.ii.20). And *'Tis not so now* both echoes and negates Othello's first sentence in the play, ''Tis better as it is' (F209; I.ii.6), in which Othello refused to be provoked by reported insult and seemed supremely confident about his honour and the workings of his fate. All in all these lines form in some of their lexicon a kind of memorial of the earlier valiant (and hubristic) hero.

It is perhaps difficult to feel much sympathy for Othello in these obsequies on honour lost. Less difficult, however, when he pub-lishes his awareness of his journey's end:

> Be not affraid, though you do see me weapon'd:
> Here is my iournies end, heere is my butt
> And verie Sea-marke of my vtmost Saile.
> Do you go backe dismaid? 'Tis a lost feare:
> Man but a Rush against Othello's brest,
> And he retires. Where should Othello go?
>
> (F3566–71; V.ii.269–74)[21]

The idea of suicide is not overtly present; but the lines induce something of awe as one hears Othello confront the fact that he is finished, self-bereft, invalid. The verbal scheme of 'to go', which started with the gone condition of Othello's occupation, which progressed through the gone condition – as Othello thought – of his fond love (''Tis gone': F2095; III.iii.450), and which has just just informed his relinquishment of all claim to virtue, 'Let it go all,' is now used to point the end of Othello's traveller's history: *Where should Othello go?* More importantly, perhaps, this awareness is expressed to a great degree in terms of the sea-imagery that features so much throughout this drama set in Venice and on Cyprus.

But Shakespeare has not indiscriminately made his characters talk of the sea; and Othello's use of sea-imagery has invariably been in contrast to, for example, Iago's. Iago's 'My Boate sailes freely, both with winde and Streame' (F1177; II.iii.59/60) expresses the nature of a pragmatic mariner, a nautical opportunist who gains as much advantage as he can from a coincidence of fair wind and fair current. Again, Iago speaks in a kind of documentary way of 'Cables of perdurable toughnesse' and of being 'be-leed, and calm'd' (F690–1 and 32; I.iii.336 and I.i.30) even when he is being metaphorical. That is, his metaphors belong in the jargon of the seaport city he serves and do not transcend it. The most obvious contrast of Iago's usage to Othello's is in Iago's 'trade of Warre' (F204; I.ii.1 – and see Chapter 1, n. 19) and Othello's 'Occupation' (F2000; III.iii.361): Iago stays inside the sailor's or soldier's job while Othello expresses his vocation. And this contrast of the mundane and the sublime is maintained when Othello alludes specifically to the sea. Othello's marine imagery has usually denoted a natural virtue – power and goodness. One example of difficulty is the 'Accidents by Flood' and the 'scapes i'th'imminent deadly breach' – in one interpretation of *breach* as 'breaking of waves on a coast or over a vessel' (*OED* sb., I.2) – at F480–1 (I.iii.135–6). Another is the 'hills of Seas' (F965; II.i.185) that Othello claims he would suffer again for the sake of the ensuing calm both actual and emotional. Another is the affliction of being 'Steep'd . . . in pouer-tie to the very lippes' – a water image at least, if not necessarily a marine one (F2745; IV.ii.51). Examples of the sea's natural virtue are in the 'Seas worth' (F232; I.ii.28) – intrinsic worth as well as ship-wreck – and in the Pontic Sea's icy current and compulsiveness, in terms of which coldly reasonable violence Othello tries to define his hot revenge. Additionally, of course, the virtue of the sea is joined by the tempering quality of the icebrook that Othello has just mentioned.

Even with Cassio, Othello shares little in his view of the sea. Cassio's sea is a courtly sea, a pleasant pander of a sea, bowing to Beauty and bearing Othello's 'tall ship' to the concave 'Bay' of female Cyprus (F843; II.i.79). In Othello's imagery the sea is, rather, a proving and uncourtly seascape. It has been as much a part of his pilgrimage as, for example, the antres vast and the deserts idle have been. In the *iournies end* passage, therefore, *Saile* as 'voyage' (*OED* sb.² [1604, citing these lines as a first recorded usage]) freshens the idea of life as a journey. It resonates from Othello's former talk of his travels and from his perceptions of the sea's virtue. *Iournie*, perhaps expressing the idea of a land-voyage (*OED, Journey* sb., II.3), might also connote in some degree the travail of Othello's travels by virtue of its sense as work done in a specific span of time (the general sense of sb., III). But it is the sea-picture that Othello develops in the following line and a half. Even in *butt*, I think, it is strongly present. Editors usually translate *butt* as 'terminal point' or 'boundary mark' (Walker, p. 222 after *OED* sb.⁴, I.1); or less convincingly as 'target' or 'goal' (thus Sanders, p. 182n, presumably after *OED* sb.⁴, II.4 and 2: 'A mark for archery practice'). This seems to suppose that Othello has been intending this particular manner of his cessation. Again, the gloss by Ross (p. 240n), that 'The butt is the structure on which the targets are placed in archery, and thus the utter limit of the aimed arrow's flight', seems inapt not only in this passage but in Shakespeare's invention of Othello as a whole. Though Shakespeare lodges him at the Sagittary and makes him speak of Cupid's toys, Othello is no Sagittarius, no archer. Insufficient attention has been given to another meaning of *butt*: as 'headland, promontory' (*OED* sb.⁸), which, the *OED* suggests, derives from a verb 'to jut out' and which it cites as a noun in '1598 Florio "Capo . . . a cape or but of any lands end" '. We still have the usage, of course, in a phrase such as the Butt of Lewis. According to this reading, Othello's life and sea-journey, having survived the actual and terrible storm at sea, will founder *Here* upon this landmass of Cyprus. One thinks of the island as an outcrop of the Italian main, as an outpost of Venice by which, emotionally, Othello has been sunk.²²

The sea-imagery persists, of course, into *Sea-marke*: 'A conspicuous object distinguished at sea which serves to guide or warn sailors in navigation' (*OED, Sea-mark* 2). But here the syntax, too, is of some interest. *And verie Sea-marke* was emended by early editors such as Theobald, Warburton and Johnson to 'The verie Seamarke'; and from the point of view of sense one can understand why, since the emendation makes for a parenthesis explaining *butt*. To retain F's version however, as modern editors do, is to retain the effective dissonance of this unexpected syntax. *And* slows the line, pointing us to the emphatic precision of *verie* and *vtmost* (which here means 'outermost' – *OED* adj., I.1). At the same time it exerts ambivalence, which is best explained – I think – as follows: *verie Sea-marke* pulls toward *vtmost Saile* semantically and syntactically; but equally it participates in a doublet with *butt*. Hence it is pulled two ways. The strange effect of this is comparable with that of two other syntactical instances in the play: the separating-out of the adverbial phrase in 'whiter skin of hers, then Snow' (see above pp. 191–3); and the repetition of *a* in 'A malignant, and a Turbond-Turke' (see below, p. 236). At these high moments of emotion, it seems, Shakespeare gives to Othello small linguistic quirks: they demand a slow delivery of the context, and they indicate an intenser mood.[23]

Such is the intensity here that Gratiano moves away from Othello. A few lines earlier he was merely *affraid*; now he goes back *dismaid* – that is, 'overwhelmed with fear . . . appalled' (*OED* ppl. adj.). To some extent Gratiano's terror may exist less in Gratiano than in Othello's sardonic exaggeration – as Othello remembers how he used to affect his enemies in battle; but, even so, it would seem to be a just reaction to the precisely menacing organisation expressed in *verie* and *vtmost* and the repetition of *Heere is my . . . heere is my*. In fact Gratiano, whose earlier theme was of suicide as a 'desperate turne' (F3496; v.ii.210), seems not to comprehend at all Othello's suicidal intent. Othello has further to explain, or to publish. Even a mere *Rush*, he claims, would make him retire. This reading of *Rush*, as a waterside plant used to cover floor or as a kind of taper, continues something of the water-imagery. It also exploits the proverbial sense of a thing of no importance (as in *OED* sb.[1],2). (Another reading, by which Othello means 'Merely supply the men for a rushing assault and Othello retires before it is made', is improbable: *but* governs *a Rush* not *Man*.) Interestingly, a vestige of sea-imagery lingers in *retires*, which was last used by Othello in the Pontic Sea simile. The virtuous Pontus never felt a retiring ebb. Othello now, bereft of former virtue, has become retirement complete.

As if to make the only mental movement possible to him, Othello now removes outside himself: he addresses himself in the third person – *Othello's brest* and *Where should Othello go?* It is as if he finds some relief from intolerable restriction by this manufacture of another presence, in which he rehearses the directly stated split of 'That's he that was Othello: heere I am' a score or so of lines later. At the same time, this self-address is reminiscent of 'Othello's Occupation's gone'; and in these few lines about journey's end is heard the same mixture of farewell and celebration. It seems that Othello's use of his own name signals a turning-away from times past and a decision made about an immediate future action. The old, gone grounds of virtuous action are positively published in their pass-

ing; and Othello moves on to a new ground. He has the motive, if
not yet the cue, for self-slaughter. He has a new cause. Unable to
move physically forward, for there is no spatial escape from his
mental torture, he can at least descend – into hell – by his own hand.
His former, elevated talk of his wife's smooth and ideally white
body is declined to the domestic simile in

> Now: how dost thou looke now? [not in Q] Oh ill-Starr'd
>   wench,
> Pale as thy Smocke: when we shall meete at compt,
> This looke of thine will hurle my Soule from Heauen,
> And Fiends will snatch at it. Cold, cold, my Girle?
> Euen like thy Chastity.
>
> (F3572–6; v.ii.275–8)

From an impossible perfection to the pallor of a corpse – with the
mention of intimate apparell suggesting the brief marital happiness
that Othello has destroyed. And, with Othello's virtue and honour
gone, the force that produced his former idealistically thrilling
language is spent – the energy of his new cause he puts to the
imaginative anticipation of torments:

> Whip me ye Diuels,
> From the possession of this Heauenly sight:
> Blow me about in windes, roast me in Sulphure,
> Wash me in steepe-downe gulfes of Liquid fire.
> Oh Desdemon! dead Desdemon: dead. Oh, oh!
> [Q *O Desdemona, Desdemona, dead, O, o, o.*]
>
> (F3577–81; v.ii.280–4)

Whether Othello does in fact finish in hell is not stated in the text.
Perhaps the sheer passion of his grief supplies an atonement sufficient for the divine pardon of his sin – if not necessarily for the
audience's forgiveness of his crime. Certainly, an Othello fixed
forever in hell would seem an unfairly afflicted figure. But, alternatively, for Othello to be brought at once into heaven would seem
an extenuation of his fault that Othello himself would vehemently
resist. The question really exists outside the play.[24] The important
fact within the text is this: that Othello fully believes in his damnation. Moreover, that he welcomes it. He turns from Gratiano and
his dead wife to address the troops of hell directly. He summons

them, commands them, encouraging them to do their worst. *This Heauenly sight* may be the dead figure of Desdemona; or it may be the heaven-given faculty of sight – literal speculation – which Othello has badly abused and which now forces him intolerably to see what he has done. On the strength of *possession* I incline to the latter reading, though on stage the former would be the more easily rendered.

About the afflictions listed here there is an opinion that arraigns Othello for choosing against mental torture, since physical pain he can the more easily endure.[25] But he could hardly enter a traditional hell and request a racking of his thoughts alone. Certainly he is consistent, this experienced traveller, in that he vividly depicts his torments inside a strange landscape. He will be punished by devils – the hellish equivalents of anthropophagi and men with heads inferior – and Shakespeare gives him something of a lexical consistency too. Hell, Othello's last visited region, has echoes of his former life and of earlier lands. *Blow*, for example, remembers the blowing of his fond love to heaven: now he will be blown by the winds of hell. And those winds are the counterpart of the wind he earlier imagined as being hushed with shame at Desdemona's sin. Again, his claims to ice-cold judgement will be mocked in his roasting – the heat of his criminal emotion will be punished in an appropriate temperature. Moreover, this roasting is to be effected in hell's own fuel of sulphur, a substance that occurs free in nature as a crystalline solid and may be taken, here, as a degraded version of Othello's chrysolite and of the pearl in his last extended speech. So his former general view of the earth with its deserts and quarries as a virtuously testing place is negated, for him at least. On such an earth Othello has no longer the right to live.

Most strongly envisaged, however, is the terrible fate contrived – in part – by the waters of his imagination. The affliction he once dismissed as endurable – of being steeped in poverty to the very lips – is now partly realised in the play from 'Steep'd' (F2745; IV.ii.51) as 'immersed' to *steepe-* as 'precipitous' (*OED, Steep* v., 1, and adj., 3). Also, the word *downe* is reused. It once sounded in Othello's scorn of effete civilisation as a 'thrice-driuen bed of Downe' (F579, I.iii.231) – as an extreme of softness; it now helps to describe the utter depths of hardship in which Othello will be steeped. Perhaps, too, the 'Antars vast' of an earlier account (F485; I.iii.140) echo in the *gulfes*: the huge empty caves once filled by Othello are taken over by the chasms whose concern is his perpetual reduction. Above all, *Wash* and *Liquid* surround Othello not with the virtuous seas of his voyagings but with an appalling penitence in which the elements of water, fire and earth combine – a landscape of flowing fire. The ease with which Othello can imagine this combination – the sheer congruity of the image – suggests something of the reorganisation of thought he has for the moment achieved. I would not make much of these lexical echoes singly; but in aggregate they do seem to indicate something of the consistency in Shakespeare's characterisation. One final point on the lexicon in this passage: all this emphasis on the heat of hell – no mention of its coldness – makes for a contrast to the *Cold, cold* nature of Desdemona's corpse, *Euen like thy Chastity*. In banishing himself to this farthest remove in temperature, Othello underlines the extreme banishment he expects. Desdemona has risen ideally to heaven; he must be gripped forever in the centre of the earth.[26]

As so often has happened, Othello's energy and organisation have become most evident at a moment of self-publication. And again that publication is practised at the cost of something else. In this instance, the near-constant publicity goes against our need that *some* meaning, *some* significance, should be derived from Othello's dreadful action. A desire exists – it has been voiced by several critics[27] – for a kind of *post mortem*, of the murderer's motive by the murderer. It is, of course, characteristic of Othello that no such introspection occurs. There is little real interest in his wonderings why. The lines

> Will you, I pray, demand that demy-Diuell,
> Why he hath thus ensnared my Soule and Body
>
> (F3605–6; V.ii.304–5)

consign not only the original responsibility for the action to Iago but also the actual inquiry to Lodovico. Additionally, the accounts of how Iago plotted with Rodorigo, and of the handkerchief's having been found by Cassio, elicit from Othello nothing beyond the comment 'O Foole, foole, foole!' (F3633; V.ii.326). This in a small way supplies yet another instance in which Othello repeats a single word for emphasis and excludes any analysis either of self or of situation; while his observation a few lines earlier, 'Il'd haue thee liue: / For in my sense, 'tis happinesse to die' (F3592–3; V.ii.292–3), suggests just how fundamentally Othello continues in his incomprehension of Iago. He seems not to have registered at all the fact that Iago's conscience will not be troubling him overmuch. 'Looke in vpon me then', he says to Gratiano (F3556; V.ii.260), meaning 'Look at me within this room'; but though in a metaphorical sense we are often looking in upon Othello's mind we do not observe much in the way of intellectual fittings. For Othello – it is generally recognised – lacks the important Hamletic traits of sharing his argument and of responding intellectually to the smirching of his ideals. Rather, one looks in upon him by means of the frequently self-betraying publications that he puts out.

This fact – that we the audience analyse Othello more than Othello does – is not to lower Othello's status as a tragic hero. That status subsists in his grief and in the eagerness with which he embraces his damnation – compounding it, indeed, by his suicide. For, in Hamlet's words, 'the Euerlasting had . . . fixt / His Cannon [*sic*] 'gainst Selfe-slaughter' (*The Tragedie of Hamlet, Prince of Denmarke*, F315–6; I.ii.131–2). And Othello's smiting of himself – the characteristic action of a man who ever made his own law and lived by it – inspired probably more of awe in a Jacobean audience than in us today. Where we interpret a merciful release *they* witnessed probably a most dreadful self-castigation. Cassio's words over Othello's corpse, 'This did I feare . . . For he was great of heart' (F3672–3; V.ii.363–4), indicate the nature of Othello's heroic action. And when Gratiano observes three lines earlier, 'All that is spoke, is marr'd', he really means it. For Gratiano is that same man who spoke of suicide and disparaged it as a desperate turn, a terrible repudiation of God's will (F3492–8; V.ii.207–12). *Mar* here means not only 'spoil' but 'damage morally' (*OED* v., 2 and 3): Gratiano means that Othello's final attempt to fix himself as an honourable killer is morally disfigured by the further sin of suicide.

Before considering how all that is spoken in Othello's final speech is *not* marred one needs to note that Shakespeare juxtaposes it against Iago's last words:

> Demand me nothing: what you know, you know:
> From this time forth, I neuer will speake word.
>
> (F3607–8; V.ii.306–7)

They are hardly eloquent in form; and yet they are highly expressive. They express Iago's contempt for Othello and for his other auditors. They also express Iago's courage and defiance as he tries to reassert his will. He has invariably until now answered Othello's

demands and inquiries in the interest of his plot; and now he
derives a certain ascendancy in refusing to dilate upon his motives
– though Othello's eventual indifference perhaps makes that ascendancy unreal. At the same time, of course, Iago's relinquishing of
words will make him powerless, since words have been his chief
weapon. It may be, indeed, that some parallel exists here with
Othello's recognition that *his* chief weapon, the sword of Spain, can
no longer be of help. Overall, however, the sentence *what you know,
you know* has the function of returning Othello's question about
Iago's motives back upon Othello. Shakespeare uses Iago to some
extent to point where the dramatic interest is at this juncture. It is
generally observed that Iago himself may not be absolutely clear
about his motives – hence, in part, his soliloquies, in which several
causes are turned over and unconvincingly proposed – and it may
well be that his resolve never to speak again is, at bottom, an
inability rationalised. Equally, though, the sentence also indicates
that Iago himself cannot explain why it is that he *has* been so
successful in ensnaring Othello. All along he has improvised, push-
ing his plot along wherever he has felt a yielding; and in the early
stages he looked for nothing beyond poisoning the Moor's delight
and making the Moor jealous. Murder, certainly, did not figure
intitially in his intent. Shakespeare has made Iago's last words
characteristically axiomatic and cryptic; but they have also, I think,
a peculiarly toneless quality which means that much of their effect
will depend on the tone that the actor himself supplies. If Iago is
interpreted as desperate and exasperated that his plot, almost
wholly successful, has been uncovered, then these lines can be
snarled. Otherwise, if Iago is interpreted as retaining his talent for
self-management, then their contempt and anger can be more
loftily expressed. The fact that Iago uses *you* – which is, I take it, the
polite singular and not a plural – helps to produce a formal, even
ceremonious, aspect to his address. And on the whole it would
seem that an aloof Iago, self-possessed, would more dramatically
project the silence as to motive that Othello himself must now fill.
Iago's silence, in fact, helps Othello towards the 'ritual' self-
presentation that convention allowed the protagonist at a drama's
end. Indeed, in his own formal pronouncement Iago too – though
strictly he is the *an*tagonist – partakes of that convention. 'I am that I
am' is his effect. The onus of explanation is now on Othello.

Lodovico even more directly helps Othello towards his final
speech. He inaugurates the lexicon of report:

LODOVICO. Oh thou Othello, that was once so good,
   Falne in the practise of a cursed [Q *damned*] Slaue,
   What shall [Q *should*] be saide to thee. [Q *thee*?]
OTHELLO. Why any thing:
   An honourable Murderer, if you will:
   For nought I did in hate, but all in Honor.

                          (F3595–9; V.ii.294–8)

To here means 'concerning', as in Schmidt (prepos, 8). Lodovico's
thou and *thee* – shortly to be eschewed for the *you* and *Sir* customary
amongst upper-class equals – closely depreciates the new Othello.
(Othello has generally to suffer a deal of disrespectful *thou*ing in this
final scene.) *Practise* may be 'method of working' (*OED, Practice* 1),
and the *cursed Slaue* may be the type of man Othello has fallen to
become, a man slavishly obedient to the commands of his blood – a
new version of being sold to slavery. However, *practise* as scheming
and conspiring (in the general senses of *OED, Practice* 6–7) seems to
rehearse Lodovico's later 'worke' as applied to Iago after Othello's
death; and this identifies Iago as the cursed slave. There is also an
echo of the accusations of witchcraft in Act I, particularly of Brabantio's 'thou hast practis'd on her with foule Charmes' and (Brabantio again) 'practises of cunning hell' (F291 and 443; I.ii.73 and
I.iii.102). This again suggests that the devilish practiser is Iago. In
any case, Lodovico explicitly invites Othello's report upon himself.
And, in Othello's immediate response, the chastened quality expressed in other half-lines in this scene is continued. (In this
respect, even Othello's 'Well, thou dost best, at F3611 [V.ii.309] – in
response to Gratiano's proposal that Iago should be tortured –
seems to suggest uninterest rather than active support.) Othello
continues to disclose an extraordinary want of interest in the details
of the practices against him. He turns instead to the promulgation
of a slogan – *An honourable Murderer* – and backs it with an explanation of having done nothing in hate but all in honour that leaves
much of Lodovico's question unanswered. It is possible to feel
much sympathy for Othello here. He is struggling to come to terms
with the deplorable error and excess of emotion he has allowed
within himself; he is struggling to resolve the contradiction in his
definition by asserting that though his act was bad his motive was
good. Conversely, it is possible to feel much exasperation, still, at
Othello's characteristic way of thinking – a thinking that excludes
so much that should be central. Here he excludes first the fact that

he *did* act in hatred – the obverse of passionate love – and secondly
the fact that the honour that impelled him was a restricted military
one, or a Spanish aristocratic one – both of them (presumably) alien
to contemporary audiences.[28]

That Othello is doing little more than justify and publish himself
is pointed by Lodovico's

> Sir,
> You shall vnderstand what hath befalne,
> (Which, as I thinke, you know not) . . .
>
> (F3612–4; v.ii.310–11)

Lodovico's earlier use of *thou* is now displaced; he uses the customary *you*, while *Sir* seems to indicate both respect and distance.
Given Iago's silence as to why, and given Othello's indifference as
to how, Lodovico has to insist on supplying Othello with the simple
facts of the plot. In the summary of events that follows, Shakespeare
may well be reminding his audience of the true explanations – some
of them sinister, none of them very complicated – that Othello
managed to overlook. He is also demonstrating yet again Othello's
incapacity; for it is only when the explanations are well in progress
that Shakespeare makes his character ask Cassio the simple question that he should have asked much earlier: 'How came you . . .
by that Handkerchiefe / That was my wiues?' (F3627–8; v.ii.322–3).

I have already discussed, at the start of Chapter 4, the dramatic
convention by which a hero is given the chance to report himself as
he dies. But the convention needs briefly mentioning again, in the
interest of demonstrating how Shakespeare utilises it here.

> The last speech of a hero is no piece of private musing, but a
> conventional *genre*. It is the moment at which the character has a
> special privilege of comment: to sum up either his own life and
> what it stood for, or the causes of his death . . . . The character is
> stepping forward from his part to speak with the voice of that
> implicit chorus which so often speaks in Shakespeare.[29]

Actually, this kind of last speech is not confined to a hero. It can be
spoken by heroines and, indeed, by any secondary character who
dies on-stage (I am thinking particularly of Aemilia as an example
of the latter). A hero's last speech is not exceptional, but an intensification of a general rule. Moreover, as Eliot observed, Shakespeare

uses the convention with particular point by making it integral with his characters; by which, I think, Eliot meant that Shakespeare's speakers infused it with their own individual style.[30] So Hamlet:

> Oh good Horatio, what a wounded name,
> (Things standing thus vnknowne) shall liue behind me.
> If thou did'st euer hold me in thy heart,
> Absent thee from felicitie awhile,
> And in this harsh world draw thy breath in paine,
> To tell my Storie.
>
> > (*The Tragedie of Hamlet, Prince of Denmarke*, F3830–5; v.ii.336–41)

Here are included not only the conventional need of report but two more Hamletic, personal preoccupations: an old looking-ahead to heavenly relief; and a constant sense of the harshness of earthly life. There may be a third concern, too, as Hamlet – who has caused so many deaths – contrives to save Horatio from infelicitous suicide.

So, too, Macbeth:

> MACDUFFE. Then yeeld thee Coward,
> > And liue to be the shew, and gaze o'th'time.
> > Wee'l haue thee, as our rarer Monsters are
> > Painted vpon a pole, and vnder-writ,
> > Heere may you see the Tyrant.
> MACBETH. I will not yeeld
> > To kisse the ground before young Malcolmes feet,
> > And to be baited with the Rabbles curse.
> > Though Byrnane wood be come to Dunsinane,
> > And thou oppos'd, being of no woman borne,
> > Yet I will try the last. Before my body,
> > I throw my warlike Shield: Lay on Macduffe,
> > And damn'd be him, that first cries hold, enough.
> > > (*The Tragedie of Macbeth*, F2463–75; v.viii.23–34)

One of Macbeth's dominant traits throughout his drama has been his stirring-on or, at other times, his defiance of a known fate; and here his soldier's braving of prophecies fulfilled is convincingly in character – particularly so since it represents a return to Macbeth's essential self after several lines of weariness and satiety. I have quoted the passage at length in order to comment, too, on another trait that Macbeth reveals at the last: his disinclination from being made a fixed figure for the time to view. In this he is like Othello, a difference being that the one fears curses, the other scorn.

Little wonder then, with all this in mind, that Othello's conven tional report on himself is so lengthy, so considered; for here the drama's need that its hero speak with more than ordinary impor-tance combines with this particular hero's dominant trait of self-publication; so that Othello becomes, as it were, double-tongued. The thin voicing of 'That's he that was Othello: heere I am' a few lines earlier (F3584–5; v.ii.286–7) – in response to Lodovico's defini-tion of Othello as 'this rash, and most vnfortunate man' – now becomes strong. In those earlier lines the third person assisted the placing of the old Othello in the past; while the new *he*, the rash and unfortunate, is barely announced in *heere I am*. In the final extended speech, however, the meekness has changed into a major promul-gation: and the whole speech can be taken as Othello's attempt to conjoin the Othello that was to the current *he* and *I* – to announce a new Othello in whom something of the former quality is restored. Broadly, this new figure is arrived at by preterite references to former deeds both good and mistaken – all of which are subsumed in the final 'virtue' of self-punishment by suicide *thus*:

> Soft you; a word or two before you goe:
> I haue done the State some seruice, and they know't:
> No more of that. I pray you in your Letters,
> When you shall these vnluckie deeds relate,
> Speake of me, as I am [Q *of them as they are*].
>   Nothing extenuate,
> Nor set downe ought in malice.
> Then must you speake,
> Of one that lou'd not wisely, but too well:
> Of one, not easily Iealious, but being wrought,
> Perplexed in the extreame: Of one, whose hand
> (Like the base Iudean [Q *Indian*]) threw a Pearle away
> Richer then all his Tribe: Of one, whose subdu'd Eyes,
> Albeit vn-vsed to the melting moode,
> Drops [*sic* in F and Q] teares as fast as the Arabian Trees
> Their Medicinable [Q *medicinall*] gumme. Set you downe this:
> And say besides, that in Aleppo once,
> Where a malignant, and a Turbond-Turke

> Beate a Venetian, and traduc'd the State,
> I tooke by th'throat the circumcised Dogge,
> And smoate him, thus.
>
> (F3648–67; v.ii.341–59)

Shakespeare fits all this into the dramatic convention by making it, virtually, a dictation of the letters that Lodovico is presumably to write. (Actually, the play's last lines, 'My selfe will straight aboord, and to the State, / This heauie Act, with heauie heart relate,' suggest Lodovico might have taken Othello's report to Venice himself.) This dictation strongly structures both the lexicon and the syntax of the speech. But, again, these are the lexicon and syntax that have been heard so often as an essential element of Othello's self-publishings; and much of the confidence that sounds here echoes the confidence expressed in the accustomed syntax of repetition heard, for example, in Othello's speech to the Senate 'Her Father lou'd me . . . ' (F473ff.; v.iii.128ff.). Here once again Othello addresses representatives of Venice with statements about himself; and here once again he uses a series of rhetorical devices – such as the winning of attention by an unassuming commencement – in a speech of skilled simplicity. A pattern both of report and of self-publication develops as follows: *Speake of me . . . Nor set downe . . . must you speake . . . Set you down this . . . And say besides . . .* On these main clauses of report and publicity most of the speech grammatically depends; for only *Set you downe this* is grammatically unnecessary – it has a summarising function similar to that of 'Such was my Processe' in the speech to the Senate (F487; i.iii.142). (That speech is discussed above in Chapter 4.) Another syntactical pattern, sometimes overlapping, is present too: *Speake of me . . . ; speake, / Of one . . . not . . . but; Of one, not . . . but; Of one, whose . . . Of one, whose.* Again, the repeated *of* makes for a syntactical similarity with the first part of the earlier speech. In that, however, the prepositioned objects were various: 'Accidents' 'the Canibals', etc. Here the object is constantly Othello, the new Othello, either *me* or *one*. This *one* has nothing of the generalised sense – equivalent to Modern French *on* and Modern German *man* – that was often used by Shakespeare (Schmidt, *One* 4). Rather, it denotes a particular person (Schmidt 3; *OED* v), the figure that Othello is dictating to Lodovico. About half the speech is occupied by these five object clauses starting with *of*; and to realise this syntactical fact is to further one's sense of the speech's theme –

which is the fixing of a figure that time will point at *un*scornfully. Lewkenor, whom Shakespeare probably read, reports the practice whereby the great generals of Venice, though always chosen as a matter of policy among foreign mercenaries, were nevertheless honoured with the titles of 'citizens & gentlemen of Venice'; and he tells specifically of one Bartholomeo Coglione of Bergamo who 'was in eternall memory of his great and glorious actions honored of our commonwealth, with his statue on horseback, set vp and erected in the fayrest and goodliest place of our Citty'. This is probably the kind of fixed figure that Othello would have wished for, the publication of himself in stone or bronze, for all to see, as a pattern of warrior virtue. With such a memorial no longer possible, he can at least hope to be judiciously reported in words, to be remembered for what he considers were his honourable motives and for his heroic end.[31]

His first line, *Soft you; a word or two before you goe*, is both a polite, Venetian way of gaining attention and a characteristically terse and understated way of exerting command. It is specifically provoked by Lodovico's directives. Othello is to forsake the freedom of his private accommodation (*this roome*); he is also to forsake his power and his command; he is to be kept a close prisoner until his trial in Venice. Such a harsh version of Othello, as a criminal to be kept in custody, needs to be softened, made less stark. Against such an extreme version, too, of the housed condition Othello must naturally also react. So, his next line, *I haue done the State some seruice, and they know't*, is voiced by the great general that he used to be; while *No more of that* sounds something of the self-possession heard in his very first line in the play, ''Tis better as it is'. Quietly and simply he reclaims from Lodovico the ascendancy in this part of the scene. The old Othello has passed, and past services are not enough to maintain him – yes, but it must be Othello himself who utters the directives still. The sentiment of 'Let it go all' is heard again, but the mood is changed. It is no longer one of dismissal and disgust; rather, it is authoritative.

In Othello's directive, *Nothing extenuate, / Nor set downe ought in malice*, there may be a double-negative construction in which *extunuate* is 'depreciate, disparage' (*OED*, v., II.5). This fits in with the theme of Othello's self-publicity: Othello is asking to be written up, as it were, rather than down. Much more probable, however, is *extenuate* as 'lessen . . . the seeming magnitude of (guilt or offence) by partial excuses' (OED v., II.7). In requesting that the report should be fair, Othello refers to two extremes: Lodovico must write neither partially nor with 'ill-will or hatred' (*OED, Malice* sb., 4). It is worth noting that, in any reading, Othello attributes to Lodovico a potential for the hatred that (according to him) he himself did not act upon. The old advising Othello – who so strongly advised Montano and Cassio after the brawl, for example, or who tried to guide Desdemona in the matter of her hand's liberality – would seem to have returned in some degree.[32]

The balance of extremes holds throughout:

> Then must you speake,
> Of one that lou'd not wisely, but too well:
> Of one, not easily Iealious, but being wrought,
> Perplexed in the extreame: Of one, whose hand
> (Like the base Iudean [Q *Indian*]) threw a Pearle away
> Richer then all his Tribe: Of one, whose subdu'd Eyes,
> Albeit vn-vsed to the melting moode,
> Drops teares as fast as the Arabian Trees
> Their Medicinable [Q *medicinall*] gumme. Set you downe this:

Moreover, the antitheses are complicated and strengthened by the qualification of *being wrought*, of *(Like the base Iudean)*, and of *Albeit vn-vsed to the melting moode*. These are three parentheses, not absolutely essential to the grammatical sense, but of major importance to Othello and to our sense of him. They create pauses, make us closely attend. All in all, it is with utmost assurance that Othello publishes to Lodovico the undiminished and considered figure that Lodovico, if he write true, must fix in Venice.

That Othello loved 'not wisely' Lodovico could truly report. *Wisely* is 'With . . . sound judgement' (*OED* adv., 1), and is connected with *Wit* as 'mental capacity' (*OED* sb., II.5 and I.2) – and therefore with Lodovico's own suspicion: 'Are his wits safe? Is he not light of Braine?' after the striking of Desdemona (F2669; IV.i.266). Even more now must Lodovico suspect the unwitting of Othello; and certainly Othello was made to love unwisely by the opportunistic and cunning wit of Iago. Additionally, the view that Othello loved *too well* is acceptable, for both *well* and *too* are intensives. (See *OED, Well* adv., III.13 and V.22a ['with qualifying abverb prefixed'], which cites this passage.) Othello *did* love too intensely for good judgement. If, conversely, *well* is read as 'in a way which is morally good' (*OED* adv., I.1), then the self-delusion of '*It is the*

Cause . . . ' would seem to have survived.

About *not easily Iealious* Lodovico's pen might pause. This phrase has provoked much argument, notably in Bradley (*Shakespearean Tragedy*, pp. 156–8), who tried to prove Othello was jealous slowly; and in Leavis (*The Common Pursuit*, p. 144), who asserted that Othello was jealous 'with extraordinary promptness'. Ridley observes, 'If Othello had said "naturally" he would have been speaking the exact truth' (p. 195n). The point is, the *OED* does in fact supply such a meaning, in *Easily* adv., 2 'Freely' (*Freely* in turn meaning 'readily, spontaneously' – *OED* adv., 1). The antithesis of *not easily . . . but being wrought* is thus fulfilled. Othello opposes two ideas: the idea of his not being naturally jealous to the idea of his having been worked into jealousy by Iago. He has not, he claims, shown a natural and prompt alacrity in becoming jealous. Of course, he is trying to speak the truth, to be just; but at the same time he himself is attempting some extenuation. True, Othello is not a Leontes, a man brought naturally to sexual jealousy by his own temperament, by his own suggestions. He needed an Iago, an external originator and authority. But Iago did work specifically on Othello's ignorance and naïveté about women; and to a great degree Othello's claim to a non-jealous nature is based, deludedly, on the austerity and denial of his former life. As a bachelor infrequenter of women Othello never had the occasion to feel 'distrustful of the faithfulness of wife . . . or lover' (*OED, Jealous* adj., 4). Another meaning of *jealous* as 'Zealous or solicitous for the preservation or well-being of something possessed or esteemed' (adj., 3) – which is not, of course, working here – does at least keep in the forefront of one's mind the fact that Othello *has* been extraordinarily zealous for his good name and that this zeal *did* greatly impel his actions once his state of sexual jealousy was established.

As for *wrought* and *Perplexed*, these are discussed above in Chapter 3 (pp. 82–3). Briefly one may recapitulate. *Wrought* is a form of the participle 'worked' and means not so much 'wrought up' or 'excited' as 'fashioned'. Othello has been worked by a master-artificer, Iago, who made Othello his very own artefact. That this *is* Othello's meaning is supported by Othello's earlier insistence on the knowledge and honesty of Iago as a major premise of his own actions. Lodovico's use of *wrought*'s noun in saying to Iago 'This is thy worke' (F3677; V.ii.367) would seem to indicate an agreement with this view of Othello as a passive victim bewildered and shaped by a virtual devil. But, of course, Lodovico has not seen or read the play. Such a view excludes all the workings by Othello's own character that have contributed to, or hardly hindered, Othello's course of murder.

In the next six lines Othello publishes a definition of what he has done and a definition of his emotional state. First, his *Iudean* or *Indian* activity. Sanders, in his recent edition of Othello, has written an admirable gloss on the relative merits of the F and Q versions and comes down decisively for Q's *Indian*. The constantly useful Hart (in the 'old' Arden edition, pp. 253–4n), who usually keeps to the text of F, finally opts for *Indian* on the strength of frequent contemporary allusions to Indians and precious stones. What I find troubling is that none of the glosses I have read (there are many in Furness, pp. 327–31n) considers the aptness of either *Iudean* or *Indian* with regard to Shakespeare's literary skill. To read Herod of Judas Iscariot into the play at this late stage when no one remotely like either of them has been earlier mentioned is, arguably, to lessen Shakespeare's artistry. Biblical characters, as opposed to obliquely biblical references, have not featured in Othello's utterance. What have featured are – Indians. That is, the 'Canibals' (F488; I.iii.143), whose English name appeared in the language midway through the sixteenth century at about the same time as the synonym 'carib'. From the 'Antropophague' of the Russias they might be differentiated by their residence in the West Indies. They were the indigenae of the Caribbean Sea, the New World, and they basely ate their fellow men. In searching for a being low in the natural order, Othello thinks of the lowest he has seen or met *personally*.[33]

At a height of the natural order is the pearl. Though stones were lower than the beasts and the plants, still pearls had a lapidary significance not only for their monetary value but for their being noble among stones. They had also, according to the *OED*, a medicinal value. In being lustrous, smooth and (frequently) white, this *Pearle* maintains the idea of perfection expressed by Desdemona's skin, but without the sepulchral attributions of 'Monumentall Alablaster' (F3243–4; v.ii.4–5). Rather, the idea is expressed in terms of the sea by whose virtuous action the pearl has been formed. The pearl is a sea-chrysolite, a symbol of intrinsic perfection. It is an example of the 'Seas worth' (F232; I.ii.28) – with this difference: that Othello's love for Desdemona was *more* valuable than the sea's worth, while Desdemona *is* the unmatchable pearl. Now, the love and the sea's worth and the object of love are compacted into an image whereby something of high value is wasted. (On the literal and figurative properties see *OED*, *Pearl* sb.l¹, I.1a and 3.) Othello compares himself with the Indian who, through ignorance, treats contemptuously either something that is more valuable than his whole race put together *or* something whose possession made the Indian, had he but known it, richer than any other Indian. Into this can be read a parallel with Othello's ignorance of Venetian ways and of women: his nine months' experience of civilisation did not enable him to discriminate and perceive his wife's precious quality.

Or rather, to be exact, Othello compares his *hand* with the base Indian. The virtuous arm of Othello's soldiership has reduced. The 'liberall hand' (F2190; III.iv.43) that Othello mistook his wife to have, i.e. an over-generous hand, has proved to belong to Othello. In the frequent synecdoche of the play, this example is not necessarily significant; but, since Othello does single out his hand as being responsible for the criminal action, the extenuating implication may be that the 'real' Othello, the essentially virtuous Othello, is less culpable. There may be something akin to Hamlet's more quibbling distribution of blame: 'Was't Hamlet wrong'd Laertes? Neuer Hamlet' – since Hamlet's madness is the culprit and since Hamlet is therefore 'of the Faction that is wrong'd' (*The Tragedie of Hamlet, Prince of Denmarke* F3684ff.; V.ii.225ff.).

Othello now defines another feature of his new figure: his expression of sorrow through weeping. From this action Othello does not dissociate himself. The eyes *are* Othello. The synecdoche is merely a conventional usage. (Compare Sonnet 61, 'It is my love that keepes mine eie awake', where *mine eie* means simply 'me'.³⁴) Here, *one* is a figure that might be called Atonement; and the trees are defined solely in terms of their 'weeping' quality. The omission of 'do' from *Drops teares as fast as* (do) *the Arabian trees* creates a long sequence of modification that extends through at least ten syllables and sits easily inside the metre in both F and Q. A slow emphasis ensues. *Arabian* asserts not only the old magic of Othello's history – he probably observed such trees (acacias) in Araby, as Bradley (*Shakespearean Tragedy*, p. 153) among others noted – but also in a connotative way the famed skills in medicine of the Arabs. Both *Medicinable* and *Medicinall* mean 'Having healing or curative properties' (*OED*, *Medicinable* A adj., and *Medicinal* adj., 1); while *Gumme* is not merely 'a viscid secretion' (*OED*, *Gum* sb.², 1) but also the trees' 'aromatic substance . . . much prized for its fragrance and medicinable properties' (*OED, Balm* sb., I.1). All in all it is a particularly virtuous vegetation that Othello recalls. It is compact of healing. And in the comparison that virtue transfers to the tears and to Othello himself. Though the eyes are overcome (*subdu'd*: *OED, Subdued* ppl. adj., which cites this passage) by sorrow, there is no loss of honour in that weakness. The *melting moode* in a soldier would have been unmanly; but now it signals a new Othello, and a new virtue. The sorrow itself is laudable – and particularly so since Othello's tears flow with balsamic profusion and speed. Importantly, the sorrow is curative not in the sense of relieving Othello of any pain but by alleviating the horror of the murder for others. The grief of the murderer goes some way to easing the audience's outrage – since the murderer himself is outraged by his deed.

Two further points can be made. Shakespeare has so deployed his comparison that the prime point of similarity is in the fluency of the tears and of the gum. Any incongruity one might have felt between the actual eyes and the actual trees is thus negated: the two sets of objects are not directly compared. Again, Shakespeare – if not Othello – may well have a specific purpose in making Othello's eyes mainly expressive of his grief. It is appropriate that Othello's repentance should be signalled by those organs that falsely received the ocular proof of Desdemona's 'guilt', those organs that obediently 'saw' what Othello wanted them to see.

Moreover, it is possible that Shakespeare has been working a motif of weak eyes, literal and metaphorical, throughout his characterisation of Othello. Othello suffered, or pretended to suffer, a 'salt and sorry Rhewme' (F2196; III.iv.48) – and even the pretence might indicate a reference to a known weakness. Schmidt, in *Rheum* 2c, reads this instance as 'moisture from the nose'. But a tendency for the eyes to water is equally probable. Certainly, *rhewme* is tears in *The life and death of King Richard the Second*:

> the Northeast wind
> Which then grew bitterly against our face,
> Awak'd the sleepie rhewme, and so by chance
> Did grace our hollow parting with a teare.
>
> (F581–4; I.iv.6–9)

Othello's salt and sorry rheum as a secreted mucous (after *OED, Rheum* 1) may well be Shakespeare's rehearsal of the later word *gumme* – which is also mucous in *OED, Gum* sb.[2] 4: 'The sticky secretion that collects in the corner of the eye'. I do not wish to over-diagnose; but it is a characteristic of good writing, and particularly of Shakespeare's, that the language in a piece of plot 'mechanism' – here leading to Desdemona's lie about not having lost the handkerchief – should also be suggestive of character. One thinks as well of why the handkerchief was dropped in the first place – when Othello rebuffed Desdemona's attempt to bind his announcedly aching head (F1916ff.; III.iii.286ff.). Even if the headache too was a pretence (it was also, of course, an allusion to cuckoldry), the impression on Desdemona and Aemilia must be of an ailing Othello, a rheumy Othello, one given to damps or aches on at least two occasions; an Othello who publicly complains and who does act somewhat as a man declined into the (damp) vault or vale of years. Again, later instances refer specifically to Othello's weeping not as a merely physiological action but as a sign of grief. These instances are: 'Why do you weepe? / Am I the motiue of these tears my Lord?' (F2736–7; IV.ii.43–4); and 'I must weepe, / But they are cruell Teares' (F3260–1; V.ii.20–1). And these, with this final assertion of lachrymosity, accumulate into an impression of deficiency in Othello's 'speculativue . . . instrument' (F620; I.iii.270) *and* in Othello *as* a speculative instrument. Had he less demonstrated his distress he might have more exercised his judgement. The qualification remains, however, that here the tears have eventually become pearls of virtue, the myrrh (as Walker notes, p. 219) of atonement and of sacrifice. One might add, further, that the tearful feminine principle has emerged in Othello to accompany the masculine principle that is continued by self-slaughter.[35]

So far Lodovico has several figures to report: the inexperienced, over-intense, perhaps over-idealistic lover; the worked-on husband confused beyond endurance; the ignorant ejector; the sincere penitent. These form a composite figure that must be set down – in the emphatic summary *Set you downe this*. This verb means not only 'put on paper' or 'relate' but also 'put on record'; and it has something of the permanently placing sense of *set* by itself (*OED, Set* v comb., 2 *Set down* c; and *Set* III). That is, it is a synonym of 'fix'. A set-down figure is a fixed figure. Othello is dictating to Lodovico the figure that he considers to be true and which he hopes will supersede both the discredited figure of the old valiant Moor and the figure broadcast by Aemilia of the gull and dolt. All these examples of *one*, composed in an emblem to be dominated by Atonement, are to be fixed onto paper and thence upon the minds of Venice present and to come.

But this composite is not yet finished. A last figure is to be incorporated: the Othello who punished himself. This *one* Othello cannot view detachedly, since the action is imminent and must involve him. So, *one* turns to *I*; while *besides* as 'moreover' (*OED* A adv., 2; Schmidt 1 adv., 1) adds urgency:

> And say besides, that in Aleppo once,
> Where a malignant, and a Turbond-Turke
> Beate a Venetian, and traduc'd the State,
> I tooke by th'throat the circumcised Dogge,
> And smoate him, thus.

Presumably, the murder of that Turk in Aleppo was the cause of Othello's 'being taken by the Insolent Foe, / And sold to slauery' (F482–3; I.iii.137–8). Aleppo was a Turkish provincial city in Syria, some 500 miles south-east of the 'Proponticke Sea', 100 miles inland from the Mediterranean. Hart (p. 255n) writes, 'In Sir Antony Sherley's *Travels* (p. 32, ed. 1825), 1599, he says: "they have a law in Turkey, that if a Christian do strike a Turk, he must either turn Turk or lose his right arm".' Evidently, Othello was not punished under that law; but in his extreme reaction Shakespeare may well be presenting an early example of Othello's prompt, even precipitate activity. Othello presents it as a just action, not done in anger but in retribution and in defence of civilised Venetian values. The biblical injunction to amputate the right hand for self-offence, when combined with the Turkish practice of cutting off hands, might have had interesting possibilities with respect to the hand that threw away the pearl; but they are not taken up. Othello's far more drastic measure of suicide effects the definition of a new Venetian hero, one who despatches the Turk that the old Othello had become. Othello kills not only the Iago in himself but also the 'Turk' who murdered Desdemona and who thereby insulted the state of Venice. In doing so he takes to himself again the virtue he had in Aleppo.[36]

Since the parallel of Othello with the Turk in Aleppo is so strongly made, it is worth considering the characteristics that they have in common. First, *malignant*. This is not closely akin to Iago's 'motive-less malignity' as attributed by Coleridge.[37] Coleridge meant ill-will, the desire to hurt (*OED* 1), a desire which is Iago's essential property. Othello, however, means 'Disposed to rebel; disaffected, malcontent' (*OED* A adj., 1 [last recorded use 1659]). Onions, in citing this passage, further specifies 'rebellious against God'. Hart again is useful here. He writes (p. 255n)

> The Venetians had a monopoly, practically, of trade in Aleppo with the Turks and Armenians, to the great annoyance of London merchants. 'There is a city in Syria named Aleppo, wherein continually are many Venetians dwelling, besides others that come yeerely'. *Hakluyt's Voyages*, i. 402 (reprint 1809), 1598. And see again pp. 441, 442.

The Turk of Othello's reference would seem to have been disaffected by reason of striking a representative of a trading-partner and traducing his Christian nation. It would seem that Othello was rebellious and disaffected not only in striking the Venetian Desdemona but in the sense also that the murderous Othello was rebelling against the real and virtuous Othello. For this rebellion, as for the murder, the punishment must be self-slaughter. There is much resonance of

> Are we turn'd Turkes? and to our selues do that
> Which Heauen hath forbid the Ottamittes.
>
> (F1289–90; II.iii.162–3)

And the dramatic irony is immense. Othello *has* turned Turk, become a renegade, treated Desdemona as the Turks could not by reason of the storm.[38]

Turbond is not a literal description, by analogy, of Othello. As an obviously visible item of clothing covering infidel beliefs in Mohammedan heads, the turban became a symbol of heathenism (*OED, Turban* sb., 1b). Othello, in killing Desdemona, has acquired a metaphorical turban to top his metaphorical Turkishness. Indeed, the name 'Othello' itself contains an orthographic element of Othoman, the founder of the Turkish dynasty *c.* 1300 who features so largely in Knolles and who, amongst a host of other suggestive details, had a trusted Christian captain called Michael Cossi or Cosse. And it is possible that Shakespeare, in the very appellation of his hero, has inscribed the tragic flaw, the 'Turkish' tendency that makes him turn and renege. From Arabic *Othmān* was derived *Ottoman* (*OED* A adj.) – or, in Othello's plural nominal use, *Ottamittes*. Perhaps to a Jacobean auditor, for whom *th* could sound as

[t], the link of Othello – or, as it were, a pre-Verdian Otello – with an Ottoman cruelty might have been more audible than to us.[39]

Circumcised, too, described a Mohammedan (and Jewish) condition. It became symbolically descriptive of non-Christian peoples (*OED* ppl. adj., 1). The prefix attracts a comparison with *Circum-scription* in Othello's *first* long speech (I.ii). Othello has proved to be, metaphorically, more circumcised – that is, un-Christian – than he was amenable to Western, 'civilised' circumscriptions. Like the actual Turk of Aleppo, too, he has *traduc'd* the state of Venice – in his case by aspersing Desdemona as well as killing her. *Traduce* here is 'speak evil of, esp . . . falsely' (*OED* v., 3); and the Latin roots of *trans-* ('across') and *ducere* ('lead') are most evocative. In his imagination Othello did push Venice from her status as a goodly city to that of a city of sin; in his imagination Desdemona did remove from virtue to being 'false as water' (F3404; V.ii.137). To see falseness in a Venetian *and* in water – the native element of Venice which yearly the Duke 'married' in a marine ceremonial and on which the trading city depended – was indeed to traduce the state.

The phrase *a malignant, and a Turbond-Turke* is stayed in the mind not only by its assonance and consonance. The curious syntax – the unnecessary and unusual second *a* – helps too. This is the only doublet, of many doublets in *Othello*, to have this feature. In earlier plays by Shakespeare it could have been merely a device for metrical scansion. But in this play, the most cunningly worked of them all, one is tempted to hear a stylistic measure. This could be one of those deviations by means of which Shakespeare helps to signal an intensification of Othello's emotion. (For other examples see above, p. 216.) The verse slows. It is not that *Turbond* is to be emphasised more than *malignant*; rather, that the whole phrase is to be elongated as Othello reviews the Turk actual and the 'Turk' that by analogy he has himself become. Once again too, as in Othello's talk of the Arabian trees, all verbal activity is excluded over a long sequence – in this case of at least sixteen syllables. There is a concentration on one place, occasion, subject, as Othello invites us to dwell upon an extraordinary and important feature in his past. All this slowness, all this concentration, makes for a highly effective contrast to the violent action that accompanies *thus*.

There are two further senses of *Turke*, however, that might be registered as enriching Othello's reference. These are *OED*, *Turk* 5a ('A human figure at which to practise shooting') and 5b ('A hideous image to frighten children'). *OED* supplies the following illustrative quotations:

> 1569 *Camden's Hist. Eliz.* (1717) Pref. 29 The shotinge with the brode arrowe, the shotinge at the twelve skore prick, the shotinge at the *Turke*.
> 1611 *Manifest Abp. Spalato's Motives* App. iii 7 All the rest were but painted posts, and Turkes of ten pence, to fill and adorne the shooting-field.
> 1598 Florio, *Manduco* a disguised or uglie picture vsed in shewes to make children afraid . . . a turke, or a bugbeare.

It would appear that fixed figures of Turks in their turbans were, to the Elizabethan/Jacobean popular imagination, what crude representations of German soldiers in their scuttle helmets were to Allied populations. It may well be that Shakespeare is playing on this popular idea of the Ottomites. The hot-blooded Moor was a vulgar image that Othello was quick to disown. Now, in Othello's view, his final figure should incorporate not only the noble Moor whose hand betrayed him, and not only the sincerely penitent Moor, but also the noble soldier who smote and unfixed the Turk he had *found* within.

I conclude both chapter and book by asking, how can the actor or director be helped by these findings of lexicon and syntax? It seems to me that several things might be useful. In particular I would have thought that the self-publication demonstrated in the last three chapters might suggest an Othello who tends, sometimes, to look at items such as stars, or moons, or imagined mortal engines, or feared fixed figures, rather than at the character(s) with whom he shares his scenes. This would contrast dramatically to an Iago who alertly looks his interlocutor in the eye. Again, I would have thought an actor might learn from the syntactical information. He might usefully emphasise Othello's characteristic repetition of single words, or of near-synonyms – such an emphasis would make for an audible simplicity. Yet again, a general slowness of delivery would point the heavy pre- and post-modification by which much of Othello's idealistic values are conveyed. Eventually, of course, one is faced by the fact that our best dramatic poet most definitely did not write 'public poetry'; and that, while his effects can be emotionally registered, his means are far less accessible. In the event, I think, one can best help the actor by taking to his performance an augmenting knowledge of Shakespeare's rich subtleties. And, again, such a knowledge is best achieved by the kind of close reading I have been attempting in these previous pages. On the advice of Heminge and Condell to the readers of the First Folio, 'Reade him, therefore; and againe, and againe: And if then you doe not like him, surely you are in some manifest danger, not to vnderstand him.'

Notes

In these notes, sources once cited are referred to by name of author/ editor and short title. The exception is for editions of Shakespeare (primarily *Othello*): these are referred to after first citation by name of editor only. Note that 'Walker' stands for the New Shakespeare edition, ed. Alice Walker and John Dover Wilson. Full details of all sources cited are given in the Bibliography, which lists Shakespeare editions before all other sources.

INTRODUCTION. TWENTIETH-CENTURY *OTHELLO*: A CRITICAL SURVEY OF SOME CRITICS

1. F. R. Leavis, 'Diabolic Intellect and the Noble Hero: or the Sentimentalist's Othello', *The Common Pursuit* (London, 1952; and Harmondsworth, 1962). The essay was first printed under a slightly different title in *Scrutiny*, 6 (1937). 'Mr Eliot and Milton' appears in the same book.
2. A. C. Bradley, *Shakespearean Tragedy: Lectures on 'Hamlet', 'Othello', 'King Lear', 'Macbeth'*, 2nd edn (London, 1905; paperback reprinted 1957) pp. 151 and 155.
3. A succinct guide to the 'schools' of *Othello* criticism to the mid-1950s is supplied in Albert Gerard's ' "Egregiously an ass": The Dark Side of the Moor. A View of Othello's Mind', *Shakespeare Survey*, 10 (1957).
4. E. E. Stoll: *Othello: An Historical and Comparative Study* (Minneapolis, 1915) pp. 21 and 23; *Shakespeare and Other Masters* (Cambridge, Mass., 1940) p. 190; *Art and Artifice in Shakespeare* (Cambridge, 1938) p. 55.
5. See T. M. Raysor's edition, *Samuel Taylor Coleridge: Shakespearean Criticism*, 2nd edn, 2 vols (London, 1960), I, 110–11.
6. For the purpose of this study both F and Q have an equal authority. I have been careful to consider any Q variant from F that has appeared important; but my main text has been F on account of its greater completion. Discussions of the textual relationship between F and Q are available in Hinman's two facsimiles. See also Sir Walter Greg, *The Shakespeare First Folio: Its Bibliographical and Textual History* (Oxford, 1955) pp. 357–74; Alice Walker, 'The 1622 Quarto and the First Folio Texts of *Othello*', *Shakespeare Survey*, 5 (1952) 16–24, and *Textual Problems of the First Folio* (London, 1953), esp. pp. 138–61. Walker summarises the findings of these last two works on pp. 121–35 of the New Shakespeare edition of *Othello*, ed. Walker and John Dover Wilson (Cambridge, 1957; paperback reprint 1969). See

also Norman Sanders' recent edition in the New Cambridge Shakespeare (Cambridge, 1984) pp. 193–207.

Alexander notes that in his edition of the *Complete Works* 'The lines are now numbered as in the great Cambridge edition of Clark and Wright' (p. v). Alexander's typesetters have not, however, invariably followed the Cambridge edition's actual lineation; so that Alexander's prose line-numbering sometimes seems inconsistent. In at least one passage the verse line-numbering seems inconsistent too.

7. Sir J. A. H. Murray, Henry Bradley, Sir W. A. Craigie and C. T. Onions (eds), *The Oxford English Dictionary* (Oxford, 1933); a corrected reissue of *A New English Dictionary on Historical Principles* (1884–1928), with four Supplements, ed. R. W. Burchfield: *A–G* (1972), *H–N* (1976), *O–Scz* (1982); *Se–Z* (1986); Alexander Schmidt, *Shakespeare-Lexicon: A Complete Dictionary of all the English Words, Phrases and Constructions in the Works of the Poet*, 3rd edn, rev. and enlarged by Gregor Sarrazin (Berlin, 1902). (1st edn 1874.)

CHAPTER 1. 'BUT TO BE FREE, AND BOUNTEOUS TO HER MINDE'

1. *My* (F and Q) is usually emended to 'me'. *Defunct, and proper,* discussed as a doublet in the last paragraph of p. 7, is a doublet only if *my* is retained. The clause is discussed on pp. 8–10.
2. William Empson, *Seven Types of Ambiguity* (Harmondsworth, 1972) p. 118 (1st edn 1930.)
3. Othello's doublets are briefly discussed in George T. Wright, 'Hendiadys and *Hamlet*,' *PMLA*, 96, 2 (Mar 1981) 168–93.
4. Chaucer, *The Franklin's Tale*, ed. Phyllis Hodgson (London, 1960) ll. 816 and 815.
5. Ibid., l. 914.
6. Ibid., ll. 9–10.
7. Ibid., ll. 39–40 and 43–4.
8. Thomas Keightley, *The Shakespeare-Expositor: An Aid to the Perfect Understanding of Shakespeare's Plays* (London, 1867) p. 299. Quoted in H. H. Furness (ed.), *Othello*, New Variorum Shakespeare, 11th edn (Philadelphia and London, 1886) p. 71n.
9. A. D. Nuttall, *A New Mimesis: Shakespeare and the Representation of Reality* (London and New York, 1983) p. 138.
10. Alice Walker, one of the few modern critics to oppose 'love-rites', reads *rights*: 'privileges' (sharing Othello's life and dangers) See p. 157 of her edition, with John Dover Wilson, of *Othello* in the New Shakespeare series.

Turkish atrocities on Cyprus are described in Richard Knolles, *The Generall Historie of the Turkes, from The first beginning of that Nation to the rising of the Othoman Familie . . .* (London, 1603). Geoffrey Bullough, *Narrative and Dramatic Sources of Shakespeare*, VII (London and New York, 1973) prints briefs extracts from Knolles but does not include the flaying of Famagusta's governor (pp. 866–7) or the massacre at Nicosia of 14,866 persons of both sexes and all ages (pp. 851–2).

11.   Knolles, *The Generall Historie of the Turkes*, p. 213. But Tamerlane, later, did not take his wife when *he* fought the Turks (p. 226). Knolles does not say why not. In Cinthio's *Gli Hecatommithi*, Shakespeare's main 'source', the Moor is troubled by the fatigue and danger he foresees his wife suffering on a sea-voyage. Of the various translations available I have used Geoffrey Bullough's in Bullough, *Narrative and Dramatic Sources of Shakespeare*, VII, 239–52.

12.   M.R. Ridley (ed.), *Othello*, Arden Shakespeare (London and New York, 1958; 1st paperback edn 1965) p. 34n.

13.   The identity of the *broken weapons* has on the whole been ignored by critics. The Duke may mean in a general way that Brabantio must make the best of the situation. But the military metaphor would seem to express some implication of the General himself as blemished but still necessary.

14.   Principal discussions of how Shakespeare's contemporaries regarded Moors are in Eldred Jones, *Othello's Countrymen: The African in English Renaissance Drama* (London, 1965); and G. K. Hunter, 'Othello and Colour Prejudice', *Proceedings of the British Academy*, 53 (1967, publ. 1968) 139–63.

15.   References in this paragraph are to Furness; H. C. Hart (ed.), *The Tragedy of Othello*, 3rd edn (London, 1923 – this older Arden edn was first published 1903); Ridley; Nuttall, *A New Mimesis*, p. 138; Hilda M. Hulme, *Explorations in Shakespeare's Language: Some Problems of Word Meaning in the Dramatic Text* (London, 1962; paperback edn, 1977) p. 20.

    Hulme discerns another possibility in *defunct*. She derives it from Latin *defungor* as defined by Thomas Cooper in his *Thesaurus Linguae Romanae et Brittanicae* (1578): 'To be deliuered, ridde, and no more troubled or chargeth with a thing: to be dispatched of a matter.' Hence *defunct* as 'free of danger, punishment, penalty incurred.' It links with *proper* as 'legally owned'. The marriage is discharged as a person in court might be discharged. (Hulme, *Explorations*, pp. 153–5.) Hart, pp. 48–9n, reads *defunct* as 'laid aside'.

    In a recent paper T. G. A. Nelson and Charles Haines specifically suggest that the repeated interruptions of Othello's conjugal activity – by the Cyprus emergency, by the brawl, by Cassio's musicians – make Othello sexually frustrated; and that this partially explains his rages. See 'Othello's Unconsummated Marriage', *Essays in Criticism*, XXXIII, i (Jan 1983).

16.   Ridley, p. 87n, notes the possible link of *defunct* with *Function*. He also reads *her Appetite* as Othello's appetite *for* Desdemona. On the representation of the old dative in personal pronouns see E. A. Abbott, *A Shakespearian Grammar: An Attempt to Illustrate Some of the Differences between Elizabethan and Modern English*, 2nd edn (London and New York, 1870) section 220.

17.   Robert B. Heilman, *Magic in the Web: Action and Language in 'Othello'* (Westport, Conn., 1977) p. 138. (1st edn Lexington, Ky, 1956.)

18.   Linked to *Rites* is Q's *vtmost pleasure* (for F's *very quality*). It means
      'every will or command' (after Schmidt, *Pleasure* sb., 2). Its reference
      is not sexual, but may be so interpreted.

19.   Madeleine Doran's essay on Iago's *if* was first published in Elmer W.
      Blistein (ed.), *The Drama of the Renaissance: Essays for Leicester
      Bradner* (Providence, RI, 1970), as 'Iago's "if-": An Essay on the
      Syntax of *Othello*'. It was reprinted, slightly revised and under the
      title 'Iago's "If-": Conditional and Subjunctive in *Othello*', in Made-
      leine Doran, *Shakespeare's Dramatic Language* (Madison, Wis., and
      London, 1976) pp. 63–91.

20.   On the loss of the subjunctive marker from plural forms see N. F.
      Blake, *Shakespeare's Language: An Introduction* (London, 1983) p. 85.

21.   *Free* as 'unhoused' is examined in Chapter 2.

22.   G. Wilson Knight, 'The *Othello* Music', *The Wheel of Fire: Interpre-
      tations of Shakespearean Tragedy with Three New Essays*, 4th edn
      (London, 1949) pp. 97–119. (1st edn 1930.) For Wilson Knight this
      scene expresses the 'harmonious marriage of true and noble minds'
      (p. 111).

23.   Cf. Desdemona's 'by his deere absence' (F609; I.iii.259) and 'What is
      the Matter (Deere?)' (F1375; II.iii.244). The first instance means 'grie-
      vous', as in *OED* adj.[2] 2. Both instances refer to the loved Othello.

24.   As is stated in Nicholas Linfield, '*You* and *Thou* in Shakespeare:
      Othello as an Example', *Iowa State Journal of Research*, 57, ii (1982)
      163–8 (see p. 170). This essay examines 'a crucially important and
      reasonably available feature of a slightly earlier English' (p. 175). See
      also Blake, *Shakespeare's Language*, pp. 6–8 and 79–80; and Charles
      Barber, *Early Modern English* (London, 1976) pp. 208–13.

25.   Brian Vickers calls Iago's comparison a 'Renaissance commonplace',
      a highly formal response to Rodorigo's formal balanced manner.
      Much of Iago's intellectual quality consists in 'an ability to vary his
      argument to suit the nature of his listener'. Brian Vickers, *The Artistry
      of Shakespeare's Prose* (London, 1968) pp. 337 and 336.

26.   Iago says 'I know my price' and talks of the 'trade of Warre' (F15 and
      204; I.i.ii and I.ii.1). One needs to be particularly careful here. Both
      price and *trade* could be ambiguous in Shakespeare's time. *Price*
      could mean 'value' (*OED* sb., B II.6 and 6b). *Trade*, with its origin in
      Old Saxon *trada* ('track'), could denote a course of life (*OED* sb., I.3).
      Both words, however, were already expressing their modern mean-
      ings. I think that Shakespeare gives Iago these modern meanings: he
      then juxtaposes Othello's more sublime vision in the use of 'Seas
      worth' and 'Occupation' (F232 and 2000; I.ii.28 and III.iii.361). See
      also Heilman, 'Iago as Economist', *Magic in the Web*, pp. 73–85.
           Love in a lexicon of finance is used more conventionally in Juliet's
      frank soliloquy on amorous rites:

              O I haue bought the Mansion of a Loue,
              But not possest it, and though I am sold,
              Not yet enioy'd . . . .

                                           (*The Tragedie of Romeo and Juliet*,
                                             F1670–2; III.ii.26–8)

The metaphor might have been more appropriately used of the arranged marriage with Paris than of the love-match with Romeo.

27.   At, for example F1491–3 (II.iii.352–3), 1086–7 (II.i.297–8), 1891–4 (III.iii.264–7).

28.   *Purchase* may also take its place in the play's legal lexicon as 'The acquirement of property by one's personal action, as distinct from inheritance' (*OED* 5).
      Lynda E. Boose observes that the *fruites* possibly ensue in the strawberry-patterned handkerchief. See 'Othello's Handkerchief: "The Recognizance and Pledge of Love"', *English Literary Renaissance*, V.3 (1975) 360–74.

29.   Desdemona's interest in 'forraine' affairs is discussed by Margaret Loftus Ranald in 'The Indiscretions of Desdemona', *Shakespeare Quarterly* XIV (1963) 127–39. 'Desdemona is not the ideal young lady of the precept books' (p. 134). She is 'innocent, yet indiscreet' (p. 139).

30.   John Bayley, *The Characters of Love*, 2nd edn (London, 1968) p. 166.

31.   Furness, p. 166n. *The Yale Edition of the Works of Samuel Johnson* ed. Arthur Sherbo, VIII: *Johnson on Shakespeare* (New Haven, Conn., and London, 1968) p. 1030.

32.   Among others, Hart, p. xxxi, notes that Desdemona's name translates as the 'unfortunate'. See also Heilman, *Magic in the Web*, p. 209.

33.   Othello's sense of fate and perdition is further discussed in Chapter 3.
      I use the word 'scene' flexibly, to denote what strictly is a 'segment'. A Shakespearean scene is generally not concluded until the stage has been cleared of all characters. See J. E. Hirsh, *The Structure of Shakespearean Scenes* (New Haven, Conn., and London, 1980) p. 15.

34.   *Watching* is 'being awake, not sleeping' (Schmidt, under *Watch* v., 1). In her earlier use, 'Ile watch him tame' (F1615; III.iii.23), Desdemona was speaking in terms of falconry. (See Schmidt, under *Watch* v., 2: 'to keep from sleep'.) As Othello watches he becomes *less* tame, of course: the dramatic irony is severe.
      Lodwick Hartley argues convincingly against *it* as the handkerchief in 'Dropping the Handkerchief: Pronoun Reference and Stage Direction in *Othello* III.iii', *English Language Notes*, 7 (1970–1) 173–6. There are no stage directions here in either F or Q apart from those for entrance and exit. If a direction for dropping the handkerchief *is* required, it should be after, not before, 'Let it alone'.

35.   *The Bridall* is the wedding feast or wedding itself (*OED Bridal* sb., 1). Desdemona uses it as a kind of non-count noun denoting a condition she still is in. This goes against Ned B. Allen's assertion that 'Shakespeare *always* while he was writing the last three acts of the play made all the characters speak as if a long time had elapsed since the marriage'. Usually, not always. Allen's admirable essay is entitled 'The Two Parts of *Othello*' in Kenneth Muir and Philip Edwards (eds), *Aspects of 'Othello'* (Cambridge, 1977) pp. 75–91. It was first published in *Shakespeare Survey*, 21 (1968). (Allen's above assertion, on p. 81, seems to go against the fact that Allen earlier found 'scarcely

any contradictions' as to time within either of the blocs formed by the first two acts and the last three [pp. 78–9].)

36.   In the Old Astronomy the sun's movement was: 'a combination of a diurnal rotation from east to west, produced by the force of the heavenly sphere, and of its own, slower motion from west to east, the latter motion resulting from the rotation of the solar sphere, and requiring a year for its completion' – Francis R. Johnson, *Astronomical Thought in Renaissance England. A Study of the English Scientific Writings from 1500–1645* (Baltimore, 1937) p. 21.

37.   The idea of Othello as the *Skilfull* one is lost in Q's 'with the skilfull / Conserues of maidens hearts'.

38.   The upper classes of Shakespeare's England enjoyed an easy public deportment between the sexes. Particularly so at the court of James I. Lawrence Stone reports, 'foreign visitors . . . noted with astonishment and shock the freedom with which it was the custom in England for persons of different sexes to greet each other by a kiss upon the lips.' He quotes, among others, John Marston's *The Dutch Courtesan* (1604), III.i: "tis grown one of the most unsavoury ceremonies . . . any fellow . . . must salute us on the lips'. He also reports the frequency around 1600 of upper-class 'topless' fashions. It would appear that other women, in other cities than Venice, had a certain reputation; and that Shakespeare's audience might be made to respond to Iago's talk of society ladies' morals from a popular knowledge not only of Venetian but of London *moeurs*. See Lawrence Stone, *The Family, Sex and Marriage in England 1500–1800* (London, 1977) pp. 520–1. The easy manners of aristocrats and royals were, of course, made use of by Shakespeare in arousing Leontes' jealousy in *The Winter's Tale*, I.ii.

39.   Othello is made to mishear, to see wrongly, and to misjudge; but one does not laugh at him. His passion and the distress of Desdemona – along with Iago's malignancy – elevate him from the comic potential of his position. A contemporary audience (one surmises) would not have been conditioned to laugh at *any* mention of the fixed figure of cuckoldry. Their mood would have been far different from that provoked by the benignly corrective gullings of *Much Ado about Nothing* or *The Merry Wives of Windsor*. The comedy in *Othello* – and there is much – derives from Iago's gulling of Rodorigo and Cassio and from Iago's self-presentation as a villain. See, for example, Russ McDonald, 'Othello, Thorello, and the Problem of the Foolish Hero', *Shakespeare Quarterly*, XXX (1979) 51–67 and Stephen Rogers, 'Othello: Comedy in Reverse', *Shakespeare Quarterly*, XXIV (1973) 210–20.

       For a fascinating discussion of the character types of the *commedia dell' arte* – on which the characters of *Othello* appear in part to be based – see B. H. de Mendonça, 'Othello: A Tragedy built on a Comic Structure', *Shakespeare Survey*, 21 (1968).

40.   Cf. 'Be innocent of the knowledge, dearest Chuck, / Till thou applaud the deed' (*The Tragedie of Macbeth*, F1204–5; III.ii.45–6); and 'No my Chucke' (*The Tragedie of Anthonie, and Cleopatra*, F2505; IV.iv.2).

41.   Empson does not comment on these two lines; but Othello's *honest*

here fits the 'Restoration' sense that Empson discerns of an unprincipled, straightforward acceptance of the natural instincts. William Empson, 'Honest in *Othello'*, *The Structure of Complex Words* (London, 1951) ch. 11, pp. 218–9.

42. Furness, pp. 302–7n, quotes from medical opinions about Desdemona's unconsciousness, recovery and death.

43. For Hulme's discussion of *lap* (in *Hamlet*) see *Explorations*, p. 119.

A clear contrast to Aemilia's set-piece 'manifesto' is Katherina's set-piece advice to women that all but concludes *The Taming of the Shrew* – if, that is, one hears the advice as 'straight'.

44. *Stubbornesse* is defined as 'roughness, harshness, in C. T. Onions, *A Shakespeare Glossary*, 2nd. rev edn (Oxford, 1919). Schmidt agrees.

45. Of 'Perchance Iago, I will ne're go home' John Barton says, 'It's a perfect example of a seemingly naturalistic line which has a much greater resonance than at first appears. . . . In the general turmoil it comes suddenly as a still line where Emilia's emotion is channelled into a single thought and she stands outside herself. Partly because she is standing up to her husband for the first time in her life, and partly because she subconsciously senses that he is about to kill her. So the line is ambiguous: it means, "I won't go home with you" and it means, "I'm going to die" ' – *Playing Shakespeare* (London and New York, 1984) pp. 200–1.

On Aemilia and on the Willow Song scene Neville Coghill writes illuminatingly in 'Revision after Performance', *Shakespeare's Professional Skills* (Cambridge, 1964) ch. 7.

Before their murders Aemilia and Desdemona are made, interestingly, to hear a similar lexicon. Compare Iago's 'Villanous Whore' (F3522; V.ii.232) with Othello's 'Out Strumpet' and 'Downe Strumpet' (F3334 and 3336; V.ii.81 and 83); and compare Iago's 'Filth, thou lyest' (F3525; V.ii.234; with Othello's 'O periur'd woman' (F3315; V.ii.66). Interestingly, too, these similar lexicons are made to reveal dissimilar characters – Iago's 'low', Othello's 'high'.

46. On the double-time scheme see Allen (n. 35 above). See also Emrys Jones, *Scenic Forms in Shakespeare* (Oxford, 1971), which argues against the existence of any such scheme.

CHAPTER 2. 'BUT THAT I LOUE THE GENTLE DESDEMONA'

1. Bernard Spivack, *Shakespeare and the Allegory of Evil: The History of a Metaphor in Relation to his Major Villains* (London and New York, 1958) p. 421.

E. J. Dobson, *English Pronunciation 1500–1700*, 2nd edn (Oxford, 1968), reports the survival of unshortened [u:] before [v] as in 'love' (II, 510). See also Barber, *Early Modern English*, p. 331.

2. Elisha Coles, *An English Dictionary*, was published in London, 1676. A reprint was issued by the Scolar Press, Menston, Yorks, in 1971.

Shakespeare's command of Latin is attested by Thomas Whitfield Baldwin, *William Shakespere's Small Latine and Lesse Greek* (Urbana,

Ill., 1944). Baldwin writes of a 'regular curriculum in the regular order' in the grammar schools across England which included the learning by rote, reading and writing of Latin (I, 493). S. Schoenbaum, *William Shakespeare: A Documentary Life* (Oxford, 1975) ch. 6, takes it as read that Shakespeare attended the excellent grammar school at Stratford and that his Latin learned there was 'not so small by the standards of a later age' (p. 57).

For a recent discussion of Shakespeare as an etymological writer see D. S. McGovern, ' "Tempus" in *The Tempest'*, *English*, XXXII, 144 (Autumn 1983) 201–14. Shakespeare emphasised or reclaimed the Latin sense in some of the new or already established English words.

3.   J. C. Maxwell, 'Shakespeare: The Middle Plays', in Boris Ford (ed.), *The New Pelican Guide to English Literature*, II: *The Age of Shakespeare* rev. edn (Harmondsworth, 1982) p. 323.

4.   Jane Adamson writes on this passage, 'To find any touch of reluctance in this one would have to be deaf to the tone, and miss the fluent, uncircumscribed and unconfined movement of Othello's voice. Nothing in it prompts us to see dormant seeds of strife . . . [Othello] has freely and gladly chosen his bond' – *'Othello' as Tragedy: Some Problems of Judgement and Feeling* (Cambridge, 1980) p. 129. I do not consider myself deaf to Othello's tone (though I do agree that his utterance has no seeds in it). Adamson seems to register Othello's rhythm of speech (though the question remains, *Can* blank verse be unconfined?) but she seems not to have examined at all the possible or probable meanings of what Shakespeare wrote. Another recent piece on *Othello*, an essay by Irene G. Dash, 'A Woman Tamed: *Othello'*, in *Wooing, Wedding and Power: Women in Shakespeare's Plays* (New York, 1981), senses reluctance in Othello but, again, makes no lexical substantiaion. Peter Alexander defined Othello's reluctance well: 'To this the reluctant pangs of abdicating bachelorhood in a Benedick or a Berowne are the merest growing pains' – *Shakespeare's Life and Art* (London, 1939) p. 163. Heilman, *Magic in the Web*, p. 171, writes of Othello's 'awareness of countervalues' and of his 'incomplete giving'. Again, however, the language is not examined.

Lewkenor's English account of Venice is *The Commonwealth and Gouernment of Venice. Written by the Cardinal Gasper Contareno, and translated out of Italian into English, by Lewes Lewkenor Esquire* . . . (London, 1599).

5.   Stone, *The Family, Sex and Marriage in England*, p. 32. Not only the canon law of 1604 but the contemporary courtesy books in Shakespeare's England condemned marriage without parental consent. Lacking Brabantio's consent, and having a secret wedding, Othello comes into *Circumscription* somewhat less than he seems to think. See also Ranald, in *Shakespeare Quarterly*, XIV; and Juliet Dusinberre, *Shakespeare and the Nature of Women* (London, 1975), which discusses the humanist and puritan arguments for the liberty and equality of women. These arguments did not prevail into statute law but affected much contemporary thinking. As so often, Shakespeare embodies in a play a current issue.

6. On Othello's inability to understand Brabantio's reaction, see Albert Gerard, '"Egregiously an ass": The Dark Side of the Moor. A View of Othello's Mind', repr. from *Shakespeare Survey*, 10 (1957), in Muir and Edwards, *Aspects of 'Othello'*, pp. 12–20. T. McAlindon indicates that in Cinthio Desdemona's parents are both alive, but that Shakespeare makes Brabantio an elderly widower who dies of shock. Nor, in Cinthio, is there any deception. In *Othello* 'we are clearly urged to consider whether the original deception is not the first of a series of concatenated deceptions' – *Shakespeare and Decorum* (London, 1973) p. 98.

7. The Duke's lines about *moderne seeming* (F448–51; I.iii.106 – 9) are attributed in F to Brabantio.

8. Murray J. Levith, *What's in Shakespeare's Names* (London, 1978) p. 55, also sees *Brabble* ('frivolous action at law') and *Ban* ('curse').

9. On the sound of *good* as in Modern English 'food' see Barber, *Early Modern English*, p. 298. On the sound in *Most, Potent* and *Noble*, see ibid., p. 294.

    Robert Louis Stevenson's 'On some Technical Elements of Style in Literature' contains one of the earliest analyses of Shakespeare's use of assonance/consonance. It was first published in *Contemporary Review*, Apr 1885, and repr. in Stevenson's *Essays in the Art of Writing*. (London, 1919) ch. 1. As might be expected, it is beautifully written.

10. My main discussions of Othello's rhetoric occur in Chapters 4–6.

11. E. A. J. Honigmann writes of these lines: 'I detect, here and there, a straining after magnificence . . . a unique fusion of the grand style and something else – one that captures the moment when ripeness approaches overripeness. I would not care to call it "an obtuse and brutal egotism", but on the other hand it affects me as more complicated than straight nobility' – 'Shakespeare's "Bombast"', in Philip Edwards, Inga-Stina Ewbank and G. K. Hunter (eds), *Shakespeare's Styles: Essays in Honour of Kenneth Muir* (Cambridge, 1980) p. 159. Inside his short essay Honigmann lacks the opportunity to 'detect' the causes of this 'straining'. His sense of near-overripeness is probably caused by the heavy modification conjoined with few verbs. I find, in fact, less straining than a heavy stressing as Othello points the superiority of his own military values over the civilian values of Venice. *I do agnize* (*OED, Agnize* v., 4: 'confess') maintains Othello's rhetorical use of modesty: he confesses as it were to an uncivil fault that the Cyprus emergency makes a virtue.

    It is worth noting Lewkenor's summary of the Venetian attitude: 'the common sence of men doth not allow these offices of warre . . . to be for themselues desired . . . it were the token of an unciuile disposition, or rather of a man hating humanitie to wish for warres, slaughters, and burnings, for this onely cause that he might be famous in matters of warre . . . warre is to be desired for the cause of peace' (*The Commonwealth and Gouernment of Venice*, p.9). Although Venice trained her youth in the galleys, she was careful to keep the foreign mercenaries she employed off her own soil. Their armed galleys were allowed into the harbour with skeleton crews only. (See ibid., pp. 131 and 137). This Venetian practice accords with Machiavelli's advice about mercenaries, that 'in peacetime you are despoiled by them' – Niccolò Machiavelli, *The Prince*, tr. George Bull, rev. edn (Harmondsworth 1981) p. 77. More an honorary Venetian than a mercenary, Othello charms persons in Venice with his tales of war and travel; but his secret marriage can be seen as a successful military operation – he *has* despoiled Venice in peacetime.

12.   'A Defence of Womens Inconstancy', in *John Donne: Selected Prose*, chosen by Evelyn Simpson, ed. Helen Gardner and Timothy Healy (London, 1967) p. 7.

13.   The relevant meanings of *Life* are expressed in *OED* sb., II ('with reference to duration') and III ('course, condition, or manner of living'). *Fresh* is 'not deteriorated or changed by lapse of time' (*OED* A adj., II.7) and 'Not exhausted or fatigued' (II.10).

14.   See Marvin Rosenberg, *The Masks of Othello. The Search for the Identity of Othello, Iago and Desdemona by Three Centuries of Actors and Critics* (Berkeley, Calif., 1961) p. 146; Hulme, *Explorations*, pp. 124–5 (though all of ch. 4 is germane); Eric Partridge, *Shakespeare's Bawdy* rev. edn (London, 1955) p. 203.

15.   Some enlightened folk, such as Sir Thomas Browne, did not consider the toad as ugly. Othello shares in the vulgar superstition of the time. See Keith Thomas, *Man and the Natural World: Changing Attitudes in England 1500–1800* (London, 1983) pp. 68–9.

      The dramatic use of animal imagery in *Othello* is discussed in: Wolfgang Clemen, *The Development of Shakespeare's Imagery*, 2nd edn (London, 1977; first published 1951) – 'Othello's fantasy is filled with images of repulsive animals such as were up to that point peculiar to Iago' (p. 132); and in Mikhail M. Morozov, 'Extract from "The Individualization of Shakespeare's Characters through Imagery" ', *Shakespeare Survey*, 2 (1949), repr. in Muir and Edwards, *Aspects of 'Othello'*. See also Wilson Knight, *The Wheel of Fire*, pp. 116–7.

16.   Furness, pp. 175–80n, excerpts from early discussions of the *Monster*.

      The *Monster* is described in terms of its eyes: this fits with the 'sight' motif of the play in which Othello sees, or thinks he sees, the ocular proof of infidelity. Also, the Latin origin of the word *monster* (*monstrum*) denoted a divine portent or warning: Iago's monster is a kind of devilish warning – it seems to interact with Othello's apprehensions about the future discussed in Chapter 1.

CHAPTER 3. 'WHO CAN CONTROLL HIS FATE?'

1.   Lewkenor, *The Commonwealth and Gouernment of Venice*, p. 229, describes the career of Sebastiano Veniero.

2.   Eldred Jones, *Othello's Countrymen*, p. 95.

3.   See Keith Thomas, *Religion and the Decline of Magic: Studies in Popular Beliefs in Sixteenth and Seventeenth Century England* (London, 1971)

pp. 442–3. There were three relevant statutes, the last enacted in 1604. The coincidence of this statute, in the same year, with the canon law against irregular marriage (see above, p. 57) and with the first performance and – possibly – the composition of *Othello* is interesting. It may suggest Shakespeare's dramatic use of topics of immediate contemporary interest.

4. The classic examination of *honest/honesty* is, of course, Empson's 'Honest in Othello'; but see also Paul A. Jorgensen, *Redeeming Shakespeare's Words* (Berkeley Calif., 1962), which discusses contemporary plays about honesty and sees *Othello* as 'a provocative study in a subject of current interest' for Elizabethans (p. 20).

5. Helen Gardner, 'The Noble Moor,' *Proceedings of the British Academy* XLI (1955) 189–205.

6. As interpreted by S. S. Hussey in *The Literary Language of Shakespeare* (London and New York, 1982) p. 29.

7. Leo Kirschbaum put the following interesting point. Aspersions about Desdemona's character are made by Iago to Rodorigo, to Cassio, to Aemilia, and to Othello: only the last of these fails to react with instant denial. See 'The Modern Othello', *English Literary History*, XL (1944) 283–96; repr. in Leo Kirschbaum, *Character and Characterization in Shakespeare* (Detroit, 1962) (see p. 148).

8. Empson (*Seven Types of Ambiguity*, p. 118) writes briefly on Desdemona's *downe-right violence, and storme of Fortunes*, 'she does not become young and helpless till she is married'.

9. Ann Pasternak Slater, *Shakespeare the Director* (Brighton, 1982) p. 81.

10. Knolles, *The Generall Historie of the Turkes*, p. 843. Rosalie L. Colie *Shakespeare's Living Art* (Princeton, NJ, 1974), discusses (p. 150) Aphrodite's island of Cyprus – to which Aphrodite, born of sea-foam, was wafted on a shell (as Desdemona on her ship).

11. It needs recording that Q attributes Cassio's lines about the elements' abeyance for the divine Desdemona to the Second Gentleman. Also, Q has 'And swiftly come to Desdemona's armes' for F's 'Make loues quicke pants in Desdemonaes Armes'.

12. Shakespeare earlier asserted Othello's rashness in Aemilia's words 'Thou art rash as fire, to say / That she was false' (F3405–6; V.ii.137–8).

13. Andrew Marvell, *The Complete English Poems*, ed. Elizabeth Story Donno (Harmondsworth, 1972).

14. *The Essayes of Michael Lord of Montaigne. Translated into English by John Florio*, 3 vols (London and New York, 1928) I, 79: 'let us remove her [Death's] strangeness from her, let us converse, frequent, and acquaint our selves with her, let us have nothing so much in minde as death, let us at all times and seasons, and in the ugliest manner that may be, yea with all faces shape and represent the same unto our imagination'.

15. Contemporary accounts of the horrors of the plague – and of how people fled to the countryside to avoid them – are in Thomas Dekker's prose and verse pamphlets: *The Plague Pamphlets of Thomas Dekker*, ed. F. P. Wilson (London, 1925).

16. A recent discussion of auxiliaries in Shakespeare is in Blake, *Shake-

speare's Language. Would, should and could all had distinguishable meanings but are often used interchangeably (pp. 95–7). See also Barber, Early Modern English pp. 253–60.

17. Moorish marriage customs included the showing of the wedding-night sheets as a proof of the bride's premarital virginity. If the handkerchief is seen as a visual reduction of the sheet then the strawberries are to be associated not only with a popular motif in needlework but also with a specifically sexual phenomenon. Shakespeare read of the Moorish marriage customs, probably, in Leo Africanus. Similar customs were known and talked of in Elizabethan Folklore. See Boose, in English Literary Renaissance, V, 3; and Lawrence J. Ross (ed.), The Tragedy of Othello the Moor of Venice Bobbs-Merrill Shakespeare (Indianapolis and New York, 1974) pp. xi and xvii.

18. Wilson Knight, The Wheel of Fire, pp. 97–9. Wilson Knight contrasts the 'aesthetic grandeur' of Othello's astral references to those of Macbeth and King Lear, in which 'man commands the elements and the stars: they are part of him'. In making the contrast, however, Wilson Knight seems to diminish the idealistic, supernal nature of Othello – and this is curious in a critic who so often, and so rightly, has stressed the 'soul' element not only of Othello but of Shakespeare's literary creation in general. See G. Wilson Knight, 'Soul and Body in Shakespeare', Shakespearian Dimensions (Brighton, 1984) ch. 1.

19. The reference to the crucifixion of Christ is generally recognised. See, for example, Furness, p. 308n.

20. Kenneth Muir (ed.), Othello, New Penguin Shakespeare (Harmondsworth, 1968) p. 215.

21. J. Copley, Shift of Meaning (London, 1961) p. 88.

22. On expanded and intensive do see Blake, Shakespeare's Language, pp. 82–4; Hussey, The Literary Language of Shakespeare, pp. 117–19; Barber, Early Modern English, pp. 263–7.
        On the composition of the page in F see Charlton Hinman, The Printing and Proof-Reading of the First Folio of Shakespeare, 2 vols (London, 1963) II, 302–5.

CHAPTER 4. 'I MUST BE FOUND' (i)

1. Giorgio Melchiori, 'The Rhetoric of Character Construction: Othello', in Shakespeare Survey, 34 (1981) 65.

2. John Holloway, The Story of the Night: Studies in Shakespeare's Major Tragedies (London, 1961) pp. 55–6; M. C. Bradbrook, Themes and Conventions of Elizabethan Tragedy (Cambridge, 1935) p. 77.

3. 'Shakespeare and the Stoicism of Seneca' (1927), in T. S. Eliot, Selected Essays, 3rd, enlarged edn (London, 1951) pp. 129–131. The essay is severally reprinted: e.g. in Laurence Lerner, (ed.), Shakespeare's Tragedies: An Anthology of Modern Criticism (Harmonds-

worth, 1968).

4. As used by Heilman, *Magic in the Web*, p. 146, of Othello's farewell to his occupation.

5. Thomas Dekker, *The Gull's Horn Book* (London, 1609) repr. in *Thomas Dekker: Selected Prose Writings*, ed. E. D. Pendry (London, 1967) p. 89. Hussey, *The Literary Language of Shakespeare*, p. 136, quotes the relevant section. Cf. also *Lucrece*: 'Collatine the publisher / Of that rich jewel he should keep unknown' (ll. 33–4) in F. T. Prince, *The Poems*, Arden Shakespeare (London, 1960).

6. G. L. Brook, *The Language of Shakespeare* (London, 1976) p. 131.

7. Honigmann, in Edwards, Ewbank and Hunter, *Shakespeare's Styles*, p. 159.

8. Ross, p. 16n.

9. As reported in John Lothrop Motley, *The Rise of the Dutch Republic*, 3 vols (London, 1904) II, 114.

10. Muir, p. 185n. A possible source of Othello's reference is Lewkenor, *The Commonwealth and Gouernment of Venice*, p. 43: 'All the citizens, as well those that beare rule and office, as those that are private men speake vnto him [the Duke of Venice] bareheaded and standing, which in these times is a signe of exceeding honor.'

11. Walker, p. 148n; Ross, p. 17n.

12. I use Doran's definitions of Othello's syntax – Doran, *Shakespeare's Dramatic Language*, p. 71.

13. Paul A. Jorgensen, *Lear's Self-Discovery* (Berkeley, Calif., 1967) pp. 63–6. The pages on *Othello* are based on ' "Perplex'd in the Extreme": the Role of Thought in *Othello*', in James G. McManaway (ed.), *Shakespeare 400: Essays by American Scholars on the Anniversary of the Poet's Birth* (New York, 1964) pp. 265–75. The essay's first printing was in *Shakespeare Quarterly*, XV (1964) 265–75.

14. See above, p. 3.

15. Abbott, *A Shakespearian Grammar*, section 202, cites this passage as an example of adverbial expression from which a preposition is omitted. *With* or *what* would seem to have been omitted from before *What Drugges . . . .*

16. In a recent, ill-advised production Othello's history was spoken rapidly – to disastrous effect. It cannot be spoken too slowly. Dobson draws one's attention to the two systems of pronunciation that broadly prevailed around 1600. One was close to Modern English. The other, more conservative and emphatic, retained far more of secondary stress. It is attractive to consider – but, of course, unprovable – that Shakespeare wrote all of Othello's utterance as a conservative contrast to a racier, more modern pronunciation in Iago. This passage in particular seems especially full of words in which such conservatism might be attempted. It is possible, for example, that *redemption* has disyllabic -ion. Certainly the several consonant strings – of, for example, [f], [l], [k] and [h] – demand emphasis. Certainly too, in Shakespeare's time, the 'schwa' of Modern English (as in 'alt*a*r' and 'alt*e*r') would not have been present to reduce the secondary stress in 'Ant*a*r' and 'Des*a*rts'; while a word such as *Antro-*

pophague could be so pronounced (I imagine) as to be virtually endless. On the two systems of pronunciation see Dobson, *English Pronunciation*, II , 445; on 'schwa', II , 759.

A conservative style overall is heard in Othello by Philip A. Smith. It is 'a formal copybook style altogether unidiomatic in its structure, uncolloquial in its nature'. Smith asserts that Othello is made to sound 'foreign' and 'culturally unassimilated', – 'Othello's Diction', *Shakespeare Quarterly* IX (1958) 428–30. I have heard such a use of English among people from Sri Lanka and the Indian sub-continent: a correct, almost over-correct, syntax – and an incomprehension of subtleties such as elision. One's impression of a 'copybook' style in Othello derives to some extent, I think, from his use of simple word-repetition as a structuring-device.

17.   Ross, p. 31n.

18.   The drawing from *Geographia universalis* is in Ross, p. 263. The quotation from Raleigh is on p. 402 of Hakluyt, *Voyages and Discoveries, The Principal Navigations, Voyages, Traffiques and Discoveries of the English Nation*, abridged edn. ed. Jack Beeching (Harmondsworth, 1972). Hart cites other contemporary works on pp. 38–9n. The monsters were popularly attributed to Russia (Scythia). Cf. *The Tragedie of King Lear*: 'The barbarous Scythian, / Or he that makes his generation messes / To gorge his appetite' (F123–5; I.ii.115–17).

19.   Bradley, *Shakespearean Tragedy*, p. 164. Leavis emphasises what he considers to be Othello's 'characteristic voluptuousness' (*The Common Pursuit*, p. 149).

20.   Othello seems to say that Desdemona pitied the dangers. This apparent hypallage is not noted in Abbott. In fact, the construction is probably elliptical: 'she did pitty [me for] them'. As Abbott says (*A Shakespearian Grammar*, p. 279), 'Elizabethan authors objected to scarcely any ellipsis, provided the deficiency could be easily supplied from the context.'

21.   Walker dislikes *feeds well*. This activity is mentioned elsewhere by Cinthio as a male vice and is an 'irrelevant interpolation which F should have deleted' (p. 184n). Walker does not take into account the place of *feeds well* in a sequence that includes Desdemona's 'greedie eare' and bent to 'deuoure vp' Othello's discourse (F494–5; I.iii.149–50); Desdemona as one of the creatures possessed of 'Appetites' (F1901; III.iii.274); and 'fed well' (F1983; III.iii.344). Healthy eating turns into promiscuous sexual appetite (Desdemona) or a gulled naïveté (Othello). Iago, of course, makes use of overeating imagery in persuading Rodorigo that Desdemona will sexually disrelish the Moor – his use of such imagery is extensive in I.iii and II.i and demonstrates how difficult it is to keep the imageries of eating and of sex apart.

22.   Clemen, *The Development of Shakespeare's Imagery*; Morozov, in Muir and Edwards, *Aspects of 'Othello'*.

23.   Othello lodges in Act I at the 'Sagitary'. Among the inns of sixteenth-century Venice no such name has been found: Thomas Elze in *Shakespeare Jahrbuch* XIV (1879) 14, in Furness, p. 25n. Abbey Jane Dubman

Hansen derives significance from Shakespeare's choice. A sagittary was not only an archer but a centaur, having the head and torso of a man but, below the hips, the anatomy of a horse. Centaurs were renowned for ferocious fighting and appalling deeds. Othello is referred to as a barbary horse (I.i) and as one likely to foam at the mouth (IV.i). Like Cassio – only more extremely – he is now a sensible man, by and by a fool, and presently a beast (II.iii). See Hansen's 'Shakespeare's *Othello*', *Explicator*, XXXV, iv (Summer 1977) 4–6. It might be added that the most famous centaur of all was one who fought in the Trojan army against the Greeks (*OED*, *Sagittary* sb., 2) – like Othello, it helped one foreign people against another foreign people. If Othello does perceive a centaur-like monster in Iago's thought, he is possibly having a premonition of his own violent nature when attacked by stallion, below-the-waist matters. On the monster see also above, pp. 72ff.

24.   Heilman, *Magic in the Web*, p. 146: 'In soliloquy he [Othello] has fewer lines than Shakespeare's other tragic heroes: he is less intelligent than they, less introspective . . . . Not only does he have a sense of audience, but he needs an audience.' More recently and dubiously it has been asserted that 'without audience, Othello isn't even a man' – Marjorie Pryse, 'Lust for Audience: An Interpretation of *Othello*', *Journal of English Literary History*, 46 (1976) 476.

CHAPTER 5. 'I MUST BE FOUND' (ii)

1.   The various instances of *it* would seem to be covered by Abbott's explanation: '*It* is sometimes used indefinitely, as the object of a verb, without referring to anything previously mentioned . . . :' Alternatively, the first three *it*s may refer to *Lust*. The *Wiu'd/her* construction has a parallel in Sonnet 94: 'They that have powre to hurt, and will doe none' (l. 1), where *none* refers back to a noun understood in verbal *hurt*. See Abbott, *A Shakespearian Grammar*, section 226; Martin Seymour-Smith (ed.), *Shakespeare's Sonnets* (London, 1963), which reprints the sonnets as they appeared in the Quarto of 1609.
2.   Kirschbaum, *Character and Characterization in Shakespeare*, p. 148.
3.   Doran, *Shakespeare's Dramatic Language*, *passim*.
4.   Hulme, *Explorations*, pp. 124–5; Onions, *A Shakespeare Glossary*.
5.   Heilman, *Magic in the Web*, p. 146.
6.   Sidney's words are excerpted from Sir Philip Sidney, *The Countess of Pembroke's Arcadia*, ed. Maurice Evans (Harmondsworth, 1977) p. 542; and Sir Phillip (*sic*) Sidney, Knight, *The Defence of Poesie* (London, 1595; facsimile edn, Menston, Yorks, 1968) sig. B.
7.   Herman Melville, '*Billy Budd, Sailor*' *and Other Stories*, ed. Harold Beaver (Harmondsworth, 1967) p. 335.
8.   Norman Sanders, the latest editor of *Othello* (New Cambridge Shake-

speare, 1984) prefers *Her name* following Walker, Hart and the non-authoritative Second Quarto of 1630.

9.   Algernon Charles Swinburne, *A Study of Shakespeare* (London, 1918) p. 183. (1st edn 1879).

10.   Steevens and Pope are referred to in Furness, pp. 210–11n. Bradley, *Shakespearean Tragedy*, pp. 367–8, thought the speech essential as a means to contrast.

11.   Bernard Shaw, *Plays and Players: Essays on the Theatre (1895–8)*, ed. A. C. Ward (London, 1952) p. 246; Bradley, *Shakespearean Tragedy*, p. 367.

12.   The comments by Leavis (*The Common Pursuit*, pp. 146–7) are specifically on this speech. Melchiori, in *Shakespeare Survey*, 34, p. 65.

13.   *The Works of George Herbert*, ed. F. E. Hutchinson (Oxford: Clarendon Press, 1941).

14.   John Donne, *The Complete English Poems*, ed. A. J. Smith (Harmondsworth, 1971).

15.   Rosamund Tuve: 'real logical inconsistencies within figures are infrequent'; 'Elizabethan images stand up to severe logical examination; both writers and readers were trained to it' – *Elizabethan and Metaphysical Imagery: Renaissance Poetic and Twentieth Century Critics* (Chicago, 1947) p. 289. Tuve also writes of the '*multiple logical bases*, upon all of which the comparison obtains' in a conceit (p. 264).

      Compare, however, Blake, *Shakespeare's Language*, pp. 42–3, on the thinking of *dramatic* poets: given auditors lacking dictionaries and a knowledge of etymology, 'authors may have been less concerned with the precise meaning of their vocabulary and the surface logic of the grammar than with such aspects as sound and rhythm'. If they were, then Shakespeare was the exception. His supreme literary gift is an ability to fuse meaning(s) with sound, with no subordination of the one to the other. See next note.

16.   The assertive meaning of this passage is assisted by the assertive consonance of [p] and [k] and by the sibilance of [s] and [z]; while the fluency Othello wishes to express is assisted by the frequency of [u:] (as in Modern English 'food') in *bloody . . . looke . . . Loue . . . vp*, and of [u] (as in Modern English 'put' by reason of there being more than one following consonant) in *Current . . . compulsiue. Course*, too, would seem to supply something to this assonance, as does *humble*; while the short vowel in *backe* and *Swallow* contributes to the assertion. (On [u:] and [u] see Dobson, *English Pronunciation*, pp. 492 and 510.)

17.   The word *lie* supplied one of the commonest of puns, particularly in 'Shakespeare, who needs and wants the words *lie, lies*, and *lying* hundreds of times in his work'. See Christopher Ricks, 'Lies', *Critical Inquiry*, 2 (1975) 121–42 (quoting from p. 128). Repr. in *The Force of Poetry* (Oxford, 1984).

18.   Heilman, *Magic in the Web*, pp. 234–6, demonstrates the scheme.

19.   Sir John Charles Bucknill, *The Medical Knowledge of Shakespeare* (London, 1860) p. 274, quoted in Furness, p. 238n.

20.   See Rosenberg, *The Masks of Othello*, pp. 176–7.

21. John P. Emery, 'Othello's Epilepsy', *Psychoanalysis and the Psycho-analytic Review*, XLVI (Winter, 1959) 30–2.

22. Thomas, *Religion and the Decline of Magic*, states that contemporary scepticism considered possession to be a natural epilepsy (p. 490) but that, popularly, internal possession or external obsession might signify bedevilment (p. 478).

   The present state of knowledge about epilepsy is stated in *Encyclopaedia Britannica Macropaedia*, 15th edn (1974) XII, 1055. Epilepsy is a 'paroxysmal disorder of the nervous system recognized by recurring attacks of loss or impairment of consciousness with or without convulsive movements'. Poison can damage brain-tissue and cause epilepsy: this kind is essentially manifested in convulsions.

23. As reported by Charlton Hinman in *The Norton Facsmile: The First Folio of Shakespeare* (New York and London, 1968) p. xix, and *The Printing and Proof-Reading of the First Folio of Shakespeare*, pp. 302–5.

24. Doran, *Shakespeare's Dramatic Language*.

25. Harold Jenkins (ed.), *Hamlet*, Arden Shakespeare (London and New York, 1982) p. 330n.

26. The 'latest editor' is Sanders, p. 155n. He chooses the clock-interpretation exclusively. Later editors on the whole are inclined to it. However, Hart (p. 201n) and Walker (p. 203n) see *time* as a figure pointing at another figure, Othello.

27. Madeleine Doran, 'Good Name in *Othello*', *Studies in English Literature* 7 (Spring, 1967) 195–217 (quoting from p. 211); Onions, *A Shakespeare Glossary*.

28. In a mid-sixteenth-century meaning as defined by William Empson in 'Honest Man', *The Structure of Complex Words*, ch. 9, p. 186.

29. It is interesting to consider – if only to dismiss – *spend* as 'give away (a garment) in payment' (*OED* v., I.1c [*c.* 1440–1575]). This reminds one that clothes were expected to last much longer, and were more valued, than they are today.

   It is also interesting to note that Iago – who is present here – picks up *spend* and *rich* to use their associations in his later talk about the filching of a good name that leaves one poor indeed (F1768ff.; III.iii.159ff.): yet another example of the skill with which Iago exploits Othello's preoccupations as disclosed by Othello's own words.

30. 'Nay but he prated, / And spoke such scuruy, and prouoking termes / Against your Honor . . . .' *Honor* here, if it is not a title, is 'Glory, renown, fame, credit, reputation, good name' (*OED* sb., 1c), not 'a fine sense of and strict allegiance to what is due or right' (sb., 2). Like reputation and opinion, honour can be internally or externally derived.

31. The literature on Othello's honour, and on Renaissance ideas of honour, is extensive. A notable addition is Barbara Everett, 'Spanish Othello: the Making of Shakespeare's Moor', *Shakespeare Survey*, 35 (1982) 101–12. Othello, though an 'any-coloured Everyman' (p. 107), has an imagination that 'is enormously, preposterously vulnerable to the sense of social shame' (p. 108); he can be seen as a Spanish Moor by temperament, in whom centuries of interbreeding have deve-

loped the 'Spanish' sense of honour that Cinthio's Moor is so devoid of. According to Jean Klene in 'Othello: "A fixed figure for the time of scorn" ', *Shakespeare Quarterly* XXVI (1975) 139–50, by this Spanish code a wife and her lover could be honourably murdered by the husband. See also Edward M. Wilson, '*Othello*, a Tragedy of Honour', *Listener*, 47 (1952) 926–7; Doran, in *Studies in English Literature*, 7; M. C. Bradbrook, '*Othello*, Webster and the Tragedy of Violence', a Folger Shakespeare Library lecture read 1981, repr. *Muriel Bradbrook on Shakespeare*, ch. 11 (Brighton, 1984); Norman Council, *When Honour's at the Stake* (London, 1973), of which chs 1 and 6 are relevant). The 'John Citizen' view of honour, and the humanists' attacks on honour as part of an aristocratic culture glorifying war, are expressed in Dusinberre, *Shakespeare and the Nature of Women*, p. 33. See also Jorgensen's chapter 'Nobility' in *Redeeming Shakespeare's Words* (one component of nobility was the being indifferent to public opinion, even to the point of despising public acclaim).

32. See John Erskine Stauffer, *Shakespeare's Derived Imagery* (Lawrence, Kan., 1953) p. 72.

33. Richmond Noble, *Shakespeare's Biblical Knowledge and Use of the Book of Common Prayer as Exemplified in the Plays of the First Folio* (London and New York, 1935) pp. 219 and 67–8.

34. Hulme, *Explorations* p. 322; Johnson, *Works* VIII, 1042.

35. Sanders, p. 155n, glosses *Cesterne* as 'cesspit' (but supplies no authority). Schmidt has merely 'a receptacle of water'.

36. Sanders' gloss (p. 155n), 'copulate and engender', does not differentiate the transitive and intransitive senses.

37. *I heere looke grim as hell* is frequently emended to 'Aye there . . . '. The emendation would seem to be unnecessary.

CHAPTER 6. 'I MUST BE FOUND' (iii)

1. Fechter's *Acting Edition* is quoted by Furness, p. 292n. For Stewart A. Baker's reading of *It* as 'blood' see 'Othello's "Cause": A New Reading', *English Language Notes*, 7 (1969–70) 96–8. The reading is based on an assertion that the scene, like many scenes in the play, begins as it were in the middle of a speech. See also Empson, *Seven Types of Ambiguity*, pp. 217–8: 'I should myself plump for *blood*: but it is no use assuming . . . that one cause can be assigned, and one thing it is the cause of.'

2. John Bayley says of Iago 'It was *because* he hates Othello that he thinks of him as a sexual rival and enemy' – *Shakespeare and Tragedy* (London, 1981) p. 205. Spivack (*Shakespeare and the Allegory of Evil*, p. 448) points out that Iago uses *And* not *for* in 'I hate the Moore, / And it is thought abroad, that 'twixt my sheets / Ha's done my Office.' Coleridge's famous phrase 'the motive-hunting of motiveless malignity' is extraordinarily apt in defining Iago's attempts to rationalise the workings of acknowledged, instinctive hate (*Coleridge: Shake-*

spearean Criticism, I.44).

3. Abbott, *A Shakespearian Grammar*, section 419a.

4. In this matter of delicate syntax, one needs to bear in mind that the relevant page of F (vv 4) was set by the frequently revisionary Compositor B and was not corrected at all – let alone back to copy. See Hinman, *The Printing and Proof-Reading of the First Folio of Shakespeare*, II, 302–5.

5. The resonances are indicated by Stauffer, *Shakespeare's Derived Imagery*, p. 50.

6. Ross, in whose edition the scriptures supply a near-constant secondary context for Shakespeare's words, heavily annotates various biblical allusions concerning God's light and the sword of divine justice (p. 216n).

7. As reprinted from the 1609 Quarto in Seymour-Smith's edition.

8. 1604 is the *OED*'s date for the *first* printed uses of *Sense* in the following substantive meanings: II.14 – 'consciousness', as in 'What sense had I, in her stolne houres of Lust?' (F1981; III.iii.342); II.15b – 'recognition', as in 'from the sence of all Ciuilitie' (F144; I.i.132); II.16 – 'Emotional consciousness', as in 'That hast such Noble sense of thy Friends wrong' (F3119; V.i.32); II.18c – 'opinion', as in 'in my sense, 'tis happinesse to die' (F3593; V.ii.293); I.9 – 'Capacity for . . . appreciation of beauty', as in 'As hauing sence of Beautie' (F833; II.i.71). With some of these definitions one might disagree: sometimes the differentiation is over-nice. But *sense* is certainly a keyword in *Othello*. Basically, Othello uses his senses but not his sense (in the modern meanings). Empson demonstrates Shakespeare's meanings of 'sensuality', 'sensibility' and 'sensibleness' in 'Sense in *Measure for Measure*', *The Structure of Complex Words*', ch. 13. See also ch. 21 ('Dictionaries'), and C. S. Lewis, *Studies in Words*, 2nd edn (Cambridge, 1967), which has a chapter on the history of *sense*.

9. Ross, p. 218n, writes on rose-allusions in the Geneva Bible. Stauffer *Shakespeare's Derived Imagery*, pp. 50–1, brings one's attention to the conicidence of soul and breath in Latin *anima*, the animating force.

10. Contrast 'cunning'st Patterne of excelling Nature' to 'that cunning Whore of Venice' (F2788; IV.ii.90). That Othello can use the same word of the same woman, and mean so differently in each instance, says much for the richness of Elizabethan/Jacobean English and also for Othello's imperceptive extremism.

11. Muir, p. 193. Ross, p. 55n, points to Sonnet 84 for another attired artist:

> he that writes of you, if he can tell,
> That you are you, so dignifies his story.
> Let him but coppy what in you is writ,
> Not maxing worse what nature made so cleere,
> And such a counter-part shall fame his wit,
> Making his stile admired every where.

Something of the same theme of true report informs Othello's final long speech: Othello advises Lodovico that an absence of malice and of extenuation alike will produce Othello 'as I am'.

Even Ridley, a champion of Q, thinks that the F version, *Do's tyre the Ingeniuer* is Shakespeare's own, and that Q's *Does beare all excellency* is 'a trifle colourless' (p. 51n).

12.   McAlindon, *Shakespeare and Decorum*, p. 80. It was about the whole of this speech that Wilson Knight (p. 104) eulogised, 'This is the noble *Othello* music: highly-coloured, rich in sound and phrase, stately . . . This speech well illustrates the *Othello* style . . . . '

13.   John Money, 'Othello's "It is the Cause . . . "': An Analysis', *Shakespeare Survey*, 6 (1953) 94–105 (quoting p. 95).

14.   The Spanish code. See Chapter 5, n.31. Bradbrook recently defined it: 'a stock-breeder's view of family life, an archaic and familial conception (with perhaps a dash of Muslim male dominance) incompatible with the British rule of law' (*Muriel Bradbrook on Shakespeare*, p. 132.)

15.   Lynda E. Boose, 'Othello's "Chrysolite" and the Song of Songs Tradition', *Philological Quarterly*, 60, iv (Fall 1981) 427–35 (quoting p. 433). The two later excerpts are from pp. 430–1 and 433.

Ross (p. 230n) on *Chrysolite*: 'Considered a perfectly hard stone, it was supposed to crack if it had any flaw . . . Early lapidaries claim for it the magical power to prevent sin and drive off devils.'

16.   *Purchase made* and *profit's yet to come* are discussed in Chapter 1, pp. 20ff.

17.   Furness, p. 317n.

18.   Shakespeare is of course concerned with morality rather than with the letter of the law; all the same it is interesting that in law Iago could not be convicted of any charge involving Desdemona's murder: 'Iago neither suggested nor even contemplated the murder of Desdemona, and therefore was not an accessory before the fact. He was scarcely guilty of criminal defamation. He persuaded his wife, Emilia, to steal the handkerchief, but she did not do so – she found it and handed it over to him, and he passed it on.' Iago could not be convicted either of the maiming of Cassio or of the murder of Roderigo – no witnesses. In law, therefore, 'Iago's only crime . . . was the murder of Emilia.' See O. Hood Phillips, QC, DCL, *Shakespeare and the Lawyers* (London, 1972) p. 153, after J. Hirschfield, 'What was Iago's Crime in Law?' *Journal of the Society of Comparative Legislation*, n.s., 14 (1915) 411.

19.   Toledo or Bilbao (Hart, p. 247n). Walker, p. 217, quotes, ' "They have a great advauntage in Spayne, to temper their blades well, bycause of the nature of their ryvers" (Palsgrave, 1530, cited O. E. D. "temper", verb 14).'

Most editors discuss the famous emendation on 'Innsbruck' from Q's spelling *Isebrookes* – and reject it. Ross accepts it, on the basis of writings on sixteenth-century arms and armour: apparently Spanish swordsmiths used German steels. See Lawrence J. Ross, 'Three Readings in the Text of *Othello*', *Shakespeare Quarterly*, XIV (1963) 121–6. The emendation was first announced by Viscount Dillon in 'Armour and Weapons', ch. 4/2 of C. T. Onions, Sidney Lee *et al.* (eds),

Shakespeare's England, 2 vols (London, 1916).

(The emendation seems to have incensed scholars into error. Walker, p. 217n, writes 'Fortescue's conj . . . is enept' – but Fortescue wrote ch. 4/1, not 4/2. Sanders, p. xii, attributes the *authorship* of the whole two volumes to J. W. Fortescue – in fact, Onions took over the editorship finally from, among others, Sidney Lee. Dillon himself helpfully supplies contemporary spelling variants – Isproka, Hysproka, Isprugk – but in his article Q's *Isebrookes* is misspellt as 'Isebrokkes'. The main objection to 'Innsbruck', I think, is that it tends to dispel the cold and Spanish qualities of a sword not only belonging to Othello but symbolising him.)

20. H. Granville-Barker, *Prefaces to Shakespeare*, 1-vol. edn (London, 1972) p. 89.

21. These lines are not in Q. Almost certainly they were omitted, as a result of compositorial 'eye-skip'. See Ridley, p. 192n.

22. The actual storm at sea was described by the Second Gentleman:

> The winde-shak'd-Surge, with high & monstrous Maine
> Seems to cast water on the burning Beare,
> And quench the Guards of th'euer-fixed Pole:
> I neuer did like mollestation view
> On the enchafed Flood.

> (F765–9; II.i.13–17)

It is generally taken as a metaphor of Othello's imminent emotional storm: a forecast of human affairs by the elements. But the sheer closeness of the metaphor needs registering. The constant Pole star seems to represent – in Shakespeare's implication – Othello. The *Guards* – the two stars of the Lesser Bear – were used by mariners as navigational aids to check or guard their course (*OED, Guard* sb., 1). Shakespeare's wording makes them also guard the Pole star: they thus become the safer guides, or the best judgement, of the constant Othello who yet voyages. The seemingly saturated burning Bear is an early example of a light put out, of a flaming minister and light of heaven quenched (cf. 'It is the Cause . . . '). The guards are quenched by the sea much as Othello's judgement is to be overcome by blood or passion. The flood or sea is *enchafed* (*OED* ppl. adj.: 'furious, excited, irritated' [1604 –]) much as Othello's blood is to be. Even *wind-shak'd-Surge* seems to have a parallel in Othello's emotions shaken by Iago. Even *high & monstrous Maine* seems to have a parallel with the barbary horse's rage, or with Othello's murderous power – which is alternatingly *high* and *monstrous*. (*Maine* seems to amalgamate an animal's mane, the high seas, and might – *OED, Mane* sb., 1; *Main*, sb.[1], II and I.1.)

23. See Furness, p. 321n, for the emendators. They followed later Quartos.

24. It is discussed by, among others, Edward Hubler, 'The Damnation of Othello: Some Limitations on the Christian View of the Play', *Shakespeare Quarterly*, IX (1958) 295–300; Robert H. West, 'The Christian-

ness of *Othello'*, *Shakespeare Quarterly*, XV (1964) 333–43.

25.   Heilman, *Magic in the Web*, p. 164: 'the tough man of war . . .equates punishment with physical torment, which . . . is just what he can best endure'.

26.   Shakespeare gives to Othello nothing of the coldness of hell that Claudio imagines: 'to recide / In thrilling Regions of thicke-ribbed Ice' (*Measure, for Measure*, F1341–2; III.i.123–4). Othello foresaw his bloody thoughts being swallowed up, engulfed in Revenge (in 'Like to the Ponticke Sea . . . '–F2103ff; III.iii.457ff); now *he* will be engulfed in fire, roasted in Iago's 'Mines of Sulphure' (F1969; III.iii.333) made actual in hell.
        Fire in itself could denote a volcanic heat, flame or glowing lava (*OED* 1c [1582–]). Sulphur is usually found in volcanic rock. Othello refers to burning inside a volcanic crater's lava. The specific nature of his periphrasis makes his imagined punishment the more vivid. It is tempting to hear Shakespeare as playing on *Wash* as 'lave' and *Liquid fire* as 'lava'; but *lava* did not enter English (from Italian *lavare*) until the eighteenth century. *Lave* derives from Old English *lafian* and Latin *lavare*.

27.   See, for example, Jorgensen, in *Shakespeare Quarterly*, XV. A lesser-known example of this critical tradition is John Money: 'Othello dies, still uncomprehending, fatally true to himself to the end' (in *Shakespeare Survey*, 6, p. 96). See also, of course, Eliot, Leavis and Heilman.

28.   See above, n. 14, and Chapter 5, n. 31.

29.   Holloway, *The Story of the Night*, pp. 55–6.

30.   Eliot, 'Shakespeare and the Stoicism of Seneca', *Selected Essays*.

31.   Melchiori, in *Shakespeare Survey*, 34, p. 66, writes on the anaphora of repeated *of* in Othello's last long speech. Q's *Speake of them as they are* is less apt: Othello's main concern is the *one* who has done the deeds. The excerpts are from Lewkenor, *The Commonwealth and Gouernment of Venice*, pp. 131–2.

32.   ' "Extenuate" is something of a synonym as well as an antonym for "set down aught in malice" ' (Baldwin, *Shakespere's Small Latine and Lesse Greeks*, II, 162).

33.   Sanders, p. 192, summarises his case against *Iudean*: 'Othello is lamenting his ignorance, stupidity, gullibility and descent to savagery, none of which is applicable to Judas. The kiss Othello gives Desdemona is hardly a sign of betrayal so much as an instinctive sexual reponse at odds with his mental conviction of her guilt. See also Richard S. Veit, ' "Like the base Judean": A Defense of an Oft-Rejected Reading in *Othello*', *Shakespeare Quarterly*, XXVI (1975) 466–9.
        Base is 'Low in natural rank, or in the scale of creation' and 'Low in moral scale' (*OED* adj., II.8 and 9.) It opposes the equation of the free and noble man with a high morality discussed in Chapter 1.

34.   The convention is strongly evident in Sonnet 145 (emphasis added):

        Those *lips* that Loves owne *hand* did make,

Breath'd forth the sound that said I hate,
To me that languisht for her sake:
But when she saw my wofull state,
Straight in her *heart* did mercie come,
Chiding that *tongue* . . .

35. A point not registered by Shakespeare's feminist interpreter Marilyn French, in *Shakespeare's Division of Experience*, paperback edn (London, 1983) pp. 204–19. (1st edn 1982.)

36. Holloway, *The Story of the Night*, p. 56: Othello 'has seen that the Turk, chief enemy of Venice, and the Moor, have become one'. In my sentence 'Othello kills not only the Iago in himself . . . ' I make some reference to Stewart's postulation: 'The true protagonist of the drama . . . is to be arrived at only, as it were, by conflating two characters . . . as interlocked forces within a single psyche' (*Character and Motive in Shakespeare*, p. 109).

37. *Coleridge: Shakespeare Criticism*, I, 44.

38. The reading of 'that / Which Heauen hath forbid the Ottamittes' as a reference to suicide seems inappropriate. (Hart, p. 105n: 'Heaven forbade the Turks to destroy themselves by doing it for them.')

    In actual history, of course, the Turks were not forbidden from harming the men of Cyprus – or the women and children. See Chapter 1, n. 10. Interestingly, Knolles reports that it was the Governor of Aleppo who with his regiment 'scoured the wals of the citie [Nicosia] round about . . . and without respect put to sword all that he met, armed or unarmed' (*The Generall Historie of the Turkes*, p. 851).

39. On *th* as [t] see Dobson, *English Pronunciation*, II, 1008–10. Other words with varying pronunciations were *Catherine, Arthur, Orthography*.

Bibliography

I. SHAKESPEARE EDITIONS

Alexander, Peter (ed.), *The Complete Works of William Shakespeare* (London and Glasgow: Collins, 1951; paperback reprint 1981).

Furness, Horace Howard (ed.) *Othello*, New Variorum Shakespeare, 11th edn (Philadelphia and London: Lippincott, 1886).

Greg, Sir Walter, and Hinman, Charlton (eds), *Hamlet, Second Quarto 1604 –5*, Shakespeare Quarto Facsimiles no.4 (Oxford: Clarendon Press, 1964 [a reprint of the 1st edn, 1940]).

Hart, H. C. (ed.), *The Tragedy of Othello*, Arden Shakespeare, 3rd edn (London: Methuen, 1923). (1st edn, 1903.).

Hinman, Charlton (ed.), *The Norton Facsimile: The First Folio of Shakespeare* (New York: Norton; and London: Hamlyn, 1968).

Hinman, (ed.), *Othello, 1622*, Shakespeare Quarto Facsimiles no. 16 (Oxford: Clarendon Press, 1975).

Jenkins, Harold (ed.), *Hamlet*, Arden Shakespeare (London and New York: Methuen, 1982).

Kernan, Alvin (ed.), *The Tragedy of Othello The Moor of Venice*, Signet Classic Shakespeare (New York: New American Library, 1963).

Muir, Kenneth (ed.), *Othello*, New Penguin Shakespeare (Harmondsworth: Penguin, 1968).

Prince, F. T. (ed.), *The Poems*, Arden Shakespeare (London: Methuen, 1960; paperback reprint, 1969).

Ridley, M. R. (ed.), *Othello*, Arden Shakespeare (London and New York: Methuen, 1958; paperback reprint 1965).

Ross, Lawrence J. (ed.), *The Tragedy of Othello the Moor of Venice*, Bobbs-Merrill Shakespeare (Indianapolis: Bobbs-Merrill, 1974).

Sanders, Norman (ed.), *Othello*, New Cambridge Shakespeare (Cambridge: Cambridge University Press, 1984).

Seymour-Smith, Martin (ed.), *Shakespeare's Sonnets* (London: Heinemann, 1963).

Sisson, Charles Jasper (ed.), *William Shakespeare: The Complete Works* (London: Odhams, 1953).

Walker, Alice, and Dover Wilson, John (ed.), *Othello*, New Shakespeare (Cambridge: Cambridge University Press, 1957; paperback reprint, 1969).

II. OTHER SOURCES

Abbott, E. A., *A Shakespearian Grammar: An Attempt to Illustrate Some of the Differences between Elizabethan and Modern English*, 2nd edn (London and New York: Macmillan, 1870).

Adamson, J., *'Othello' as Tragedy: Some Problems and Judgements of Feeling* (Cambridge: Cambridge University Press, 1980).

Adamson, W., 'Unpinned or Undone? Desdemona's Critics and the Problem of Sexual Innocence', *Shakespeare Studies*, 13 (1980) 169–86.

Alexander, N., 'Thomas Rymer and *Othello'*, *Shakespeare Survey*, 21 (1968) 67–77; repr. in Muir and Edwards, *Aspects of 'Othello'*.

Alexander, P., *Shakespeare's Life and Art* (London: James Nisbet, 1939).

Allen, N. B., 'The Two Parts of *Othello'*, *Shakespeare Survey*, 21 (1968); repr. in Muir and Edwards, *Aspects of 'Othello'*.

Andrews, M. C., 'Honest Othello: The Handkerchief Once More', *Studies in English Literature*, 13 (1973) 273–84.

Armstrong, E. A., 'Hidden Images', *Shakespeare's Imagination* (London: Lindsay Drummond, 1946; and Lincoln, Nebr.: University of Nebraska Press, 1963).

Arnold, A., 'The Function of Brabantio', *Shakespeare Quarterly* VIII (1957) 51–6.

Auden, W. H., 'The Joker in the Pack', *The Dyer's Hand* (London: Faber and Faber, 1962); repr. in *Selected Essays* (London: Faber and Faber, 1964).

Babb, L., 'The Physiological Conception of Love in the Elizabethan and Early Stuart Drama', *PMLA*, 56 (1941) 1020–35.

Bailey, R. W. (ed.), *Early Modern English: Additions and Antedatings to the Record of English Vocabulary 1475–1700* (Hildesheim: Olms, 1978).

Baker, S. A., 'Othello's "Cause": A New Reading'. *English Language Notes*, 7 (1969–70) 96–8.

Baldwin, T. W., *William Shakespere's Small Latine and Lesse Greeke*, 2 vols (Urbana: University of Illinois Press, 1944).

Barber, C., *Early Modern English* (London: André Deutsch, 1976).

Barton, J., *Playing Shakespeare* (London and New York: Methuen, 1984).

Bayley, J., 'Love and Identity: *Othello'*, *The Characters of Love: A Study in the Literature of Personality*, 2nd edn (London: Chatto and Windus, 1968). (First published 1962.)

——, 'The Fragile Structure of *Othello'*, *The Times Literary Supplement*, 20 June 1980, pp. 707–9.

——, *Shakespeare and Tragedy* (London: Routledge and Kegan Paul, 1981) esp. pp. 200–20.

Benson, M., *Erring Othello* (London: Coleman, 1970).

Berry, R., 'Pattern in *Othello'*, *Shakespeare Quarterly*, XXIII (1972), 3–19.

Bethell, S. L., 'Shakespeare's Imagery: The Diabolic Images in *Othello'*, *Shakespeare Survey*, 5, (1952) 62–80; repr. in Muir and Edwards, *Aspects of 'Othello'*.

Black, M., *Poetic Drama as Mirror of a Will* (London: Vision Press, 1977) esp. pp. 78–92.

Blake, N. F., *Shakespeare's Language: An Introduction* (London: Macmillan, 1983).

Bland, D. S., 'Shakespeare and the "Ordinary" Word', *Shakespeare Survey*, 4 (1951) 49–55.

Bodkin, M., *Archetypal Patterns in Poetry* (London: Oxford University Press, 1934 and 1968) esp. pp. 333–4.

Boose, L. E., 'Othello's Handkerchief: The 'Recognizance and Pledge" of Love', *English Literary Renaissance*, V, 3 (1975) 360–74.

——, ' "Lust in Action": *Othello* as Shakespeare's Tragedy of Human Sexuality', (doctoral dissertation, University of California at Los Angeles, 1976.) *Dissertation Abstracts International*, 37: 11–12 (1976) pp. 7136-A to 7137-A.

——, 'Othello's "Chrysolite" and the Song of Songs Tradition', *Philological Quarterly*, 60, iv (Fall 1981) 427–35.

——, 'The Father and the Bride in Shakespeare', *PMLA* 97 (1982) 325–47.

Bradbrook, M. C., *Elizabethan Stage Conditions: A Study of their Place in the Interpretation of Shakespeare's Plays* (Cambridge: Cambridge University Press, 1932; paperback 1968).

——, *Themes and Conventions of Elizabethan Tragedy* (Cambridge: Cambridge University Press, 1935; paperback reprint 1960).

——, 'Shakespeare the Jacobean Dramatist', in Muir and Schoenbaum, *A New Companion to Shakespeare Studies*.

——, '*Othello*, Webster and the Tragedy of Violence', the Folger Shakespeare Library's annual Shakespeare birthday lecture, 1981, *Muriel Bradbrook on Shakespeare* (Brighton: Harvester Press, 1984) ch. 11.

Bradley, A. C., *Shakespearean Tragedy: Lectures on 'Hamlet', 'Othello', 'King Lear', 'Macbeth'*, 2nd edn (London: Macmillan, 1905; paperpack reprint 1957). (1st edn 1904).

Brook, G. L., *The Language of Shakespeare* (London: André Deutsch, 1976).

Brower, R. A., *Hero and Saint: Shakespeare and the Graeco-Roman Tradition* (London: Oxford University Press, 1971) esp. pp. 1–28.

Bruce, F. F., *The English Bible: A History of Translations from the Earliest English Version to the New English Bible*, new rev. edn. (London: Lutterworth, 1970).

Bullough, G., *Narrative and Dramatic Sources of Shakespeare*, VII (London: Routledge and Kegan Paul, 1973).

Burgess, C. F., 'Othello's Occupation', *Shakespeare Quarterly* XXVI (1975) 208–13.

Campbell, L. B., *Shakespeare's Tragic Heroes* (London: Methuen, 1961). (First published Cambridge, 1930).

Castiglione, Baldassar *The Book of the Courtier*, tr. Sir Thomas Hoby (1561) intro. J. H. Whitfield (London: Dent, 1974).

Cercignani, F., *Shakespeare's Works and Elizabethan Pronunciation* (Oxford: Clarendon Press, 1981).

Chambers, E. K., *William Shakespeare: A Study of Facts and Problems*, 2 vols (Oxford: Clarendon Press, 1930).

Charlton, H. B., *Shakespearean Tragedy* (Cambridge: Cambridge University Press, 1948).

Chaucer, Geoffrey *The Franklin's Tale*, ed. Phyllis Hodgson (London: Athlone Press, 1960).

Cinthio, G. B. G., *De Gli Hecatommithi* (Venice, 1566) tr. Geoffrey Bullough, in Bullough, *Narrative and Dramatic Sources of Shakespeare*, VII, 239–52.

Clemen, W. H., *The Development of Shakespeare's Imagery*, 2nd edn (London: Methuen, 1977) esp. pp. 119–32 (1st German edn 1936; 1st English edn 1951.)

——, 'Some Aspects of Style in the *Henry VI* Plays', in Edwards, Ewbank and Hunter, *Shakespeare's Styles*.

Coghill, N., *Shakespeare's Professional Skills* (Cambridge: Cambridge University Press, 1964) (Preface and chs 6–7.)

Cohen, E. Z., 'Mirror of Virtue: The Role of Cassio in *Othello*', *English Studies*, 57 (1976) 115–27.

Coleridge, S. T., *Samuel Taylor Coleridge: Shakespearean Criticism*, ed. T. M. Raysor, 2nd edn, 2 vols (London: Dent, 1960).

Coles, Elisha *An English Dictionary* (1676), facsimile edn (Menston, Yorks: Scolar Press, 1971).

Colie, R. L., *Shakespeare's Living Art* (Princeton, NJ: Princeton University Press, 1974).

Colman, E. A. M., *The Dramatic Use of Bawdy in Shakespeare* (London: Longman, 1974).

Cooke, K., *A. C. Bradley and his Influence in Twentieth-Century Shakespeare Criticism* (Oxford: Clarendon Press, 1972).

Copley, J., *Shift of Meaning* (London: Oxford University Press, 1961).

Council, N., *When Honour's at the Stake* (London: Allen and Unwin, 1973).

Dash, I. G., 'A Woman Tamed: *Othello*', *Wooing, Wedding and Power: Women in Shakespeare's Plays* (New York: Columbia University Press, 1981).

Dekker, T., *The Gull's Horn Book* (1609) in *Thomas Dekker: Selected Prose Writings*, ed. E. D. Pendry (London: Edward Arnold, 1967).

——, *The Plague Pamphlets of Thomas Dekker*, ed. F. P. Wilson (London: Oxford University Press, 1925).

Dillon, Viscount, 'Armour and Weapons', ch. 4/2 of C. T. Onions, Sidney Lee *et al.* (eds), *Shakespeare's England*, 2 vols (Oxford: Clarendon Press, 1916).

Dixon, P., *Rhetoric*, Critical Idiom Series no. 19 (London: Methuen, 1971).

Dobson, E. J., *English Pronunciation 1500–1700*, 2nd edn, 2 vols (Oxford: Clarendon Press, 1968).

Donne, John, *The Complete English Poems*, ed. A. J. Smith, corrected reprint (Harmondsworth: Penguin, 1973).

——, 'A Defence of Womens Inconstancy', *John Donne: Selected Prose* chosen by Evelyn Simpson, ed. Helen Gardner and Timothy Healy (Oxford: Clarendon Press, 1967).

Doran, M., 'Good Name in *Othello*', *Studies in English Literature*, 7 (Spring 1967) 195–217.

——, 'Iago's "If–": Conditional and Subjunctive in *Othello*', in *Shakespeare's Dramatic Language* (Madison and London: University of Wisconsin Press, 1976), rev. reprint of 'Iago's "If–": An Essay on the Syntax of *Othello*' in E. W. Blistein (ed.), *The Drama of the Renaissance: Essays for Leicester Bradner* (Providence, RI: Brown University Press, 1970).

Draper, J. W., 'Shakespeare and the Turk', *Journal of English and Germanic Philology*, 55 (1956) 523–32.

Dusinberre, J., *Shakespeare and the Nature of Women* (London: Macmillan, 1975).

Edwards, P., Ewbank, I-S., and Hunter, G. K. (eds), *Shakespeare's Styles: Essays in Honour of Kenneth Muir* (Cambridge: Cambridge University Press, 1980).

Eliot, T. S., 'Shakespeare and the Stoicism of Seneca', *Selected Essays*, 3rd, enlarged edition (London: Faber and Faber, 1951). (1st edn, 1927.)

Elliott, G. R., *Flaming Minister: A Study of 'Othello' as Tragedy of Love and Hate* (Durham, NC: Duke University Press, 1953).

Emery, J. P., 'Othello's Epilepsy', *Psychoanalysis and the Psychoanalytic Review* XLVI (Winter 1959) 30–2.

Empson, W., *Seven Types of Ambiguity*, 3rd edn (Harmondsworth: Penguin, 1961). (1st edn London: Chatto and Windus, 1930.)

——, 'Honest Man', 'Honest in *Othello*', 'Sense in *Measure for Measure*', 'Dictionaries', *The Structure of Complex Words*, chs 9, 11, 13, 21 (London: Chatto and Windus, 1951).

Encyclopaedia Britannica Macropaedia, 15th edn, ed. Warren E. Preece (Chicago, etc.: H. H. Benton, 1974).

Engler, B., 'How Shakespeare Revised *Othello*', *English Studies*, 57 (1976) 515–21.

Evans, B. I., *The Language of Shakespeare's Plays* (London: Methuen, 1952).

Everett, B., 'Reflections on the Sentimentalist's Othello', *Critical Quarterly*, 3 (1961) 127–39.

——, 'Spanish Othello: The Making of Shakespeare's Moor', *Shakespeare Survey*, 35 (1982) 101–12.

Ewbank, I-S., 'Shakespeare's Poetry', in Muir and Schoenbaum, *A New Companion to Shakespeare Studies*.

——, 'The Word in the Theater', in Muir, Halio and Palmer, *Shakespeare: Man of the Theater*.

Farnham, W., *The Shakespearean Grotesque, its Genesis and Transformation* (Oxford: Clarendon Press, 1971).

Fiedler, L. A., *The Stranger in Shakespeare* (London: Croom Helm, 1973; St Albans: Paladin, 1974).

Flatter, R., *The Moor of Venice* (London: Heinemann, 1950).

Fleissner, R. F. 'The Moor's Nomenclature', *Notes and Queries* no. 223 (1978) 143.

Foakes, R. A., 'Poetic Language and Dramatic Significance', in Edwards, Ewbank and Hunter, *Shakespeare's Styles*.

Fraser, J., '*Othello* and Honour', *Critical Review*, 8 (1965) 59–70.

Fraunce, Abraham, *The Arcadian Rhetorike* (1588) facsimile edn (Menston, Yorks: Scolar Press, 1969).

French, M., *Shakespeare's Division of Experience* (London: Jonathan Cape, 1982; paperback London: Sphere, 1983).

Fripp, E. I., *Shakespeare, Man and Art*, 2 vols (London: Oxford University Press, 1938).

Frye, N., *Fools of Time: Studies in Shakespearean Tragedy* (London: Oxford University Press, 1967).

Frye, R. M., *Shakespeare and Christian Doctrine* (Princeton, NJ., and London: Oxford University Press, 1963).

Gamble, G. Y., 'Shakespeare's *Othello* IV.ii.482–86' *Explicator* LXXV,iii (Spring 1977) 35–6.

Gardner, H., 'The Noble Moor', *Proceedings of the British Academy*, 41 (1955) 189–205; repr. in Anne Ridler (ed.), *Shakespeare Criticism 1935–60*, World's Classics (London: Oxford University Press, 1963) and as *The Noble Moor* (Folcroft, Penn. Folcroft Press, 1955).

——, '*Othello*: A Retrospect 1900–1967', *Shakespeare Survey*, 21 (1968) 1–11;

repr. in Muir and Edwards, *Aspects of 'Othello'*.

Gerard, A., ' "Egregiously an ass": The Dark Side of the Moor. A View of Othello's Mind', *Shakespeare Survey*, 10 (1957); repr. in Muir and Edwards, *Aspects of 'Othello'*.

Godfrey, D. R., 'Shakespeare and the Green-Eyed Monster', *Neophilologus*, 56 (1972) 207–19.

Goldsmith, U. K., 'Words out of a Hat? Alliteration and Assonance in Shakespeare's Sonnets', *Journal of English and Germanic Philology*, 49 (1950) 33–48.

Granville-Barker, H., *Prefaces to Shakespeare*, 1-vol. edn (London: Batsford, 1972). '*Othello*' was first issued in 1930.

Greg, W. W., *The Shakespeare First Folio: Its Bibliographical and Textual History* (Oxford: Clarendon Press, 1955).

Hakluyt, Richard, *Voyages and Discoveries: The Principal Navigations, Voyages, Traffiques and Discoveries of the English Nation*, abridged edn, ed. Jack Beeching (Harmondsworth: Penguin, 1972).

Halliday, F. E., *The Poetry of Shakespeare's Plays* (London: Duckworth, 1954).

Hansen, A. J. D., 'Shakespeare's *Othello*', *Explicator* xxxv, iv (Summer 1947) 4–6.

Hapgood, R., '*Othello*' in Stanley Wells (ed.), *Shakespeare: Select Bibliographical Guides* (London: Oxford University Press, 1973).

Harris, B., 'A Portrait of a Moor', *Shakespeare Survey*, 11 (1958) 89–97.

Hartley, L., 'Dropping the Handkerchief: Pronoun Reference and Stage Direction in *Othello* III.iii', *English Language Notes*, 8 (1970–1) 173–6.

Hawkes, T., 'Iago's Use of Reason', *Studies in Philology*, 58 (1961) 160–9.

Heilman, R. B., *Magic in the Web: Action and Language in 'Othello'* (Lexington: University of Kentucky Press, 1956; and Westport. Conn.: Greenwood Press, 1977).

—— , ' "Twere Best not Know Myself": Othello, Lear, Macbeth'. in J. G. McManaway (ed.), *Shakespeare 400: Essays by American Scholars on the Anniversary of the Poet's Birth* (New York: Holt, Rinehart and Winston, 1964).

Herbert, George, *The Works of George Herbert*, ed. F. E. Hutchinson (Oxford: Clarendon Press, 1941).

Hinman, C., *The Printing and Proof-Reading of the First Folio of Shakespeare*, 2 vols (Oxford: Clarendon Press, 1963).

Hirsh, J. E., *The Structure of Shakespearean Scenes* (New Haven, Conn., and London: Yale University Press, 1980).

Holloway, J., *The Story of the Night* (London: Routledge and Kegan Paul, 1961;.

Holmes, M., *Shakespeare and Burbage* (Chichester: Phillimore, 1978).

Honigmann, E. A. J., 'Shakespeare's Bombast', in Edwards, Ewbank and Hunter, *Shakespeare's Styles*.

—— , 'Secret Motives in *Othello*', *Shakespeare: Seven Tragedies. The Dramatist's Manipulation of Response* (London: Macmillan, 1976) ch. 6. (See also chs 2 and 3.)

Hoskyns, Sir J., *Directions for Speech and Style* (1599/1600) ed. H. H. Hudson, Princeton Studies in English no. 12 (Princeton, NJ: Princeton

University Press, 1935).

Hubler, E., 'The Damnation of Othello: Some Limitations on the Christian View of the Play', *Shakespeare Quarterly* IX (1958) 295–300.

Hulme, H. M., *Explorations in Shakespeare's Language: Some Problems of Word Meaning in the Dramatic Text* (London: Longman, 1962).

—— , 'Shakespeare's Language', in James Sutherland and Joel Hurstfield (eds), *Shakespeare's World* (London: Edward Arnold, 1964) pp. 136–55.

Hunter, G. K., 'Othello and Colour Prejudice', *Proceedings of the British Academy*, 53 (1967, published 1968) 139–63.

Hussey, S. S., *The Literary Language of Shakespeare* (London: Longman, 1982).

Hyman, S. E., *Iago: Some Approaches to the Illusion of his Motivation* (London: Paul Elek, 1971).

Janus, L. A., 'The Telling Word: The Soliloquy in *Hamlet, Othello,* and *Macbeth*' (doctoral dissertation, University of Maryland, 1972). *Dissertation Abstracts International* 33:5–6 (1972) p. 2331–A.

Jeffrey, D. L., and Grant, P. 'Reputation in Othello', *Shakespeare Studies*, 6 (1970) 197–208.

Johnson, F. R., *Astronomical Thought in Renaissance England: A Study of the English Scientific Writings from 1500–1645* (Baltimore: Johns Hopkins Press, 1937; reissued New York, 1968).

Johnson, Samuel, *The Yale Edition of the Works of Samuel Johnson,* ed. Arthur Sherbo, VII: *Prefaces,* VIII: *Johnson on Shakespeare* with an introduction by Bertrand H. Bronson (New Haven, Conn., and London: Yale University Press, 1968).

Jones, Eldred, *Othello's Countrymen: The African in English Renaissance Drama* (London: Oxford University Press for Fourah Bay College, 1965).

Jones, Emrys, '*Othello, Lepanto* and the Cyprus Wars', *Shakespeare Survey*, 21 (1968); repr. in Muir and Edwards, *Aspects of 'Othello'*.

—— , *Scenic Form in Shakespeare* (Oxford: Clarendon Press, 1971).

Jorgensen, P. A., *Shakespeare's Military World* (Berkeley, Calif.: University of California Press, 1956).

—— , 'Noble' in *Coriolanus*' and 'Honesty in *Othello*', *Redeeming Shakespeare's Words* (Berkeley, Calif.: University of California Press, 1962). 'Honesty . . . ' first appeared in *Studies in Philology*, 47 (1950) 557–67.

—— , *Redeeming Shakespeare's Words* (Berkeley, Calif.: University of California Press, 1962).

—— , ' "Perplex'd in the extreme": The Role of Thought in *Othello*', *Shakespeare Quarterly*, XV (1964) 265–75; repr. in J.G. McManaway (ed.), *Shakespeare 400: Essays by American Scholars on the Anniversary of the Poet's Birth* (New York: Holt, Rinehart and Winston, 1964).

—— , *Lear's Self-Discovery* (Berkeley, Calif.: University of California Press, 1967) esp. pp. 63–6.

Joseph, Sister M., *Shakespeare's Use of the Arts of Language* (New York: Columbia University Press, 1947).

Kirsch, A., 'The Polarization of Erotic Love in *Othello*', *Modern Language Review*, 73 (1978) 721–40.

Kirschbaum, L., 'The Modern Othello', *English Literary History*, XI (1944) 283–96; repr. in *Character and Characterization in Shakespeare* (Detroit:

Wayne State University Press, 1962).

Klene, J., 'Othello: "A fixed figure for the time of scorn" ', *Shakespeare Quarterly*, XXVI (1975) 139–50.

Kliger, S., 'Othello: The Man of Judgement', *Modern Philology*, 40, viii (1951) 221–4.

Knight, G. W., 'The *Othello* Music', *The Wheel of Fire: Interpretations of Shakespearean Tragedy with Three New Essays*, 4th rev. and enlarged edn (London: Methuen, 1949; paperback reprint 1961). (1st edn London: Oxford University Press, 1930).

——, 'Soul and Body in Shakespeare', *Shakespearian Dimensions* (Brighton: Harvester Press, 1984) ch. 1.

Knights, L. C. 'Rhetoric and Insincerity', in Edwards, Ewbank and Hunter, *Shakespeare's Styles*.

Knolles, Richard *The Generall Historie of the Turkes, from the first beginning of that Nation to the rising of the Othoman Familie: with all the notable expeditions of the Christian Princes against them. Together with the Lives and Conquests of the Ottoman Kings and Emperours Faithfullie collected out of the best Histories, both auntient and moderne, and digested into one continuat Historie untill this present yeare 1603* (London, 1603).

Kökertiz, H., *Shakespeare's Pronunciation* (New Haven, Conn.: Yale University Press, 1953).

Leavis, F. R., 'Diabolic Intellect and the Noble Hero: or the Sentimentalist's Othello', *The Common Pursuit* (London: Chatto and Windus, 1952; and Harmondsworth: Penguin, 1962) First printed under a slightly different title in *Scrutiny* 6 (1937).

Lees, F. N., 'Othello's Name', *Notes and Queries*, 216 (n. s., 8) (Apr 1961) 139–41.

Lerner, L., 'The Machiavel and the Moor', *Essays in Criticism* 9 (Oct 1959) 339–60.

——, *Love and Marriage: Literature and its Social Context* (London: Edward Arnold, 1979) esp. pp. 16, 53ff.

——, (ed.), *Shakespeare's Tragedies: An Anthology of Modern Criticism* (Harmondsworth: Penguin, 1968).

Levith, M. J., *What's in Shakespeare's Names* (London: Allen and Unwin, 1978).

Levitsky, R., 'All-in-All Sufficiency in *Othello*', *Shakespeare Studies*, 6 (1970) 209–21.

Lewis, C. S., *The Discarded Image* (Cambridge: Cambridge University Press, 1964).

——, *Studies in Words*, 2nd edn (Cambridge: Cambridge University Press, 1967).

Lewkenor, L., *The Commonwealth and Gouernment of Venice. Written by the Cardinal Gasper Contareno, and translated out of Italian into English, by Lewes Lewkenor Esquire. With sundry other Collections, annexed by the Translator for the more cleere and exact satisfaction of the Reader. With a short Chronicle in the end, of the liues and raignes of the Venetian Dukes, from the very beginninges of their Citie.* (London, 1599) Extracts in Bullough, *Narrative and Dramatic Sources of Shakespeare*, VII.

Linfield, N., 'You and Thou in Shakespeare: Othello as an Example', *Iowa*

State Journal of Research, 57, ii (1982) 163–78.

Long, M., *The Unnatural Scene: A Study of Shakespearian Tragedy* (London: Methuen, 1976).

McAlindon, T., *Shakespeare and Decorum* (London: Macmillan, 1973).

McDonald, R., 'Othello, Thorello, and the Problem of the Foolish Hero', *Shakespeare Quarterly*, XXX (1979) 51–67.

McGee, A., 'Othello's Motive for Murder', *Shakespeare Quarterly*, XV (1964) 45–54.

McGovern, D. S., ' "Tempus" in *The Tempest*', *English*, XXXIII, 144 (Autumn 1983) 201–24.

McGuire, P. C. '*Othello* as an "Assay of Reason" ', *Shakespeare Quarterly*, XXIV (1973) 198–209.

McLauchlan, J., *Shakespeare: 'Othello'* (London: Edward Arnold, 1971).

Macey, S. L., 'The Naming of the Protagonists in Shakespeare's *Othello*', *Notes and Queries*, 223 (1978) 143–5.

Machiavelli, Niccolò, *The Prince*, George Bull, rev. reprint (Harmondsworth: Penguin, 1981).

Mack, M., 'The Jacobean Shakespeare: Some Observations on the Construction of the Tragedies', in J. Russell Brown and B. Harris (eds), *Jacobean Theatre*, Stratford-upon-Avon Studies, no. 1 (London: Edward Arnold, 1960).

Mahood, M., *Shakespeare's Wordplay* (London: Methuen, 1957; paperback reprint 1968).

Marovitz, S. E., 'Othello Unmasked: A Black Man's Conscience and a White Man's Fool', *Southern Review*, 6 (1973) 108–33.

Marsh, D. R. C., *Passion Lends Them Power* (Manchester: Manchester University Press, 1976) esp. pp. 89–140.

Marvell, Andrew, *The Complete English Poems*, ed. Elizabeth Story Donno (Harmondsworth: Penguin, 1972).

Mason, H. A., *Shakespeare's Tragedies of Love: An Examination of the Possibility of Common Readings of 'Romeo and Juliet', 'Othello', 'King Lear' and 'Anthony and Cleopatra'* (London: Chatto and Windus, 1970).

Maxwell, J. C., 'Shakespeare: The Middle Plays', in Boris Ford (ed.) *The New Pelican Guide to English Literature*, II: *The Age of Shakespeare* (Harmondsworth: Penguin, 1982).

Melchiori, G., 'The Rhetoric of Character Construction', *Shakespeare Survey*, 34 (1981) 61–72.

Melville, Herman, *'Billy Budd, Sailor' and Other Stories*, ed. H. Beaver (Harmondsworth: Penguin, 1967).

Mendonça, B. H. de, '*Othello*: A Tragedy Built on a Comic Structure', *Shakespeare Survey*, 21 (1968).

Money, J., 'Othello's "It is the cause" ', *Shakespeare Survey*, 6. (1953) 94–105.

Montaigne, Michel de, *The Essays of Michael Lord of Montaigne. Translated into English by John Florio*, 3 vols (London: Dent, 1928).

Moore, J. R., 'Othello, Iago and Cassio as Soldiers', *Philological Quarterly*, 31 (1952) 189–94.

Moore, P., *The Development of Astronomical Thought* (Edinburgh: Oliver and Boyd, 1969).

Morozov, M. M., 'Extract from "The Individualization of Shakespeare's

Characters through Imagery" ', *Shakespeare Survey*, 2 (1949); repr. in Muir and Edwards, *Aspects of 'Othello'*.

Motley, J. L., *The Rise of the Dutch Republic*, 3 vols (London: John Murray, 1903).

Muir, K., 'The Text of *Othello*', *Shakespeare Studies*, 1 (1965) 227–39.

——, *Shakespeare's Tragic Sequence* (London: Hutchinson, 1972).

——, *The Sources of Shakespeare's Plays* (London: Methuen, 1977).

Muir, K and Edwards, P. (eds), *Aspects of 'Othello': Articles Reprinted from 'Shakespeare Survey'* (Cambridge: Cambridge University Press, 1977).

Muir, K., Halio, J.L., and Palmer, D.J. (eds), *Shakespeare: Man of the Theater. Proceedings of the Second Congress of the International Shakespeare Association 1981* (London: Associated University Presses, 1983).

Muir, K., and Schoenbaum, S. (eds), *A New Companion to Shakespeare Studies* (Cambridge: Cambridge University Press, 1971).

Murray, E. K. M., *Caught in the Web of Words: James A. H. Murray and the 'Oxford English Dictionary'* (New Haven, Conn., and London: Yale University Press, 1977).

Nelson, T. G. A., and Haines, C., 'Othello's Unconsummated Marriage', *Essays in Criticism*, XXIII, i (Jan 1983) 1–18.

Nevo, R., *Tragic Form in Shakespeare* (Princeton, NJ: Princeton University Press, 1972) esp. p. 194.

Nicolson, M., ' "The New Astronomy" and English Literary Imagination', *Studies in Philology*, 32 (1953) 428–62.

——, 'The Telescope and Imagination', *Modern Philology*, 32 (1934–5) 233–60.

Noble, R., *Shakespeare's Biblical Knowledge and Use of the Book of Common Prayer as Exemplified in the Plays of the First Folio* (London: SPCK; and New York: Macmillan, 1935).

Nowottny, W., 'Justice and Love in *Othello*', *University of Toronto Quarterly*, 21 (1951–2) 330–44.

——, 'Shakespeare's Tragedies', in Sutherland and Hurstfield, *Shakespeare's World*.

Nuttall, A. D., *A New Mimesis: Shakespeare and the Representation of Reality* (London: Methuen, 1983).

Onions, C. T., *A Shakespeare Glossary*, 2nd rev. edn (Oxford: Clarendon, Press, 1919).

——, *'Othello': A Concordance to the Text of the First Folio*, Oxford Shakespeare Concordances (Oxford: Clarendon Press, 1971).

The Oxford English Dictionary, ed. Sir J. A. H. Murray, Henry Bradley, Sir W. A. Craigie and C. T. Onions (Oxford: Clarendon Press, 1933), a corrected reissue of *A New English Dictionary on Historical Principles*, (1884–1928), with four supplements, ed. R. W. Burchfield: *A–G* (1972); *H–N* (1976); *O–Scz* (1982); *Se–Z* (1986).

Partridge, E., *Shakespeare's Bawdy* rev. edn (London: Routledge and Kegan Paul, 1955).

Phillips, O. H., *Shakespeare and the Lawyers* (London: Methuen, 1972).

Proser, M. N., '*Othello* and *Coriolanus*: the Image of the Warrior', *The Heroic Image in Five Shakespearean Tragedies* (Princeton, NJ: Princeton University Press, 1965).

Prosser, E., *Hamlet and Revenge* (London: Oxford University Press, 1967; 2nd rev. edn 1971).

Pryse, M., 'Lust for Audience: An Interpretation of *Othello*', *Journal of English Literary History* 46 (1976) 461–78.

Puttenham, George, *The Art of English Poesie* (1589), English Linguistics 1500–1800, no. 110, ed. R. C. Alston (Menston, Yorks: Scolar Press, 1968). Another edition is that edited by G. W. Willcock and A. Walker (new edn Cambridge: Cambridge University Press, 1970).

Quirk, R., 'Shakespeare and the English Language', in Muir and Schoenbaum, *A New Companion to Shakespeare Studies*; and Quirk, *The Linguist and The English Language* (London: Edward Arnold, 1974).

Quirk, R., Greenbaum, S., Leech, G., and Svartvik, J. (eds), *A Grammar of Contemporary English* (London and New York: Longman, 1972).

Raleigh, Sir W., *Shakespeare* (London: Macmillan, 1907).

Ranald, M. L., 'The Indiscretions of Desdemona', *Shakespeare Quarterly*, XIV (1963) 127–39.

Ransom, J. C., 'On Shakespeare's Language', *Sewanee Review*, 55 (1947) 181–98.

Ricks, C., 'Lies', *Critical Inquiry* 2 (1975) 121–42; repr. in *The Force of Poetry* (Oxford: Clarendon Press, 1984).

Rogers, R., 'Endopsychic Drama in *Othello*'. *Shakespeare Quarterly*, XX (1969) 205–15.

Rogers, S., '*Othello*': Comedy in Reverse'. *Shakespeare Quarterly*, XXIV (1973) 210–20.

Rosenberg, M., *The Masks of Othello: The Search for the Identity of Othello, Iago and Desdemona by Three Centuries of Actors and Critics* (Berkeley, Calif.: University of California Press, 1961).

Ross, L., 'Three Readings in the Text of *Othello*', *Shakespeare Quarterly*, XIV (1963) 121–6.

——— , 'Shakespeare's "Dull Clown' and "Symbolic Music" '. *Shakespeare Quarterly*, XVII (1966).

——— , 'World and Chrysolite in *Othello*', *Modern Language Notes*, 76 (1961) 683–92.

Rossiter, A. P., '*Angel with Horns' and other Shakespeare Lectures*, ed. G. Storey (London: Longmans, Green, 1961).

Rubinstein, F., *A Dictionary of Shakespeare's Sexual Puns and their Significance* (London: Macmillan, 1984).

Rymer, Thomas *The Critical Works of Thomas Rymer* (incl. 'A Short View of Tragedy . . . '), ed. C. A. Zimansky (New Haven, Conn.: Yale University Press; and London: Oxford University Press, 1956).

Salgādo, G., *Eyewitnesses of Shakespeare: First-Hand Accounts of Performances 1590–1890* (London: Sussex University Press, and Chatto and Windus, 1975).

Salmon, V., 'Sentence Structures in Colloquial Shakespearean English, *Transactions of the Philological Society*, 1965, pp. 105–40. (This journal is bound in Senate House Library as *Philological Society's Transactions*.)

——— , 'Some Functions of Shakespearian Word-formations'. *Shakespeare Survey*, 23 (1970) 13–26.

Sanders, N., correspondence with Stanley Wells, *The Times Literary Supple-*

ment, 7 Sep 1984, p. 995.

Schäfer, J., *Documentation in the O. E. D.: Shakespeare and Nashe as Test Cases* (Oxford: Clarendon Press, 1980).

Schmidt, A., *Shakespeare-Lexicon: A Complete Dictionary of all the English Words, Phrases and Constructions in the Works of the Poet*, 3rd edn, rev. and enlarged by G. Sarrazin (Berlin: Reimer, 1902). (1st edn, 1874.)

Schoenbaum, S., *William Shakespeare: A Documentary Life* (Oxford: Clarendon Press with the Scolar Press, 1975).

Schücking, L. L., *Character Problems in Shakespeare's Plays: A Guide to the Better Understanding of the Dramatist* (London: Harrap, 1922).

Schwartz, E., 'Stylistic "Impurity" and the Meaning of *Othello'*, *Studies in English Literature 1500–1900*, 10 (1970) 297–313.

Scragg L., 'Iago – Vice or Devil?', *Shakespeare Survey*, 21 (1968),

Sewell, A., *Character and Society in Shakespeare* (Oxford: Clarendon Press, 1951).

Shaw, G. B., *Bernard Shaw: Plays and Players, Essays on the Theatre (1895–8)*, ed. A. C. Ward (London: Oxford University Press, 1952).

Shirley, F. A., *Swearing and Perjury in Shakespeare's Plays* (London: Allen and Unwin, 1979) esp. pp. 110–24,

Sidney, Sir Philip *The Countess of Pembroke's Arcadia*, ed. Maurice Evans (Harmondsworth: Penguin, 1977).

—— , *The Defence of Poesie*, (1595), facsimile edn (Menston, Yorks: Scolar Press, 1968).

Siegel, P. N., 'The Damnation of Othello', *PMLA* 68 (1953) 1068–78.

—— , *Shakespearean Tragedy and the Elizabethan Compromise* (New York: New York University Press, 1957) ch. 8.

Sisson, C. J., *New Readings in Shakespeare*, 2 vols (Cambridge: Cambridge University Press, 1956).

Skulsky, H., *Spirits Finely Touched: The Testing of Value and Integrity in Four Shakespearean Plays* (Athens, Ga: University of Georgia Press, 1976).

Slater, A. P., *Shakespeare the Director* (Brighton: Harvester Press, 1982).

Smith, P. A., 'Othello's Diction', *Shakespeare Quarterly*, IX (1958) 428–30.

Smithers, G. V., 'Guide-lines for Interpreting the Uses of the Suffix -ed in Shakespeare's English', *Shakespeare Survey*, 23 (1970) 23–37.

Snow, E. A. 'Sexual Anxiety and the Male Order of Things in *Othello'*, *English Literary Renaissance*, 10 (1980) 384–412.

Snyder, S., *The Comic Matrix of Shakespeare's Tragedies: 'Romeo and Juliet', 'Hamlet', 'Othello', and 'King Lear'* (Princeton, NJ: Princeton University Press, 1979).

Spencer, T., *Shakespeare and the Nature of Man* (Cambridge: Cambridge University Press, 1943).

Spivack, B., *Shakespeare and the Allegory of Evil: The History of a Metaphor in Relation to his Major Villains* (London: Oxford University Press; New York: Columbia University Press, 1958).

Spurgeon, C. F. E., *Shakespeare's Imagery and What It Tells Us* (Cambridge: Cambridge University Press, 1935).

Stanislavsky, K. S., *Stanislavsky Produces 'Othello'*, tr. H. Nowak (London: Geoffrey Bles, 1948; republ. New York: Theatre Arts, 1984).

Stauffer, J. E., *Shakespeare's Derived Imagery* (Lawrence: University of

Kansas Press, 1953).

Steiner, G., *The Death of Tragedy* (London: Faber and Faber, 1961).

Stempel, D., 'The Silence of Iago', *PMLA*, 84 (1969) 252–62.

Stevenson, Robert Louis, 'On Some Technical Elements of Style in Literature', *Contemporary Review*, Apr 1885; repr. in Stevenson, *Essays in the Art of Writing*, 7th edn (London: Chatto and Windus, 1919).

Stewart, J. I. M., *Character and Motive in Shakespeare* (London: Longman, 1949).

Stockholder, K. S., ' "Egregiously an ass": Chance and Accident in *Othello'*, *Critical Inquiry*, 2 (1975) 121–42.

Stoll, E. E., *Othello: An Historical and Comparative Study*, Studies in Language and Literature no. 2 (Minneapolis: University of Minnesota, 1915).

—— , *'Othello', Art and Artifice in Shakespeare: A Study in Dramatic Contrast and Illusion* (Cambridge: Cambridge University Press, 1938) ch. 2.

—— , 'Othello the Man', *Shakespeare and Other Masters* (Cambridge, Mass.: Harvard University Press, 1940) ch. 5.

Stone, L., *The Family, Sex and Marriage in England 1500–1800* (London: Weidenfeld and Nicolson, 1977).

Sutherland, J., 'How the Characters Talk', in Sutherland and Hurstfield, *Shakespeare's World*.

Sutherland, J. and Hurstfield, J. (eds), *Shakespeare's World* (London: Edward Arnold, 1964).

Swinburne, A. C., *A Study of Shakespeare* (London: Heinemann, 1918). (1st edn London: Chatto and Windus, 1879.)

Thomas, K., *Religion and the Decline of Magic: Studies in Popular Beliefs in Sixteenth and Seventeenth Century England* (London: Weidenfeld and Nicolson, 1971).

—— , *Man and the Natural World: Changing Attitudes in England 1500–1800* (London: Allen Lane, 1983; and Harmondsworth: Penguin, 1984).

Thompson, A., *Shakespeare's Chaucer: A Study in Literary Origins* (Liverpool: Liverpool University Press; and New York: Barnes and Noble, 1978).

Tillyard, E. M. W., *The Elizabethan World Picture* (London: Chatto and Windus, 1943; and Harmondsworth: Penguin, 1963).

Traversi, D., *An Approach to Shakespeare*, II: *From 'Troilus and Cressida' to 'The Tempest'*, 3rd, rev. edn (London: Hollis and Carter, 1969). (First published 1938.)

Tuve, R., *Elizabethan and Metaphysical Imagery: Renaissance Poetic and Twentieth Century Critics* (Chicago: University of Chicago Press, 1947).

Veit, R. S., ' "Like the base Judean": A Defense of an Oft-Rejected Reading in *Othello'*, *Shakespeare Quarterly*, XXVI (1975) 466–9.

Vickers, B., 'Shakespeare's Use of Rhetoric', in Muir and Schoenbaum, *A New Companion to Shakespeare Studies*.

—— , *The Artistry of Shakespeare's Prose* (London: Methuen, 1968).

Vyvyan, J., *Shakespeare and the Rose of Love: A Study of the Early Plays in Relation to the Medieval Philosophy of Love* (London: Chatto and Windus, 1960).

—— , *Shakespeare and Platonic Beauty* (London: Chatto and Windus, 1961).

—— , *The Shakespearean Ethic* (London: Chatto and Windus, 1959).

Wain, J. (ed.), *Shakespeare, 'Othello': A Casebook* (London: Macmillan, 1971).

Walker, A., 'The 1622 Quarto and the First Folio Texts of *Othello'*, *Shakespeare Survey*, 5 (1952) 16–24.

—— , *Textual Problems of the First Folio* (Cambridge: Cambridge University Press, 1953) esp. pp. 138–61.

Watson, C. B., *Shakespeare and the Renaissance Concept of Honour* (London: Oxford University Press, 1961; London: Greenwood Press, 1977).

Watson, G. (ed.) *The New Cambridge Bibliography of English Literature*, I: *600–1660* (Cambridge: Cambridge University Press, 1974).

Wells, S., correspondence on Knolles and the completion date of *Othello*, in *The Times Literary Supplement*, 20 July 1984, p. 811 and 28 Sep 1984, p. 1089. See also Sanders, N.

West, R. H., 'The Christianness of *Othello'*, *Shakespeare Quarterly*, XV (1964) 333–43.

Whitaker, V. K., *Shakespeare's Use of Learning: An Inquiry into the Growth of his Mind and Art* (San Marino, Calif: Huntington Library, 1961). (First published 1953.)

Widdowson, H. G., 'Othello in Person', in Ronald Carter (ed.), *Language and Literature: An Introductory Reader in Stylistics* (London: Allen and Unwin, 1982) pp. 40–52.

Willcock, G. D., 'Shakespeare and Elizabethan English', *Shakespeare Survey*, 7 (1954).

—— , 'Shakespeare and Rhetoric,' *Essays and Studies*, 29 (1943) 50–61.

Wilson, E. M. '*Othello*, A Tragedy of Honour', *Listener*, 47 (1952) 926–7.

Wright, G. T., 'Hendiadys and *Hamlet'*, *PMLA*, 96 (1981) 168–93.

Wright, G. T., 'The Play of Phrase and Line in Shakespeare's Iambic Pentameter', *Shakespeare Quarterly*, XXXIV (1983) 147–58.

Index

References to Othello, Desdemona, Iago, Aemilia and Cassio are so numerous only the more important ones are indexed. Words discussed in the text are listed in italics. The titles of Shakespeare's plays are taken from the First Folio. Aemilia (Folio spelling) is listed under 'E'.

276